D1208222

ENGLISH LITERATURE
DURING THE LIFETIME
OF SHAKESPEARE

THE EARLIEST ILLUSTRATION TO "SHAKESPEARE"

This earliest illustration of a play attributed to Shakespeare, is a pen drawing made in 1595 and preserved among the Harley Papers, belonging to the Marquis of Bath, at Longleat (vol. i, p. 159ᵛ). The drawing represents scene 1, i, 104, from *Titus Andronicus* and to it is appended forty-two lines of that scene in the beautiful handwriting of Henry Peacham, author of *The Complete Gentleman*, who became later a writing-master. This drawing was first reproduced by Mr. E. K. (now Sir Edmund) Chambers, in *The Library*, Fourth Series, vol. V, 1926, with an interesting note on its provenance, to which this note is indebted. It was calendared in 1907 (H. M. Comm, Longleat Papers, vol. ii, p. 43) and is made up of a single sheet endorsed on a spare page, "Henrye Peachams Hande, 1595." Peacham must have copied his lines from the quarto of Titus of 1595, now extant in only one copy in the possession of Mr. H. C. Folger. It is of interest to students of the drama to note the primitive conception of a Roman toga as worn by Titus, the contemporary Elizabethan costumes of the guard and the ink bestowed on a realization of Aaron who was, like Othello, a Moor.

THE EARLIEST ILLUSTRATION TO "SHAKESPEARE"

ENGLISH LITERATURE
DURING THE LIFETIME
OF SHAKESPEARE

Revised Edition

BY
FELIX E. SCHELLING
PROFESSOR IN THE UNIVERSITY OF PENNSYLVANIA
Author of "Elizabethan Playwrights,"
"The English Lyric," etc.

NEW YORK / RUSSELL & RUSSELL

PREFACE

The following pages attempt to tell once more, and as far as possible at first hand, the fascinating story of Elizabethan literature. But the tale has been somewhat compressed to treat what preceded the birth of Shakespeare with brevity, and what followed his death merely by indications and suggestions. This compression has seemed the more justifiable because Shakespeare's own work, thus contemplated in what surrounded it, gives to the subject a closer unity, and because the transition from literature, as an Elizabethan conceived and practised it, to what it came to be regarded in the time of Charles I, was well on its way by the year 1616.

This book departs in method from the customary arrangement of material by way of annals. It has neither listed authors in the order of their birth nor books in the chronology of their publication; but it has sought to view the subject in large by the recognition of a succession of literary movements, developments, and varieties in poetry, drama, and prose, at times identified with a great name, at others grouped merely because of subject-matter or likeness in origin or purpose. It is believed that the reader can experience no greater difficulty in seeking for Jonson, for example, in half a dozen chapters, than he might undergo in an effort to trace, let us say, the pastoral form of poetry through the scattered annals of a score of poets, ordered with chronological precision. It is the writer's conviction that until the history of literature cuts loose from the tyranny of biography, as history at large has long since cut loose, little progress can be made toward the realization of the higher aims of literary study. These he believes to consist less in the acquisition of a mass of information — however desirable information may be — about books, authors, and borrowings, about style and the bare bones of plays, than in the recognition of those unseen influences, literary and other, by which even the greatest man becomes

v

the product of his age. These higher aims he finds, too, in the ideals that great men have set up to write for and to live by, and in the nature of the artistry which, in as many differing beautiful forms as the forms of nature, results from this finest phase of the activity of men.

History now chronicles the common man. Literature should chronicle the common book, if we are to have a full understanding of the age. For a knowledge of the relations of minor authors, the quality, even the short-comings and inferiorities of their work, give us a mean level from which to judge the heights attained by choicer spirits. This book offers no apology for its treatment of the works of minor poets, dramatists, and pamphleteers where such treatment is demanded for the completeness of the picture. On the other hand it makes no claim to exhaustiveness, as neither its plan nor the demands of a just proportion could support such a claim.

The drama was the most potent form of Elizabethan artistic expression. It is obvious that in it Shakespeare literally dominated his age, as he radiated after his time a wider literary influence than that of any other English author. Shakespeare accordingly dominates this book, the history of literature in his age. For not only is the romantic drama his sovereign domain, but in the lyric, too, Shakespeare expressed the highest reach of his time. From the historical point of view, however, other men equally affected their fellow-subjects of Elizabeth and James. Sidney, Spenser, Donne, and Jonson, in poetry; Lyly, Hooker, Bacon, and the translators of the English Bible, in prose: these were the effective spirits of the time to be recognized as such not only for the divergent rays that each, as a lens, spread after far and wide, but for the converging light that each drew to himself from his predecessors, ancient, modern, foreign, or contemporary at home.

The short quotations from Elizabethan writers that occur in this book have been frankly modernized; as what may be lost of the flavor of quaintness is more than compensated in ready intelligibility to the modern reader. So, too, old titles have been curtailed at need and rendered into modern spelling, except where custom demands, as in *The Faery Queen*, for example, or *The Defense of Poesy*, a species of compromise. In this edition the text has been submitted to a thorough revision, where the discovery of new material has been made or where newer views have obtained as to certain matters among scholars. For example, we now know that Marlowe's opponent in the quarrel that cost him his life was one Ingram Frazer and that Frazer was pardoned by the Queen for his deed. An illustration of a current change in scholarly opinion is that which rejects Shakespeare's earlier alleged affiliation with the Earl of Leicester's and Lord Strange's players and refers them to the unsuccessful company under the patronage of the Earl of Pembroke which was disrupted in 1593, the year before we find Shakespeare's name among the Lord Chamberlain's men.

Lastly, the bibliography presents in alphabetical arrangement a list of authors who were writing or publishing during the lifetime of Shakespeare. It purposes to give in condensed form a representation of their literary activity and to indicate where their works may be read in modern available editions. The bibliography, too, has been thoroughly revised, not merely to bring it up to date with respect to new reprints of Elizabethan authors, but also to add in citation the best of the many new books of commentary and criticism which the unexampled activity of scholars in this fertile field has put forth within the last few years. Attention is called to the Supplementary List which adds especially to this latter bibliographical feature.

CONTENTS

CHAPTER V

LYLY AND THE DRAMA AT COURT

CHAPTER VI

MARLOWE AND HIS FELLOWS IN THE POPULAR DRAMA

CHAPTER VII

THE PAMPHLET AND THE PROSE OF CONTROVERSY

CHAPTER VIII

THE PASTORAL LYRIC AND THE SONNET

CHAPTER IX

SHAKESPEARE IN COMEDY AND IN CHRONICLE HISTORY

CHAPTER X

VERNACULAR DRAMA OF DEKKER, HEYWOOD, AND MIDDLETON

CHAPTER XI

LATER ANTHOLOGIES AND LYRICS TO BE SET TO MUSIC

CHAPTER XII

EPIC, NARRATIVE, AND PASTORAL VERSE

CHAPTER XIII

JONSON AND THE CLASSICAL REACTION

CHAPTER XIV

SHAKESPEARE, WEBSTER, AND THE HEYDAY OF ROMANTIC TRAGEDY

CONTENTS

CHAPTER XV

TRANSLATION IN VERSE AND PROSE

CHAPTER XVI

HISTORY, DIVINITY, AND OTHER PROSE OF CONTEMPO-
RARY COMMENT

CHAPTER XVII

ELIZABETHAN SATIRE, THE EPIGRAM, AND THE
" CHARACTER "

CHAPTER XVIII

BACON, JURIST, PHILOSOPHER, AND ESSAYIST

CHAPTER XIX

DONNE AND HIS PLACE AMONG LYRICAL POETS

CHAPTER XX

DRAMA AT THE UNIVERSITIES, THE PASTORAL DRAMA, AND THE MASQUE

CONTENTS

CHAPTER XXI

SHAKESPEARE AND THE NEW DRAMA OF FLETCHER

ERRATA

p. 66, l. 1   *for* Dolei *read Ariosto*
p. 134, l. 20   *for Poisy read Poesy*
p. 166, l. 22   *for* Bandello *read* Boccaccio
p. 250, l. 16   *for* higer *read* higher
p. 261, l. 11   *for Nortward read Northward*
p. 262, l. 2   *for* embarassment *read* embarrassment
p. 282, l. 30   *for* Boisteau *read* Boistuan
p. 283, l. 3   *for* Boisteau *read* Boistuan
p. 309, l. 20   *for* four *read* five
p. 309, l. 21   *for* 1954, the other *read* 1594 and 1597,
p. 436, l. 14   *for* Fuillerat *read* Feuillerat
p. 438, l. 31   *for* Gosson, Setphen *read* Gosson, Stephen
p. 448, l. 33   *for* 1, *Return read* 1, *The*
p. 450, l. 38   *for* Mudrer *read* Murder
p. 451, l. 6   *for* Haslitt *read* Hazlitt
p. 462, l. 35   *for* Fauset *read* Fausset
p. 463, l. 32   *for The Gulls' Handbook read The Gull's Handbook*
p. 464, l. 17   *for* Pedantins *read* Pedantius

p. 468, 2nd col., l. 30:   *The entry under Beaumont*—not the author of *Britain's Ida, 218—should appear under Spenser*
p. 469, 1st col., l. 16   *for* 193 *read* 192
p. 469, 2nd col., l. 11   *for* Boisteau *read* Boistuan

ENGLISH LITERATURE DURING THE LIFETIME OF SHAKESPEARE

CHAPTER I

THE LITERATURE OF FACT

WHEN Shakespeare was born, in the year 1564, Elizabeth had been on her throne for six years and had already gained, by the steadiness of her conduct and the wisdom of her counsels, the loyal affections and support of her people. King Henry's reign towards its close had degenerated into a reign of terror; and incompetency ruled throughout the government of the child Edward. More recent had been the bloody reprisals of unhappy and bigoted Queen Mary in her misguided endeavors to restore officially to her country the supplanted older faith. England had swung in these three reigns from Rome to Geneva, and from Geneva back to Rome, impelled by the fiat of monarchs and not by popular revulsions of belief. But these things were now memories of the past. What neither the example of Lutheran Germany nor the despotic will of Henry could effect, the fires of Smithfield had accomplished. England was at last become, if not wholly Protestant, at least once and forever hostile to the pretensions of Rome; and the menace of an ill-assorted union of England with Spain, the danger that England might sink, like the Netherlands, into a mere province of the universal Spanish dominion, had vanished with the resolute refusal of Elizabeth to accept the hand of King Philip.

In 1564 Queen Elizabeth was thirty-one years of age, a capable and imperious sovereign, skilled in the tortuous diplomacy of the age, unerring in her power to discern and employ men competent for the task of government, and devoted with the whole strength of her keen intellectual nature to the welfare of England. The queen's subjects at large knew little of her niggardliness in money affairs, of her want of religious conviction, or the doubles and turns of the royal policy in its frequently short-sighted opportunism; but her immediate servants had learned that even by devious courses and without the stay of a strong moral principle, Elizabeth might be trusted to steer a course safe and true among the quicksands of international intrigue; and in their trust was begotten the larger trust of the nation. Elizabeth had acquiesced in the accomplished fact of the French recovery of Calais; but she wrested from Francis and Mary Stuart, a year or two later, the withdrawal of the French garrison from the Scottish town of Leith and the acknowledgment that the realms of England and Ireland appertained of right to her. Elizabeth failed to obtain the papal recognition of her legitimacy and her right to succeed to the crown; but she curbed the reactionary zeal of her sister's clergy as she held in leash the violence of expectant Protestantism, and in the chaos of the religious uncertainty of the first few years of her reign achieved the foundations of a toleration of opinion, if not of worship, which the other European countries of her age knew not. Moreover Elizabeth was committed now, once and for all, to the policy of her father by the passing of the act of royal supremacy in the church, by her restoration of the prayer-book, and by her decisive refusal either to admit a papal nuncio into her realm or to send an envoy to the Council of Trent.

It is difficult to realize the poverty of English literature in the first years of Elizabeth's reign and appreciate how little the age had advanced, despite the new learning, towards the flowering time that was so near at hand. Aside from sermons, controversial pamphlets, and chronicle histories, the chief books reprinted in these years were Elyot's *Governor*, the *Utopia* of Sir Thomas More, now turned into English, and the *Colloquies* of Erasmus. In poetry the *Songs and Sonnets of Henry Howard, Earl of Surrey, Sir Thomas Wyatt and Others*, popularly known as *Tottel's Miscellany*, attained a third edition by the year of the accession of the queen; and the notable, if lugubrious, collection of historical "complaints," *The Mirror for Magistrates*, a second in 1563. Other poetry there was little, if we except Tusser's easy rimes on *The Hundreth Good Points of Husbandry*, Churchyard's "flyting," as the Scotch call such literary squabbling, with one "Camell," and the *Eclogues* of Barnabe Googe. In the drama as little had appeared. An interlude or so of John Heywood, *Lusty Juventus*, *The Nice Wanton*, and *Thersites*, these were nearly all. Perhaps the *Diccon of Bedlam* of the Stationers' Register of 1563 was *Gammer Gurton's Needle*, though of this we can not be sure. But an interest in poetry was awakening. Chaucer's complete works, Lydgate's *Siege of Thebes* and Langland's *Vision of Piers Plowman*, all were reprinted in 1561; and the works of John Heywood appeared collected in the following year. The ancients, too, were now translated into English. Besides Surrey's earlier attempts of 1557, Phaer's translation of Vergil's *Æneid* came two years later, carried on to nine books by 1562; while Jasper Heywood and Alexander Nevile set forth four of the Senecan tragedies in English, and Nicholas Udall, the well known author of *Ralph Roister Doister* (long since written but not yet printed), "newly corrected" his *Publius Terentius, Flowers of Latin Speaking*. Translations in part of Sallust, Cicero, Plutarch, Quintius Curtius, Cato, and Cæsar were printed within these few years, and Guevara's popular *Golden Book*, Castiglione's *Courtier*, and Macchiavelli's *Art of War* were Englished for the unlettered. More suggestive of what was to come was the translation of two Italian stories, *Titus and Gisippus* and *Romeus and Juliet*, both shortly to be employed as subjects for drama; while the beginnings of that deep interest in everything Italian that characterizes Elizabethan literature at large are disclosed in the informing works of William Thomas, his *History of Italy*, his Italian *Grammar*, and *Dictionary* of that language.

The mental awakening of England, which some still dare to call the Renaissance, and the similar earlier awakening in Italy offer two marked contrasts: a difference in character and a difference in the tardiness with which that movement proceeded to its results in the northern country. In Italy the Renaissance had been for the most part unmoral, and the highest æsthetic perception and scholarly tastes had often existed in men whose lives were marked by moral obliquity and blackened with crime. There the pleasures of the world's newly stirred curiosity were largely the virtuoso's delight in profane learning. When this reached deeper, it stimulated the frank philosophical cynicism of Macchiavelli's *Prince*, or raised ideals of the perfect man living in society as depicted in *The Courtier*. In Italy, the new world which the study of the ancients had opened to the spirit of man reacted immediately and mainly on literature, art, and society. In England, on the contrary, the new learning, as it was there called, took on from the first a more practical and a more ethical turn. The attitude of such men as Erasmus, Sir Thomas More, and those who brought the study of Greek to England was notable for its moral tone. The new knowledge was to be studied as a means to the better understanding of man in his relations to man and in his obligations to God. This was wide of the virtuoso's pleasures in the beauties of ancient classical art and the niceties of ancient classical learning; and hence it was a long time in England before the spirit of the new learning was felt to the full in works of art. In a word, although the bud was swelling and ready to burst about the time that Shakespeare was born, the flower of the Renaissance came into bloom only after Queen Elizabeth had been on her throne for a generation. The poetical activities of Sidney and of Spenser begin, at earliest, in the late seventies, and Lyly's *Euphues* appeared in 1579. It is doubtful if Marlowe, much less Shakespeare, wrote anything permanent before 1586; and Hooker and Bacon first emerge from controversy into authorship in the nineties. It is true that certain qualities which came to distinguish Elizabethan poetry are discoverable in Wyatt and Surrey, both of whom died while Henry VIII was yet reigning, and it is equally certain that men like Roger Ascham, the famous tutor to the children of that sovereign, and Latimer, one of the most eloquently outspoken of Henry's preachers, presaged, in form as well as in matter, certain abiding characteristics of Elizabethan prose. Nevertheless, it is the fruit and not the flower of promise that we gather in the harvest; and little has the student of English poetry or English prose to lose (if we except some half-dozen books, all of them already mentioned), who begins his study of Elizabethan literature with the works which appeared, in print at least, at a time subsequent to the birth of Shakespeare.

It is a commonplace of English history that the vigilant and centralized monarchy of Henry VII fostered in Englishmen a sense of nationality to which they had become almost complete strangers during the long feuds of the Wars of the Roses. The national consciousness, once reawakened, waxed strong in the earlier days of Henry VIII; and, though submitted to a terrible ordeal in the political and religious persecutions that followed, answered with enthusiasm the appeals of Elizabeth to patriotism and rested firm in its appreciation of her good government at home and her success in foreign politics. Literature responded at once to this awakened national spirit in a renewed interest in the past evinced in the translation and republication, for example, of such history as Ralph Higden's *Polychronicon* and in a revival of the popularity of works like Lydgate's *Falls of Princes* and Malory's *Morte Darthur* in which the historical instinct vies with the love of romance. A little later came the heyday of the English chronicle history which flourished in prose, in verse, at large and in epitome, in collections and in separate tracts, poems, and dramas. Sidney died too early to have felt to the full the literary reflex of this revival of national spirit. But it was this spirit no less than the love of poetry which inspired a familiar passage of *The Defense of Poesy*, which quotation can never stale: "Certainly I must confess my own barbarousness, I never heard the old song of Percy and Douglas that I found not my heart moved more than with a trumpet: and yet is it sung but by some blind crouder with no rougher voice than rude style."

The amount and variety of the literature of the sixteenth century which took English historical and legendary themes for its subject-matter are things commonly forgotten. This literature began towards the end of the reign of Henry VIII with Grafton's printing and continuation of the metrical chronicle of Hardyng and his edition of Hall. In the two succeeding reigns such books were discouraged; Gardiner even discerned concealed heresy in the political examples of *The Mirror for Magistrates*, and the projected publication of that work, in 1555, was stayed. On the accession of Elizabeth the publication of historical literature began anew with a third edition of the *Chronicle* of Fabyan. In 1563 Grafton brought out *An Abridgment of the Chronicles of England* which attained a fourth edition in 1572. He was rivaled in this undertaking by John Stow in 1565 with *A Summary of English Chronicles* which ran through ten editions up to 1604 and was the accepted short history of England of its day. Before a decade had elapsed John Foxe's *Acts and Monuments*, first published in 1563 and popularly known as *The Book of Martyrs*, had gone into a second edition; Grafton had abridged his *Abridgment* which still stretched, however, "from the creation of the world to the year 1566," and extended it into his *Chronicle at Large and Mere History of the Affairs of England and the Kings of the Same*, 1569; while Stow, in association with Bishop Parker, brought to the press three earlier Latin chroniclers, Matthew of Westminster, Matthew of Paris, and Thomas of Walsingham, and was busily at work in gathering materials for his *Chronicles of England*, 1580, and his *Annals*, first printed in 1592. In 1577 was published the most important of Elizabethan prose histories, *The Chronicles of England, Scotland and Ireland*, by Ralph Holinshed, a second edition appearing under the title, *Chronicles of England from William the Conqueror*, in 1587. To this enumeration of chronicles may be added the scattered biographies of historical personages from *The Life of Cardinal Wolsey* by Cavendish, written in the reign of Mary, and Sir John Hayward's several lives of English kings, to Bacon's *Life of Henry VII*, dating late in the reign of King James.

Nor was the prevalent interest in English history less notable among the poets whose flights, if by no means so sustained as those of the chroniclers, were far more frequent. *The Mirror for Magistrates* was one of the earliest fruits of the Elizabethan press. It is commonly spoken of as projected by Sir Thomas Sackville, one of the authors of *Gorboduc*, though he was really no more than the contributor of the one "legend," that of the Duke of Buckingham, which reached a real poetic level on a plane of mediocrity. The work was originally undertaken in consequence of the revived popularity of Lydgate's *Falls of Princes*. This origin gives to *The Mirror for Magistrates* a medievalism of tone which is enhanced by the sameness of mood, the moralizing, the somewhat old-fashioned versification of the majority of the "legends," and their connection by an artificial thread. *The Mirror* was a growth and accretion. The nineteen "legends" which constitute the first edition, that of 1559, are the work of six writers, of whom William Baldwin is the chief. They concern events from the days of the two Roger Mortimers and Thomas of Woodstock (1329–1392) to the tragedy of George, Duke of Clarence (1478). The second edition, 1563, reprinted these "legends," and added eight more by several authors, three of whom had already contributed to the first. Nearly all these "legends" concern personages of the time of Richard III. In 1574, John Higgins added seventeen "legends" of mythical and Roman Britain; and, as they preceded the other stories in point of time, called the new book *The First Part of the Mirror for Magistrates*. Four years later a rival continuation called *The Second Part of the Mirror for Magistrates* "containing the Fall of the unfortunate Princes of this Land from the Conquest of Cæsar unto the coming of Duke William the Conqueror" was published, the work of Thomas Blennerhasset, Baldwin's work thus becoming the third part. Blennerhasset's collection contains twelve "legends." In 1587 Higgins added to his "first part" no less than twenty-three stories, into which several Roman emperors intrude with a few further tales of modern personages by Churchyard and others. The last edition of *The Mirror*, 1610, picks and chooses from the earlier ones and adds eleven "legends," one by Drayton, the rest by the editor, Richard Niccols. We have thus a corpus of nearly a hundred "legends" varying in length from fifty to four hundred lines each, the work of some fifteen authors, extending over a period of fifty years and appearing in eight issues. We shall defer inquiring into the historical epics of Daniel, Drayton, and Warner to a later place in this book. All were of this general type. This impetus towards historical writing continued far into the reign of King James; although it was in the more patriotic times of Elizabeth that it reached its height and begot in the English drama that peculiarly typical and effective group of plays which is known as the English chronicle histories.[1]

Turning more specifically to the early prose chronicles, it is to be remembered that the learned in Tudor days still looked askant upon any work of a solid nature written in the vernacular prose. The sanction of centuries of scholarship demanded the use of the learned tongue, and when men came to cast their thoughts into English, it was with apologies for such a departure from custom and wont. For example it is thus that the learned Ascham writes in 1545:

And although to have written this book either in Latin or Greek had been more easier and fit for my trade in study, yet nevertheless, I supposing it no point of honesty, that my commodity should stop and hinder any part either of the pleasure or profit of many, have written this English matter in the English tongue for English men.

Elsewhere Ascham makes clear the condition of the time:

And as for the Latin or Greek tongue, everything is so excellently done in them, that none can do better. In the English tongue, contrary, everything in a manner so meanly, both for the matter and handling, that no man can do worse. For therein the least learned for the most part, have been always most ready to write. And they which had least hope in Latin, have been most bold in English; when surely every man that is most ready to talk, is not most able to write.

These passages of Ascham present by no means the biased and prejudiced opinion of a scholar who failed to appreciate the work of his own age in dwelling in the past. As a matter of fact, few of the familiar books of the modern world were

[1] The foregoing three paragraphs are repeated in part from the author's *English Chronicle Play*, 1902.

in existence when Ascham wrote. As Macaulay put it: "In the time of Henry VIII and Edward VI, a person who did not read Greek and Latin could read nothing, or next to nothing. The Italian was the only modern language which possessed anything that could be called a literature. All the valuable books then extant in all the vernacular dialects of Europe would hardly have filled a single shelf. England did not yet possess Shakespeare's plays and *The Faery Queen*, nor France Montaigne's *Essays*, nor Spain *Don Quixote*; . . . . Chaucer, Gower, Froissart, Comines, Rabelais nearly complete the list."

It was in the nature of things, then, that books so thoroughly national as those which discoursed of English deeds and English heroes should be cast in the English mold. Sir Thomas More might write in Latin of his imaginary commonwealth in Utopia, or Bacon, much later, shudder to trust his weighty philosophical cargo in the same vessel with *The Faery Queen* or *Hamlet;* but when it came to the glorification of English deeds and English kings, the English tongue was clearly the only fitting medium. We may thus affirm that this outburst of historical and kindred writing had much to do with the development of English vernacular prose, and in confirming thoughtful men to a preference for their own tongue over outworn and medieval Latin.

Once more, nearly all early Elizabethan English prose moved in the leading-strings of Latin. "It had been more easier and fit for my trade in study," says Ascham once more, "to have written this book either in Latin or Greek"; and when that excellent old teacher discourses of pedagogy his thoughts are riveted on the study of the classics. To write good prose was then to emulate Cicero; to write good English was to transfer Latin terms and Latin constructions to the modern tongue. To the present day we recognize a difference between the formality of the bookish tongue and everyday colloquial speech. And that difference arose out of the Latin foundations of English style. Until recently grammarians of English used an antiquated Latin desk full of pigeon-holes, if it may so be put, elaborately constructed to contain, each in its place, the many rules of Latin grammar. True, it might be difficult to find English material to fill all these compartments allotted to rules and exceptions. But for what was language given us, if not that the grammarians might wreak their ingenuity upon it? And so our tongue was contorted and analyzed, distinguished and subtilized until nearly every pigeon-hole in the Latin desk was filled. Here, again, was a recognition of the effect of Latin on English. But it is to be most carefully observed that, though often devout almost to slavishness in the worship of classical models, the writers of Elizabeth's day recognized to the full — as some others have not — that to confuse the vocabularies of two tongues is to write in neither. The Latinism of the Elizabethans is a Latinism of construction, not a Latinism of vocabulary. They could write "without all question" (*sine omni dubitatione*), speak of "the ill" (*mali*) for bad men, or say, like Milton,

He, *after Eve seduced*, unminded shrunk
Into the wood fast by;

but it was reserved for Sir Thomas Browne, a subject of Charles II, to write "Embrace not the *opacous* and blind side of *opinions*, but that which looks most *luciferously* or *influentially* unto goodness"; and for Dr. Samuel Johnson, a subject of the Georges, to define, for simplicity's sake, a fit as "a paroxysm or exacerbation of any intermittent distemper."

By far the most interesting of the prose chronicles of England, enumerated above, is that of Holinshed; for aside from the importance and excellence of this work, it was to this book that Shakespeare turned most frequently for the material of his chronicle plays. Ralph, or Raphael, Holinshed is first met early in the reign of Elizabeth as a translator or utility writer in the printing office of one Reginald Wolfe. Wolfe seems to have been a man of ambition and ideas. He had designed a universal history and a cosmography which was to include elaborate illustrations and maps. He had inherited the notes of the indefatigable librarian and antiquary of Henry VIII, John Leland, who in his peregrinations claimed to have visited "almost every bay, river, lake, mountain, valley, moor, heath, wood, city, castle, manor house and college in the land," who sought to collect manuscripts from the dismantled monasteries for the king's library, and who sedulously hived information and antiquarian, topographical, and literary material for more than thirty years. But "after five and twenty year travail spent therein," Wolfe died, and his successors, alarmed at the impracticable magnitude of his undertaking, reduced his plan to a history and description of the British Islands.

Holinshed continued in their employ, and became responsible for the greater part of the work. But others, likewise, were associated in it: among them William Harrison, at that time chaplain to Lord Cobham, Edmund Campion, the notable Jesuit missionary and martyr, and Richard Stanihurst, an eccentric Irish scholar and translator of Vergil. Stanihurst contributed the greater part of the history of his own country, adapting it chiefly from Giraldus Cambrensis. Holinshed was assisted likewise in that part of his work which dealt with Scotland; and his sources here were chiefly the histories of Hector Boece and John Major. It is to Harrison that we owe the delightful prefatory *Description of England*, the foundation book of any knowledge at first hand of the England of Elizabeth. Several qualities conspire to give this work its permanent value. First of all, Harrison tells us what we want to know, from the order of the nobility and the constitution of bishoprics to the nature of the houses people lived in, the clothes they wore, and the hour at which they dined. Secondly, Harrison's style is ever direct, colloquial, and racy in its originality of view and command of idiomatic English. Again, the personality of Harrison, which is always present, is most engaging in his honesty, outspokenness, and sanity of attitude. The *naïveté* of Harrison's nature, too, is unceasingly entertaining. It was this that caused him to find nothing irrelevant in a digression as to how he obtained tulips for his garden from Holland or in the circumstantial details of Mrs. Harrison's brewing of March beer. Harrison includes the commonplace and discusses the obvious, and as neither the commonplace nor the obvious of the England of his day is such to the reader of the twentieth century, he contrives to give us the "very age and body of the time, his form and pressure."

Thus, in the chapter devoted to the degrees of people in the commonwealth of England, we are informed with a searching insight into human nature quite applicable to to-day:

Whosoever studieth the laws of the realm, whoso abideth in the university, giving his mind unto his book, or professeth physic and the liberal sciences, or beside his service in the room of a captain in the wars, or good counsel given at home, whereby this commonwealth is benefited, can live without manual labor, and thereto is able to bear the port, charge, and countenance of a gentleman, he shall for money have a coat and arms bestowed upon him by heralds (who in the charter of the same do of custom pretend antiquity and service, and many gay things), and thereunto, being made so good cheap, be called master (which is the title that men give to esquires and gentlemen), and reputed for a gentleman ever after.

Elsewhere, affording more direct information, Harrison tells us:

With us the nobility, gentry, and students do ordinarily go to dinner at eleven before noon, and to supper at five, or between five and six at afternoon. The merchants dine and sup seldom before twelve at noon, and six at night, especially in London. The husbandmen dine also at high noon as they call it, and sup at seven or eight; but out of the term in our universities the scholars dine at ten. As for the poorest sort they generally dine and sup when they may, so that to talk of their order of repast it were but a needless matter.

To return to Holinshed, his part in the *Chronicles*, aside from general supervision, was the compiling of the history of England from the coming of Brute to 1577. As thus issued, Holinshed's *Chronicles* appeared in two large folio volumes illustrated with portraits, pictures of battles, and the like and enjoyed an immediate success. Holinshed died in 1580, and the second edition, of 1587, was edited by John Hooker *alias* Vowell with the help once more of several co-workers, notable among them John Stow, author of the *Survey of London*. The style of Holinshed's *Chronicles* is clear and dignified, though little distinguished by the graces. The editors strove to get at the truth as they understood it, and quoted an enormous array of authorities. Moreover the work is patriotic and Protestant to the core, and absolutely honest in its faiths and convictions. However, the Elizabethan conception of history was limited. It knew nothing of historical perspective and weighed scarcely at all the relative importance of the events which it detailed. It knew very little of historical portraiture, but followed the caricatures which partisanship had created, and repeated the tales which gossip had forged. Comets and pestilence were God's portents of his intervention in the affairs of men. Droughts and tempests, like contemporary murders and trials for witchcraft, were fit subjects for its pages with the progresses of kings and the falls and misfortunes of princes. Between More's distorted "biography" of Richard III, the enemy of the House of Lancaster, and Bacon's historical portraiture of the first Tudor Henry, there is little historical writing approaching our modern ideals and conceptions; for the method of annals, the facile and thoughtless art of the narrator, the simplicity of the repeater of tales and rumors, mark Hall, Holinshed, and Stow alike. Shakespeare used his materials in Holinshed, as elsewhere, honestly, even faithfully; and it is always a new surprise to turn from one of his historical plays to the corresponding passages in Holinshed and realize how close is his following:

Shortly after happened a strange and uncouth wonder, which afterward was the cause of much trouble in the realm of Scotland, as ye shall after hear. It fortuned as Macbeth and Banquo journied towards Forres, where the king then lay, they went sporting by the way together without other company, save only themselves, passing through the woods and fields, when suddenly in the midst of a land, there met them three women in strange and wild apparel, resembling creatures of elder world, whom when they attentively beheld, wondering much at the sight, the first of them spake and said: 'All hail, Macbeth, thane of Glamis!' (for he had lately entered into that dignity and office by the death of his father, Sinell). The second of them said: 'Hail, Macbeth, thane of Cawdor!' But the third said: 'All hail, Macbeth, that hereafter shalt be king of Scotland!' . . .

Herewith the aforesaid women vanished immediately out of their sight. This was reputed at the first but some vain fantastical illusion by Macbeth and Banquo, insomuch that Banquo would call Macbeth in jest, king of Scotland. . . . But afterwards the common opinion was, that these women were either the weird sisters, that is (as ye would say) the goddesses of destiny, or else some nymphs or fairies, indued with knowledge of prophecy by their necromantical science, because every thing came to pass as they had spoken.

Which of us reading this passage for the first time could fail to be surprised that the words "the weird sisters" are borrowed thence by Shakespeare? Indeed, considering Shakespeare's employment of this ancient quarry and the permanence of the ideas which cultivated men and women have derived from his plays, it may be questioned whether our general conception of the personages of earlier English history have not been derived more from Holinshed than from any other writer. Prince Hal, a wild and roistering youngster, reformed by responsibility into a model sovereign; Hunchback Richard, malevolent, unrepentant, capable of any crime; "Good Duke Humphrey"; Margaret, Queen of Henry VI, "the she wolf of France"; cool, calculating Bolingbroke; wronged, pathetic, and unhappy Katherine, who does not recognize these popular portraits? And what student of history does not know to how large a degree they are perversions of historical facts?

Even more popular than the *Chronicles* was Foxe's *Book of Martyrs*, printed again and again between its first appearance in 1563 and the end of the century. John Foxe had studied at Oxford and resigned his fellowship at Magdalen in 1545 in consequence of his Protestant convictions. Thereafter he lived much abroad, but returned to England on the accession of Elizabeth and died, in 1587, a prebend at Salisbury. He appears to have sacrificed preferment in the church to conscientious scruples as to surplices and ceremonials; and it is to his credit that he plead, though in vain, that mercy might be accorded the much persecuted Anabaptists. The portentous title of Foxe's remarkable work reads: "*Acts and Monuments* of these latter and perilous days, touching matters of the Church, wherein are comprehended and described the great persecutions and horrible troubles that have been wrought and practised by the Romish Prelates, especially in this Realm of England and Scotland, from the year of our Lord, a thousand unto the time now present." It was later augmented, first by Foxe and then by others, to include "a universal history of the church" at least so far as it concerned Christian martyrdom. A late edition of Foxe (1804) contains 2123 large pages in double columns of rather small print, in three volumes, which it is an effort for any but an athlete to wield. Foxe's book received the sanction of the bishops, and an order of the Anglican Convocation of 1571 "placed it in the hall of every bishop in England." In Protestant households of standing it lay ever at hand for the old to ponder and for the young to devour. Foxe is vivid, picturesque and circumstantial. He had a thesis to defend for the illustration of which the unchristian conduct of Christian men in all ages afforded him only too many terrible examples. His work is a huge party pamphlet and is often distorted, unhistorical, and unfair. But it was not more distorted or unfair than were the works which attacked it; and its stanch patriotism and Protestantism, albeit the latter was fanatical, wrought wonders in knitting Englishmen together to repel alike the invasion of Spain and the more insidious efforts of the Jesuits' missions to reclaim Protestant England to the mother faith of Rome.

There remains a kindred topic. If Englishmen in their re-awakened national consciousness "joyed to read the doings of brave Talbot against the French" and the martial deeds of Edward against the Bruce or Percy against Douglas, no less intense was their interest in their present world, in the adventurous spirit that animated Drake to compass the globe or Essex to "singe the beard of the Spanish king" at Cadiz. Martin Frobisher and Sir Francis Drake, Sir John Hawkins and Sir Humphrey Gilbert, what heart of English speaking man but warms at the mention of these valiant sea dogs, "old England's ever memorable worthies," their daring on many seas, their buccaneering, their grasp after Spanish gold, their trust in God and in England! Richard Hakluyt — or Hacklewit, which attests his English origin — was a man of one idea, and that was geography and the history of discovery. He tells us that while a student at Oxford, "I read whatever printed or written discoveries and voyages I found extant, either in Greek, Latin, Italian, Spanish, Portugal, French or English languages." Later he became a lecturer on cosmography and was among the first to show "the new lately reformed maps, globes, spheres and other instruments of this art, for demonstration in the public schools." In 1582 Hakluyt published his first work, *Divers Voyages touching the Discovery of America*, and he continued almost to the date of his death, in the same year with Shakespeare, an unwearied collector and investigator in the field of his choice. Like Harrison, Hakluyt was a clergyman and his various livings and preferments gave him the means and the leisure to prosecute his favorite work. Hakluyt's most noteworthy undertaking was *The Principal Navigations, Voyages and Discoveries of the English Nation* "made by sea or overland to the remote and farthest distant quarters of the earth at any time within the compass of these 1500 years, 1589." The range of this work is extraordinary and the zeal with which the editor labored, collecting, translating, and adapting every account of a voyage on which he could lay hands is altogether unparalleled. The slave trade of Sir John Hawkins and his barter and buccaneering among the Spaniards of the West Indies; Sir Francis Drake and his amazing success in rifling unprotected Peru, with his circumnavigation of the globe to escape reprisal; Sir Humphrey Gilbert's search after gold and the northwest passage, and the heroic death that he found at sea: such are some of the themes of this prose laureate of England's earliest geographical expansion. Variously enlarged and rewritten as it was in later editions, Hakluyt's *Principal Navigations* constitutes a marvelous and exceedingly circumstantial piece of evidence of the astonishing activity that preceded the laying of those foundations on which the future empire of England beyond the seas was to rest. While at first curiosity, and then patriotism, seem to have called Hakluyt to his task, he displays a consistent interest in the growth of trade and in the economic aspects of his subject, as we should call them to-day; and again and again we meet with him in the counsels of the newly founded East India

Company or in projects and petitions promoting colonization in Virginia and elsewhere. Hakluyt belongs to other fields than those of literature and yet the dead level of his utilitarian prose is not unbroken at times with a smack of the larger utterance of his age. Hakluyt was only the greatest of his class, like Holinshed among the chroniclers. Hakluyt's avowed successor was Samuel Purchase (1577-1626), a Cambridge man, parson of St. Martin's Ludgate. *Purchase his Pilgrims*, as he called his collection of voyages, was published in 1625 and is a work decidedly below that of Hakluyt in style, arrangement, and editorial judgment. In an earlier work of Purchase, entitled his *Pilgrimage*, he had put together a species of gazetteer of previous English voyages of discovery. Besides these greater works, many lesser pamphlets attest English adventures on the sea and in strange lands. *The Last Fight of the Revenge*, described by Sir Walter Raleigh in 1591, is cast in remarkably vivid and honest prose, and may be taken as typical of the epic height which this literature of fact attained at times in the hands of greater writers. The Revenge, single handed, had fought fifteen Spanish ships of war for fifteen hours:

All the powder of the Revenge to the last barrel was now spent, all her pikes broken, forty of her best men slain, and the most part of the rest hurt. In the beginning of the fight she had but one hundred free from sickness, and four score and ten sick, laid in hold upon the ballast. A small troop to man such a ship, and a weak garrison to resist so mighty an army. By those hundred all was sustained, the volleys, boardings, and enterings of fifteen ships of war, besides those which beat her at large. On the contrary, the Spanish were always supplied with soldiers brought from every squadron: all manner of arms and powder at will. Unto ours there remained no comfort at all, no hope, no supply either of ships, men, or weapons; the masts all beaten overboard, all her tackle cut asunder, her upper work altogether rased, and in effect evened she was with the water, but the very foundation or bottom of a ship, nothing being left overhead either for flight or defense. Sir Richard finding himself in this distress, and unable any longer to make resistance, ... commanded the master gunner, whom he knew to be a most resolute man, to split and sink the ship; that thereby nothing might remain of glory or victory to the Spaniards.

It was then that the Spanish admiral offered honorable ransom and a return to England for all; for he admired the desperate courage of his foes. At last Sir Richard, who was sorely wounded, was conveyed aboard the admiral's ship. From a Dutch writer, who had at first hand the Spanish report of this encounter, we learn that, on the Spanish galleon after the fight, and wounded among his enemies, Sir Richard "would carouse three or four glasses of wine and in a bravery take the glasses between his teeth and crush them in pieces and swallow them down." He was dying, and he longed for death. When the supreme moment came "he spake these words":

Here die I, Richard Grenville, with a joyful and quiet mind, for that I have ended my life as a true soldier ought to do, that hath fought for his country, queen, religion, and honor, whereby my soul most joyfully departeth out of this body, and shall always leave behind it an everlasting fame of a valiant and true soldier that hath done his duty as he was bound to do.

Into the corresponding works of the poets we can not enter here. They were more imaginative and reconstructive, and therefore less true to the actualities of stirring Elizabethan life. The true epic of such an age of action must be close to the deeds it depicts, though this represents but one phase of multiform Elizabethan life. We shall meet with higher ideals than these which are tethered to fact and national welfare, but we shall meet with no truer exponents of the material side of the national spirit that made modern England than Holinshed's chronicles of the political and social past of the nation, than Foxe's affirmation and justification of the Protestant position, or Hakluyt's thousand and one tales of the distant gropings and graspings after empire that laid the beginnings of greater Britain and her dominion over the sea.

CHAPTER II

LITERATURE OF THE COTERIE

THE medieval conception of the true gentleman excluded books, and culture by means of books. "When amongst knights or gentlemen," says Guevara, "talk is of arms, a gentleman ought to have great shame to say, that he read it, but rather that he saw it. For it is very convenient for the philosopher to recount what he hath read, but the knight or gentleman it becomes to speak of things that he hath done." The gentleman of the Renaissance added to the medieval virtues, which were prowess in war and wisdom at the council table, the new qualities of a love of learning and a taste and knowledge in the arts. The large and diverse interests of Sir Philip Sidney, the mirror and pattern of the Elizabethan gentleman, included athletic address on the tilting field, the theory and practice of war, the training of the courtier and the diplomat, a deep seated veneration for the classics, and the modern man's acquaintance with his own and foreign modern literatures. To Sidney were dedicated, among many other books, Spenser's *Shepherds' Calendar*, the first edition of Hakluyt's *Voyages*, and philosophical writings of the Italian skeptic and philosopher, Giordano Bruno; for Sidney was equally interested in the future of English letters and of English colonial empire beyond the seas, in the introduction of foreign meters to beautify English poetry, and in the preservation of the balance of Protestant power against the intrigues and encroachments of Philip of Spain.

In that beautiful book, *The Courtier* of Baldassare Castiglione, we have an engaging picture of the little court of Urbino in the early years of the sixteenth century. There the graces of conduct and the virtues of kindliness abounded; and a sweet and unaffected converse, combined with innocent merriment, all presided over by the grave but courteous duchess of that state. This circle was doubtless not so brilliant as the notable assembly which met in Florence at the fiat of Lorenzo the Magnificent, where Pulci, Ficino, Pico, and Poliziano discoursed learnedly and eloquently of state, art, literature, and philosophy. But at Urbino there was a comity of spirit, a "sweet conversation that is occasioned of an amiable and loving company"; and while we may recognize in its externals traces of that worldliness, lightness, and vanity which rise to the surface like froth in any current of social life, it held before it wholesome and gracious ideals, honoring gentleness and delicacy in man no less than in woman and offering a conclusive refutation to the charge that the Italy of the Renaissance was hopelessly abandoned and corrupt. A similar court was that of Margaret of Navarre, patroness of poets and lover of literature, Platonism, and the amenities of gentle social life. Without here anticipating, it is clear that the Sidneian circle of the Countess of Pembroke, that was to come, was not without its precedent in foreign lands.

Modern English poetry found its earliest cultivation in the select circles of the court. The old sacred drama, originating in the church, had come out into the public places of the market towns; it flourished in York, Chester, Coventry, and was popular and provincial. So, too, the ballad, that truest example of folk-poetry, was tied neither to place nor to poet, but was an utterance of the people at large. On the other hand, Chaucer was a poet of London and the court; Gower, a wealthy gentleman of Kent, attendant on his king, and learned and dull in three languages; while the best of the Scotch Chaucerians, from King James to Dunbar, were either royal or in the royal service. So when English poetry revived to shake off the traditions of medievalism, the first awakening was at court. Henry VIII was an accomplished and affable young man, a lover of the arts, a good musician, and not without claim to an humble rank as a poet; and he was surrounded by "a crew of courtly makers," foremost among them Wyatt and Surrey who were imbued with like tastes and talents. Neither Wyatt nor Surrey intrinsically amount to very much. In form they limp only too often to the tiresome

tune of what was known as Poulter's measure, a verse of alternate sixes and sevens:

> So feeble is the thread, that doth the burden stay,
> Of my poor life, in heavy plight that falleth in decay;
> That but it have elsewhere some aid or some succors,
> The running spindle of my fate anew shall end his course.

Inexpressibly tiresome is this kind of thing when prolonged
to any degree. In substance, too, the Wyatt-Surreian lover,
faint-hearted, languishing, and despairing, begets in the
modern reader, according to mood, disgust or mocking laughter. Yet there are better things in both poets; and historically
their importance is unquestionable. Wyatt experimented in
English verse, counting his syllables; Surrey attained a
smoothness and ease such as no one had reached in England
since Chaucer. Both poets attempted new meters as well
as novel-subject matter, derived from Italy and France.
Wyatt, before its rage in the latter country, had introduced the
sonnet into England; and, with it, that close imitation and
translation of Petrarch, master of the sonneteers, and of the
Petrarchists of France, which was to become so distinguishing
a characteristic of Elizabethan lyrists. The sonnet thus took
the English fancy and became, in time, one of the noblest of
English lyrical forms. The French *ballade*, on the contrary,
also employed by Wyatt, was so little understood that Wyatt's
first editor, Grimald, misprinted it; and save for Charles
Cotton in the Stuarts' reign, the *ballade* remained unknown
to English until revived in our own day. On the other hand,
Surrey in more facile versification confirmed the practice of
the sonnet and attempted an imitation of the Italian *versi
sciolti*, a free or unrimed verse of ten syllables, known to
English literature as blank-verse. Surely it was no small
service to point the way to "Marlowe's mighty line," to be
the first to practise a measure immortalized by Shakespeare
and Milton. Surrey's translation of parts of the *Æneid* is
the earliest English blank-verse. Nor is the metrical form
of these two early Tudor poets their only claim on our consideration. In them appears for the first time in English

the subjective note that has come so markedly to distinguish modern poetry. It was this, though it marked little more than disconsolate love, that was recognized in *Tottel's Miscellany*, and in *The Gorgeous Gallery of Gallant Inventions*, Clement Robinson's *Handful of Pleasant Delights*, and *The Paradise of Dainty Devises*, the anthologies of like character, if inferior repute, that followed *Tottel* in the seventies.

What Wyatt and Surrey groped for in the lyric of art, George Gascoigne, chief of poets between their time and Spenser's, furthered with a certain originality and force of his own. Gascoigne was born, we now know, in 1542 and educated at Cambridge, the Middle Temple, and Gray's Inn. Of honorable family but far from rich, Gascoigne gravitated naturally to court and remained, with an interval of service as a soldier in the Low Countries, a courtier and protégé at one time of Lord Grey de Wilton, at last of Elizabeth herself. It was in the congenial society of his fellows of the Inns of Court that Gascoigne first became an author and his versatility in poetry, drama, and prose was as great as his contemporary reputation. Under the title of *A Hundreth Sundry Flowers bound up in one Small Posy*, Gascoigne had attempted, by 1572, songs and sonnets in the manner of Surrey, elegies, autobiographical and narrative poems, in excellence well above the best work of his immediate contemporaries, a satire in blank verse of considerable merit entitled *The Steel Glass*, and three dramas, each somewhat a departure in its own kind. The prose writings of Gascoigne also deserve attention for a directness and simplicity of style and a freedom from Latinism rare in his day. To Gascoigne belong the earliest set treatise on versification in the English language and the first attempt to imitate, on the basis of an English story, the "novels" of Italy already popular in England in the translations of Painter, Fenton, and others. Gascoigne's story, *The Adventures of Master Ferdinando Jeronimi* (otherwise *Master Freeman Jones*) enjoyed, like some of his poetry, a repute not a little enhanced by allusions and innuendoes of a scandalous nature. Yet Gascoigne was one of the choir of poets that welcomed Queen Elizabeth to Kenilworth at the command of the Earl of Leicester during the festivities there in 1575. Gascoigne's poetry is always egotistic, it is often autobiographical. He was overwhelmed at times with repentance for "his youth misspent" and employed his later days in penning devotional pamphlets and eulogizing the queen in what seems a measurably successful endeavor to serve in the royal employ. Gascoigne was not a scholar though he was a cultivated man of the world; and both in his sensible little treatise, *Certain Notes of Instruction concerning the Making of Verse and Rime in English*, and in his practice of the art of poetry, he maintained an attitude of remarkable independence alike of classical models and of modern foreign influences.

Gascoigne's literary associates include such now forgotten names as Francis Kinwelmarsh, his coadjutor in the translation of the tragedy *Jocasta*, Alexander Nevile, translator of Seneca, Barnabe Googe, writer of *Eclogues*, and Thomas Churchyard, general pamphleteer. Other poetical contemporaries were the Earl of Oxford, Humphrey Gifford, Matthew Grove, and Thomas Howell. George Whetstone's prosaic Muse celebrated Gascoigne's obsequies. But among the commendatory verses prefixed to the *Posies*, one set is signed with initials that may stand for Gabriel Harvey, Spenser's Hobbinol and Mentor of the Areopagus, whilst to *The Steel Glass* we find prefixed a series of verses signed "Walter Rawely of the Middle Temple." Indeed, when Gascoigne died, in 1577, Spenser had already passed to his master's degree at Cambridge and but two years remained to the publication of *The Shepherds' Calendar* and the broad daylight of Elizabethan poetry. As for Sidney, though but twenty-two years of age, he was already abroad on an embassy to the Emperor of Germany and the poetry of *Astrophel and Stella* was soon to be seething in his brain.

Philip Sidney was the son of Sir Henry Sidney, Lord Deputy of Ireland and President of Wales, one of Elizabeth's most tried and faithful servants; his mother was sister to Robert Dudley, the great Earl of Leicester who courted Queen Elizabeth so assiduously. The Sidneys were of better blood than the Dudleys. Sir Henry appears to have been too honest to become wealthy; but Philip, as his eldest son, with birth the most honorable and as nephew and possible heir to Leicester, started with much that fortune could give. Sidney enjoyed, too, the best of educations, going to Shrewsbury School and thence to Oxford. It was at Shrewsbury that Sidney formed his enduring friendship with Fulke Greville. Sidney was a grave and precocious youth and employed the leisure of his attendance at court in travel abroad, or in study. His interests were general — history, "plantation," as colonization was called, politics, philosophy, science, and literature. An idea of the diversity of Sidney's talents may be gleaned from the fact that he was prized by William the Silent as "one of the ripest and greatest counselors of estate in Europe," esteemed by the learned Languet for his scholarship, appreciated for his love of philosophy by Giordano Bruno, intimate with Drake, Frobisher, and Sir Humphrey Gilbert for his interest in adventurous voyage and colonization, and beloved by the poets — Spenser foremost among them — for his poetry. "There was not an approved painter, skilful engineer, excellent musician, or any other artificer of fame that made himself not known to him," says Greville.

Like the poetry of Wyatt and Gascoigne, that of Sidney and of Spenser maintained a tradition and a cult. Confined to a limited and select circle, it emulated in its practice and its patronage of the arts the amenities of Italian courts such as that of Urbino and in its theories about literature and its experiments in poetry, the group of writers known in France as the *Pléiade*. The *Arcadia*, written in the seclusion of Penshurst, the seat of the Earl of Pembroke, read to a group of intimate friends there, page by page, and dedicated to the author's beloved sister; *The Faery Queen*, allegorically setting forth the doings of the queen and noble personages of her court, as much a book of the ideal man and of ideal conduct in life as *The Courtier* itself; Lyly's *Euphues*, the popular novel of the moment, no less the work of an attendant at court and no less addressed to a select and limited audience: all of these belong to the literature of the coterie. And so do Lyly's dramas and in a sense likewise, *A Midsummer-*

Night's Dream, perhaps prepared to celebrate the marriage of that "universal patroness of poets, Lucy Harington," to the Earl of Bedford in the royal presence. Sidney's poetry was, in even a narrower sense than this, literature of the coterie. From certain letters exchanged between Spenser and Gabriel Harvey, we learn that, in the late seventies, there existed in London a species of literary club called the Areopagus, which interested itself in poetry, experiments in versification, and other literary matters. This intimacy of the young poets and courtiers of the time is interestingly illustrated in many poems and especially in the "two pastorals made by Sir Philip Sidney upon his meeting his two worthy friends Sir Edward Dyer and Mr. Fulke Greville." A couple of stanzas will show the relation:

> Join, mates, in mirth with me,
> Grant pleasure to our meeting,
> Let Pan, our good god, see
> How grateful is our greeting.
> Join hearts and hands, so let it be;
> Make but one mind in bodies three.

> Sweet Orpheus' harp, whose sound
> The steadfast mountains moved,
> Let here thy skill abound
> To join sweet friends beloved.
> Join hearts and hands, so let it be;
> Make but one mind in bodies three.

"This happy blessed trinity," as it is called in another stanza, was the heart of the Areopagus. About these three were clustered a chosen few that were interested in poetry and in theories about it. Spenser, then newly come to court, could not fail to be drawn into such a brotherhood, whilst Gabriel Harvey, the pedantic and somewhat unwise but zealous Cambridge don, friend and self-constituted Mentor of Spenser, surveyed the proceedings from afar and amused himself — if not others — by writing censorious or jocular letters to Spenser on the subjects of the discussion, all of which letters, as we have seen, Harvey carefully preserved and printed a few years later for general edification and for the particular aggrandisement of his own importance.   Later members of the Areopagus were Samuel Daniel and Abraham Fraunce, like Harvey a champion and practicer of English hexameter verse.

The Areopagus entered heart and soul into a discussion of the most pressing literary problem of the day, the relative merits of ancient and modern versification.   This question had been first mooted in print in England by the excellent Ascham, in his *Schoolmaster*, printed in 1570, two years after the author's death.   Gascoigne wrote his sensible little treatise as we have seen, some five years later, laying down rules of thumb for the making of English verse; and King James followed, exercising his boyish pen in the same momentous subject in the preface to a volume which he entitled *Essays of a Prentice in the Divine Art of Poesy*, 1586.   With the example of Roman literature before them, a literature based on that of Greece and successful in the main only where it had faithfully followed its prototypes, it was not surprising that men, educated in the classics, should conceive that the salvation of English literature was to be reached only in a slavish following of the ancients.   Long were the discussions of Harvey, Spenser, and others concerning the quantities of English words.   Thomas Drant, the translator of Horace, set up a system, the rival of Harvey's.   William Webbe, a tutor of St. John's College, Cambridge, in *A Discourse of English Poetry*, 1586, ventilated his opinion "touching the reformation of our English verse" and "travestied" a poem or two of *The Shepherds' Calendar* into sapphics; Stanihurst, even doing six books of the *Æneid* into some of the most astonishing vernacular hexameters that have ever been perpetrated in the name of poetry.   Sidney alone of his time discerned the larger issues of this controversy, and, recognizing the beauties of Italian poetry as well as those of the classics, conducted a marvellously complete set of experiments in classical meters and Italian forms: the more marvellous when we remember his preoccupation and the extraordinary variety of interests that claimed his attention and his time.

Not to pursue this topic too far, it may none the less be recorded that an elaborate and important treatise on *The Art of English Poesy*, published in 1589 and attributed to George Puttenham, upholds the possibilities of English versification in the course of an exhaustive discussion of matters historical, rhetorical, and fantastic concerning poetry and language at large. Indeed, the latest guns in this long controversy were not fired until the very last years of Elizabeth's reign when Thomas Campion, musician and lyric poet, and Samuel Daniel, one of the last of the Sidneian circle, measured swords on the subject in their tracts, entitled respectively *Observations on the Art of English Poesy* and *A Defense of Rime*, 1602 and 1603.

But let us return to Sidney and his experiments in exotic forms of verse. Sidney's *Astrophel and Stella*, offers a complete vindication of the sonnet, practised in a dozen different forms, to adoption into the English language. In the poems which diversify the *Arcadia*, may be found experiments in the *terza rima*, the dignified and exquisite verse of the *Divina Comedia* of Dante; in the *canzone* and in the *sestina*, intricate interlacings of successive stanzas; and in the madrigal, a dainty little verse-form, commonly written for music. There likewise are as successful achievements in classical sapphics, anacreontics, elegiacs, and hexameters as may be devised in a tongue which is compelled, as is English, to substitute, as a governing feature, accentual stress for the classic principle of quantity, and an arbitrary ascription of quantity to English syllables for that nice system which the genius of classical prosody had invoked. In a word, Sidney tested by exhaustive experiment the possibilities of both classical and Italian metrical forms transplanted into English verse. He died before he made known his verdict. But when it is recalled that no poem of his was published in his lifetime, we cannot affirm that he was absolutely satisfied with his results.

But we are not without knowledge of Sidney's larger tenets as to literature and art. The age was full of literary controversy. Ascham had inveighed against riming and the running of the letter with "the Gothic barbarism" that fostered it; but he had warned the age against "the Siren enchantments of Italy" and declared "an Italianate Englishman an incarnate devil." Gascoigne, on the other hand, was content to treat of English verse as it was, and waste no time either in abuse or in praise of foreign matters. Another question of the day was raised by the new and surprising up-growth and popularity of vernacular plays acted on improvised stages in public taverns and other resorts. In 1579 Stephen Gosson wrote a book which he entitled *The School of Abuse*, "a pleasant invective against poets, pipers, players, jesters, and such like caterpillars of the commonwealth." This, as its title sets forth, was one of a series of attacks upon the stage and its abuses — attacks which were often extended Puritanically to include all art. Gosson was a renegade actor and playwright and exhibits much of the zeal and rancor of the reclaimed. Whether in impudence or in honest mistake, he dedicated his *School* to Sidney, and "was for his labor scorned," reports Spenser, "at least if it be in the goodness of that nature to scorn." Gosson was almost immediately answered by Lodge in a *Defense of Poesy, Music, and Stage Plays*, a book of much eloquence and suavity; and soon after Sidney wrote his own *Defense*, not for publication, but for circulation among his friends.

Sidney's *Defense of Poesy* is a work of genuine and fervid enthusiasm, remarkable in its breadth and liberality, and of a nature comparable at least in its effects to Lessing's famous *Laocoon*. Sidney transcended the limits of Gosson's petty objections to consider on wide and philosophical grounds the nature of poetry, its relation to history and to philosophy, and eloquently to plead its divine origin and its beneficent influence on human life. Nor is it a serious criticism of this work to acknowledge the influence upon it of "current continental criticism." But admirable as *The Defense* was in its day, the historical value of this little treatise is even greater; for it defines for us the position of a talented, judicious, and independent young critic about the time that Spenser was beginning *The Faery Queen* and Shakespeare was still wandering, a mischievous rather than a dreamy lad, among the lanes of

Warwickshire. *The Defense of Poesy* must have been written soon after 1580, though it first appeared in print in 1595. It is not, then, surprising that we should find Sidney expressing discontent with poetry and declaring that besides Chaucer, *The Mirror for Magistrates,* Surrey's lyrics and *The Shepherds' Calendar,* "I do not remember to have seen but few (to speak boldly) printed that have poetical sinews in them." In the light of this date of writing, Sidney's praise of *Gorboduc* and his decided preference of Sophocles and Euripides over the English dramatists Edwards and Preston, most popular of their time, is in no wise amazing. Five or six years were yet to elapse before *Tamburlaine* was to sound a new era for English drama, and Gascoigne and Whetstone represented the height to which the English dramatic genius had by that time attained. Equally interesting is Sidney's attitude of criticism towards the new Euphuistic prose, which had already fallen into the abuses of excess. He puts his finger on three of its distinctive features, declaring of alliterative writers that they pursue the "coursing of a letter, as if they were bound to follow the method of a dictionary"; likening the undue use of ornament to "those Indians" who are "not content to wear ear-rings at the fit and natural place of the ears, but they will thrust jewels through their nose and lips because they will be sure to be fine." But the living value of *The Defense* lies in the liberality and lofty ideality of its conception of poetry and in its affirmation of poetry's true function in life. We have here no petty dallying with the "toys of wit," as Puttenham denominates poems, fit only "to fill the vacant hours of time of idle courtiers and gentlewomen," but the serious assignment of poetry to that concrete representation of human ideals in forms of imperishable beauty, which has formed an essential part of every true definition of this subtlest of the arts since philosophers began to define.

Let us now turn to the poetry of Sidney. *Astrophel and Stella* (like the rest of Sidney's work) was printed after his death, appearing first in a surreptitious edition in 1591, and procured for the printers by Thomas Nash. This earliest sequence of its kind in the language consists of one hundred

and ten sonnets with a few intercalated lyrics in other measures. The series was indubitably inspired by the sonnets of
Petrarch and the Platonic ideals of love therein upheld by the
Italian poet's cult of his ideal mistress, Laura. Moreover,
Sidney was acquainted not only with Italian poetry, but with
French poetry, notably Ronsard, and the rest of the *Pléiade* as
well. He followed their guidance as to the professional manner
of writing a sonnet, if we may put it so, precisely as he might
imitate an ancient meter or observe any other poetic convention. Until lately it has been customary to recognize in
the fervor of the poetry of *Astrophel and Stella* the poetical
expression of a leaf from Sidney's life; and his age appears to
have accepted his sonnets as such. According to this view,
Astrophel and Stella sets forth the story of Sidney's love for the
Lady Penelope Devereux, daughter of the first Earl of Essex
who was much attached to Sidney and had suggested a match
between the two as early as 1576, when Philip was twenty and
Penelope a little maid of twelve. But Sidney, proving unwilling, whether from disinclination to marry at all, ambition
to achieve a higher position than was his before doing so, or
indifference, another match was at once arranged for Stella,
and she was married to the young Lord Rich, who, to say the
least, neglected her. As to Sidney, he soon found out to his
disquiet that, having lost Stella forever, he had really never
ceased to love her; and being a man of poetic temperament
— the temperament that seeks consolation and relief in artistic
expression — Sidney spoke out his heart in rime.

Of late, however, it has been maintained that although
"Sidney's pursuit of the favor of Lady Rich, a coquettish
friend of his youth who married another," may have "led him
to turn sonneteer," "he wrote under the glamour of Petrarchan
idealism, and held that it was the function of the 'lyrical kind
of songs and sonnets' to sing 'the praises of the immortal
beauty' and of no mundane passion."[1] According to this idea,
"detachment from the realities of ordinary passion, which
comes with much reading about love in order to write on the

[1] See Sidney Lee, *Elizabethan Sonnets*, i, xliii; Courthope,
English Poetry, ii, 227-233.

subject, is the central feature of Sidney's sonnets"; and it is
shown triumphantly that Sidney borrowed idea after idea
from Petrarch, Ronsard, and others, addressing the Thames
only because Ronsard had similarly addressed the Rhone,
and apostrophizing night, sleep, and the power of Stella's eyes
only because Petrarch had said all these things before him.

These parallels need not be questioned either in bulk or
in detail. But it may well be queried if their mere existence
is in itself sufficient to deprive the story adumbrated in Sidney's
sonnets of all subjective basis in fact. However deeply Sidney
may have been affected by the study which we know he made
of the poetry of Italy and France, and whatever was to be the
general practice of English sonneteers to come, there is neither
anything improbable in the situation nor in the emotions detailed in *Astrophel and Stella*. The following sonnet has been
found to parallel one of Petrarch's; it may none the less have
certain reference to the joustings of May, 1581, in which Sidney and his friend Greville appeared as challengers, clothed
with a sumptuousness and attended by a state that recalled the
tourneys of the Middle Ages:

> Having this day my horse, my hand, my lance
> Guided so well that I obtained the prize,
> Both by the judgment of the English eyes
> And of some sent from that sweet enemy, France;
> Horsemen my skill in horsemanship advance,
> Town folks my strength; a daintier judge applies
> His praise to sleight which from good use doth rise;
> Some lucky wits impute it but to chance;
> Others because of both sides I do take
> My blood from them who did excell in this,
> Think Nature me a man-at-arms did make.
> How far they shot awry! the true cause is,
> Stella looked on, and from her heavenly face
> Sent forth the beams which made so fair my race

And this other sonnet:

> Stella, think not that I by verse seek fame,
> Who seek, who hope, who love, who live but thee;
> Thine eyes my pride, thy lips mine history:
> If thou praise not, all other praise is shame.

Nor so ambitious am I as to frame
A nest for my young praise in laurel tree;
In truth, I swear, I wish not there should be
Graved in my epitaph a poet's name.
Ne, if I would, could I just title make,
That any laud thereof to me should grow,
Without my plumes from others' wings I take:
For nothing from my wit or will doth flow,
Since all my words thy beauty doth endite,
And Love doth hold my hand and makes me write.

Assuredly such poetry rings with more than the trivial music of a mere Petrarchan imitator; or all instinct for poetry must go for naught.

Besides *Astrophel and Stella* the greater part of Sidney's poetry is found strewn incidentally through the pages of his romance, the *Arcadia*. It may be said in general of the poetry of the *Arcadia* that it seems less spontaneous than the sonnets of *Astrophel*, less poetry of direct emotion; and yet we may wrong Sidney here if we fail to recognize that delicacy and elaboration of workmanship, in any art, need not necessarily destroy that sincerity of impulse which is the life principle of all the arts. The metrical experiments unconsidered, there remains much in the poetry of the *Arcadia* worthy of the author of the burning lines of *Astrophel and Stella*

Sidney's poetry is imitative of the loveliest melodies of contemporary French and Italian poetry, and resonant with deeper notes of the music of the classics. It was Sidney who popularized the pastoral mode as well as the sonnet in England. The first served its turn in offering to the poets of the Elizabethan spring-time a delicate and artistic convention in which to cradle their first fledglings. The sonnet had been written before, as we have seen, but never with such success, in a variety so Italian, or in a sequence which so emulated the beauty and glory of the sonnets of Dante and Petrarch. The popularization of the "conceit" is a more doubtful service of Sidney to the literature of his time. Sidney's romantic temper delighted in the ornament of detail, and no grace was to him too trivial or bizarre to lavish on the decoration of divine poesy. Though thus our first great poet to fall under the spell of the petty "conceit" with its extravagant figure and far-fetched metaphor, Sidney erred in this less from mere delight in these petty baubles of ingenuity than from the passionate current of a poetical eloquence that carried great thoughts like trifles and trifles like great thoughts on its impetuous torrent. More certain immediate services to the literature of his age were those in which Sidney proved by experiment the real possibilities and limitations of classical prosody as applied to the construction of English verse; and laid, by a liberal application of ancient and Renaissance Italian theories to modern conditions, the foundations of English æsthetics and criticism. But whether for the earnestness and eloquence of his theories or for the fervor and sincerity with which he applied them, it may be said that Sidney was the poet he was because he was the man he was. In the words of his loving and faithful Jonathan, Fulke Greville, whose *Life of Sidney* is one of the sweetest and manliest tributes to true friendship that literature knows: "His very ways in the world did generally add reputation to his Prince and country, by restoring amongst us the ancient majesty of noble and true dealing; as a manly wisdom that can no more be weighed down by an effeminate craft than Hercules could be overcome by that effeminate army of dwarfs. And this was it which I profess I loved dearly in him, and still shall be glad to honor in the good men of this time: I mean that his heart and tongue went both one way, and so with every one that went with the truth; as knowing no other kindred, party, or end. Above all he made the religion he professed the firm basis of his life."

CHAPTER III

THE NEW CULTIVATED PROSE

IT has been said that a list of the earliest Elizabethan books written in prose is chiefly a list of literary curiosities; and to a certain degree this is true, though we are coming more and more to understand that modern English prose was not the invention of John Dryden or of any other subject of King Charles, but had already been formed in all its essential particulars in the age that produced Hooker, Bacon, our English Bible, and the prose of Shakespeare and Jonson. But much had to go before results such as these; and English prose no less than English verse was compelled to pass through the period of experimentation and to test the value of exotic models before it came to its own. We have already heard of Elizabethan Latinism and how it was a Latinism of structure and idiom rather than a Latinism of vocabulary. When learning left the school and the cloister to inhabit likewise the court, new ideals were added both to the conception of life and to that of literature. Scholarship had its conventions; and so, too, had social life. There was a correct way (as to which scholars agreed) in which to write the learned language, then, be it remembered, no dead tongue. Might there not be an equally correct way in which to write modern English, a way in which the graces and elegance of court life might be expressed in contradistinction to the common tongue which men spoke in the streets and taverns?

John Lyly, the Euphuist, was of a Hampshire family and born about 1554. He was the grandson of William Lilly, the grammarian, and a student of Magdalene College, Oxford. Anthony à Wood, the gossipy biographer of Oxonians, tells us that Lyly "was always averse to the crabbed studies of logic and philosophy," and that he did "in a manner neglect academical studies, yet not so much that he took not the

degrees in arts, that of master being completed in 1575."
Lyly seems to have sought the patronage of Lord Burleigh
as far back as 1574; and he must have gone up to London
and begun attendance on the court soon after taking his master's degree. Lyly was especially desirous of obtaining the
Mastership of the Queen's Revels, and several letters of his
relative to this remain. Lyly began his career with *Euphues,
the Anatomy of Wit*, registered in 1578 and published in the
next year. The book was an immediate success, and Lyly
probably spent the better part of 1579 in writing the second
and longer part, called *Euphues and his England*, which
appeared in 1580. Some idea of the esteem in which this
book was held may be gained from one or two contemporary
opinions. Thus Webbe in his *Discourse of English Poetry*,
1586, comparing the achievements of the ancients with modern
writers, says:

Among whom I think there is none that will gainsay, but Master
John Lyly hath deserved most high commendations, as he which
hath stepped one step further therein than any either before or since
he first began the witty discourse of his *Euphues*. Whose works,
surely in respect of his singular eloquence and grave composition of
apt words and sentences, let the learned examine and make trial
thereof thorough all the parts of rhetoric, in fit phrases, in pithy sentences, in gallant tropes, in flowing speech, in plain sense and surely, in
my judgment, I think he will yield him that verdict, which Quintillian
giveth of both the best orators Demosthenes and Tully, that from
the one, nothing may be taken away, to the other, nothing may be
added.

Again and again we find Lyly's praises sung by his contemporaries with but few dissenting voices. As late as 1633 the
publisher of Lyly's collected plays exclaims: "Our nation
are in his debt, for a new English which he taught them.
Euphues and his England began first that language. All our
ladies were then his scholars, and that beauty in court, which
could not parley Euphuism, was as little regarded as she
which now there speaks not French."

The volume which so took the English world of its day
by storm is a love story of the slenderest possible construction

in which is told the adventures in England and elsewhere of Euphues, a young Athenian gentleman of wealth and position, thus offering the greatest possible number of opportunities for conversation, argument, and satirical comment on topics most of them of contemporary interest and moment. The plot, such as it is, hardly moves at all, and little or no characterization is attempted. It is neither for plot nor character that *Euphues* was written; except so far as these things are necessary to serve as the foundations on which to construct fine dialogue, rhetorical speeches, and moral discourses. But a distinction must be drawn between the first part, *Euphues, the Anatomy of Wit*, which is in the main a philosophical essay addressed to gentlemen and students, and *Euphues and his England*, in which the author appeals directly "To the Ladies and Gentlewomen of England," declaring that "*Euphues* would rather lie shut in a lady's casket than open in a scholar's study"; and that "there shall be nothing found that may offend the chaste mind with unseemly terms and uncleanly talk." The second part of *Euphues* is therefore much less satirical and more interested in the refinements of choice society, more concerned with the intricacies of polite love-making and the repartee of smart conversation among gentlemen and gentlewomen. While neither a book of essays,—much less of philosopy,— a book of deportment and polite conduct, nor a story in any wise worked out as to plot or character, it is yet not altogether extravagant to say that in *Euphues* we have the earliest important piece of English fiction, the slender beginnings of that sea of writing realistic and romantic in which the modern reader finds his solace and his delight. As M. Jusserand has pointed out, with *Euphues* commences in England the literature of the drawing-room

And yet it is remarkable how, in its many aspects, Lyly's work has been understood and misunderstood. Charles Kingsley called it, not without justice,"as brave, righteous, and pious a book as a man need look into"; and the year 1900 saw it abused in print as "a piece of square-toed, finical vacuity," whatever that may mean. The most complete failure to represent *Euphues* and Euphuism — though we may say with Dr. Horace Howard Furness, "it stabs, to couple this word with that great and dear memory"— was Sir Walter Scott's in his character of Sir Percie Shafton in *The Monastery*. As to Euphuism the word is constantly misused,[1] although the subject has been now so thoroughly discussed that there is no excuse for any misunderstanding.

Euphuism is a rhetorical prose style. It is concerned neither with the choice of subject-matter nor with vocabulary. Hence the common use of the word to denote a florid and poetic style, the chief features of which are foreign and far-fetched words, is indefensible. Euphuism is concerned wholly with grammatical structure and syntax, and its purpose is the inducement of an artificial emphasis by means of antithesis and repetition in sentence form and relation. Its sentences are elaborate in their antithetical or parallel structure, they are balanced and pointed, and constructively as symmetrical as possible. The means used to produce all this is complicated and yet not unreducible to certain very definite categories. In the first place, Lyly is very fond of oratorical question and response, a device too familiar to need illustration. Secondly, he employs figurative language in a deliberately artificial manner, often taking familiar natural objects and stringing them together in similitudes, all illustrating the same point. For example: "As therefore the sweetest rose hath his prickle, the finest velvet his brack, the fairest flower his bran, so the sharpest wit hath his wanton will, and the holiest head his wicked way." Again, Lyly carried to excess the fondness of his age for allusion to classical and mythical history, revelling with delight in that rediscovered world in a true spirit of the Renaissance. Thus he asks: "Did not Giges cut Candaules' coat by his own measure? Did not Paris, though he were a welcome guest to Menelaus, serve his host a slippery prank?" Opening his book at random, we find Diogenes, Pythagoras, Socrates,

[1] See especially Mr. Courthope's perverse employment of the word in connection with poetry. The authoritative monograph on the topic is that of C. G. Child, *John Lyly and Euphuism*, Münchener Beiträge, vii, 1894.

Plato, Milo, Lycurgus, Lacedemonians, and Thessalians all on one page. Scarcely less pervasive and excessive are the figures and illustrations which Lyly derives from nature perverted, what has been dubbed Lyly's "unnatural natural history." "It is like to fare with thee as with the eagle, which dieth neither for age nor with sickness, but with famine, for although thy stomach hunger yet thy heart will not suffer thee to eat." "I have read, that the bull being tied to the fig-tree, loseth his strength; that the whole herd of deer stand at the gaze, if they smell a sweet apple; that the dolphin by the sound of music is brought to the shore." No trick of Lyly has called forth so much ridicule as this; but is it much more unnatural than our own contemporary "animal story," which, under guise of an accurate chronicle of nature (to which Lyly made no pretense) ascribes to the beasts of the fields and the prairies manlike qualities of thought and reasoned action which would do credit to the talking dragons and diabolical werewolves of the dark ages?

But more distinctive than all these artificial similitudes and illustrations is Lyly's equally deliberate employment of certain devices for rhetorical emphasis. Alliteration, which is the correspondence of the initial sound of words otherwise dissimilar, is as old as the language. As is universally known, it was a chief distinguishing trait of Old English verse, and it remains one of the graces of modern English poetry. Lyly makes use of this familiar device in the subtlest possible manner, simply, continuously, transversely. He plays with words of like sound or similar sound, producing what is technically know as assonance and annomination, and employs all this to emphasize and ornament a larger likeness of clause and phrase.

Cast not your eyes on the beauty of women, lest ye cast away your hearts with folly; let not that fond love, wherewith youth fatteth himself as fat as a fool infect you; for as a sinew, being cut, though it be healed, there will always remain a scar; or as fine linen stained with black ink, though it be washed never so often, will have an iron mole: so the mind once mangled or maimed with love, though it be never so well cured with reason, or cooled by wisdom, yet there will appear a scar, by the which one may guess the mind hath been pierced and a blemish whereby one may judge the heart hath been stained.

Here the whole passage is balanced and antithetical as are equally its various members; it begins with a play on words (*cast* not your eyes, *cast* away your hearts); alliteration is present in "*fatteth* himself *fat* as a *fool*," "*mind* once *maimed* and *mangled*," "*cured* with reason, *cooled* with wisdom." The antithetical words *reason* and *wisdom* chime, as well as *cured* and *cooled*. Lastly parisonic antithesis is illustrated in the "*mind maimed* with love, *cured* with reason, *cooled* by wisdom"; whilst the Euphuistic similitudes are pervasive, albeit we are for once spared a piece of unnatural nature lore. In a word, Lyly uses alliteration continuously or transversely for ornament to mark parallel or antithesis. All of these devices are more or less constantly present in Lyly's earlier prose whether in *Euphues* or in his dramas.

Euphuism was not the invention of Lyly, although most highly developed in his hands. It is a style of marked and unmistakable character discoverable in English literature as early as 1532, reaching its height between 1579 and 1590, and continuing even beyond that in Lyly's imitators. Ascham and his contemporaries were chiefly engaged in writing clearly, although Ascham himself employs antithesis with effect. In 1557 appeared North's *Dial of Princes*. In this book is found an occasional use of parisonic balance, simple alliteration, and figurative allusions in argumentative illustrations. This, North seems to have derived in part from a French translation of the works of Antonio de Guevara, a Spanish writer of history and familiar letters whose *Epistolæ Aureæ* enjoyed great reputation in the reign of Henry VIII, and was translated into English early in Elizabeth's reign. In 1577 appeared a book entitled *Pettie his Palace of Pleasure*, a collection of stories translated from the French. The style of this work retains and augments the peculiarities already noted in North, and adds allusions to fabulous natural history and the device of oratorical question and response, thus anticipating Lyly in every one of the characteristics of Euphuism. What Lyly did then was to heighten these devices and maintain their quality. This, added to the sententious force and persuasive morality of his book, gave it its success. That this was not due alone to its style is proved by its superior popularity over Pettie's book. *Euphues* reached a twelfth edition in the year 1636, and then was left unreprinted until 1868.

The vogue of *Euphues* called forth a swarm of imitators, and the new literature of the boudoir was thus launched in England once and for all. M. Jusserand in his scholarly and entertaining work, *The English Novel in the Time of Shakespeare*, tells how the word "Euphues" was played on in the titles of books. There was *Zelauto, the Fountain of Fame*, . . ."containing a delicate disputation . . . given for a friendly entertainment to Euphues," by Anthony Munday, 1580; there was *Euphues his Censure to Philautus*, 1587, and *Menaphon, Camilla's Alarm to slumbering Euphues*, two years later, both by Robert Greene, poet, dramatist, pamphleteer, and enemy of Shakespeare. There was *Rosalynd, Euphues Golden Legacy* by Thomas Lodge, 1590, delightful original of *As You Like It;* and *Arisbas, Euphues amidst his Slumbers* by John Dickenson, 1594. But far more than the title of *Euphues* was followed in Barnabe Riche's *Don Simonides*, 1581, who travels abroad like Euphues and then comes to England to meet Philautus, Euphues' friend in Lyly's story. In *Zelauto*, likewise, a gentleman of station comes, after other travel, to view "the happy estate of England," and learn "how a worthy princess governed their commonwealth." Other books more or less in Lyly's manner were Melbancke's *Philotimus*, 1583, Warner's *Pan his Syrinx*, 1584, and Emanuel Ford's popular *Parismus*, 1598, with further like stories by Munday, Lodge, Greene, and others.

Although the earlier of these productions make a determined effort to imitate the artificialities and mannerisms of Lyly's style, few succeeded to any degree; and they certainly added nothing to the devices for emphasis and other rhetorical niceties for which Lyly must always stand notoriously eminent among writers of English prose. Greene made almost no use of such features of Euphuism as its fabulous natural history, and he carried its other mannerisms to no inordinate length. Thomas Nash's vigorous and vernacular English lent itself with difficulty for a passing moment to a style so alien to his own. Lodge is the most confirmed of the Euphuists after the master himself; but in the best of Lodge's work, as for example his *Rosalynd*, the story and the characters have taken a place of importance — as they do likewise in the best fiction of Greene — which clarifies the Euphuistic manner and marks a step forward in the history of English fiction as well as in English prose. In a word, no follower of Lyly was so purely a rhetorician as he, and no one wrote his story so unabashedly for its moral and the opportunities which it offered to discourse at large. By the year 1590, Euphuism had nearly worked itself out, later prose preserving only "its spirit of scrupulous neatness . . . with an occasional use of balanced antithesis and alliteration." Even Lyly's own work — we have only prose plays from which to judge — shows a gradual abandonment of his favorite devices in the interest of a purer and less conscious style.

Next to the mistakes about Euphuism, the commonest misapprehension as to Elizabethan prose is that which groups the prose of Sidney's *Arcadia* with that of Lyly. It is said that every educated man carries about with him a definition of poetry of his own making and adoration. Without raising a question, more difficult to lay than a ghost, one thing may be affirmed: whatever poetry may be, it is never rhetoric; and where rhetoric abides and rules, poetry is not. Not only is *Euphues* not poetic, but Lyly's plays are poetry neither in form nor in spirit; and they owe their success to much the qualities that distinguish his other prose. The late Mr. Henley went even further, to deny to Lyly's dainty little verses, "Cupid and my Campaspe played at cards for kisses," the title of a lyric and to class it with epigrams. The essence of Sidney's work is his poetry; as Professor Dowden less fittingly said of Shelley, "his life, deeds, and words all sang together"; and the *Arcadia* in its nature, conduct, style, and impetus is the complete and permanent antithesis of Euphues and Euphuism. Nor need we qualify this statement, remembering Sidney's experiments in exotic poetical forms and the extraordinary part which he played in introducing the "conceit" into English poetry, any more than we need doubt the sincerity of any true art because its methods are ornate and ingenious.

The Countess of Pembroke's Arcadia, as Sir Philip called his romance, was written during his retirement in partial disgrace with the queen, in 1580. It was addressed to his intimate friends, dedicated to his sister, and never intended for publication. It remained in manuscript some years after Sidney's death, but was fortunately not destroyed as he had intended. In 1590 a piratical edition appeared and fourteen other editions followed within a century. The *Arcadia* was thus one of the most popular stories of the age, and the parent, like *Euphues*, of a long line of prose romances. It was translated into foreign languages and used as material for other writings at home. The underplot of *King Lear*, to mention only one example, is derived from an episode of the *Arcadia*, that of the blind king of Paphlagonia, and a dozen other plays levied upon it.

The *Arcadia* is more a heroic romance than a pastoral. The pastoral atmosphere of the earlier parts is not maintained. As to material, Sidney's story is the very opposite of *Euphues*, being rich in event, stirring in adventure, and full of imagination, sentiment, and poetry. The main story relates the fortunes and adventures of two young princes, who disguise themselves, the one as an Amazon, the other as a shepherd, to win the love of two fair princesses. The heroines are the daughters of Basilius, a king whose caution for their welfare and future causes him to remove his court to a country lodge. The course of the story is much entangled and full of glorious and romantic adventure, it is diversified with no less than seven episodes each of them a completely wrought story, and the end is left to the reader's imagination, as the whole is unfinished. Thus not only the style but the content of the *Arcadia* is poetical. It was one of the prime theories of Sidney that it was spirit and not form which made poetry. He says: "It is not riming and versing that maketh a poet, no more than a long gown maketh an advocate." And elsewhere: Verse is "but an ornament and no cause to poetry: sith there have been many most excellent poets that never versified, and now swarm many versifiers that need never answer to the name of poets." In view of such ideas we must expect to find a close relation in Sidney's *Arcadia* between the subject-matter and the form of expression. Arcadianism is then not only a prose style, but a variety of the art of fiction. Sidney's aim is the "feigning notable images of virtues, vices, or what else, with that delightful teaching which must be the right describing note to know a poet by." Arcadianism is an emotional medium for the expression of lofty and heroic thought. If we consider it on the side of mere style, the diction of the *Arcadia* is what we might expect of a scholar and a courtier. It is thoroughly English and remarkably free from words which have since become obsolete. Compound words are not frequent and poetical words can not be considered a feature. The salient characteristics of the Arcadian style are its habitual employment of bold and natural imagery for plain and direct speech, in the extreme degenerating into conceit; the use of antithesis with accompanying alliteration, balance, and iteration to give emphasis to thought and feeling; and the general employment of a loose and cumulative structure of sentence. It was no vain boast of the age to declare that Sidney had reclaimed English prose from the excesses of the cultivated style. The influence of the *Arcadia* was more permanent than that of Euphuism, if less easy accurately to trace; for Sidney's "bold feigning of notable images," even his striking and original "conceits," fell in with the spirit of a poetical and imaginative age as no rhetorician's studied devices could hope to do. But who can deny the permanent value to literature of these consistent and thorough experiments in the art of writing elegant prose ? From the leading-strings of an outworn tongue, from the precedents and unchallenged usages of "Tully," *Euphues* led writers to a contemplation of the niceties and elegancies of vernacular English and taught them the possibilities of their own tongue. Nor was this education confined alone to the writers of books. The beauty and clarity of the diction of Elizabethan letters, even of documents, not too much clogged by contact with the law, has often been remarked. Some of the queen's own English letters show a grace and feeling for the phrase which we may be sure, with all Elizabeth's natural endowments, came not wholly unstudied.

It was a fortunate day for English literature that both in verse and in prose it should so happily have passed the age of experiment. What Sidney did for foreign meters in English verse, Lyly accomplished for English prose. Sidney proved that although we might compass the hexameter, the sapphic, the canzon, or the madrigal in English, it would be better to be true to the genius and spirit of English verse. Lyly showed the possibilities of a highly organized and rhetorical style in prose; but, living longer than Sidney, withdrew from its excesses himself when he saw growing up about him a vigorous and idiomatic English speech alike removed from the pedantry of Latinism and the affectations of courtly preciosity. But the lesson that Lyly had to impart once learned, it was in the nature of the Elizabethan spirit to revert to the more spontaneous, the more flowing and imaginative prose of Sidney and to prefer the fine abandon of his tumultuous eloquence to the nice devices of Lyly's ingenious invention. It was Matthew Arnold's stricture on English prose at large, that it is a prose in which the imagination has been too busy, and the rational faculty not busy enough. This criticism finds its earliest justification in the prose of Sidney which chose rhetoric for its antithesis, not for its example. It was Lyly who was dainty, artificial, allegorical, the rhetorician of finished art and studied phrase. The limit of such literary art is the epigram and beyond this it can not attain. Sidney, in contrast to all this, is natural; although of a strong artistic bent, romantic in temper, seeking literature as an outlet to feeling, not as an art to be loved only for its own sake: the goal of such art is lyricism. And in lyricism the barrier between prose and poetry, wherever you erect it, is once and for all broken down.

CHAPTER IV

SPENSER, "THE NEW POET"

"THIS place have I purposely reserved for one," wrote William Webbe in 1586, "who if not only, yet in my judgment principally, deserveth the title of the rightest English poet that ever I read. That is the author of *The Shepherds' Calendar*, intituled to the worthy Master Philip Sidney, whether it was Master Spenser or what rare scholar of Pembroke Hall soever . . . I force not greatly to set down. Sorry I am that I can not find none other with whom I might couple him in this catalogue in his rare gift of poetry." And even earlier, in his entertaining "gloss" to the *Calendar*, "E. K.," the poet's friend, had declared: "I doubt not so soon as his name shall come to the knowledge of men and his worthiness be sounded in the trump of fame but that he shall . . be . . . beloved of all, embraced of the most and wondered at of the best." Seldom has a poet so leaped with a bound as did Spenser into the esteem and appreciation of his countrymen; and even more rarely has such a feat been accomplished by the means of an art so singularly ideal and free from the transient qualities that commonly make for immediate poetic repute.

In the *Prothalamion*, Spenser has recorded London as the place of his birth and nurture. His father's family was of northeast Lancashire, numerous and respected there and elsewhere. Thus Spenser's connections were good and he was born, if humbly for his station, a gentleman. The year of his birth was 1552, and he was one of several children. He was educated at the Merchant Tailors' School, then newly founded and under the head-master, Richard Mulcaster, a man neither unknown to the history of education nor to that of the drama. The future dramatists, Kyd and Lodge, were among his schoolmates. Spenser was the recipient of bounty granted "to certain poor scholars of the schools about London," and went up to Cambridge, matriculating as a sizar — a term equivalent to servitor at Oxford — at Pembroke College, in May, 1569.

But Spenser had appeared in print even before he went to Cambridge. *The Theater of Voluptuous Worldings*, 1569, is the translation of a moral tract, originally in Flemish prose and the work of one John van der Noodt. It was translated first into French and then into English. Prefixed were a score of woodcuts illustrating certain poems of Petrarch and Du Bellay and portraying matter more or less relevant to the moral tract. Four of these poems, translations of Du Bellay into unrimed decasyllabic lines, have been assigned to Spenser, because in a collection of poems, avowedly his, published in 1591, they reappear under the title, *Complaints*, with certain revisions.

Spenser's works disclose that he acquired at college not only a competent knowledge of the classics but a very considerable acquaintance with French and Italian poetry. As to authors in his own tongue, he accepted Chaucer above all as an inspiration and example; although Spenser's temperament and his ideals of art were vastly in contrast with the robuster genius of the father of English poetry. Spenser's interest in Skelton is less easy to explain, although the poet in Skelton is discoverable to him who will seek the tiny sweet kernel within the thick and bitter rind. Among Spenser's intimates at the University was Gabriel Harvey, the adviser of the Areopagus, a man who must have had somewhat in him above mere pedantry to have inspired Spenser's affection. Edward Kirke, too, soon to introduce to the public *The Shepherds' Calendar*, must have been close to the poet in these early days. John Still, once alleged the author of *Gammer Gurton's Needle*, and Thomas Preston, the author of that extraordinary hotch-potch of moral, history, farce, and tragedy, *Cambyses*, were both of them contemporary with Spenser at Cambridge. But we know nothing of any intimacy of Spenser with them. Nash and Marlowe were to come a decade later.

Spenser was not a very healthy young man; and he left

college, after taking his mastership in 1576, going to live with his own people in Lancashire. It was there that he met and loved the young woman celebrated in his pastorals as Rosalind. Aubrey's story that Rosalind was a kinswoman of Sir Erasmus Dryden, the grandfather of the great poet, may be dismissed; and a more recent identification of the lady with one Rose Dyneley, at least provisionally, accepted. Whatever the truth, it is certain that this Rosalind preferred another, not Spenser, for her Orlando, and that some charming and plaintive poetry was the result.

The circumstances of Spenser's coming up to London to seek his fortune are not altogether clear. Through his association with Harvey or through some unknown recommendation, he gained an introduction to Sidney and a place in the household of the Earl of Leicester about 1578. Between this and 1580, Spenser appears to have traveled on the continent, perhaps as far as Rome, and also into Ireland on services for the earl. These were the days of growing friendship with Sidney, who loved all poets, and of the Areopagus and the letters interchanged between Harvey and Spenser relative to the new classical measures in English. Spenser seems to have experimented, like Sidney, with hexameters and other ancient forms of verse. We hear also of nine comedies, called after the Muses and written after the manner of Ariosto, of a poem entitled *Dreams* prepared for the press with a comment by Kirke, and of a prose tract, *The English Poet*, apparently in the nature of Sidney's *Defense of Poesy*. But all have been irretrievably lost. Several other poems are believed to have been recast into parts of *The Faery Queen* and other extant poems. In December, 1579 *The Shepherds' Calendar* was entered at the Stationers' Company. *The Faery Queen*, likewise, must have been well under way before Spenser left the protection of Leicester in 1580.

It is a remarkable example of the confidence of genius that Spenser should deliberately have set himself against several of the fashions of his day, notwithstanding that he was more or less affected by them. Although his natural affinities were with Harvey and the classicists, Spenser's good sense and musical ear saved him from the absurdities of the attempt to in

troduce classic meters into English. But it was not only from
pedantry that he rescued himself. Though full of the spirit
of the Italian Renaissance in its larger embodiments as represented in the epics of Tasso and Ariosto, Spenser had little in
common with the Italianated style that dealt in "dainty antithesis and alliteration, ingenuity of simile," and far-fetched
comparison. Spenser held "the laboriously small literature"
of Italy in undisguised disdain. In consequence of this feeling
he even dared to employ at times Chaucer's obsolete language
in protest against the foreign words which were at the moment
crowding into English. Other motives, too, led Spenser to a
love of antiquated expressions. There is a charm about the
unusual, especially in sound, which the ear of Spenser, attuned
to musical impressions, found it difficult to resist. Unquestionably Spenser abused at times his mastery over language
and, though he rarely invented new words, he frequently distorted old ones. It has been held that many of his alleged
archaisms are really referable to actual provincial usage in the
Lancashire of his day, and that more of them may be otherwise
justified. But when all has been said, Spenser must be acknowledged much of a tyrant over words, twisting and con-
torting, at times, his pitiable subjects at his royal will. In
this Spenser differed immeasurably from Shakespeare who extended a beneficent rule over thousands of subjects in the world
of speech that had remained hitherto unreduced to citizenship
in the realm of literary acceptance.

The Shepherds' Calendar, "containing twelve allegories
proportionable to the twelve months," was registered in December, 1579, dedicated "to the noble and virtuous gentleman,
most worthy of all titles both of learning and chivalry, Master
Philip Sidney," and modestly signed "Immerito." The Dedicatory Epistle to Harvey was written by E. K., that is Edward
Kirke, Spenser's friend at college, who also supplied the quaint
"gloss" or running comment that accompanies the text. *The
Shepherds' Calendar* is the first successful attempt to write
poetical pastoral eclogues in English. Spenser appears to have
found his inspiration in the pastorals of Battista Spagnuoli,
commonly known as Mantuan, one of the foremost Latin poets

of the Italian Renaissance, and in those of Clement Marot, a French religious free-lance who was alternately in favor and exiled from the courts of Marguerite d'Alençon and Francis I. But the pastoral mode had already crept into England in Alexander Barclay's satirical and allusive *Eclogues*, 1513, and in those of Barnabe Googe, 1563, who, as well as Turberville, had translated pastorals of Mantuan into English; while long before the Scottish poet, Robert Henryson, had set a standard of idyllic excellence in his perfect little poem, *Robyn and Makyne* (albeit likewise of French extraction), which none was to equal save Marlowe, Breton, and Lodge in times to come.

Notwithstanding that *The Shepherds' Calendar* is thus imitative of foreign poets, written in a mode which seems strained and artificial to us to-day, and weighted by a conservative adherence to an archaic vocabulary and an obsolete system of rhythm in parts, the poem was an immediate success, and Spenser was enthusiastically hailed as "the new poet" in a chorus of praise. Spenser lived to see five editions of the *Calendar*. It was translated into Latin by John Dove in 1585, and commended by critics like Webbe and Nash, by personal friends such as Sidney, and fellow poets like Drayton. And indeed in the *Calendar* we recognize at once the presence of a consummate artist, a powerful grasp of ideas, a pictorial and vivid style, and an extraordinary power over metrical form in calling forth the music of the language. Already we find Spenser's fondness for allegory asserting itself in the personages of these eclogues. Colin is Spenser himself; Hobbinol, his friend Harvey; Menalcas, the fortunate rival of the poet for the hand of Rosalind.

But *The Shepherds' Calendar* is more than a set of eclogues on amorous and trifling subjects. It contains underneath a thin disguise of pastoral form, a deep undercurrent of sturdy and independent opinion. For example Archbishop Grindal, as the wise shepherd Algrind, receives Spenser's unstinted praise. Grindal had set himself in opposition to the court in an attempt to educate and liberalize the clergy, and had manfully refused to yield to the queen on what he considered

a question of conscience. It was a brave thing for the young
poet, awaiting preferment, to speak so boldly as he did on the
side of liberality and justice.   This conduct was of a piece
with the candor of Spenser's later satire of the courtly delay
and corruption of the time which he voices in his excellent
satirical poem, *Mother Hubberd's Tale,* and elsewhere.

The Shepherds' Calendar and the *Arcadia* set the pastoral
fashion, and thereafter this became for a decade or more the
prevailing literary mode. This mode was common to verse
and prose, to the epic, dramatic, and lyric form, and it mingled
with every other conceivable manner of writing which the teem-
ing inventivenesss of an age that doted on originality could
bring forth. The *Arcadia* had contained pastoral lyrics; but
the lyrics of *The Shepherds' Calendar* may have preceded them.
It is somewhat strange that Spenser should never have written
pastoral or other lyric for itself. The "Song to Eliza," "Perigot and Willie's Roundelay," and the majestic "Lament for
Dido," all included in their variety of beautiful meters in the
Calendar, disclose how varied and perfect was Spenser's
lyrical art. Yet in them all, as in the glorious poetry of the
Prothalamion and the *Epithalamion,* we have the large and
leisurely poetical utterance so distinctive of Spenser. Spenser
has none of the brevity, the concentration, the concrete expres-
siveness, the short holding phrase that distinguishes the best
of Elizabethan lyrists. Rarely can he catch with the instinct
of some lesser men the fleeting joy or sorrow of the moment.
Spenser's Muse is like some stately galleon of the age, built
high above the water, bearing on in stately course, her bil-
lowy sails all set and gay with a thousand floating pennons.
She needs the broad ocean for her course, but she is a gallant
sight to behold, and little pinnaces shrink before her regal
progress.

In July, 1580, Spenser was appointed secretary to Arthur
Grey de Wilton, Lord Deputy of Ireland, and accompanied
him to Dublin. Although Spenser returned to England for
two brief visits, Ireland thenceforth became his home, until
the rebellion drove him back to London as a refuge shortly
before his death. The successive posts and employments in

the service of the government held by Spenser we need not detail here. He was for some years Clerk of Chancery (1581–1588), and later clerk of the Council of Munster (1588–1594). He was well paid for his services to the crown, and acquired at different times a considerable landed estate, living, amongst other places, at New Abbey in county Kildare, and at Kilcolman Castle, near to Doneraile in county Cork. Nor was Spenser without associates in Ireland. There were then as now many cultivated gentlemen on what may be called the civil list of the colonial office. One Lodowick Bryskett, a fellow Irish official, became an intimate friend of Spenser's. Bryskett was of Italian extraction, and had traveled on the continent as the companion of Sidney. His *Discourse of Civil Life*, 1606, the translation of an Italian philosophical work, has a peculiar interest from his description in it of a party of literary friends who met at his cottage near Dublin, chief among them Spenser. Here Bryskett tells how Spenser encouraged him "long sithence to follow the reading of the Greek tongue, and offered me his help to make me understand it"; how he requested Spenser to discourse to the party of moral philosophy . . . "whereby virtues are to be distinguished from vices"; and how Spenser excused himself on the plea that he had already undertaken "a work tending to the same effect." Another intimacy, the outcome of Spenser's life in Ireland, was the friendship of Walter Raleigh, the "Shepherd of the Ocean" of *Colin Clout*. Raleigh lived not far from Spenser and visited him at Castle Kilcolman. To him on one of these visits Spenser submitted the first three books of the *The Faery Queen*; and Raleigh, delighted with the work, induced Spenser to return to England to seek a publisher. This Spenser did, arriving in London in October, 1589, about the time that Shakespeare was beginning his apprenticeship to the stage. All this matter and Spenser's own delight in the gracious reception which he met at court from Cynthia and her maids is charmingly, allegorically, and pastorally set forth in *Colin Clout's Come Home Again*, printed in 1595. Spenser arranged for the publication of the first three books of *The Faery Queen*, and in 1590 they appeared with the dignified and graceful dedication to Queen Elizabeth, the well-known prefatory letter to Sir Walter Raleigh declaring the intention of the author, and numerous sonnets to illustrious people who had shown favor to the poet.

Spenser's literary triumph was all that he could wish; but he did not succeed in getting employment which would remove him from savage Ireland and bring him nearer the court. He, too, experienced the delays and doubts of attendance on royal favor. According to a well-known anecdote Elizabeth was so pleased with *The Faery Queen* — as well she might be, for never has woman been so royally flattered — that she determined to give Spenser a pension of five hundred pounds per annum, a large and munificent gift, considering the purchasing value of money in that age. But Burleigh demurred that so much money should be paid for a song. The queen then told her thrifty secretary to give Spenser what in his judgment he thought was fit for a poet, and the pension was granted at fifty pounds. This is the basis of the notion that Spenser was poet laureate. The office did not exist in Spenser's day, nor in Daniel's, the unofficial successor of Spenser to the favors of the court. Ben Jonson was the first poet laureate.

In a well-known passage of *Colin Clout*, Spenser touches on his poetical contemporaries with generous appreciative comment. Each poet is veiled, after the fashion of the time, under a pastoral name, and among them Spenser certainly mentions Alabaster, Churchyard, Raleigh, Daniel, Sidney, and some minor writers, while the surmises of scholars have considerably extended the list of identifications. The whole passage concludes:

> And there, though last not least, is Ætion,
> A gentler shepherd may no where be found:
> Whose Muse, full of high thoughts' invention,
> Doth like himself heroically sound.
> All these, and many others moe, remain,
> Now after Astrophel is dead and gone:
> But while as Astrophel did live and reign,
> Amongst all these was none his paragon.

All these do flourish in their sundry kind,
And do their Cynthia immortal make:
Yet found I liking in her royal mind,
Not for my skill, but for that shepherd's sake.

Astrophel is of course Sidney whose memory Spenser everywhere reveres. It was becoming and courtier-like in Spenser
thus to attribute the royal recognition to his friendship with
Sidney and not to his own poetic merit. As to Ætion, the
adjective "gentle" in this passage immediately suggests
Shakespeare. We may not always remember that the epithet
is Jonson's, to be found with a dozen other good things about
the great dramatist in the famous lines prefixed to the first
folio edition of Shakespeare's works. "Gentle" is now once
and for all the Shakespearean epithet, and the heroically
sounding Muse of this passage has been applied to him (Shakespeare). But it has also been applied to Sack-ville; and it is
equally applicable to Rowland, the self-assumed pseudonym
of Michael Drayton, a poet who must have been well known
to Spenser in 1595. It must be confessed that Shakespeare
— a player and only on sufferance acquainted with men of
Spenser's court circle — was certainly unlikely to be so addressed by "the new poet" in the year 1595, so soon after the
earliest heir of Shakespeare's invention had seen the press.
And yet the two greatest poets of the age may have met. If
they did into what insignificance fall the royal fields of cloth of
gold and other ceremonious meetings of august worldly sov-
ereigns. Did Spenser find "our Shakespeare" truly gentle?
And was Spenser to Shakespeare the "poet's poet?"

In 1590 appeared *Daphnaïda*, an elegy on Lady Douglas,
and a volume entitled *Complaints*. Strange as it must seem
to us, some of the matter of *Muiopotmos*, an allegorical story
of the proud butterfly swept into a spider's web, and the satirical beast epic, *Mother Hubberd's Tale* gave offense, and part
of the work was suppressed. The publisher's promise of another volume of small poems was never fulfilled.

In 1592 Spenser fell in love once more and wooed and won
for his wife Elizabeth Boyle, a woman of position and culti-

vation, well worthy of the poet's addresses. Spenser's beautiful sonnet sequence, *Amoretti*, is, in part at least, the poetical record of this courtship. The *Epithalamion* which celebrated his marriage, in June, 1594, has been truly described as "one of the grandest lyrics in English poetry." These two works were printed in 1595, as was *Colin Clout;* and at the close of this year Spenser brought three more books of *The Faery Queen* to London and they appeared the next year. Once more was Spenser received by the best people of England, staying at Essex House with the earl, and penning the fine *Prothalamion* for a double wedding held there. Spenser was also engaged during this visit in writing his prose tract, *A View of the Present State of Ireland.* This clear and able paper of state is marred by its attitude which allows no rights to the down-trodden Irish. The gentle and kindly poet was one of the English invaders that approved and even took part in the raids of devastation that wasted unhappy Ireland. He was also one of those who was rewarded with the confiscated estates of rebels, a reward which was to bring to him a speedy and terrible retribution. In an examination of the social culture and civilization of the reign of Elizabeth we must not forget that much of the last was as yet superficial. Bear-baiting and bull-baiting were no uncommon amusements, to say nothing of cock-fighting, in praise of which worthy Roger Ascham wrote a book, unhappily now lost. Those who delight in what they choose to call historical "realism," have been at pains to tell us how Queen Elizabeth used to beat her maids of honor, and how she actually boxed my Lord of Essex on the ears one day when she was scolding him, a chastisement which the young coxcomb doubtless richly deserved. Add to this the habit of public execution, drawing and quartering, and the exhibition of heads and mangled limbs on the parapet of London Bridge, and we have illustrations alike of the childish petulance of the queen and of the brutality of the age.

In Elizabeth's day the Irish were little better than savages. They had been given no opportunity to become civilized, and were not eager to seize one. They continued, almost to our own day, the objects of the injustice and rapacity of their more powerful neighbor. To Spenser, Ireland was a horrible but beautiful wilderness, whose beauties and his own loneliness among them he both celebrates and deplores. He detested the Irish as an inferior race. Neither his age nor his position could make his judgment in this matter fair. As a man we know Spenser to have been kindly, gentle, and estimable, with few of the weaknesses vulgarly attributed to poets. It is no small credit to the taste of the Elizabethan age that their contemporaries gave to Shakespeare and to Spenser that rank to which it was left to comparatively modern appreciation to restore them. Spenser was as highly honored by the queen as could be expected, considering his birth and the fact that he exhibited no very marked political qualifications. As to his flattery of her, it was a mere fabric of imaginative gallantry and devotion, the result of a grateful and loyal nature. How manly after all, is his greatest piece of flattery, the dedication of *The Faery Queen*, and what a glorious assumption of equality it conveys: "To the most high, mighty, and magnificent empress, renowned for piety, virtue and all gracious government Elizabeth, by the grace of God, Queen of England, France, and Ireland, and of Virginia, Defender of the faith, her most humble servant, Edmund Spenser, doth in all humility dedicate, present, and consecrate these his labors to live with the eternity of her fame."

In 1597 Spenser returned to Ireland in failing health. He was appointed sheriff of Cork; and in the year following, the Tyrone Rebellion broke out. The English were taken unawares, massacre and outrage followed. In October of that year Kilcolman Castle was sacked and burnt, and Spenser fled to Cork with his wife and four children. According to Jonson, one of his children perished in the flames. In December Spenser came to London, the bearer of dispatches from Sir Thomas Norris, governor of Munster, and died at an inn in Westminster the next month, January, 1599. The tradition goes that he died in poverty. It seems improbable, however, that the holder of a crown pension and bearer of official dispatches, so well known and honored as Spenser, should so have perished. He was ruined in a sense by the destruction of his Irish castle and the spoiling of his estate. This is the origin of the story. Spenser's funeral was sumptuous, and attended by the poets and the nobility. He was buried in Westminster Abbey near to Chaucer.

And now as to Spenser's famous book, *The Faery Queen*. Fortunately for our understanding of its scope and meaning, we have Spenser's own interesting letter to Raleigh. Therein we learn that *The Faery Queen* is "a continued allegory or dark conceit," and that "the general end thereof . . . is to fashion a gentleman or noble person in virtuous and gentle discipline."

Which for that I conceived should be most plausible and pleasing, being colored with an historical fiction, the which the most part of men delight to read rather for variety of matter than for profit of the ensample, I chose the history of King Arthur, as most fit for the excellency of his person, being made famous by many men's former works, and also furthest from the danger of envy and suspicion of present time.

After naming as his examples Homer, Vergil, Tasso, and Ariosto, Spenser continues:

By ensample of which excellent poets, I labor to portray in Arthur, before he was king, the image of a brave knight, perfected in the twelve private moral virtues, as Aristotle hath devised; the which is the purpose of these first twelve books, which if I find to be well accepted, I may be perhaps encouraged to frame the other part of politic virtues in his person after that he came to be king.

Then follows a justification of the allegorical method and an explanation of how Arthur saw "in a dream or vision the Faery Queen with whose excellent beauty ravished, he awaking, resolved to seek her out; and so being by Merlin armed, he went to seek her forth in faery land."

In that Faery Queen I mean glory in my general intention, but in my particular I conceive the most excellent and glorious person of our sovereign the queen and her kingdom in faery land. And yet, in some places else I do otherwise shadow her. For considering she beareth two persons, the one of a most royal queen or empress, the other of a most virtuous and beautiful lady, this latter part in some places I do express in Belphœbe fashioning her name according to your own excellent conceit of Cynthia, Phœbe and Cynthia being both names of Diana.

It will thus be seen how this elaborate plan carries out the idea, already suggested in Spenser's words to Lodowick Bryskett "to represent all the moral virtues, assigning to every virtue a knight to be the patron and defender of the same, in whose actions and feats of arms and chivalry the operations of that virtue whereof he is the protector are to be expressed, and the vices and unruly appetites that oppose themselves against the same to be beaten down and overcome." This stupendous plan was never completed. The six finished books give the legend (each in twelve cantos, averaging fifty or sixty stanzas each) of Holiness, Temperance, Chastity, Friendship, Justice, and Courtesy; while a fragment of two "Cantos on Mutability" is supposed to have belonged to a seventh book (not necessarily seventh in order) on Constancy. The legend that *The Faery Queen* was actually finished may be dismissed as improbable. The poem as it stands contains about four thousand stanzas, or between thirty and forty thousand verses, and is of a quality of sustained poetical excellence, unequaled in any other poem of the language.

As *The Faery Queen* remains to us, it is like some fragment of ancient sculpture, the more beautiful from its incompleteness. However, such is its exquisite detail and such its chainlike quality of unity in continuance, that it is probable that we are not much the losers by this. Indeed, with all its elaborate plan, *The Faery Queen* must be pronounced one of the most plotless epics in existence. Moreover the narrative, despite its graces and variety, is repetitious, if continuous; and whether we "prick o'er the plain" with the Knight of Holiness, descend with Sir Guyon to the caves of Mammon, or follow Sir Arthegal's aquatic duel with the Paynim Pollente, again and again recur the seemly images of knightly prowess, the brave encounters, the contrasted braggadocio or caitiff knights, the fair disconsolate virgins, Una-like, and the Vivianlike Duessas, all-seeming fair but foul within. I never read

The Faery Queen without thinking of those rare and costly tapestries which decked in ancient days the halls of princes. Here is the same soft richness of color and of texture, the dim remoteness to anything like actual life, the delicate care of detail, and the same enchanting decorative effect. Of such art we feel that it is loving and leisurely; its very progress is like that of the shuttle in the loom, now forward, now back. Neither weaver nor poet can be conceived as hurried or as otherwise than content to add, hour after hour and thread after thread, the beautiful colors that grow insensibly into a pattern, ever recurrent and conventional, but ever holding, as with a soft compulsion, our approval and affection.   Take these stanzas, some three of many more, descriptive of Belphœbe, type of virgin perfection and sufficiency:

> Eftsoon, there steppéd forth
> A goodly lady clad in hunter's weed,
> That seem'd to be a woman of great worth,
> And by her stately portance born of heavenly birth.

> Her face so fair, as flesh it seeméd not,
> But heavenly portrait of bright angel's hue,
> Clear as the sky, withouten blame or blot,
> Through goodly mixture of complexions due;
> And in her cheeks the vermeil red did shew
> Like roses in a bed of lilies shed,
> The which ambrosial odors from them threw,
> And gazer's sense with double pleasure fed,
> Able to heal the sick and to revive the dead.

> In her fair eyes two living lamps did flame,
> Kindled above in th' Heavenly Maker's light,
> And darted fiery beams out of the same,
> So passing piersant, and so wondrous bright,
> In them the blinded god his lustful fire
> To kindle oft essayed, but had no might;
> For with dread majesty and awful ire,
> She broke his wanton darts and quenchéd base desire.

> Her ivory forehead, full of bounty brave,
> Like a broad table did itself dispread,
> For love his lofty triumphs to engrave,
> And write the battles of his great godhead:

> All good and honor might therein be read;
> For there their dwelling was. And when she spake,
> Sweet words, like dropping honey, she did shed;
> And 'twixt the pearls and rubies softly brake
> A silver sound that heavenly music seemed to make.

No wonder that it was once profanely said that nothing but Spenser's death could possibly have prevented *The Faery Queen* from going on in the same bloom, fragrance, and vitality forever.

Two allegories underlie the story of *The Faery Queen*, one figuring forth abstract virtues and religious qualitites, the other the concrete presentation of the same. Thus the Red-Cross Knight of the first book signifies Holiness in the abstract. In the concrete this figure stands, somewhat unfittingly, for the Earl of Leicester. Belphœbe, the Virgin Warrior, is militant Chastity in the abstract; but, like all unwedded and feminine abstractions of the age, in the concrete is Queen Elizabeth. The allegory of *The Faery Queen* is sometimes moral, sometimes political, sometimes religious and even personal, although there can be no doubt that Spenser not infrequently avoided the possibility of too close an identification. With this uncertainty as to Spenser's personages, *The Faery Queen* has been most happily compared to a wide landscape, viewed from a point of vantage on one of those days when, although the heavens are fair, the mist is driving in from time to time from the sea. As you look out over the plain, you see some village, apparently familiar; but before you identify the spire on its church, down sweeps the mist and the baffling semi-luminous cloud covers all. In the reading of the poetry of Spenser we may well follow the witty suggestion of one of his fellow poets. "Poetry," says Sir John Harington, "is one kind of meat to feed divers tastes. For the weaker capacities will feed themselves with the pleasantness of the history and the sweetness of the verse; some that have stronger stomachs will, as it were, take a further taste of the moral sense; and a third sort, more high conceited than they, will digest the allegory."

Nothing is more erroneous than to suppose that Spenser

borrowed his perfect stanza of *The Faery Queen* from the
Italian. The sonnet and the famous *ottava rima* (*a b a b a b
c c*) were both used by Spenser and may have suggested, be-
tween them, the advantage of a long and well-knit stanza.
A more likely original than either of these is to be found in
Chaucer's rime royal (*a b a b b c c*), used in *Troilus and
Cresside* especially,which by the insertion of a line(*a b a b b c b c*)
between the last two verses becomes Chaucer's stanza of
The Monk's Tale. One step more, the addition of the final
alexandrine, and we have the Spenserian stanza (*a b a b b c
b c c*). But this step was a great and original one, and takes
Spenser's stanza out of the group of "five stress" verses,
giving it a character entirely new. The Spenserian stanza
is Spenser's own, and is certainly to be regarded as one of
the happiest inventions in formal versification. Its adaptation, moreover, to the style and subject of *The Faery Queen*
is perfect; for the Spenserian stanza combines the advantage
of a beautiful integral form, of sufficient scope to admit every
variety of cadence, with the unusual additional faculty of
linking well stanza to stanza. It is therefore an admirable
form for a continuous narrative, made up of successive vi-
gnettes; and has very properly been likened to a broad and
beautiful river, flowing in graceful curves with a "steady,
soft, irresistible sweep forwards." The extraordinary smoothness of Spenser's versification further justifies this comparison
together with the agreeable recurrence of the rime, so cadenced
as not too strongly to mark the end of each verse. The final
alexandrine is inexpressibly beautiful, seeming as it does to
round up each stanza with a graceful *retardo*, and, by its
excess over the other lines, to break the monotony of the
succession of decasyllables:

> Nought under heaven so strongly doth allure
> The sense of man, and all his mind possess,
> As beauty's lovely bait, that doth procure
> Great warriors oft their rigor to repress,
> And mighty hands forget their manliness;

Drawn with the power of an heart-throbbing eye,
And wrapped in fetters of a golden tress,
That can with melting pleasance mollify
Their hardened hearts enured to blood and cruelty.

So whilom learned that mighty Jewish swain,
Each of whose locks did match a man in might,
To lay his spoils before his leman's train:
So also did that great Œtean Knight
For his love's sake his lion's skin undight;
And so did warlike Antony neglect
The world's whole rule for Cleopatra's sight.
Such wondrous power hath women's fair aspect
To captive men, and make them all the world reject.

The Spenserian stanza is really less monotonous than blank-verse, even with Milton, in all his varied powers, as its exponent, to say nothing of stanzas ending in a couplet and shorter quatrains. Many poets have tried to improve Spenser's stanza; none have succeeded either in writing it more gracefully than Spenser or in inventing a better. The Spenserian stanza is technically an extremely difficult one, both from its length, the intricacy of the rime, and the necessity of long sustained excellence. Spenser accomplished all these technical demands with an ease that must remain the despair of all his imitators.

The paradox of Spenser's genius lies in his combination in harmonious union of a passionate love of the sensuously beautiful with the purest and sternest ethical spirit of his time. This it is that makes Spenser alike the poet of the Renaissance and the poet of the Reformation. The combination of these apparently repugnant elements is exemplified to a still higher degree in Milton, the poet who owes most to Spenser. We must say "apparently repugnant elements," for it is assuredly no essential of the flower of art that it spring from the offal of sensuality and irreligion, nor of purity in morals and religion that all that is bright and joyous in the world be held in contempt. It is this union of the elements of beauty with moral truth that gives Spenser a poetic dignity such as Tennyson enjoyed in our own day.

Spenser, like Tennyson, is one of the greatest pictorial artists in words, and a consummate craftsman in the handling of that varied succession of sounds and qualities of tone in which the technique of verse consists. But Spenser is, in a sense, the last of the medieval poets. With all the decorative glory of the Renaissance his own, its imagery, its power to compel words to the expression of ideas, the figure beneath all this elaboration often discloses the hard angular lines of didactic allegory. It is not Spenser's truth to nature nor his insight into human life and conduct, his sense of design, nor his ability to tell a connected story that makes him great. For, if the truth be confessed, he has none of these things in unusual measure, and we scarcely remember a character or an episode in his great epic, or, if we do, it leaves the impression of an agreeable arabesque in which the design was pleasing for color and graceful of curve, but not memorable or distinctive, nor indeed at all times comprehensible. Spenser's mind was in full sympathy with the strong, refining, and ennobling influences of the age which produced Sidney, the first English gentleman. Its loyalty, its spirit of adventure, its sensitiveness and delicacy of sentiment, all found an echo in his poetry, toned with a deep and fervent religious sense that has the effect of sanctifying the melodious words in which he conveyed his pure and beautiful thoughts. The saving grace of Spenser is first his devotion to the beautiful, which no Keats nor Shelley more profoundly worshipped; and, secondly his lofty moral impulse, involving an ideal code of conduct for man and a devout faith in good. In Spenser the worship of the beautiful did not breed the passion of disappointment which it bred in Keats, nor the defiant revolutionary attitude to which it impelled Shelley; although the moral impulse of Spenser, no less than that of Shelley, was a reforming impulse. But where Shelley was revolutionary, and at times vituperative of the tyrants, the dungeons, and wrongs of suffering humanity, Spenser sought ever to reform by an appeal to the uplifting effects of calm and exquisitely wrought poetry and by dwelling with the passion and insistence of a lover on the beauty of holiness.

CHAPTER V

LYLY AND THE DRAMA AT COURT

THE accession of Queen Elizabeth found England without a genuine drama. The old sacred plays that had flourished all over England, in the ports and market towns, even in boroughs and rural villages, were extinct or, where lingering, moribund. The new drama of art was not, as yet. True, the reigns of Henry, Edward, and Mary abounded in interludes, moral, educational, religious, and, above all, controversial. Moreover John Heywood, first name on the honorable rôle of English dramatists, had amused the court of Henry VIII with witty and free-spoken interludes; and in them for the first time unmistakably, the artistic process was set loose, and English drama absolved from its ancient intent to guide, edify, and instruct. The interludes of Heywood are as French as the sonnet of Wyatt is Italian. But the difference between *Respublica*, a controversial morality written to inculcate Roman Catholic principles, or *King Johan*, a controversial morality written to intrench Protestant prejudice, and the interludes of Heywood, is the difference between preaching and literature, a difference from the point of view of art comparable alone to that between midnight and daylight

A contrast has been suggested between the medieval ballad and the courtly lyric of art which found its way into England in the days of Henry VIII; and the origins of modern English poetry and much else have been found in the select court circle, the coterie, which emulated the cultivation of the better small courts of Italy. A similar antithesis exists between the old sacred drama and the new regular drama of the reign of Elizabeth. The old drama was, as all know, first clerical in that the priests were the earliest actors and promoters of it, just as the drama itself was in its essence a form of worship. Soon all this was changed and the drama, once secularized, fell into the hands of the trade guilds and became bourgeois and the care of the citizens of towns. A popular nature inhered in the old sacred drama almost to the end, notwithstanding that both morality and interlude were often employed as entertainments at court, in the schools, and in the universities themselves. The new regular drama, then, was separated from the past not only in its character as an amusement and an art; but, in its quality as a product of the literature of the court, it was equally in contrast with the old popular drama of the citizens. The earliest Elizabethan dramatists were scholars, gentlemen, and courtiers; then came the school-masters and semi-professional poets; lastly, the actors as playwrights and the professional dramatists. Elizabethan drama originated at court, in the universities, and among the young lawyers of the Inns of Court; it progressed to the schools and singing choirs and thence to the inn-yards and taverns of London.

The familiar story tells how Nicholas Udall, sometime head-master, first of Eton and then of Westminster School, wrote the earliest English Comedy, *Ralph Roister Doister*, in the reign of King Edward or earlier; how it was written in imitation of the *Miles Gloriosus* of Plautus and acted by the boys of his school in place of the usual Latin play at Christmas; but it is sometimes forgotten that Udall was not only a school-master but a professional playwright who devised pageants for the coronation of Queen Anne Boleyn and dramatic performances for Queen Mary. Of William Stevenson, author of another of the earliest regular English comedies, *Gammer Gurton's Needle*, we know very little. This was a university play and may have been acted as early as 1560. Its authorship was long ascribed to Bishop Still, then given to John Bridges, and now settled as Stevenson's. *Gammer Gurton* is modeled on the interludes of Heywood, and tells in plain and very vernacular language how a whole village is set by the ears by the loss of a needle and the chicanery of a mischievous rascal known as Diccon of Bedlam. *Ralph Roister Doister* is a more decorous play if less vigorous and is concerned with the foolish and presumptuous suit of Ralph, a vain braggart, for the hand of the merry but virtuous Dame Custance. The power of both comedies is in their honest representation of actual life. On the other hand, romance came into regular dramatic form in tragedy and at the hands of Thomas Sackville and Thomas Norton, two young students of the Inner Temple; and the name of their play was *Gorboduc* or *Ferrex and Porrex*. Here the model was Seneca, the moralist and philosopher of Neronian Rome, though the story was borrowed from that mythical lore which Englishmen of the day included in the history of their country. Gorboduc was king of England. Like Lear he unwisely divided his kingdom before his death between his two sons, Ferrex and Porrex, a procedure which ended in the destruction of all. Now this tale resembles that of the sons of King Œdipus of Thebes who likewise divided a kingdom and fought to the death over it; and this tragedy Seneca treated in his *Phœnissæ*, whence in all probability its attraction for the young English students of law. *Gorboduc* was acted before Queen Elizabeth in January, 1561, and is memorable alike as the first regular English tragedy and as the first play to be written in English blank-verse.

Plautus and Seneca continued favorite models with English dramatists throughout the entire reign and for diverse reasons. Plautus is genuinely clever and, despite all his burlesque and farce, a dramatist of repute; English comedy could have found no better model, limited though his subjects are, and tending, though his characters do, to types. Seneca, on the contrary, was only the most available model for tragedy. His plays were not even intended for acting; and their florid rhetoric, moralized commonplaces, and exaggerated horrors were but a crude example to young English tragedy. Moreover it was a mistaken idea of the usages of the ancients as exemplified in Seneca that long kept Italian tragedy, and after it that of France, in classical leading-strings to the detriment of the highest art. It is impossible here to mention the many plays that followed on these various models; suffice it to say that from the sixties onward the drama flourished steadily, furnishing many notable examples. Thus, Gascoigne followed *Gorboduc*, a few years after, with a Senecan tragedy *Jocasta*,

and adapted from the Italian of Dolei a comedy called
Supposes whence Shakespeare had a part of his *Taming of the
Shrew*.   In the seventies Robert Wilmot rewrote a play (originally by himself and others) called *Tancred and Gismunda*,
a romantic tragedy levying on Italian rather than classical
sources.   Whetstone, much about the same time, wrote his
Promos and Cassandra whence Shakespeare derived his grave
comedy, *Measure for Measure*.   A play on the story of Romeo
and Juliet is alluded to as "lately set forth on stage," two
years before Shakespeare was born.   And an interlude of
The Cruel Debtor, registered four years later, may not impossibly be an earlier version of a play called *The Jew*, wherein
Gosson tells us was depicted "the greediness of worldly
choosers (Portia's unsuccessful suitors) and bloody minds of
usurers (Shylock's implacable pursuit of Antonio)."   In
nothing are we more apt to mistake than in the supposition
that Shakespeare was identified with the beginnings of English
drama.   The drama in a general sense was at least three hundred and fifty years old when Shakespeare began to write, and
plays of the type of his own had long been popular before he
was out of his boyhood.

The history of the drama up to the coming of the Armada
is bound up with the tastes and the fashions of the court.   In
view of the centralized power of the Tudors and the formation
about the person of the sovereign of a brilliant and cultivated
court, the personal character of the monarch came more and
more to affect society and the literature and art which mirrored it.   Whatever may be said of the fickleness and men-
dacity, the doubles and turns, of her Macchiavellian politics,
Queen Elizabeth must have been a remarkable woman as well
as a magnificent and august sovereign to have inspired in men
of gravity and wisdom, as well as in those of more elastic temper, those emotions of mingled loyalty and gallantry which
glow in nearly all who knew her personally, and which may
be regarded as one of the most admirable testimonies to her
fortunate reign.   Elizabeth had acquired many courtly Italian
accomplishments to gloss, if not to refine, a genuine English
spirit which was by no means lacking in coarseness.   Dis-

liking religious feeling and mistrusting sectarian zeal, Elizabeth had inherited a love of form and pageantry, which latter had flourished with masking at her father's court. These traits resulted in the royal encouragement of ceremonials, functions, and amusements, the drama among the rest. As a consequence the office of the revels, to which fell the supervision of plays and the allowance of their performance, was increased in importance, entertainments were constantly devised for the court and for the royal progresses, and the taste for such things, growing on what it fed, soon demanded the services of professional actors and playwrights.

The actors of the time of Elizabeth were of several classes. There were first the gentlemen of the Inns of Court, of the universities, occasionally the courtiers themselves; these were all non-professionals. There were, secondly, the boys of the public schools and the singing schools attached to the royal chapels and to the cathedral of St. Paul's. These soon became practically professionals. Lastly, there were the adult professional actors, a class at first held in great contempt and often verily little better than vagabonds, but destined, as time went on, to claim among its numbers such actors as Burbage, Alleyn, and Shakespeare, men who retired honored and rich from the profession which their talents had graced.

The plays of Sackville and Gascoigne are occasional plays. They were acted by amateur actors and staged by the authors themselves. But amateur performances could not long content the cultivated and critical audiences that gathered about the queen; and the professional actor soon emerged in answer to the demand for better music and finer histrionic art. During the first two decades of the reign nearly a dozen names of school-masters and choir-masters who were likewise the managers of theatrical companies, appear. Among them was Richard Edwards, Master of the Chapel between 1561 and 1567 and the author of an extant play called *Damon and Pythias*, and a lost *Palæmon and Arcyte*, on the theme of Chaucer's *Knight's Tale* and Fletcher's *Two Noble Kinsmen*. To Richard Bower, predecessor of Edwards, has been assigned *Appius and Virginia*, an indifferent production still extant.

Edwards' successor also, William Hunnis, was pamphleteer, musician, poet, playwright, and manager as well. Even more important, as a manager if not a playwright, was Richard Ferrant, Master of Windsor, who associated his children with those of Hunnis, and converted part of the priory buildings of the Dominicans or Blackfriars into a playhouse which he ran successfully for three or four years, passing on his lease at his death in 1580 to the Earl of Oxford, and his management to Lyly, his lordship's secretary. Other figures, such as Sebastian Wescott of Paul's, William Elderton of Westminster, and Richard Mulcaster of the Merchant Tailors' School remain more shadowy; though some of the plays that they staged are extant. Such are the anonymous *Queen Hester* and *Horestes.* Another, *Cambyses*, by Thomas Preston, fellow of King's College, Cambridge, in 1564, where and when his play was acted before the queen, long remained the butt of contemporary ridicule for its bombast and extravagant rant, attracting again and again the pungent satire of Shakespeare.

The new professional actors, trained by masters such as Edwards and Hunnis, were the pupils of the great schools, Eton and Westminster, or the boys who sang in the choirs of the royal chapel or of the cathedral of St. Paul's. This custom of training choir-boys to entertain the court and the nobility extends back into very early times. It soon became mixed with a custom of different origin, the performance in the schools on festival occasions of classical plays for the practice in Latin involved. For the better service, moreover, of the royal chapels, it had long been customary to issue letters patent, permitting choir-masters to take good voices for training to the royal service, a power which was soon abused. For the choir-master was thus converted into a theatrical manager and added an eager pursuit of popular favor to his former duty as purveyor of entertainment to the court. In 1597 one Nathaniel Giles, then master of the chapel, under a commission of this kind, actually kidnapped boys on their way to school and delivered them over to Henry Evans, who had just taken a lease from James Burbage of the newly renovated Blackfriars' Theater. According to the complaint of Henry Clifton, the father of one of these boys, to the Star Chamber, the children were restrained in their liberty and compelled to learn their parts at the point of the rod. Clifton's son was released; but seven other boys, whose names appear in this complaint, remained in this servitude, indubitably with the connivance if not the approbation of the queen's council. Indeed it has recently been affirmed that the status of this troupe of the Children of the Chapel Royal acting at Blackfriars was that of a company under the direct patronage of the queen, established not only with her knowledge but carrying out her will.[1] Certain it is that this company became a very important one, playing many of the most difficult and successful plays of the age; and that it continued at the Blackfriars under the later name of the Children of the Queen's Revels until the lease of that theater was resumed by Shakespeare and Burbage's company in 1609. The boy companies continued throughout the reign of Queen Elizabeth powerful rivals even of the best professional actors, though they were not infrequently "inhibited," as the term went, for indulging in satire and other abuses, and were at last practically suppressed.

The most interesting person whose career as a playwright falls among the school-master and choir-master managers is John Lyly. Born within a year of Spenser, Lyly was thus ten years Shakespeare's senior. From College, he removed to court to enjoy the patronage of Burleigh and the Earl of Oxford, for whom he appears at one time to have managed a company of players. The publication of his novel, *Euphues*, in 1579, as we have seen, brought Lyly an immediate and, for his time, an extraordinary reputation; and a second part, in the following year, confirmed it. Lyly was possessed of an ambition to hold a post in the office of the revels, for which he was better fitted than any man in England. But notwithstanding recent affirmations to the effect that Lyly became in 1585 the Clerk Controller of the Revels, besides holding the post of the Vice Master of the Children of St. Paul's, neither of these statements can be substantiated. Lyly was at one time

[1] See C. W. Wallace, in *Nebraska University Studies*, 1908, viii, 240 ff. This opinion has not been confirmed.

a member of Parliament and a writer in the contemporary prose of controversy, but his tastes naturally turned him to the drama and to the devising of entertainments for the court.

Eight comedies remain to attest the dramatic activity of Lyly which was confined for the most part within the decade of the eighties. All of them, except one, deal in a manner both fanciful and romantic with material ultimately of classical derivation; and three are commonly supposed to conceal an allegorical significance underneath a seemingly mythological story. Thus *Endimion* and *Sappho and Phao* are alleged to figure forth intrigues within the intimate circle that surrounded her majesty, the latter alluding especially to the visit of the Duc d'Alençon and his offer for Elizabeth's hand; whilst Midas, the foolish Phrygian king in whose grasping hand all things were turned to gold, alludes to England's arch enemy, King Philip of Spain. The remaining plays seem devoid of allegorical design. Among them, *Campaspe* tells the story of Alexander's infatuation for the fair Theban captive of that name and his magnanimous release of her affections to the painter Apelles. Interspersed as it is with the humors of Diogenes in his intercourse with Alexander and the philosophers, the whole is a pleasing comedy and it deserves the praise which it has received as a love tale well told. *Mother Bombie* reverts to a closer following of the method of Roman comedy, dealing in a well-constructed and clever plot with the familiar situation of children exchanged in infancy, and parents the dupes of clever and intriguing servants. *Galathea*, *Love's Metamorphosis*, and *The Woman in the Moon* are best described under the general designation of pastoral comedies of a mythological type. The last alone is written in verse. All contain some allegory, but it is in none of these cases as complete as that of *Endimion* or *Midas*, and may be suspected as intended to convey little more than the customary "concealed" compliment to the queen. Except for *Love's Metamorphosis*, all the comedies of Lyly are relieved by farcical scenes usually sustained by pages and servants. But few of his comedies are wanting in topics of serious gravity.

Endimion remains by far the most interesting of the dramas of Lyly, alike for its intrinsic qualities and for the circumstance that it is most typical of the style and method of its author. The allegory, too, of *Endimion* is elaborately conceived and carried out with ingenuity and address. This has given rise to many theories and surmises among scholars in which the date of the presentation of the play is involved and its relations to certain intrigues of the intimate court circle of Elizabeth is affirmed and denied. This drama, which is otherwise called *The Man in the Moon*, is based on the well-known classical myth of the sleep of Endimion on the slopes of Mount Latmus and of the goddess Diana, enamored of him and impulsively awakening him by her kiss. Obviously if this myth was to be applied in any wise to the queen — and it appears to have been impossible for any Elizabethan poet to name Diana, Cynthia, Semele, or any other mythical virgin without such an allusion — some change must be made in the story. Lyly therefore represented the kiss as a boon extorted only after entreaty and as a sovereign condescension free from the slightest taint of an earthly affection. It is Endimion who is enamored, not Cynthia, the queen; and his affection is of the nature of that reverent adoration of beauty in womanhood which has long been recognized as one of the distinctive "notes" of Renaissance poetry. It has been customary to interpret the allegory of this play, like that of *The Faery Queen*, as of a double intent, the one abstract and relating to the contrasts of the love inspired by heavenly and earthly beauty, love, free or tainted with amorous desire, the other concrete, referring to actual persons, their relations and intrigues. Not only is Cynthia the queen, but Endimion is the Earl of Leicester. Tellus, the earth and foil to the goddess, the moon, is either the Countess of Sheffield or Mary Queen of Scots; and the minor personages fall more or less into their places according as we interpret the events of the whole play as referring to Elizabeth's discovery, in 1579, of Leicester's marriage with the Countess of Essex through the French ambassador, M. de Simier, or prefer the more recent interpretation that places the play at 1585 and refers the allegory to the historical duel of Elizabeth with Mary of Scotland. It is but fair to say that recently a protest has been raised against these concrete historical interpretations of *Endimion;* Lyly's comedy has been studied anew and the whole allegory referred to the abstractions of the contrasts and relations of heavenly and earthly beauty as set forth in the conventionalized fashion of contemporary love-making.[1] To this we may give a qualified assent, remembering, however, that inconsistency in its conduct and denial by the author can be urged as no real objections to allegory in any age, and that it was peculiarly the nature of English allegory in Lyly's time to conceal a concrete as well as an abstract significance.

While no author can be judged as a dramatist by short extracts, the following may suffice to show the quality of Lyly's refined and Euphuistic diction as well as the nature of his allegorical flattery of the queen in this play.

Endimion. O fair Cynthia, why do others term thee unconstant, whom I have ever found unmovable? Injurious time, corrupt manners, unkind men, who finding a constancy not to be matched in my sweet mistress, have christened her with the name of wavering, waxing and waning. Is she inconstant that keepeth a settled course, which since her first creation altereth not one minute in her moving? There is nothing thought more admirable or commendable in the sea than the ebbing and flowing; and shall the moon, from whom the sea taketh this virtue, be accounted fickle for increasing and decreasing? Flowers in their buds are nothing worth till they be blown; nor blossoms accounted till they be ripe fruit; and shall we then say they be changeable for that they grow from seeds to leaves, from leaves to buds, from buds to their perfection? . . . Tell me, Eumenides, what is he that having a mistress of ripe years and infinite virtues, great honors and unspeakable beauty, but would wish that she might grow tender again? getting youth by years and never decaying beauty by time; whose fair face neither the summer's blaze can scorch nor winter's blast chap, nor the numbering of years breed altering of colors. Such is my sweet Cynthia, whom time can not touch because she is divine, nor will offend because she is delicate. O Cynthia, if thou shouldst always continue at thy fulness, both gods and men would conspire to ravish thee. But thou to abate the pride of our affections

[1] See P. W. Long in *Publications of the Modern Language Association*, xxiv, 1909.

dost detract from thy perfections; thinking it sufficient if once in a
month we enjoy a glimpse of thy majesty; and then to increase our
griefs thou dost decrease thy gleams, coming out of thy royal robes,
wherewith thou dazzlest our eyes, down into thy swathe clouts, be-
guiling our eyes; and then —

Eumenides. Stay there, Endimion, thou that commitest idolatry
wilt straight blaspheme, if thou be suffered. Sleep would do thee
more good than speech: the moon heareth thee not, or if she do,
regardeth thee not.

When all has been said, Lyly's *Endimion* remains a brilliant piece of court comedy, skilfully constructed and admirably sustained. The transition from *Horestes* and *Cambyses* to *Endimion* is the transition from the botching of the
tyro to the professional touch of the artist. True it is that
these court plays of Lyly are rhetorical and decorative, superficial and limited in any appeal to the modern reader by
reason of their occasional nature; none the less his contributions to the drama are tangible and definite. It was Lyly
who gave to English comedy ease of dialogue and natural
witty retort; who gave to drama likewise fluency and finish of
style. He drew for the first time portraits of the cultivated
men and women of his day in the easy intercourse of good
society, and he restrained exorbitant medieval allegory to a
modest and subsidiary place. He was inventive, too, and
happy in uniting the diverse classical and other elements out
of which he fashioned his plays. Indeed it may be affirmed
that he is the superior of many of his successors in these as in
some other qualities of his art. It was an innovation in
Lyly to write his plays — all except one — in prose, and it
is not to be denied that his prose, Euphuistic though it is in
some of his earlier productions, is wanting neither in idiomatic
force and effectiveness nor in grace and elegance. In a
word, it was Lyly who raised the entertainments of the court
from the haphazard of amateurishness to a professional
standard, giving to the drama for the first time artistic form
and unity.

Lyly's earliest rival at court was George Peele, whose
first drama, *The Arraignment of Paris*, was acted before the

queen between 1581 and 1584. Peele, son of the clerk of
Christ's Hospital, was educated there and at Oxford, where
his interest in the drama seems to have been inspired by a
kinsman, William Gager, the author of several Latin plays.
In these plays Peele appeared as an actor and he is related to
have translated while at college one of the *Iphigenias* of
Euripides, but whether into English or into Latin remains
uncertain. From college Peele went to court, where the slender
patronage he mustered could not have carried him far. Before
long he gravitated to the popular stage then occupied by
Wilson and Tarlton. Peele led a riotous and Bohemian
life and became a peg, so to speak, on which to hang knavish
stories and worse. Possessed as he was at times of no mean
lyrical gift, Peele is imitative and eclectic in the drama and
constantly follows in the wake of others. Thus his *Arraignment of Paris* is a clear effort to outdo Lyly in his own court
drama and a bid for the patronage of the court; his *Battle
of Alcazar* frankly imitates Marlowe's *Tamburlaine;* his
Edward I is an inferior chronicle play, disfigured by an attempt to gain momentary popularity by a gross misrepresenta-
tion of one of the Spanish-born queens of England; and his
David and Bethsabe is an ill-advised if poetical revival of the
Bible play in the guise of a chronical history. Peele seems to
have been possessed of an uncontrollable bias towards burlesque; for on this ground alone can we explain his *Old Wives
Tale* in which the absurdities and extravagances of old romance
are ridiculed with delightful effect. *Locrine*, which belongs
to the same source in mythical British history as *King Lear*,
is an extravagant attempt to popularize Senecan blood and
horror on the public stage. Although never avowed by Peele
as his, it seems almost unquestionably of his authorship,
and is perhaps truly read as a take-off on other like productions of his time. Peele's work must all have been written
while Lyly was still active, for he died prematurely, in 1597,
worn out by disease and a dissolute life.

Peele's *Arraignment of Paris* is a dramatic version of the
old myth of Œnone's unhappy love for Paris combined with
his award of the golden apple of Até to Venus on her promise

to bestow on him the most beautiful woman in the world. But Peele at this point adapted mythology to the exigencies of a graceful flattery of royalty, borrowing his idea from an old poem addressed to the queen by Gascoigne some half-dozen years before. Paris, on complaint of Juno and Pallas to Jove, is summoned to attend an action "entered in the court of heaven." The parties meet at "Diana's bower," and so equal are the claims of all three that Jove is perplexed until Apollo suggests:

> Refer this sentence where it doth belong:
> In this, say I, fair Phœbe hath the wrong;
> Not that I mean her beauty bears the prize,
> But that the holy law of heaven denies
> One god to meddle in another's power;
> And this befell so near Diana's bower,
> As for th' appeasing this unpleasant grudge,
> In my conceit she hight the fittest judge.

Diana accepts the duty of deciding, and, having sworn each god and goddess to obedience, declares:

> There wons within these pleasant shady woods
> Where neither storm nor sun's distemperature
> Have power to hurt by cruel heat or cold,
> . . . . . a gracious nymph,
> That honors Dian for her chastity,
> And likes the labors well of Phœbe's groves;
> The place Elizium hight, and of the place
> Her name that governs there Eliza is;
> A kingdom that may well compare with mine,
> An ancient seat of kings, a second Troy,
> Y-compassed round with a commodious sea:
>
> . . . .
>
> She giveth laws of justice and of peace;
> And on her head, as fits her fortune best,
> She wears a wreath of laurel, gold and palm;
> Her robes of purple and of scarlet dye;
> Her veil of white, as best befits a maid:
> Her ancestors live in the house of fame:
> She giveth arms of happy victory,
> And flowers to deck her lions crowned with gold,

This peerless nymph, whom heaven and earth beloves,
This paragon, this only, this is she,
In whom do meet so many gifts in one,
On whom our country gods so often gaze,
In honor of whose name the Muses sing;
In state Queen Juno's peer, for power in arms
And virtues of the mind Minerva's mate,
As fair and lovely as the Queen of Love,
As chaste as Dian in her chaste desires:
The same is she, if Phœbe do no wrong,
To whom this ball of merit doth belong.

And after further fitting ceremony, the distance from the stage to the throne is traversed and the prize is conveyed into the royal hand of the true Eliza. There are more beautiful and poetical lines than these just quoted from *The Arraignment*, for the comedy abounds in exquisite lyrics, and in charming poetry and imagery, but none could better disclose the quality of these plays of courtly compliment. It may be surmised that so admirable a piece of poetical flattery would have meant preferment and fortune to a pretty fellow like Sidney, Greville, or Harington, had any one of them devised it; Peele was too lowly to have received more than a brace or two of angels for his play, and these we may believe he speedily spent in the honor of her majesty's health and to the detriment of his own. In the maintenance of the perspective of literary history we must recognize in Peele's *Arraignment of Paris*, printed in 1584, a metrical facility, an ease and grace of expression in verse, remarkable when we recall that at that date Marlowe was still at Cambridge and Shakespeare indistinguishable as yet among his fellow yeomen of Warwickshire.

And now let us turn to the presentation of these earlier plays at court and to some of the means by which they were commended in action to their auditors. Shows, maskings, and allegorical devices had been so long familiar to the English court that when the regular drama emerged from the chaos of medieval dramatic conditions, all of those things were at once adopted. An early use, for example, of dumb shows or tableaux as we should call them, is to be found in such plays as *Gorboduc* and *Tancred and Gismunda*. In the first the shows were extraneous to the action of the drama though illustrative of it, as for example the parade of a company of "harquibusiers" in order of battle to betoken "tumults, rebellious arms, a civil war." In *Tancred* the tableaux were for the most part made up of groupings of the personages of the tragedy. In both, the dumb show eked out defective action and appears to have been derived from an Italian device. Costume at court was always elaborate and costly, as the extant inventories of the accounts of the office of the revels still attest with their entries of silk, velvet and damask, embroidery and cloth of gold and silver. The fitness of this apparel for the scene and purpose in hand is often far to seek: a friar is clad in russet velvet with sleeves of yellow, Turks wear caps unlike either fez or turban, and the Greek worthies seem in one case to have been actually labeled with the name of each on breast and back.

The drama of the court was staged from the earliest times with properties, though not with scenes in our modern sense involving flies in perspective. These were called "players' houses" in the accounts of the revels, and were constructed of canvas stretched on frames and painted. Arbors, fountains, trees, mountains, castles, battlements, and palaces are among the scenes thus enumerated, and they were "steered" by means of "long boards" or raised and lowered by pulleys. Some must have been of considerable size, for cities, hills, and forests were sometimes represented and the transportation of them by water was deemed of sufficient importance to receive a separate entry in the accounts.[1] These evidences derived from the office of the revels are corroborated when we come to look at the plays still extant. Trees appear on the stage in Lyly's *Gallathea* and *Love's Metamorphosis*, a palace in *Midas*, a fountain and castle in *Endimion*. *The Misfortunes of Arthur*, by Thomas Hughes and others, acted in 1587, represented "the house appointed for Arthur" as

[1] See A. Feuillerat, *Documents relating to the Office of the Revels*, 1908, pp. 20, 116, 129, 331, 349.

well as Mordred's house. *Mother Bombie* calls for a row of some half-dozen houses, among them a tavern; and the action traversed the stage from house to house after the manner of medieval pageantry. Gascoigne's *Supposes*, like several early plays, calls for a balcony. Curtains were in constant use; they were commonly drawn apart on rings run on wires, but in one case at least they appear to have been raised up and down.

In general when a play was given at court or in one of the halls of the university the whole room was fitted and decorated for the purpose. An interesting account of the arrangement of the Common Hall of Christ's Church College, Oxford, for the queen's visit of 1566 has come down to us, the work of one John Bereblock. The hall was paneled with gilt, arched and frescoed to represent an ancient Roman palace. A large stage, "many steps high," was erected across the upper end on which were reared "palaces and well-equipped houses" for the actors and masquers. Scaffolds were raised about the room with a lofty seat and golden canopy for the queen; and especial attention was given to the brilliant lighting of the entire room by "cressets, lamps, and burning candles." It has recently been maintained that the private theaters, such as Blackfriars, that of the Paul's boys, and Whitefriars, were evolved out of these halls of the court and university, occasionally fitted for the performance of plays; and that their structure and their practices in time reacted on the conditions ruling the public stage. On the dissolution of the monasteries by Henry VIII the property of the Blackfriars on the embankment north of the Thames and east of old Fleet Street, now Bridge Street, reverted to the crown. Thither in Edward's day the office of the revels was removed with its furniture and apparel for the customary performances at court; and here, in all likelihood, the actors for court performances rehearsed in the time of Sir Thomas Cawarden, Master of the Revels from 1546 to 1560. Here, too, Ferrant established his theater in the eighties and John Lyly, combining the children of the chapel with those of Paul's, staged his *Campaspe* and *Sappho and Phao*. So that when, in 1596, James Burbage acquired the title to the old Priory House in Blackfriars and refitted it as a playhouse he was really making no serious innovation. The new Blackfriars, thus remodeled, cost Burbage upwards of £800 and has recently been compared favorably as to size as well as equipment with the contemporary public playhouse, the Globe. It was furnished with galleries and "lord's rooms," or private boxes, and, while it may have accommodated no more than half as many auditors as the Globe, had an ample stage and sufficient tiring-rooms. The rental of Blackfriars, on its remodeling, to the Children of the Royal Chapel was likewise no more than the maintenance of what must long have been the conditions of this house.[1]

Of Lyly's qualities as a dramatist and his place among the playwrights of school and court enough has been said. But Lyly's influence was wider than this and more lasting. It affected the court entertainments which continued in classical plays, pastorals, masques, and other entertainments, despite much influence from the contemporary popular drama, all the way to the closing of the theaters in 1642, and was the true source of a distinct and separable stream of growth, paralleling the popular drama of Shakespeare. The first prominent successor of Lyly, as the accredited entertainer of the court, was Samuel Daniel, who outlived Shakespeare three years and wrote favorable specimens of that exotic form of the drama, the pastoral. Overlapping Daniel in his later career was Ben Jonson, the master of the English masque. That the grace and easy mastery of the amenities of court life which Lyly shows were the example, with much else, of both of these can admit of no serious doubt. More interesting to us, Lyly profoundly affected the earlier comedy of Shakespeare, a theme that will claim, with the consideration of the earlier popular drama, our attention in the next chapter.

[1] On this whole topic see the recent researches of C. W. Wallace in *Nebraska University Studies*, April-July, 1908, and A. H. Thorndike, *Shakespeare's Theater*, 1916.

CHAPTER VI

MARLOWE AND HIS FELLOWS IN POPULAR DRAMA

IN the last chapter we were concerned with the drama of the schools and the court, with beginnings based on a study and imitation of classical ideals, with amateur actors, and, in a sense, with amateur authors as well. This drama, like most of the non-dramatic literature of the age — the sonnets and romance of Sidney, the poetry and allegory of Spenser, and the cultivated prose of Lyly — was the literature of the select and cultivated few, and to a certain degree existed as the shibboleth of a clique. We turn now to something very different, to the drama of the people acted in inn-yards and by strolling players, written, as acted, professionally and before long to develop, in the plays of Kyd, Marlowe, and Shakespeare, to a degree of excellence not hitherto known.

Strolling players and mountebanks are traceable far back into the Middle Ages, and link on to the minstrel as the minstrel goes farther back to the Anglo-Saxon *gleomon* or *scop*. The patronage of players' companies by nobles is likewise no innovation of Tudor times, though, as the drama grew in popularity, this patronage became more a form for the players' protection than the mark of any intimate relation. The Earl of Leicester, whose seat of Kenilworth was in Warwickshire near to the town of Stratford, was an early patron of actors and took a company abroad with him as early as 1585. By some this company has been thought to continue into that which Shakespeare afterwards joined, variously known as Lord Strange's, the Chamberlain's, the King's, and by other titles according to its successive patrons. By others the first step in this succession has been denied, and the origin of Shakespeare's company referred to a troupe under the patronage of Lord Strange, mentioned as performing "feats of tumbling and activity" at court in January, 1580.[1] The best opinion now refers Shakespeare's earlier affiliations to neither of these companies, but to that of the Earl of Pembroke, a company of brief existence which, however, achieved an extraordinary success with Marlowe's *Edward II* and other plays, in 1592; but, owing to the plague, was disrupted in the following year. In this association Shakespeare probably met Peele and Marlowe, revising historical plays of theirs on Henry VI, which afterwards appeared in the first folio. Two years later Shakespeare became a member of the Chamberlain's company and remained such through its various changes of patron to the end. Earlier there had been other successful companies, the Queen's players in the eighties at the Theater in Shoreditch, and the Admiral's men, who, under the leadership of the great actor, Edward Alleyn, creator of several rôles of Marlowe, united temporarily in 1591 with Lord Strange's men, who were associated with James Burbage, the builder of the Theater. In 1592 these two companies were acting together at the Rose. The Chamberlain's men acted first at the Theater, then briefly at the Curtain nearby, until their final removal to the new Globe on Bankside in 1598.

The circumstances of the building of the Globe theater and the formation of a theatrical company to act there have recently been placed in a new light by the researches of Professor Wallace, whose discoveries have already been alluded to in this book. It appears that when, in 1597, the Burbage brothers met with difficulty in renewing the lease for the ground on which the Theater stood, they determined to exercise a right, reserved in their deed, and remove to the Bankside the material out of which the building had been constructed. To insure the success of this venture they associated with them five actors — Shakespeare, Heming, Philips, Pope, and Kempe — and organized "a sharing company, the first of its kind in the theatrical world." The new lease of the site for the Globe was so arranged that the two Burbage brothers acquired half of it, the five associated actors the other half, the total rental being £14 10s. Shakespeare thus held

[1] W. W. Greg, *Henslowe's Diary*, Part II, 68-71.

originally a tenth interest in the Globe; and this continued up to 1610, when the five actors admitted Henry Condell to a share, reducing the share in the whole of each of the now six owners of the actors' half to one twelfth. In 1612 a further admission of William Osteler as a sharer reduced the share of each of the now seven actor-sharers of the Globe to one fourteenth. The Burbages continued to own their half as before. To continue this digression into Shakespeare's relations to Blackfriars, in 1608 this house, also the property of the Burbages, was leased to the Children of the Queen's Revels who were suppressed as a company in that year by the order of King James. Immediately after, Richard Burbage, the owner, leased the Blackfriars to a theatrical company of seven persons, retaining a seventh both for himself and his brother Cuthbert, and giving five others, among them Shakespeare, Heming, and Condell, each a share like his own. The total rental was £40 a year. In 1614 Shakespeare owned one seventh of the Blackfriars and one fourteenth of the Globe. The original cost of these shares was merely the rent of the ground and the obligations for building and management. They became in time very valuable; but the statement in the legal complaint of the time from which these facts were gathered that the value of such a share as Shakespeare's in each of these theaters was £300 is of course excessive, as such statements for claim of damage always are. It may be noted in passing that Heming and Condell are the fellow-actors of Shakespeare who signed their names to the prefatory matter of the folio edition of his collected works in 1623.[1]

But if we are to appreciate the conditions under which the popular drama sprang into life in Elizabeth's time, we must understand the nature of the playhouses of the day and learn under what circumstances they came to be built. Earlier popular theatrical performances followed the traditions of wandering minstrels and were acted for the most part in taverns or other public places, not infrequently in yards and open spaces. The inn-yard is the original of the Elizabethan popular playhouse; and the common features of the inn were

[1] See C. W. Wallace in *The Times*, October 2 and 4, 1909.

reproduced when structures intended specifically for the public acting of plays came to be built.

Let us turn, however, first to a consideration of the ground. Elizabethan London was to our modern ideas a small city, certainly not much exceeding a hundred thousand inhabitants. It lay along the Thames, then a clear and swiftly flowing stream, from the Tower to Temple Bar, and, like most medieval towns, was surrounded by a wall. London was ruled by a lord mayor, elected yearly, and by a council which was made up of men prominent in the trade guilds of the city. A certain gravity and seriousness naturally characterized such "city fathers," and their care extended to the minuter welfare of the citizens. For this reason quite as much as because many of the citizens were Puritan in their leanings, the theater was never approved in the councils of the lord mayor. For aside from the vanity and ungodliness that they found in many plays, they recognized in such concourses of the disorderly element of the city, a menace to the public peace and (most important of all) to the public health. The plague in Shakespeare's age was a very real danger; and the general ignorance of hygienic rules and popular carelessness in matters of cleanliness rendered it at times a veritable terror. Laws were passssed closing both churches and playhouses when the mortality from the plague rose to a certain percentage; and, when buildings for theatrical purposes were projected, the lord mayor succeeded in forbidding the erection of any such building within the precincts of the city. His jurisdiction however stopped without the several gates in the city walls and at the middle point of London Bridge, which alone connected London with Southwark on the Surrey side or Bankside. Under these conditions, we find the earliest playhouses just beyond the walls or across the river in Southwark. Thus the Theater, the first regular playhouse to be erected in London, was built in the parish of Shoreditch in 1576, and near it in Moorfields the Curtain arose in the following year. Shoreditch was a borough on the main thoroughfare north, without Bishopsgate. The Theater was built by James Burbage, father of the famous actor, Richard. It was demol-

ished in 1598 and the materials used in part for the building
of the Globe. But the Bankside was soon recognized as a
more favorable location for the erection of playhouses. The
Bankside had long been in use as a playground and place of
license and diversion. Bull-baiting and bear-baiting were
among its amusements and the two old arenas for these purposes existed long before the theaters. The Globe, the Rose,
the Hope, and the Swan were the four Elizabethan theaters
of the Bankside. All of them were built within the decade of
the nineties and, in the order named above, they ranged
irregularly along the river shore to the right of him who crossed
London Bridge from the city or to the left of the bridge and
the Church of St. Saviour's, as one looks at a map or a view
of old London. There were other theaters besides these, the
one at Newington Butts, back from the river in Southwark;
the Fortune, a new and fine theater for its day, built in 1600
by Edward Alleyn in St. Giles, Cripplegate, in rivalry with
Shakespeare and his Globe. And there were the private
theaters of Blackfriars, Whitefriars, and that of the boys of
St. Paul's; but these latter ones do not concern us here.

The last few years have witnessed much interest in the
construction of these old Elizabethan playhouses and in the
probable manner in which Elizabethan plays were staged.
Unfortunately the evidence at hand is sparse and, what is
worse, at times, conflicting: moreover, it has been occasionally
somewhat unwisely assumed that it is possible to reduce the
whole problem to a typical stage. Undoubtedly the playhouses of Elizabeth differed as the theaters of to-day and what
may have been true of one may possibly not have been true of
all. This is not the place for discussion; of some things,
however, we may feel reasonably sure.

The Elizabethan public playhouse was ordinarily a cir-
cular or octagonal structure built about an open space or
yard to which there was but one public entrance at which
"gate money" might be charged. Within, the yard was open
to the sky and here the "groundlings" as they were called
stood to see the play. As to three fourths of its circumference
the yard was surrounded with galleries, two or three, and in

them sat the auditors of better station; although the highest gallery must have been as undesirable then as to-day. In the fourth part of the circumference and opposite the entrance door, the stage was situated, jutting far out into the yard so that the groundlings stood on three sides of it. The stage of Shakespeare's time was primarily a platform for declamation, not, as with us, a place for a picture set in a frame. The roof over the stage was supported by two pillars or "pilasters" as they were called; but they appear to have stood back from the front of the stage, and it is doubtful whether they were near the two edges or not, rather, placed closer together so as to produce the effect of a structure near the middle of the stage and thus leave space for free action not only in front but around each pillar at the side. There has also been much question as to whether or not a curtain was strung between the pilasters. Certainly no drop curtain, such as we now use, was employed on a public stage before the Restoration. As there are many references in the stage directions of old plays to curtains (or traverses as they were sometimes called), it has been thought that, if they were not stretched between the pilasters, they were draped to hang beneath the balcony or gallery that ran across the back of the stage, thus dividing the stage into the part before the pilasters, the part between the pilasters and the curtain, and the corridor or alcove under the balcony. The opinion of the present writer leans to a curtain between the pilasters, thus bringing out the action on the back part of the stage to a point immediately behind them rather than concealing it in the shadow of the balcony. As to the balcony itself, it, too, was furnished with curtains and was employed wherever an upper window, a battlement, or other eminence was necessary to the action. The music, of the use of which between the acts and elsewhere there is abundant proof, was doubtless at times placed in a part of of the balcony which was in the nature of a gallery and may have been arranged diagonally at its two extremities.[1]

Among the many questions concerning the Elizabethan stage none has been waged more fiercely than that which

[1] See W. Archer in *The Quarterly Review*, April, 1908.

concerns the presence or absence of scenery on the stage. On the one hand all scenery has been denied; but we hear in at least two authentic passages of its existence in such a phrase as Jonson's (1600) "'Slid, the boy takes me for a piece of perspective," and in Dekker's words (1609): "Stand at the helm and steer the passage of the scenes." [1] Though this has been interpreted to mean no more than " run the play " or control the course of the action. It must be allowed that there was no such system of perspective by means of back curtain and side flies as we have now in use; but it is defiant of both evidence and probability to deny to the Elizabethan popular stage many scenic properties of considerable size and variety. Thrones of state, trees, buildings of importance enough to be designated "castles," hangings suggesting the rigging of a ship, even landscapes and cities find mention again and again, and we should be impelled to believe in the use of such properties, were the evidence less certain than it is, from the influence that performances at court must in time have exerted on the popular stage.

That the use of properties such as these was often very crude and insufficient according to our modern ideas must be granted. The Elizabethan stage has been thought by some to have inherited from medieval conditions the practice of what has been called simultaneous scenery. Heavier properties must frequently have remained on the stage though often incongruous to the action which appears at times to have moved from one part of the stage to another. When the action was about the throne set in the center, a presence chamber was conjured with imagination's inward eye. When the action sidled to a tree in a box to the left it was transferred to the country-side. To escape this incongruity (to our modern ideas), some have imagined that heavy properties were confined to the space back of the curtain into which they might be lugged from the tiring-room and concealed by the curtain when not in use. Attempt has even been made to divide Shakespeare's plays into a strict alternation of scenes before

[1] See Gifford-Cunningham, *Jonson*, ii, 210; *The Gulls' Hornbook*, Grosart, *Dekker*, ii, 248. But see also *Mod. Lang. Rev.*, xv, 166.

the curtain and scenes behind, to allow of such shifts of the properties. However, of late it must be confessed that a very good case has been made out for a liberal modification of some such system, based on a study of the staging of theatrical productions from the medieval times up and, more especially, from the Restoration backward.[1] None the less we may believe that not a little of the setting of the Elizabethan stage was content to symbolize the scene by some important object suggesting it, and to be little hurt by incongruities which would destroy the illusion to modern auditors. With the intervention of incidental music and the employment, where there was need, of the curtain which divided the rear stage from the front, the action of an Elizabethan play must have been carried on continuously all over the stage and gallery. Indeed, those who have seen Shakespeare simply staged with next to no scenery and acted without division by waits between acts or scenes, have recognized how much our old drama has to gain by a reversion to earlier and less elaborate methods of histrionic representation.

As to the acting of an Elizabethan play, it is to be remembered that the performance was for men and acted by men. The employment of women to act on the stage of the day would have been thought a disgrace and a scandal. In fact, in stricter Elizabethan times no woman of character would think of attending a common playhouse; and when later, she did, she wore a mask. Women's rôles were taken by boys who appear to have become remarkably skilful in their difficult profession, though none ever attained the rank of such men as Burbage and Edward Alleyn, the leaders in male parts and the creators of the chief rôles of Shakespeare and Marlowe. The performance of a play, in old times, must often have been a very disorderly proceeding, for gallants were tolerated on the very stage itself and disturbances often arose among the auditors, breaking up the performance and ending at times in affrays and bloodshed. It is impossible not to sympathize with the mayor and his council in their honest endeavors to abate such nuisances and in their wider looks askant at the

[1] See especially V. E. Albright, *The Shakesperian Stage*, 1909.

theater, in general, as an innovation of doubtful character.
The Elizabethan drama could not plead, like the old sacred
drama, that it instructed men in the gospel. It could not claim,
like the morality, that it existed to teach right living, or like
the Latin school plays to impart confidence to the boys who
acted and improve their Latin pronunciation. The new
drama had no excuse for its existence, and existed only to
amuse. There was a long struggle between the city and the
court about the professional players and their theaters, the
city passing laws against actors and plays, pleading their
wickedness and licentiousness, the danger to the public peace
and to the public health. On the other hand the court pro-
tected the actors, who commonly gave as an excuse for their
popular performances that they must practise if they were to
perform before the queen, and, claiming the protection of
some noble as patron, thus escaped the rigor of the laws against
"rogues, vagabonds, and common players."

As time went on the actors thrived and rose in the social
scale. In Greene's tract *A Groatsworth of Wit Purchased
with a Million of Repentance*, notorious for its attack on
Shakespeare, we find the following little colloquy on this
subject:

What is your profession? said Roberto. Truly, sir, said he, I
am a player. A player! quoth Roberto, I took you rather for a
gentleman of great living; for, if by outward habit men should be
censured, I tell you you would be taken for a substantial man. So
am I, where I dwell, quoth the player, reputed able at my proper cost
to build a windmill. What though the world once went hard with
me, when I was fain to carry my fardel a foot-a-back; . . . it is
otherwise now; for my very share in playing apparel will not be sold
for two hundred pounds.

The player here represented may have been one Robert
Wilson of the queen's company of actors in 1583, the author
of three or four extant plays in which the old morality is
mingled with newer ideas. Elsewhere, he tells us "the twelve
labors of Hercules have I terribly thundered on the stage and
placed three scenes of the devil on the highway to heaven."
Another early popular actor and playwright was Richard

Tarlton, who was famed for his clown's parts and for antics and humors that found a place in the jest-books of the time. Tarlton was of the humblest origin and in the height of his success kept a tavern in Gracechurch Street. He died in 1588, the year of the Armada, but he was long outlived by the fame of his extemporal wit, a variety of extemporaneous embroidering on the part assigned that drew from Shakespeare in later times the terse words of Hamlet: "Let those that play your clowns speak no more than is set down for them."

Not only is the number of these early pre-Shakespearean plays of the common stages very great, but their variety is extraordinary. Besides the English historical subjects already suggested in Tarlton's *Famous Victories of Henry V* (a crude production, not unknown to Shakespeare), and plays like the anonymous *Troublesome Reign of King John* (another Shakespearean "source"), there was a domestic comedy like *Grim the Collier of Croyden*, or *Tom Tyler*, a diverting interlude in which an attempt to tame a shrewish wife proves amusingly abortive. There was also domestic drama, represented in the able and effective *Arden of Feversham*, a tragedy which some have ascribed to Shakespeare, others to Thomas Kyd. And there was, besides the semi-moralities of Wilson, romantic drama dealing with knights and fair ladies, Greene's *Orlando Furioso* and *The Thracian Wonder*, turned to probably satirical references in such a play as *Fair Em, the Miller's Daughter of Manchester*. Without pursuing this enumeration further here, it is demonstrable that nearly all the notable varieties of the Elizabethan drama were already presaged in rudimentary form before the morality went out of vogue. Not only did Shakespeare invent no solitary kind of play not already well known to the stage before him; but no one of his great predecessors — Marlowe, Greene, Lyly, Peele, or Kyd — invented a new variety of drama. It is important to recognize how fully the soil had been prepared for the great harvest that was to follow, how an humble but by no means despicable growth had already covered these previous times, and how the playhouse, the organized company, an audience eager for the drama and accustomed to it, all had been created before the great and memorable playwrights of the time came forward to assume their inheritance.

The three great influences that made Elizabethan drama are now before us. First, the influence of the classics — Plautus for comedy, Seneca for tragedy — exemplified in *Ralph Roister Doister* on the one hand and *Gorboduc* on the other. Secondly, the influence of the popular vernacular farce, English to the core though touched by French example: in comedy illustrated in *Gammer Gurton* or *Tom Tyler*, and pure of any foreign contact in the murder play, *Arden of Feversham*. Thirdly, the influence of Italy and the spirit of romance, already suggested in Lyly's courtly plays, in *Tancred*, and in Whetstone's *Promos and Cassandra*, and soon to become the distinguishing characteristic of the great dramas of Marlowe, Shakespeare, and Webster.

With Lyly and Peele, it is customary to place Lodge, Greene, and Nash as well as Kyd and Marlowe, to call them indiscriminately "university wits" or by a like designation to dilate upon their short and abandoned lives and the precise similarlity of their alleged careers. Kyd was not a university man; and Lyly, at least, was no Bohemian. Lodge, despite early escapades, lived far into the reign of James, a respectable physician, and wrote, besides *Marius and Sylla*, hardly any drama certainly traceable as his. Nash's part, too, in the drama is slight, and consists of one masque-like production, *Summer's Last Will and Testament,* of *Dido, Queen of Carthage*, a tragedy written in conjunction with Marlowe, and a lost Latin comedy. Nothing could be more uncritical than the habitual grouping of these "predecessors of Shakespeare."

Of Peele enough has been said above as to how he transferred his interests in the drama, first from the university to court and thence to the popular stage of Wilson and Tarlton. Peele's art was imitative, as we have seen, his life dissolute, his end untimely; but his satirical consciousness of the absurdities of the popular plays about him — plays that he imitated in *David and Bethsabe* and especially in *Edward I*, while he parodied them in *The Old Wives Tale* and in

Locrine — is not without its interest to the history of the drama.

Greene, too, was a man of disordered life, although the candor of his revelations concerning himself and the circumstance of his enmity to Shakespeare have conspired perhaps somewhat to exaggerate his bad name. Greene was a busy pamphleteer as well as playwright, and death overtook him, as it overtook Marlowe, in the midst of his sins. Greene's work, like of Peele's, was imitative and eclectic. In *A Looking Glass for London and England*, which he wrote with Thomas Lodge, he gives us work of the morality type, little above the plane of Wilson, though superior in execution. In *Orlando Furioso* he outdid the excesses of the heroical romance; in *Alphonsus of Aragon* he essayed the "high astounding terms" of Marlowe's *Tamburlaine*. None the less Greene's genuine contribution to Elizabethan drama is both considerable and peculiar. In *The Scottish History of James IV* he has given us a serious comedy of very considerable worth, memorable for the fine and pathetic pictures of true womanhood represented in both his heroine, Ida, and the queen. In *Friar Bacon* he dramatized the story of that famous English necromancer and contrasted his white and harmless magic with the black art of Marlowe's *Faustus*, which was at the moment holding the stage. Though truer to nature and more peculiarly Greene's own are the charming scenes in this comedy which tell of the love and courtship of the Fair Maid of Fressingfield who is wooed for his prince but won for himself by the young Earl Lacy, after a manner familiar to American readers of Longfellow's *Courtship of Miles Standish*. Equally successful and characteristic of Greene, is his apotheosis of the English yeoman in *George a Green or the Pinner of Wakefield*. This hero impounds an earl's horses that have trespassed on the town's corn, defeats Robin Hood himself at quarterstaff, and cleverly traps and captures the king's enemies. For all these services King Edward, who happens that way, asks George to demand what he will. And his reply is that the king may use his influence

to induce old Grimes, his "leman's father," to consent to that
maiden's marriage with him.   This granted, the king adds:

Now, George, it rests I gratify thy worth:

.   .   .   .

Kneel down, George:
George.   What will your majesty do?
Edward.   Dub thee a knight, George.
George.   I beseech your grace, grant me one thing.
Edward.   What is it?
George.   Then let me live and die a yeoman still:
So was my father, so must live his son.
For 'tis more credit to men of base degree,
To do great deeds, than men of dignity.

Can we not imagine how at this the pit must have risen to a
man?   And what could be a better example of the truly popular nature of this new people's drama?

Could Greene have lived and led a less disordered life,
could he have developed leisurely and harmoniously instead
of driving an overworked pen for bread, Shakespeare might
not have been without a rival in comedy worthy his best
efforts.   The pathetic story of Greene's end, his miserable
death from his own excesses, his touching letter to his wronged
and deserted wife that she see those paid who had buried him
out of pity, is known to every student, as well as his notorious
address to his quondam acquaintance, Marlowe, Peele, and
Lodge "who spend their time in making plays."   It was
sheer envy that prompted the dying Greene rancorously to
attack the rising young Shakespeare, to call him "an upstart
crow beautified with our feathers," to imagine Shakespeare
so elated with his own success that he had become "in his own
conceit the only shake-scene in a country."   But there was
another side, Greene was a genuine poet, an able playwright,
a successful pamphleteer, all this despite his reckless life and
wasted time.   Such a man must have known of possibilities
within which we can not reconstruct from the broken remains
of his work.   Infinitely above the painstaking achievements of
mediocrity is the comparative failure of an irregular genius
such as Greene's.

English romantic tragedy reached fruition all but simultaneously in two great plays, *Tamburlaine* in two parts by Christopher Marlowe, and *The Spanish Tragedy* by Thomas Kyd. Both plays were certainly on the stage a year or more before the coming of the Armada; but which is the earlier has never been absolutely determined, for neither exhibits the slightest borrowing from the other and each expresses an independent phase of tragic art.

Until recently we have known very little of Thomas Kyd; now we can tell — thanks to Professor Schick of Munich and to Mr. Boas and his researches — that Kyd was born in 1558, in London, and attended the Merchant Tailors' School where Lodge and Spenser were among his school-fellows. Kyd's father was a scrivener or lawyer's clerk and Thomas may have followed that "trade of noverint" as it was called. He appears not to have gone to either university, but was admitted to the literary circle of the Sidneys and Pembrokes and enjoyed the intimate acquaintance of Marlowe. The poets at one time occupied together the same room, a circumstance that drew Kyd into suspicion of sharing also in Marlowe's alleged atheistical opinions. Kyd was even imprisoned on charges connected with this association and lost all chances of patronage therefore. Indeed, whether for this cause or for some other, Kyd was disowned by his parents, who renounced the administration of the goods of their deceased son in December, 1594.

The height of Kyd's activity as a dramatist was concentrated within a very few years, those between 1584 and 1589. *The Spanish Tragedy* was doubtless his earliest dramatic work and the companion play called *The First Part of Jeronimo* is best considered not Kyd's, but a production subsequently written by another on account of the popularity of Kyd's tragedy. A second and less successful drama of much the type of *The Spanish Tragedy* is *Soliman and Perceda*, dating 1588, and assuredly of Kyd's authorship. The translation of a tragedy by Garnier called *Cornelia*, published in 1592, and a lost play on Hamlet, 1587, complete the tale of Kyd's dramatic labors.

The Spanish Tragedy is the most typical of the tragedies of Kyd. The story details the revenge of a father, the Marshal Hieronimo, for the murder of his son, who has been slain under circumstances that leave the father uncertain of the slayer and incapable of redress. Madness, actual or pretended, and hesitancy to act add to the difficulties of Hieronimo; but, discerning at length in the Prince Lorenzo the true instigator of the murder, and with revenge for that reason even more than ever beyond his reach, Hieronimo pulls down general ruin on his enemies and himself, in a play devised to bring about the catastrophe. The interest of *The Spanish Tragedy* centers in the vital personage Hieronimo. This became one of the favorite rôles of Edward Alleyn and was revised and amplified on revival by Ben Jonson. The popularity of Kyd's tragedy lasted a generation; seven quartos up to 1608 and repeated allusions attesting its vogue and reputation. Nor is it to be denied that this popularity was deserved. *The Spanish Tragedy* is effective melodrama, bold, striking, dramatically efficient, and not untrue to the broader outlines of life. The text affords many examples of the rhetorical diction so beloved of the playgoers of the earlier days of Elizabeth and taken off, not altogether unkindly, by Shakespeare in the speech of the player in *Hamlet* and in the soldier's account of the battle at the opening of *Macbeth*. The following passage is Kyd, not Shakespeare:

> There met our armies in their proud array:
> Both furnished well, both full of hope and fear,
> Both menacing alike with daring shows,
> Both vaunting sundry colors of device,
> Both cheerly sounding trumpets, drums and fifes,
> Both raising dreadful clamors to the sky,
> That valleys, hills, and rivers made rebound
> And heaven itself was frighted with the sound.
>
> .   .   .   .   .   .
>
> Now, while Bellona rageth here and there,
> Thick storms of bullets rain like winter's hail,
> And shivered lances dark the troubled air;
>
> .   .   .   .   .   .

On every side drop captains to the ground
And soldiers, some ill-maimed, some slain outright:
Here falls a body sundered from his head;
There legs and arms lie bleeding on the grass,
Mingled with weapons and unbowelèd steeds,
That scattering over-spread the purple plain.
In all this turmoil, three long hours and more
The victory to neither part inclined,
Till Don Andrea with his brave lanciers
In their main battle made so great a breach
That, half dismayed, the multitude retired.

. . . .

Till, Phoebus waning to the western deep,
Our trumpeters were charged to sound retreat.

Although the direct influence of Seneca on Kyd is patent to the most casual reader, the novel and apparently original plot of *The Tragedy*, its swift action, inventive episode, and real passion mark something new. There had been no play up to its time alike so well constructed and possessed of personages so vitally conceived.

Another interesting thing about Kyd is the unquestionable fact that he was the author of a play called *Hamlet*, on the stage at least as early as 1589, though now irretrievably lost. This play appears to have been of a Senecan character and it is interesting to notice that the situation of the *Hamlet* that we know and that of *The Spanish Tragedy* offers a striking parallel. *Hamlet* is the story of the revenge of a son for the murder of his father; *The Spanish Tragedy*, as we have seen, the story of the revenge of a father for the murder of his son. In both the fundamental idea is revenge under circumstances justified by the impossibility of other redress, revenge heightened in difficulty of attainment by the hesitancy of the protagonist and by his real or pretended madness.

Christopher Marlowe was born at Canterbury in February, 1564, and was thus some two months Shakespeare's senior. His station in life was not much higher, as his father was a shoemaker and tanner, though he acted likewise as clerk of St. Mary's. Marlowe was a precocious boy and from the King's school at Canterbury he went up to Cambridge which he finally left with a master's degree in 1587. Of his early life in London we know as little as of Shakespeare's. It can not be proved that Marlowe was an actor, but we know that most of his plays were written for the Admiral's company and that Alleyn acted in them. Marlowe's career must have been well under way before the coming of the Armada and it is not impossible that he was a dramatist of repute before he attained his higher degree at Cambridge. Unlike Shakespeare and Jonson, Marlowe appears not to have served an apprenticeship to the drama, but leaped to immediate fame by that daring production *Tamburlaine*, which was on the stage by 1587. Thereafter his works followed year after year until seven dramas, his in whole or in part, were credited to his name with we know not how much other journeyman work in unacknowledged collaboration with others. Marlowe, as we make it out, was one about whom men held definite opinions; he had enemies and many friends, among the latter Raleigh and Sir Thomas Walsingham of Chislehurst. Marlowe must have known his contemporaries, the playwrights, thoroughly well. Nash collaborated with him, while Shakespeare alludes to him tenderly in *As You Like It*. Marlowe was unorthodox in his opinions and unwisely frank in uttering them; but it is difficult to believe the author of *Faustus* an atheist. There are no actual evidences that Marlowe led a loose life, although the sensuousness of his poetical imagination is indubitable. He was killed in a quarrel in 1593 by one Ingram Frazer, who was pardoned soon after for his deed by the queen. The stories that Marlowe ended his life blaspheming, the allegations as to his atheism and abandoned life are inventions which have gathered about his name since his death to adorn a fanciful example of the depravity of the player and the unorthodox; and, strange, as it may appear, priest and Puritan combined to draw the monster.

Seldom has any poet begun his career with so definite and purposeful an ideal as Marlowe. If we are to judge from the conscious pronouncement of the prologue to *Tamburlaine*, Marlowe set his face from the first against the trivialities of the comic stage, which he designates as "such conceits as clownage keeps in pay," and against the old tumbling, running measures, illustrated in such plays as *Gammer Gurton*. It was force, dignity, and passion that Marlowe demanded of the romantic drama and in choosing blank-verse he fixed the medium of serious drama for generations to come. *Tamburlaine* was a splendid gage of promise for a youth of twenty-three to throw down to his age. The two parts of *Tamburlaine* — for the popularity of the first part soon demanded a second — are best described as an heroic epic in dramatic form. The tale of the Scythian conqueror of the eastern world and his rise from a shepherd to be king over kings is told in language befitting so heroic a theme, and if it dilates at times into the extravagant and bombastic, it is pervaded none the less throughout with fire, poetry, and genuine passion. The popularity of *Tamburlaine* was immediate and it begot in hands less forcible a long line of like heroical plays.

The second dramatic venture of Marlowe was the dramatizing of the world-story of Faustus. How exactly the poet came by the theme is not altogether clear, as the earliest extant translation of the German *Faust-buch* bears date 1592 and Marlowe's tragedy was certainly on the stage four years earlier. The play, as we have it, seems sketchy and incomplete. Moreover, it is disfigured with scenes of precisely the type of clownage which Marlowe had so reprobated in the prologue of *Tamburlaine*. Yet, with both these shortcomings, *Faustus* is a surprisingly effective tragedy in which the throes and agonies of the unhappy hero who had bartered his soul for a few short years of power and pleasure in this world, are set forth with a distinction of phrase, a quality of poetic imagery and a poignant appreciation of the agony of hopeless repentance unequaled in English drama. Least justifiable of all are quotations from the dramas, for here everything depends on the situation in hand, the personages, and the unity of the complete whole; yet, possibly better in the following than in some more striking passage, may the reader discern alike the

temper of Faustus in his inordinate lust after power as well
as the limpid and effective diction of Marlowe:

> Oh what a world of profit and delight,
> Of power, of honor, of omnipotence
> Is promised to the studious artisan!
> All things that move between the quiet poles
> Shall be at my command: emperors and kings
> Are but obeyèd in their several provinces,
> Nor can they raise the wind or rend the clouds;
> But his dominion that exceeds in this
> Stretcheth as far as doth the mind of man;
> A sound magician is a mighty god:
> Here, Faustus, tire thy brains to gain a deity.

But the good and the evil angel, after the manner of the old
morality, are ever at hand with their alternate promptings:

> O Faustus! lay that damnèd book aside
> And gaze not on it lest it tempt thy soul,
> And heap God's heavy wrath upon thy head.
> Read, read the Scriptures: that is blasphemy.

And the other replies:

> Go forward, Faustus, in that famous art,
> Wherein all Nature's treasure is contained:
> Be thou on earth as Jove is in the sky,
> Lord and commander of these elements.

The angels disappear and Faustus continues in soliloquy:

> How am I glutted with conceit of this!
> Shall I make spirits fetch me what I please,
> Resolve me of all ambiguities,
> Perform what desperate enterprise I will?
> I'll have them fly to India for gold,
> Ransack the ocean for orient pearl,
> And search all corners of the new-found world
> For pleasant fruits and princely delicates;
> I'll have them read me strange philosophy
> And tell the secrets of all foreign kings;
> I'll have them wall all Germany with brass,
> And make swift Rhine circle fair Wertenberg,
> I'll have them fill the public schools with silk,
> Wherewith the students shall be bravely clad;

> I'll levy soldiers with the coin they bring,
> And chase the Prince of Parma from our land,
> And reign sole king of all the provinces.

In *The Jew of Malta* Marlowe found a less universal theme, but constructively he produced a better play. It is Marlowe's misfortune that his indignant and revengeful Jew should be thrown inevitably into contrast with Shylock. Barabas is the incarnation of superhuman revenge (not greed, for that is secondary to him), as Tamburlaine depicts inordinate lust of empire, and Faustus inordinate lust of knowledge and supernatural power. To compare Barabas, therefore, to Shylock, who remains ever human, is unfair, for the very terms of Marlowe's art demand a different scale of values. *The Jew of Malta* is a lurid and terrible play: but it must have been most effective on the stage. To upbraid Marlowe for following the popular conception of his day as to the race whose badge is sufferance is as preposterous as it is to read into Shakespeare a humanitarian spirit which belonged not to his time.

The last of the unaided plays of Marlowe is *Edward II*, in its source and more general characteristics a chronicle history like much that had gone before; but, in its conception of an unkingly king in struggle with his surroundings, in the pity and the terror of his fall, a tragedy, worthy to hold place beside Shakespeare. The advance in dramatic construction of *Edward II* over Marlowe's previous plays is alone enough to set at rest, once and for all, the notion that Marlowe's genius was not dramatic. Almost anything might have been predicted of a poet who at less than thirty had compassed the overwhelming pathos of the closing scene of this tragedy. But Marlowe was dead at the opening of the year 1594, leaving however behind him a repute, foremost among the poets and dramatists of his day, and affecting subsequent drama, for his images of dilation and heroic resolve, for his genuine passion, power over the phrase and poetry, more than any man of his time.

Of *Dido, Queen of Carthage*, in which, according to the quarto of 1594, Nash assisted Marlowe, and of *The Massacre at Paris*, the last of Marlowe's works, but a word must suffice. *Dido* was acted (unlike the other plays of Marlowe) by the Children of the Chapel and may have been written early, though the blank-verse is mature. The whole play is less vital than the rest of Marlowe's work. *The Massacre* exhibits haste in composition and exists only in a corrupt text. It is interesting as the earliest extant play to lay under contribution the annals of France and to employ them in much the way that the English chronicles were to be so largely used by Shakespeare and others.

The new romantic drama that sprang into being in the years immediately preceding the Armada is referable above all to the influence and example of Kyd and Marlowe, the former marking the steps from Seneca, the latter showing a freer spirit all his own. Among the many plays inspired by their example may be mentioned Peele's *Battle of Alcazar*, Greene's *Alphonsus of Aragon* and *Selimus*, if the latter be his, the anonymous *Wars of Cyrus*, and other conqueror plays, as they have been called from their immediate inspiration in *Tamburlaine*. Of more general though no less certain suggestion in Kyd and Marlowe are the several plays on Titus of which we hear about this time, the only one surviving being *Titus Andronicus*, variously accredited and denied to Shakespeare. A play of like class is *Lust's Dominion*, written at latest in 1600, but published for the first time long after. This melodramatic production reproduces a queen of the extravagant lust of Tamora, a Moor of equal wickedness with Aaron, and otherwise imitates *Titus Andronicus*. *Lust's Dominion* has been identified with *The Spanish Moor's Tragedy*, mentioned in *Henslowe* as the work of Dekker, Haughton, and Day. It is certainly not Marlowe's.

With the death of Marlowe and Kyd, Elizabethan drama was well launched on its conquering career: for it had gained by this time not only dramatists to depict life, transfigured with the illumination of poetry, but it had found as well, in men like Alleyn and Burbage, actors to interpret the written word on the stage. Edward Alleyn, through his marriage with the daughter of Philip Henslowe, an exploiter of plays for the rivals of Shakespeare's company, acquired the financial support necesssary to success on the boards,and became notable in tragedy, especially for the chief rôles of Marlowe's plays. Alleyn inherited Henslowe's wealth and, with money gained by his own talents, retired, like Shakespeare later, a substantially rich man. Richard Burbage's career was not dissimilar. His father, James Burbage, was a joiner by trade and became, through this, concerned in the erection of the Theater in Shoreditch, first of Elizabethan playhouses. The interest of the family in the stage continued through three generations, Richard holding large shares in the Theater, the Globe, and Blackfriars and making a reputation on the tragic stage that placed him at the head of his profession. Burbage's association throughout his life was with the company to which Shakespeare was attached; and it was he who created the most important tragic rôles of the great dramatist. A lifelong friendship existed between the two, and of late their names have been discovered in an association not hitherto suspected. It appears that in March, 1613, the steward of the Earl of Rutland paid Shakespeare "forty-four shillings in gold" for a design of an "impresa" or semi-heraldic pictorial badge with its attendant motto, and an equal sum to Burbage for "painting" the same and "making it in gold." The invention of devices of this kind was a fashionable pursuit of scholarly and literary men of the day, and we hear of Sidney, Daniel, Camden, Jonson, Donne, and Drummond, all as variously interested in them. The connection of Shakespeare's name with pictorial art is new, but in no wise surprising. As to Burbage, there is a picture of him in Dulwich College which purports to be the work of his own brush. The notion that he may likewise have painted, in 1609, the portrait of Shakespeare on wood from which the Droeshout engraving of the title-page of the first folio was subsequently copied, must be pronounced fanciful. Burbage continued on the boards long after the retirement of Alleyn, dying in 1619, three years after the death of Shakespeare.

CHAPTER VII

THE PAMPHLET AND THE PROSE OF CONTROVERSY

COULD you or I have had the good fortune to have strolled out into the narrow streets of Elizabethan London, along Cheapside, past the Standard where culprits were displayed in the stocks or the pillory, and where condemned books were burned by the common hangman; into Gracious Street or Bishopsgate where were many taverns still used as cheaper playhouses; or back to St. Paul's Churchyard where the scriveners and stationers chiefly congregated, we should have been struck by the sight on all sides of bright and conspicuous signs, marking not only shops with their wares displayed on booths, but private houses as well. Your blue-coated servant might be a very intelligent and trustworthy fellow, but to give him a letter for delivery, addressed as we address letters with name, street, and number, would have been to nonplus him hopelessly. Such was the dilemma of Capulet's servant, who, given a written list of persons to invite to his master's feast, was compelled, as he put it, "to resort to the learned." "To my very dear friend, Antonio at the Elephant in the south suburb" would have reached Sebastian's friend in *Twelfth Night*, precisely as a meeting might have been arranged between two bookish friends at the shop of Thomas Fisher at the Sign of the White Hart in Fleet Street, seller of *A Midsummer-Night's Dream*, or of Thomas Heyes in Paul's Churchyard at the Sign of the Green Dragon, for whom one of the quartos of *The Merchant of Venice* was printed.

It is improbable that three out of ten of the general population of the London of Elizabeth could read or were habituated to writing more than their names. Shakespeare's father affixed his mark, and it has been declared that the art of reading and writing remained a mystery to Judith, Shakespeare's daughter. Be these bits of gossip true or false, it is plain that the age attached no such importance to what Carlyle calls "the mystery of alphabetic letters" as do we. Now, we know scarcely any education save that which comes through books, and illiteracy is a brand and a stigma. Such was not Elizabeth's age. The London of Shakespeare's time could not have numbered a hundred and twenty thousand souls, and there was no other large city in England. With a reading public thus limited in numbers and by illiteracy, it is amazing how many books the Elizabethan and Jacobean press put forth. What proportion of the population of a modern British or American city would buy the collected edition of a popular contemporary playwright at say twenty or twenty-five dollars a volume? That was about the comparative price of the first folio of Shakespeare in 1623, the year of its publication. The exhaustion of the first edition of this work in nine years, with a possible ten thousand readers in all England, means little less than the twentieth thousand of some cheap passing novel of to-day with the possibility of fifty or — if it cross seas — a hundred million purchasers.

It is often affirmed that the theater of Shakespeare absorbed to itself the functions of the newspaper, including those of our magazines, reviews, and other like publications. But the theater was not alone. The pamphlet already existed, and the pamphlet and the broadside were the forerunners of the modern newspaper. The works of the pamphleteers, of Breton, Rowlands, Greene, Nash, Dekker, and many others, are often among the rarest of books. No one thought of preserving such productions any more than we think of treasuring old newspapers; and they were read as thoughtlessly and destroyed as carelessly as we read and destroy newspapers to-day. The Elizabethan pamphlet is any piece of ephemeral printing, from a prognostication of the weather or a ballad turned into rime because of some recent event, to a tract of political, religious, or other comment, or an account of the queen's last progress. Within this range almost every conceivable variety of writing is possible: anecdote, from the jest-book or piece of rimed doggerel to the prose tale of low life or complete romantic story; realistic pictures and writings-up of contemporary rogues and vagabonds or exposures of the tricks of thieves and sharpers; "characters," biographies, travels, real and imaginary, autobiographical and other sketches. The pamphlet was rarely political, for there were pains and penalties attendant upon political freedom of speech, but it was often on matters of religious controversy, social satire, and personal lampoon. We are as apt to forget all this in thinking of the great age of Spenser and Shakespeare as we are apt to forget those clogs about the necks of our own culture, the commoner newspapers, the commoner books, and the common thoughts with which they overlay and overwhelm us. Though just as now there are able men who give their best talents to our own daily and monthly press, so in the old time an occasional man, capable of enduring work, bartered his talents to the needs of the moment and rested content with the repute of a day.

All this is incipient journalism, only requiring a keener interest in that modern acquired need of our daily lives which we call news, the organization by which that need is supplied, and regular publication assured, completely to parallel the modern newspaper. Much of this fleeting literature has perished and much more of it was produced by anonymous authors or by those whose names are now practically forgotten; and yet enough remains to surprise us with its bulk and variety and with the productiveness of some of those who contributed to it. Thus, for example, an enumeration of the jest-books that appeared in print between the time of Shakespeare's coming to London and the year of his death comprehends a dozen or more titles in which the names of Skelton, Scoggin, and Tarlton recur. Peele, the dramatist, was notorious for his *Merry Conceited Jests*, collected in 1607; and Richard Edwards, in his day, and Robert Armin, a later actor, contributed each his share to a variety of anecdote which neither then nor now is creditable either for its wit or its decency. Of wholesomer nature were the collections of popular tales, best represented in the work of Thomas Deloney, variously described as "a jig-monger" or "the balleting silk-weaver." This trades-

man's laureate, as he has likewise been called, was the author
of such books as *Jack of Newbery*, *Thomas of Reading*, and
The Gentle Craft, all printed in the nineties and concerned
with tradesmen heroes. It was from the last of these pamphlets that Dekker borrowed the plot of his *Shoemakers' Holiday*, including the immortal personage Simon Eyre; and, in
a second story of the same book, Rowley found the story of
another play, his *Shoemaker a Gentleman*. As to the fecundity
of some of these pamphleteers, it may be noted that the article
on Thomas Churchyard, in *The Dictionary of National Biography*, contains over fifty titles of works of his; Grosart's
edition of Nicholas Breton prints some forty tracts in verse
and prose, all of this general class; and the same editor's edition of the prose writings of Robert Greene fills eleven crown
octavo volumes. Greene and Lodge were more than pamphleteers; for, aside from the plays of the former, each contrived to give distinction even to some of his more fugitive
tracts. Breton, too, concealed in much rubbish many a gem
of dainty pastoral verse and discloses a pervading kindliness
of spirit unusual in his class. While Thomas Nash, despite
the rancor of his personalities and the passing and trivial nature of his controversies, must always be reckoned among the
masters of vigorous, idiomatic English prose.

Of the several pamphleteers, then, that it is here possible
to notice, Thomas Churchyard was the earliest. An older
contemporary of Gascoigne, born in 1520, but living on to
1604, Churchyard affected the broadside in verse and was fond
of historical and quasi-historical subjects. His best known
work is his contribution of the story of Jane Shore to Baldwin's edition of *The Mirror for Magistrates*, 1563; but he likewise told the vicissitudes of his own career as a soldier in
Scotland, Ireland, and on the continent, describing the siege
of Leith, "the lamentable and pitiful wars in Flanders," and
the "calamity of France," this last in 1579. Somewhat later he
wrote several tracts on the projected voyages of Sir Humphrey
Gilbert and Martin Frobisher, moralized upon the late earth-
quake, described the queen's progresses into the country to
visit her nobles, and never lost an opportunity lugubriously

to celebrate the obsequies of statesman or notable courtier. Churchyard affected the letter in his titles: *Churchyard's Chipps, Churchyard's Choice, Churchyard's Chance, Churchyard's Challenge.* His *Worthies of Wales*, 1587, is accounted the best of his works; their journalistic character is plain; for few events, from Sidney's death and the Babington conspiracy to Essex's folly, escaped his indefatigable pen.

Nicholas Breton, though later born, was even longer lived and no less continuously industrious. Of better birth and greater refinement than Churchyard, Breton seems to have been urged to a literary career by the example of his step-father, the poet Gascoigne, who left him a love of learning although he dissipated his estate. Breton was a minor satellite of the charmed circle of the Countess of Pembroke to whom he dedicated more than one of his booklets; and his literary work extends from 1577 quite through the reign of King James to embrace much excellent devotional prose and poetry and several exquisite pastoral lyrics. Considering his voluminousness, Breton maintains a remarkable uniformity of style and diction. He was, moreover, a writer of unusual versatility, writing verse and prose, satirical, romantic, religious, and pastoral, with equal ease and success, and with a charming and equable flow of good spirits — cheerful, fanciful, and pathetic at will. *Wit's Trenchamour*, 1597, in its interlocutors, an angler and a scholar, and the talk about fish and fishing with which it opens, is suggestive of its famous successor, Walton's *Complete Angler:* but the dialogue takes a different turn. *A Discourse between a Scholar and a Soldier, The Praise of Virtuous Ladies, An Old Man's Lesson and a Young Man's Love* are sufficiently described in their titles. Several of Breton's pamphlets are satirical and three of these in verse contain the word Pasquil — *Pasquil's Madcap, Pasquil's Fool's Cap, Pasquil's Pass* — on their titles. But there is nothing bitter in Breton's nature; even his satire is full of humanity and kindly merriment, and the just and modest value that he puts on his own efforts, calling them *Toys for an Idle Head, A Post with a Packet of Madcap Letters, I Pray You be not Angry,*

Against Murmurers and Murmuring, disarms anything in the nature of hostile criticism.

Among Breton's many dialogues, moral, fanciful, religious, and other, it is of interest to find several in form of short essays imitating the manner and even the subjects of Bacon. *Fantastics* "discants of the quarters, months and hours of the year with other matters"; but *Characters upon Essays, Moral and Divine*, 1615, not only deals with Baconian abstractions, such as Honor, Love, War, and Resolution, but is dedicated in respectful terms, confessing the imitation, to "my worthy, honored, truly learned and judicious Knight, Sir Francis Bacon." *The Good and the Bad, a Description of the Worthies and Unworthies of this Age*, 1616, partakes more of the variety of writing, recently come into the vogue of the moment in the "character," of which more below. Lastly, the larger class of Breton's devotional tracts, both prose and verse, exhibit a simple-hearted piety and kindly charity of heart which further endear this engaging old writer to our recollection.

Of less literary worth, though similar in his career, was Samuel Rowlands, whose activity lies between 1598 and 1628 and who died two years later. Rowlands' productivity almost equals Breton's and includes many religious tracts and satires of such asperity that some of the author's works were ordered to be publicly burnt. Rowlands imitated greater men in a large group of writings on the low life of London, its thieves, beggars, and "roaring boys," as they were called; and a certain ready-handed ability marks, as well his *High Way to Mount Calvary*, *'Tis Merry when Gossips Meet*, as his *Terrible Battle between the Two Consumers of all the Earth, Time and Death*.

The greatest of the early pamphleteers is Robert Greene, whose place among the predecessors of Shakespeare has already claimed our attention. Greene's earliest prose work was written under the direct influence of Lyly whose style he imitated and whose long disquisitions on the nature of love and the processes of courtship he specially emulated. Greene's *Mamillia* was entered as early as 1580 and was followed, before the end of the decade, by more than a dozen other love-pamphlets. *Mamillia* is the not ineffective story of a fickle and wavering young man, Pharicles, at length reclaimed to virtue and to matrimony by the beautiful and steadfast Mamillia. Among the others, *Euphues his Censure of Philautus* is interesting as an intended continuance of Lyly's famous story; *Perimedes the Blacksmith* contains in its preface much valuable matter by way of allusion to the contemporary relations of the predecessors of Shakespeare; and *Pandosto* is memorable for having furnished in the beautiful tale of *Dorastus and Fawnia* no unworthy original of *The Winter's Tale*. Greene is often clever in the manner in which he frames or introduces his stories. Thus *Planetomachia*, as its name imports, is a dispute amongst the planetary gods as to which had most potently affected the doings of men, and stories are told by way of illustration. In *Penelope's Web* that dutiful wife discourses with her maidens by night, of love and adventure, as she unweaves the thread that she has spun all day; in *Euphues' Censure* the interlocutors are the heroes of the Trojan war. Some of these productions are mere "dissertations on love clothed in a story." In nearly all, Greene holds up a high ideal of womanhood and maintains Lyly's conception of "a cleanly story fit for ladies to read."

With the threatened arrival of the Armada, Greene forsook love themes to sound the note of war. *The Spanish Masquerado* is a book of the moment such as we might expect from a stanch patriot and Protestant in a time of national peril. "In the attempted invasion of the Spaniards he saw the hand of God directed towards England for the purpose of awakening her religious enthusiasm; in Englishmen he saw God's weapon for the punishment of Spaniards for their pride and dishonesty." This production is only historically of any interest.

Greene soon returned to his love stories, imitating the *Arcadia* in *Menaphon*, a pastoral of great beauty, esteemed by some the best of his work, and assuming a deeper and more moral tone in *The Mourning Garment*. Nor did he leave behind him a more charming and finished story than *Philomela*, which was written in the year preceding his death. Greene began now, too, to levy more and more upon his own adventures and experiences, and to dispute more deeply on vice and passion, as in his *Farewell to Folly* and in the two touching books, *A Groatsworth of Wit Purchased with a Million of Repentance* and *Greene's Repentance*, with which he closed his career. There remains a notable class of Greene's writings, the series which deals with the impostors and sharpers with which London was infested, the haunts and tricks of which Greene knew with the closest personal acquaintance. Some half-dozen pamphlets of various lengths on cosenage and cony-catching (the old words used to designate such deceits), belong to the years 1587 and 1592. They were followings of a type long since set, of which more below. Greene's handling of such topics is frank and realistic but never prurient or unclean. His words are marked by the same honest outspokenness and sincerity which characterized all his utterances concerning himself. It would be difficult to find a truer, a more wholesome story of a fallen and reclaimed womanhood than may be read at the conclusion of the tract called by the cumbrous title, *A Disputation between a He-Conycatcher and a She-Conycatcher;* precisely as it would be impossible to find a more touching story than the autobiographical account which Greene gives us in his *Groatsworth of Wit* of his own pathetic and untimely death. That story has been told so often that it may here be passed by and another passage preferred which almost equally expresses the nature of these autobiographical pamphlets. After relating the careless wickedness of his life at the University of Cambridge and in Italy, his pose as a "malcontent," his extravagance in attire, Greene proceeds to tell how he became "an author of plays and a penner of love pamphlets," and one "young yet in years though old in wickedness." At this period, he continues:

Yet let me confess a truth, that even once, and yet but once, I felt a fear and horror in my conscience; and then the terror of God's judgements did manifestly teach me that my life was bad, that by sin I deserved damnation, and that such was the greatness of my sin, that I deserved no redemption. And this inward motion I received in Saint Andrew's Church in the City of Norwich, at a lecture or sermon then preached by a godly learned man, whose doctrine, and the manner of whose teaching, I liked wonderful well: yea (in my conscience) such was his singleness of heart, and zeal in his doctrine, that he might have converted me, the most monster sinner of the world. . . .

At this sermon the terror of God's judgements did manifestly teach me that my exercises were damnable, and that I should be wiped out of the book of life, if I did not speedily repent my looseness of life, and reform my misdemeanors. . . .

But this good motion lasted not long in me; for no sooner had I met with my copesmates, but seeing me in such a solemn humor, they demanded the cause of my sadness: to whom when I had discovered that I sorrowed for my wickedness of life, and that the preacher's words had taken a deep impression on my conscience, they fell upon me in jesting manner, calling me Puritan and precisian and wished I might have a pulpit, with such other scoffing terms, that by their foolish persuasion the good and wholesome lesson I had learned went quite out of my remembrance: so that I fell again with the dog to my old vomit, and put my wicked life in practice, and that so thoroughly as ever I did before.

Is it always necessary that we should remember Robert Greene as the man who first maligned Shakespeare, or even as the poet whose ungoverned life and repentant spirit has served to point many a moral and adorn many a tale? Greene never ceased to look up. He never failed to adore the sun and the pitiful heavens, although his feet faltered sadly in the miry ways of the world. If we add our voices to the chorus of Shakespearean praise, may we not save a tear for this, his fallen rival?

Of Thomas Lodge as a poet, rare lyrist like Greene that he was, and memorable for delicate and charming *Rosalynd*, original of *As You Like It*, it is not the place to write much here. As to his prose, in his *Defense of Plays*, 1579, Lodge had taken a part, honorable to his taste and learning, in the controversy which Stephen Gosson had started concerning the wickedness of plays. The subsequent pamphlets of Lodge include a variety of stories and discussions more or less Euphuistic or couched in the manner of Greene. Lodge was a far traveler and wrote one story while at sea on an expedition against the Spaniards, another on a voyage while in the Straits of Magellan, entitled *A Margarite of America*, published in 1596. This may be commended to those who think that the accident of geographical position should determine such questions, as the earliest specimen of "American literature," as it preceded Sandys translation of Ovid made in the wilds of Virginia by some twenty years, and Mistress Anne Bradstreet, "the tenth Muse, sprung up in America," by sixty or more.

From these lighter pamphlets, the fringe of fiction, we turn to the more forbidding prose of controversy. In one of the latest of his pamphlets, *A Quip for an Upstart Courtier*, 1592, Greene had incidentally described Gabriel Harvey, the Cambridge don, Mentor of Spenser and would-be intimate of Sidney, as "the son of a rope-maker of Saffron Walden," which unquestionably he was. Absurdly touched by this in his family pride, Harvey attacked Greene abusively in his *Four Letters and Certain Sonnets*, and it is even said visited the obscure lodgings in which Greene had meanwhile died to collect material concerning his wretched and unhappy end to exult over. This conduct stung Nash to reply, not so much because he had been an especial intimate of Greene's as because he detested Harvey's conduct and recognized in him an excellent subject for his own satirical quill. Thomas Nash was born in 1567, a minister's son of Lowestoft. He left Cambridge prematurely, according to Harvey, because he had played "the varlet of clubs in a satirical Latin play called *Terminus et non Terminus*." The literary life of Nash in London began about the year 1588, and his first work was apparently *The Anatomy of Absurdity*. Nash was influenced in this work, as were others temporarily, by the fashionable mannerism of Lyly, though his vigorous prose was far from being subdued by Euphuistic affectations. In the *Epistle* to Greene's *Menaphon* Nash reviewed contemporary literature with the vivacity and contemptuousness of extreme youth. It is notable though that the young critic attacks the abuses of the style of his day, especially the bombastic style of Kyd and the "Thrasonical huff-snuff," as he dubs it, of such translators as Phaer and

Stanihurst, while he lavishes eloquent words of praise on true poetry, and upholds patriotically the credit of England. To "our English Italians" who declare that "the finest wits our climate sends forth are but dry-brained dolts in comparison of other countries," Nash names Chaucer,Lydgate, and Gower; and he adds: "One thing I am sure of, that each of these three have vaunted their meters with as much admiration in England as ever the proudest Ariosto did his verse in Italian." And then he continues:

> Should the challenge of deep conceit be intruded by a foreigner to bring our English wits to the touchstone of art, I would prefer divine Master Spenser, the miracle of wit, to bandy line for line for my life in honor of England against Spain, France, Italy and all the world. Neither is he the only swallow in our summer.

But to return to Nash's controversy with Harvey, it was in his *Wonderful Astrological Predictions* and *Strange News of the Intercepting of Certain Letters* that Nash assailed Harvey in 1591 and 1592. Harvey replied in *Pierce's Supererogation or New Praise of an Old Ass;* and Nash in the epistle to a serious book called *Christ's Tears over Jerusalem* offered honorable amends and reconciliation. But Harvey was not made of magnanimous stuff and stood in suspicion of Nash's offered hand, which Nash accordingly withdrew with dignity in a new epistle to the same work. So things rested until 1596 when, having heard that Harvey had boasted that he had silenced him, Nash put forth his *Have with you to Saffron Walden, or Gabriel Harvey's Hunt is Up*, "containing a full answer to the eldest son of the halter-maker." "For brain power, for prodigality and ebulliency of wild wit, for splendid fight," says Grosart, "for ridicule deepening into scorn, scorn rippling into laughter, for overwhelming absurdity of argument, and for biting, scathing words, this satiric book stands alone in the literature of its kind." Nor is this praise excessive. Upon the publication soon after of a weak reply by Harvey entitled *The Trimming of Thomas Nash*, the whole thing became a stench in the nostrils of the public and it was ordered by the Bishop of London "that all Nash's books, and Dr.

Harvey's books be taken wheresoever they may be found, and that none of the same books be ever printed hereafter." This meant, after the quaint custom of the time, a public burning of all the confiscated copies of both books, a ceremony held at the Standard in Cheapside and superintended — at least at times — by the common hangman.

But this was not Nash's only literary warfare. Elizabeth's system of uniformity in religion rested on compromise; and the growth of Calvinistic ideas among the Puritans imperiled this equilibrium towards the end of her reign. The Puritans made episcopacy the especial object of their attacks because the institution savored, to their minds, of popery and upheld many usages under the Act of Uniformity to which they could not in conscience subscribe. The bishops, too, had other enemies besides the Puritans. Many a gentleman, ruffling it at court, recalled that his forefathers had founded his estate on the dismantling of monasteries; and would have been little loath to repeat a like spoliation of the church. Moreover, the pride and ostentatious wealth of some of the bishops must have raised the question among the poorer brethern of their own clergy as to the administration of Christian offices in a manner at times so unchristian. The Martin Marprelate Controversy, as it was called from the pen-name assumed by the authors of the attacking party, arose about 1588, among the Puritans, out of these considerations and especially in consequence of the immense authority which the union of church and state had thrown into the hands of the bishops of the Established Church. The Puritan party resented what amounted to the conversion of a difference in religious opinion into a capital crime; and being unable to reach the impersonal power residing in the high commission, appealed in print from the crown to the people.

For the control of political and religious opposition and criticism, the press had long been subjected to a rigid censorship, and the right to print confined to a designated number of printers in London and elsewhere. In 1585 Archbishop Whitgift took a new step against the liberty of printing by obtaining a decree of the Star Chamber which restricted the right to print to London and the two universities. By this decree the number of printers was still further limited. Only a member of the Stationers' Company could maintain a press and, on misuse, this press was subject to instant confiscation under order to the warden of the company from the Bishop of London, who, with the Archbishop of Canterbury and the official licenser alone could authorize the publication of any book. None the less the Puritan party opened their press attack on the bishops, in 1588, with a violent dialogue, *Diotrephes*, written by John Udall, a minister of Kingston, who had been dispossessed for his Calvinistic leanings. The press of the printer of this tract was broken up and he was deprived of his license. John Penry, a Welshman of reforming instincts, whose tract, *The Equity of an Humble Supplication*, had been suppressed in the previous year, now took Udall's place in the van of the Puritan advance, while his party, nothing daunted, continued their attacks. Although the government sought to reach their masked enemies, tract after tract issued from a press moved from place to place and concealed in the houses of various country gentlemen. Among the pamphlets so published were *Martin Marprelate's Epistle*, 1588, leveled against Dr. Bridges of Salisbury, *Martin's Epitome* and *Hay Any Work for Cooper* (both in the next year), the last a reply to a serious *Admonition to the People of England* by Thomas Cooper, Bishop of Winchester. At last the government succeeded in seizing the press and in prosecuting, under torture, Barrow and Penry, two of the suspected writers, both of whom were executed. Udall died after leaving prison in 1592. This pamphlet war continued well into 1590; but it gradually died out in the following years.

The merits of this dead question need not concern us. There can be no doubt as to the violence and scurrility of both sides. Who Martin Marprelate really was has never been ascertained. The *nom de guerre* probably covered the writings of several persons. Among the popular defenders of the bishops, on the other hand, both Lyly and Nash were active. A pamphlet called *Pap with a Hatchet*, 1589, has been confidently attributed to the pen of the former. Nash certainly contributed no less than three such works in 1589 and 1590: *A Countercuff given to Martin Junior, The Return of Pasquil* and *Pasquil's Apology*. *A Mirror for Martinists, Martin's Month's Mind,* and *An Almond for a Parrot* have also been assigned by some to Nash. Both Nash and Lyly are said to have ridiculed the Martinists in plays on the stage. The anonymous reply, *Hay Any Work for Cooper,* has been considered the best of the Marprelate tracts themselves; Lyly's *Pap,* and the pamphlets of Nash, the ablest of the replies. It is of interest to note that Bacon, safe man of compromise that he was, raised his voice against this as against other religious contentions in his able *Controversies in the Church,* 1589. Of the style of these papers in general it is not necessary to speak: they range through all the degrees of satire and burlesque to a grossness and acridity of personal invective which was in keeping with the coarseness of the times. One of Nash's editors condemns his author's "fine nose for the carrion of anecdote," and for the "terrorism" and literary blackmail of his malignant and vehement denunciation of the Martinists. In violence and scurrility Nash little surpassed the violence of militant Puritanism.

But controversy was not the sum total of Nash's art in prose. His *Christ's Tears over Jerusalem* is a serious tract in which, under the guise of lamentation over the fate of Jerusalem, the author bewails the woes and shortcomings of his own city and age. In the social and satirical pamphlets, *Pierce Penniless* and *Lenten Stuff or the Praise of Red Herring,* we have Nash's more characteristic work. Quaint learning, a keen and observant eye, much knowledge of the world and its ways, an exuberant fund of humorous anecdote, a clever power to give a witty turn to thought and phrase, and a copious command of the language of encomium and especially that of vituperation: all these things are characteristics of the remarkable prose of Thomas Nash.

Lastly, there remains by Nash one piece of genuine fiction, *Jack Wilton or the Unfortunate Traveler.* This vigorous burlesque and melodramatic story has the distinction, as M. Jusserand has pointed out, of being the earliest picaresque romance in the English language and the only production of its kind in its age. *The Unfortunate Traveler* relates the adventures of a lively stripling, Jack Wilton, who lives successfully by his wits in various parts of Europe. He begins as a page with tricks upon a tapster for which he is soundly whipped as he deserves; but, rising in fortune, becomes servant to the Earl of Surrey, elopes with an Italian lady, and actually passes himself off for the earl. It is worthy of remembrance that the adventures of Surrey in this book, like Defoe's *Memoirs of a Cavalier* over a century after, were taken as actual facts by later writers and incorporated in sage biographies. Indeed Nash shares with Defoe that delightful art of "grave, imperturbable lying" or, to put it less opprobriously, of faithful likeness to actuality in trifling details which is one of the most precious possessions of the true novelist. It is impossible not to deplore that talents such as those of Nash — his power of vision, his mastery over language, his gaiety of spirit, eloquence, and rapid ease — could not have been better enlisted than in petty ephemeral pamphlet warfare and in the exploitation of passing literary fashions. But when all has been said to mark these limitations and conditions of his art, Nash must remain conspicuous, nay unexampled, in the annals of English prose not only for his inexhaustible Rabelaisian humor, his merry malevolence, and for his confident mastery over the vocabulary of Billingsgate, but likewise for his power over the telling realistic stroke and a copious flow of idiomatic vigorous English, alike removed from the alienisms of the Latinists, the niceties and affectations of the Euphuist, and the Arcadian flower of speech and ornament. Here is part of a humorous description by Nash of Harvey's bulky volume, *Pierce's Supererogation*:

O 't is an unconscionable vast gorbellied volume, bigger bulked than a Dutch hoy, and far more boisterous and cumbersome than a pair of Swisser's omnipotent galleas breeches. But it should seem he is ashamed of the incomprehensible corpulency thereof himself, for at the end of the 199th page he begins with 100 again, to make it seem little (if I lie, you may look and convince me); and in half a quire of paper besides hath left the pages unfigured. I have read that the giant Abtaeus' shield asked a whole elephant's hide to cover it, *bona fide* I utter it, scarce a whole elephant's hide and a half would serve for a cover to this Gogmagog, Jewish Talmud of absurdities. . . . But one epistle thereof, to John Wolfe, the printer, I took and weighed in an ironmonger's scales, and it counterpoiseth a cade of herring and three Holland cheeses. You may believe me if you will, I was fain to lift my chamber door off the hinges, only to let it in, it was so fulsome a fat bona-roba and terrible Rounceval.

Lastly as to Elizabethan pamphleteers, we turn to Thomas Dekker, who to his repute as the follower of Greene in the drama we must add that of the chief successor of both Greene and Nash in the pamphlet. Of the life of Dekker word will be found elsewhere; suffice it here to say that Dekker was a voluminous writer of pamphlets, upwards of a score being listed and accredited to his authorship between 1598 and 1637, the year of his death. Nor is their range less than that of previous pamphleteers. Thus *Canaan's Calamity* and *The Four Birds of Noah's Ark* are devotional, respectively in verse and prose. *The Wonderful Year* is a vivid picture of the low life of London, especially of London lying sick with the plague, from which Defoe, in his *Journal of the Plague*, disdained not to borrow. *The Bachelor's Banquet* is a free adaptation of a well-known French tract, *Les quinze joyes de marriage*, while the delightfully satirical *Gulls' Hornbook*, in which the Jacobean gallant is anatomized in all his folly, is an equally free rewriting of Dedekind's *Grobianus*. Dekker worked once more the rich vein of Greene's conycatching tracts in his *Bellman of London* and its several additions and amplifications, and he diversified all with his ready wit, his fund of anecdote, and the occasional play of a poetical spirit which we must lament to find thus wasted on mere production of copy. Dekker's pamphlets are an invaluable fund of information on contemporary social manners and customs and have yet to offer much in their obscurer parts to a fuller understanding of the greater works of the age. For example, the single little chapter, now very well known, in *The Gulls' Hornbook*, which tells "how a gallant should behave himself at a playhouse," contains a mine of information concerning the theater of Shakespeare, its settings, the price of admission, how the gal-

lants abused the privileges of the stage, how the unfortunate
playwright and actor were beholden to them not only for their
patronage but for permission to be heard at all, and other like
matters.

As I open at random one of the five volumes of a modern
edition of Dekker's prose, I find an account of the poet's visit
to the Bear Garden on the Bankside where the bear set upon
by dogs puts the visitor in mind of "hell, the bear . . . like
a black rugged soul that was damned and newly committed
to the infernal churls, the dogs, like so many devils in-
flicting torments upon it." And much pity is moved in the
author's humane breast when "a company of creatures that
had the shapes of men and the faces of Christians . . .
took the office of beadles upon them and whipped Monsieur
Hunkes," the famous blind bear, with long sticks till the blood
ran from his hairy shoulders. It was not for the bear that the
later Puritans condemned the royal game of bear-baiting. In
another place we read:

Thus sports that were invented for honest recreation, are by the
wicked abusing of them, turned to men's confusion: and not only in
these games before rehearsed, but also in those that are both more
laudable and more lawful. For in the tennis court, cheating hath a
hand; yea, and in shooting (which is the noblest exercise of our
English nation), arrows do now and then fly with false feathers.

Could anything have a more modern ring?

But the pamphleteers could occasionally rise above contemporary conditions. Many are the passages of memorable
eloquence that might be culled from their works. Here is a
rhapsody of Nash on poets, with which this chapter may well
conclude:

Destiny never defames herself but when she lets an excellent poet
die. If there be any spark of Adam's paradised perfection yet em-
bered up in the breasts of mortal men, certainly God hath bestowed
that, his perfectest image, on poets. None can come so near to God
in wit, none more contemn the world. Seldom have you seen any
poet possessed with avarice; only verses he loves, nothing else he
delights in. And as they contemn the world, so contrarily of the

mechanical world are none more contemned. Despised they are of the world because they are not of the world. Their thoughts are exalted above the world of ignorance and all earthly conceits. As sweet angelical choristers they are continually conversant in the heaven of arts. Heaven itself is but the highest height of knowlege. He that knows himself and all things else knows the means to be happy. Happy, thrice happy are they whom God hath doubled his spirit upon and given a double soul unto to be poets.

CHAPTER VIII

THE PASTORAL LYRIC AND THE SONNET[1]

THE age of Elizabeth was above all the age of song. Music then flourished as a diversion and accomplishment to a degree which has not been known since in England; and that form of poetry which is nearest to music, the lyric, reached a height as memorable for its variety as for its extraordinary excellence. A lyric is primarily a poem that sings, as an epic is primarily a poem that tells. But while the song-like quality deserves all the emphasis which it has received, the modern lyric demands an equal recognition of the subjective or personal quality which characterizes it. The lyric is concerned with the poet and with the interpretation of his thoughts, sentiments, and emotions. It is the inward world of passion and feeling that is here celebrated, as opposed to the outward world of sequence in time. It is the individual singer, dignified by the sincerity and potency of his art, that unfolds his own moods and emotions to our sympathy and understanding, not a mere voice, the instrument by which we are introduced to the protracted wanderings of Ulysses or the heroic deeds of Beowulf. Several corollaries follow from this conception of the dual character of the lyric. It must deal with passion and emotion in their simplicity as contrasted with the drama which is busied with both in their complexity. The lyric must be emotion clothed in beautiful and musical language; it must be free from the intrusion of mere story or description, except so far as each may serve as the foundation of a mood. Above all, it must remain free of any intent to teach, argue, or explain; for its address is ultimately, like that of all true art, an address to the feelings, to the emotions, and only mediately to the understanding. Inasmuch as the lyric demands a grasp of the subtler forms

[1] The initial paragraphs of this chapter are based on the author's Introduction to *Elizabethan Lyrics*, 1895.

of human passion and emotion, combined with a consummate mastery of form and of the music of speech, it is but natural that all literatures should display the lyric among the latest of literary growths. Despite what must be admitted as to an impersonal lyrical quality inhering in much early popular poetry, an age, in which the gift of lyric expression is widely diffused, must be alike removed from the simplicity and immaturity which is content to note in its literature the direct effects of the phenomena of the outside world and no more, and from that complexity of conditions and that tendency to intellectualize emotion which characterize a time like our own. In an age lyrically gifted, we may look for innumerable points of contact between the spirit of the time and its literature, for the most beautiful and fervent thoughts couched in the most beautiful and fervent language; in such an age we may expect the nicest adjustment and equilibrium of the real and the ideal, each performing its legitimate function and contributing in due proportion to the perfect realization of truth in its choicest form, beauty. Such an age was that of the Elizabethan lyric, which bloomed with a flower-like diversity of form, color, and fragrance from the boyhood of Shakespeare far into the century that knew Milton and Dryden.

The origin of the modern lyric of art in the poetry of Wyatt, Surrey, and their followers has already been sufficiently indicated. *Tottel's Miscellany* is the first book of modern English lyrical poetry, and it includes what the following generation regarded as the best of the lyrical output of the reign of Henry VIII. Although *The Paradise of Dainty Devises*, published in 1576, gathered what was intervening, and although the lyrics of Gascoigne, Turberville, and some few others, their contemporaries, deserve consideration, the outburst of the true Elizabethan lyric scarcely preceded that of other forms of the literature of the century. In 1575, Spenser, Greville, Lodge, and Greene were already at Cambridge, whilst Lyly, Peele, and Watson remained at Oxford, which Sidney had just quitted to be introduced at court and to proceed upon his foreign travels. The influences that made these men poets were thus at work while they were students at the universities, and within the ten years that followed each had made a name for himself in literature.

The Elizabethan lyric, with all its variety and its frequently high poetic attainment, is peculiarly conventional and imitative of precedent and example. For this reason we find it subject to a succession of fashions as to form and manner, following now the dainty unrealities of the pastoral mode, then inclosed within the formal bounds of French and Italian sonnet practice, and again fashioning its winged words to be set to music.

From 1580 to 1590, for example, it was the custom to express lyrical sentiment for the most part in the terms of the pastoral. The world became a glorified sheep-walk, its inhabitants nymphs and shepherds devoted to the cult and sway of love, and flitting their time carelessly away in discussions of the divine passion combined with a conventionalized appreciation of flowers and fine weather. The pastoral mode, to be sure, was by no means confined, in England or elsewhere, to the lyric. Originating in Italy with the revival of an interest in ancient poetry, especially the *Georgics* and *Bucolics* of Vergil, the pastoral took many forms, such as the eclogue, pastoral drama, prose romance, and lyric. All of these spread to France and Spain, and later reached England in as great a variety as that in which they flourished abroad. We have thus the eclogue, illustrated in *The Shepherds' Calendar;* the pastoral romance told in prose in Lodge's *Rosalynd;* glorified into a tale of valor and adventure as in the *Arcadia;* and told in verse and allegorized into a moral scheme of life in *The Faery Queen.* Again, there is the pastoral drama, which came for the most part later. The pastoral lyric occurs first as an incidental song in the midst of the narrative or descriptive eclogue and continues in this use in the romance, eclogue, and masque, only later developing into a separate poem free from special application. Spenser was the first English pastoralist to include songs in differing meters within the dialogue of the eclogue. Such are the "Song to Eliza" and "The Lament for Dido" in "April" and "November" respectively of *The Shepherds' Calendar.*

Similarly, Sidney inserted many lyrics in the prose of his *Arcadia*. Spenser never wrote a lyric for its own sake. Nor did Sidney nor Shakespeare, very often, for that matter. All Spenser's lyrics are incidental, like the two songs just mentioned, or of specific application like the larger *Prothalamion* and *Epithalamion*, and even the *Amoretti*, if we consider that sequence as a whole. The influence that separated the lyric from its place in the eclogue, romance, or drama was its use as the words for music; and we find the pastoral tone showing itself in the first madrigals and songs intended to be sung and in the anthologies, such as *England's Helicon*, 1599, in which occur several poems, parted from their context.

Coming thus from Italy, where it had been cultivated for two or three generations, the pastoral lyric combined with a certain fantasticality, conventional phraseology, and fondness for conceit, a delightfully childlike abandonment to the senses, a joy in beauty, light, and life itself which disarms the very criticism which at times it deserves. Indeed, the average of this variety of lyric is not nearly so high as we might suppose. The lesser poems of *England's Helicon* — admirable collection though it be at large — the volubility of Anthony Munday, the long-spun mediocrity of Nicholas Yonge, even the fluent but somewhat attenuated strain of Breton when he is not quite at his best, all go to attest the truth of this assertion. But if we turn to the greater men that practised the pastoral mode, or to the best work of many minor poets — Sidney and Spenser aside, to Lodge, Greene, Peele, Breton at his best, Barnfield and Drayton at times, even Constable, and Marlowe assuredly in one poem — we find the pastoral lyric rising above its conventions into the domain of the finest literature and exhibiting a simplicity, a freedom from consciousness, a happiness in metrical effect, an engaging sweetness and tenderness united with a love of nature, genuinely and artistically expressed.

> In time of yore when shepherds dwelt
>   Upon the mountain rocks,
> And simple people never felt
>   The pain of lovers' mocks;

But little birds would carry tales
  'Twixt Susan and her sweeting,
And all the dainty nightingales
  Did sing at lovers' meeting:
Then might you see what looks did pass
  Where shepherds did assemble,
And where the life of true love was
  When hearts could not dissemble.

Then *yea* and *nay* was thought an oath
  That was not to be doubted,
And when it came to *faith* and *troth*
  We were not to be flouted.
Then did they talk of curds and cream,
  Of butter, cheese and milk;
There was no talk of sunny beam
  Nor of the golden silk.
Then for a gift a row of pins,
  A purse, a pair of knives
Was all the way that love begins;
  And so the shepherd wives.

Thus sings that sweet pastoralist, Nicholas Breton. Nor is
Robert Greene behind with the music of his "Shepherd's
Wife's Song":

Ah, what is love? It is a pretty thing,
As sweet unto a shepherd as a king;
    And sweeter too:
For kings have cares that wait upon a crown,
And cares can make the sweetest love to frown.
    Ah then, ah then,
If country loves such sweet desires do gain,
What lady would not love a shepherd swain?

And what lover of old poetry ever forgets "that smooth song
made by Kit Marlowe," "Come live with me and be my
love," so beloved of Izaak Walton; or Barnfield's

As it fell upon a day,
In the merry month of May,

long and far from unreasonably attributed to Shakespeare
himself? The pastoral mode continued in vogue to the end

of Elizabeth's reign and after; but in the following decades
it declined and soon ceased to be the dominant lyrical strain.

But if this decade is superficially the period of the pastoral,
there is in its poetry a deeper undertone not only in the artistic
seriousness of Spenser, but in the sincerity and passion of
Sidney, of both of whom enough has already been said. In
the collection known as *Cælica* which embodies the lyrical
poetry of Sidney's friend, Fulke Greville, there is a new and
independent spirit, a widening of the sphere of the lyric theme
to include non-erotic sentiment, and an all but complete
abandonment of the classic imagery and allusion which long
continued elsewhere to be one of the chief excrescences of the
ornate and elaborated style of the time. The queen, with all
the poetry of adulation that was lavished on her, was not
often addressed in terms as cabalistic as these:

> Cynthia, because your horns look divers ways,
>   Now darkened to the east, now to the west,
> Then at full glory once in thirty days,
>   Sense doth believe that change is nature's rest.
> Poor earth, that dare presume to judge the sky:
>   Cynthia is ever round, and never varies;
> Shadows and distance do abuse the eye,
>   And in abused sense truth oft miscarries:
> Yet who this language to the people speaks,
> Opinion's empire, sense's idol, breaks.

Some of the later lyrics of Greville have a fullness and
intricacy of thought and a disdain for prevalent conventional
poetical mannerisms that would do credit to Donne himself,
who, whether influenced by a possible contact with the poetry
of Greville or not, was at least of a kindred cast of mind.
So, too, the devotional poetry of Robert Southwell, written
mostly in the years immediately following 1592, shows an
independence of the literary influences of the moment (save
for the one matter of "conceit") that discloses how deeply
that faithful priest and true poet was immersed in the mission
that brought him undeservedly to a traitor's scaffold. Southwell was educated at Douay and took up, like Parsons and
Campion, the dangerous Jesuits' mission of reconverting

England. His two volumes, *St. Peter's Complaint* and *Mæon-iæ*, appeared in 1595, the year of his execution. Southwell deserved the high repute in which he was held in his time for his fervor, originality, and genuine piety; and his use of an older fashioned verse, for the most part, than that of his immediate day did not obscure his worth. Even Jonson declared that although "Southwell was hanged, yet so he [himself] had written that piece of his, "The Burning Babe," he would have been content to destroy many of his [own poems]."

Different in almost every respect from Greville and Southwell, to whom poetry was the outlet respectively of philosophic ponderings and devotional yearning, was the poetry of Thomas Watson and of Barnabe Barnes who continue the Italian impulses given to English poetry by Sidney as Greville continued Sidney's strength if not his fervor of thought. Watson's *Hecatompathia or Passionate Century of Love* was published in 1582 and was thus contemporary with, if it may not have preceded, the writing of *Astrophel and Stella*. Watson was a Londoner; he studied at Oxford and appears to have died a young man about 1593. He is frankness itself as to his inspiration, ostentatiously noting many of his sources among Italian, French, and classical authors, and even occasionally ridiculing them. In 1593 Watson issued a second similar collection of amorous verse, this time in true sonnet form, which he called *Tears of Fancy or Love Disdained*, holding much the same attitude and pursuing the same method. But this time he omitted definite mention of his sources. The interests of Watson in foreign sources extended to music and, between the two volumes just named, he published a book entitled *Italian Madrigals Englished*, 1590, thus taking his place (though only as a translator) as the earliest of a long line of lyrists writing words for music. Barnabe Barnes was born about 1569 and died in 1609. Barnes was the son of a bishop, an Oxford man, and much traveled abroad. As the friend of Gabriel Harvey he was traduced by Nash. An intimacy seems to have existed between Barnes and the minor sonneteer, William Percy, and both were interested in the drama as well as in lyrical poetry. Barnes' *Parthenope and*

Parthenophil, 1593, is a sequence of sonnets interspersed with canzons, sestinas, and other poems of Italian form with which he seems to have experimented almost as fully as did Sidney The rediscovery of Watson and Barnes within recent times has caused critics somewhat to overrate their facile ability to catch the general Renaissance spirit in its lighter moods, even although both poets justify praise by occasionally reaching high levels.

But before we pass on to a consideration of the sonnet, a salient mannerism in the general poetical style of these earlier poets must claim our attention. In Elizabethan English the word "conceit" meant commonly little more than idea, thought, or conception. It came, however, soon to involve the notion of wit, fancy, and ingenuity; and, as applied to literature and to poetry in particular, was used both of the thought itself and of the rhetorical device by means of which the thought was expressed. Gascoigne thus advises: "If I should declare my pretence in love, I would either make a strange discourse of some intolerable passion or find occasion to plead by the examples of some history, or discover my disquiet in shadows *per allegoriam*, or use the covertest means that I could to avoid the uncomely customs of common writers." It is this conscious avoidance of "the uncomely customs of common writers" that begets the conceit or, otherwise expressed, the effort on the part of the poet to deck out his thought in striking, apt, and original figures of speech and illustration. It is obvious that such an effort easily degenerates into ingenuity, far-fetched metaphor, extravagance, and want of taste; for all these things came in time to characterize the conceit to such an extent that the original idea was lost, and a conceit came restrictedly to mean "any conventional device of the poet — fancy, figure, or illustration — used to give individual, transcendant expression to the thing he has to say." The conceit was not the invention of any single English poet; nor is it any longer held that Gongora, or Marino, or any other foreign poet is specifically responsible for it in English literature; though it certainly developed under the influence of Petrarch and in the hands of his followers in Italy, France, and England in their attempt to outdo the hyperbole of their master's ingenious imagery.

As already intimated, to Sidney belongs the doubtful honor of popularizing the conventional conceit in England, and from his sonnets the conceit descended to his heirs, lawfully and unlawfully begotten, the sonneteers. But Sidney's own use of the conceit was not confined to his poetry. True, Stella's brow is alabaster crowned with gold, the door of her face is red porphyry locked with pearl, the porches (which endure the name of cheeks) are of red and white marble; her lover shares her heart and she yields him her frontiers; her eyes serve him with shot, her lips are his heralds, her skin his armor, her flesh his food; the ink as he uses it runs to Stella's name, pain moves his pen, his paper is pale despair. But in the prose of the *Arcadia* also, Urania, putting her foot in a boat is said to divide her heavenly beauty between sea and shore; Philoclea's hand at Zelmane's lips stands like a hand in a book pointed to noteworthy words; and Pamela's eyes dissolve in tears and leave only crimson circles behind.[1] Outside of the sonneteers — of whom more shortly — Father Southwell elaborated the conceit most extravagantly and at times absurdly. Christ's tears are pools of Heshbon, baths of grace where happy spirits dive, turtle-doves bathed in virgin milk, and half a dozen other things as strange. He drinks the drops of the heavenly flood and bemires his Maker with returning mud; Peter's heart was not thawed by the fire before which he sat, its hell-resembling heat did freeze it the more. Drayton, too, though comparatively free from the conceit in his sonnets and pastorals, fell into the fashion in his *Heroical Epistles*, a work naturally pitched in a high key, though he later gave up the employment of such devices.

The next decade, the last of the sixteenth century, is the time of the sonnet. Introduced into the language by Wyatt, first practised in sequence and raised to the standard of exquisite poetry by Sidney, the Elizabethan sonnet appears to

---

[1] For the material of these paragraphs on conceit and these illustrations I am indebted to an unpublished paper on the topic by my friend and colleague, Professor C. G. Child.

have owed, almost from the first, nearly as much to France as to Italy. The first and surreptitious edition of *Astrophel and Stella*, uttered by Nash in 1591, included not only Sidney's sequence, but "sundry other rare sonnets of divers noblemen and gentlemen," notably twenty-eight sonnets of Samuel Daniel. Daniel, an Oxford man of good family, had already been introduced at court and encouraged by the Countess of Pembroke. Daniel's inspiration is thus directly traceable to Sidney. At the time of this publication of his sonnets, Daniel was apparently abroad, as he appears to have acted at various times as a tutor to the young nobility. The poet resented this premature publication of his work, and in the following year put forth a true edition of his *Delia*, which included the sonnets already published together with many others and a narrative poem, *The Complaint of Rosamund*. Daniel's poetry was so well received that in the next year, 1594, he issued another edition, called *Delia and Rosamund Augmented*. Neither of these poems was without its effect upon the non-dramatic poetry of Shakespeare. And indeed Daniel deserved his popularity; for versatility of expression, choiceness and polish of diction, grace and leisurely dignity of style, all are his; though no one could be carried away by his fervor, and the flowers of his ornamentation seem artificial at times. The same year (1592) brought forth *Diana: the Praises of his Mistress in Certain Sweet Sonnets* a short collection, afterwards enlarged and the work of Henry Constable who is described as "a Roman Catholic gentleman who lived much in exile by reason of his religion." Constable was also highly esteemed by his age for his "pure, quick and high delivery of conceit," and he practised his art with a clearer understanding of the technical demands of the Petrarchan sonnet than any man of his time.

With Daniel and Constable begin clear traces of the immediate influences of the French sonneteers on those of England. Even the titles of these two series are suggestive of their borrowings, the one from a series of dizains by Maurice Sève, entitled *Delie*, the other from Desportes' *Les Amours de Diane*. Michael Drayton too, in his *Idea's Mirror, Amours in*

Quartorzains, 1594, took over the title, *L'Idée*, from a collection of sonnets by Claude de Pontoux, 1579, and is otherwise indebted to the French poets. But the chief borrower from France in the sonnet, as in his other lyrical poetry, is Thomas Lodge whose *Phillis Honored with Pastoral Sonnets*, a production of no inconsiderable poetical merit, was printed in 1593. Ronsard and Desportes especially were pillaged by Lodge; Desportes by Constable and Drayton; while Barnabe Barnes in his *Divine Century*, was more than inspired by Du Bartas and Jacques de Billy. But the Italians and the ancients were equal quarries for these free-booters of poetry. Aside from the universal imitation of Petrarch and his school, even Spenser disdained not to translate Tasso in some of his *Amoretti;* and, to the scandal and employment of modern minute scholarship, he neglected to make note of his borrowings. When all has been said on this topic a protest must be raised, as it is not fair to make too much of a practice that was as common to the age and, in general, as ingenuous and free from concealment as piracy on the high seas against the commerce of Spain. We have seen how Watson, in his *Passionate Century of Love*, ostentatiously noted the sources of most of his poems and even the details of his treatment. Watson differed only in this petty pedantry from his contemporaries and successors in this art of lifting gold from the poetical coffers of those who have had the impertinence to precede us. We may doubt whether these foreign influences, so much exploited of late, did much more than "facilitate literary effort by providing plenty of material ready at hand," and justify Ben Jonson's recognition, among the "requisites" of a poet or maker, of *imitatio*, or the power "to convert the substance or riches of another poet to his own use."

Sonneteering now became the fashion, and sequence after sequence, in repeated editions, issued from the press. Drayton added the writing of sonnets to his multiform literary activities. Watson gave over Latin poetry and converted his translations into sonnet form, entitled *The Tears of Fancy or Love Disdained*. Giles Fletcher, in his *Licia*, turned from travel and diplomacy; the author of *Zepheria* and Sir John Davies from the law; Spenser from epic poetry and Shakespeare from the stage to sonneteering; whilst every small gentleman, Percy, Lynche, Griffin, or Smith, in his *Cælia, Diella, Fidessa*, or *Chloris*, emulated the raptures of Sidney and the finished similitudes of Petrarch in the public poetical courtship of his real or imaginary fair beloved.

The Italian form of the sonnet, as is well known, involved two parts, the octave and the sestette, the first displaying but two rimes, usually inclusive (that is, arranged *a b b a a b b a*), the sestette frequently three (for example, *c d e c d e*), but variously arranged. There are many theories about the Italian sonnet; as a matter of fact, it was practised even among orthodox Italian poets with considerable freedom. Wyatt attempted the Italian mode; Surrey frankly Anglicized the sonnet by converting it into a series of three alternately riming quatrains, each with new rimes, followed and concluded with a couplet. And the majority of Elizabethan sonneteers — with Sidney, Constable, and Barnes as notable exceptions — accepted Surrey's form. This form (*a b a b, c d c d, e f e f, g g*) has been immortalized by Shakespeare, who even emphasized the effect of the final couplet by bringing the sense habitually to a pause immediately before it. It would not be difficult to argue that in substituting English habits of verse — such as the alternate rime (*a b a b*) for the inclusive (*a b b a*), such as the final couplet for the avoidance of it, and a variety of rimes for the Italian paucity — the form practised by Shakespeare and his compeers represents a truer translation of the sonnet into English than a closer imitation of foreign exotic conditions. Opprobrious names belong, assuredly, to no sincere form of art. Triumphant usage has hallowed the Shakespearean form of the sonnet.

Elizabethan sonnet sequences fall naturally into certain well-defined groups. The majority are devoted to the celebration of the passion of love: some, as Sidney's, Drayton's *Idea*, Spenser's *Amoretti*, and Shakespeare's, suggesting by means of successive lyrical moods a more or less connected love story, on greater or less probable basis in fact; another class dealing with the praises of a mistress or lamenting her hardness of heart, as *Phyllis*, *Cynthia*, and *Diana* or Watson's *Tears of Fancy*. Another class are little more than loosely connected series of amatory verse, as Willobie's *Avisa*, 1594, J. C.'s *Alcilia*, 1595, Breton's *Arbor of Amorous Devices*, 1597, or Tofte's *Alba*, 1598. Still others are collections of poems amatory and other, as Greville's *Cælica*, having nothing in common with the sonnet except a certain unity of thought and brevity of form. Two interesting short series of sonnets disclose a healthy revulsion against this excess of sentiment and sugared similitude. These are Chapman's *Coronet for his Mistress, Philosophy*, 1594, and the *Gulling Sonnets* of Sir John Davies in the next year. The first appeals to a higher inspiration than that which animates the "Muses that sing Love's sensual empery," and is a fine and elevated continued poem, linked sonnet to sonnet by the repetition of the last line of the first to the first line of the next sonnet, and so on after the manner of a "coronet." The sonnets of Sir John Davies, as their title implies, are pure "take-off" on the absurdities of the sonneteering tribe who were fair game for the clever courtier's raillery.

But by no means were all Elizabethan sonnets amatory. Second, but far from unimportant, was the devotional or religious sonnet, often written in sequences emulating the length, if not the extravagances, of the amatory sequences themselves; and sometimes, as in the case of Constable's *Spiritual Sonnets to God and his Saints*, in their day unpublished, and the *Divine Century of Spiritual Sonnets* of Barnes, 1595, the work of the same poets. The most persistent writer of devotional sonnets of his age was Henry Lok (or Locke) who printed, in 1597, *Sundry Sonnets of Christian Passions*, "sundry" here equaling one hundred and one. A previous hundred, devoted to "meditation, humiliation and prayer," merciful Time has allowed to perish; but upwards of sixty more, denominated "a few to divers," were collected by the printer and reprinted in our own day. As to Lok, he appears to have been a good man, practising a kind of piety that makes this world a hideous place to live in. As to inspiration or the slenderest runnel of song, he has absolutely neither.

To have been born such a man as Lok in the age of Shake-speare was the very quintessence of the irony of fate. But Lok represents a dismal fall from the average poetical competency of Elizabethan devotional sonneteering. The "spiritual sonnets" of either Constable or Barnes could furnish examples comparable at least with the average level of either in worldly poetry; while the two short series of Donne, *La Corona* and his *Holy Sonnets*, both of questionable date, contain individual poems worthy of Donne's great repute, as this famous *Sonnet on Death* will show:

> Death, be not proud, though some have callèd thee
> Mighty and dreadful, for thou art not so;
> For those whom thou think'st thou dost overthrow
> Die not, poor Death; nor yet canst thou kill me.
> From rest and sleep, which but thy picture be,
> Much pleasure, then from thee much more must flow:
> And soonest our best men with thee do go,
> Rest of their bones, and souls' delivery.
> Thou art slave to Fate, chance, kings, and desperate men,
> And dost with poison, war, and sickness dwell,
> And poppy or charms can make us sleep as well,
> And better than thy stroke; why swell'st thou, then?
> One short sleep past, we wake eternally,
> And Death shall be no more; Death, thou shalt die.

The religious sonnet ran into hybrid varieties in some cases, as in Thomas Roger's *Celestial Elegies in Quartorzains*, 1598, a mingling of the sonnet fashion with the obituary poem, so dear to the age, in the old edition bordered with black and embalmed, so to speak, in a style suggestive of the Senecan-funereal manner of the *Mirror for Magistrates* or the lugubrious solemnity of Blair's *Grave*. In 1600 Breton used the sonnet form as the stanza for a continuous religious poem, called *The Soul's Harmony*, and the second part of Davies of Hereford's *Wit's Pilgrimage*, in 1610, is cumberously entitled *Soul-Passions*, "and Other Passages Divine, Philosophical, Moral, Pietical and Political."

A third use to which the Elizabethan sonnet was put, was that of the occasional poem, most frequently in obituary, dedicatory, or other form addressing a patron. Roger's *Celestial Elegies*, just mentioned, is an example of the extended use of the sonnet for the first purpose. Four sonnets "to Sir Philip Sidney's soul" accompanied the first edition of that poet's *Defense of Poesy*, 1595. It was the fashion to prefix at times long series of dedicatory poems to important works. Among works, so introduced by sonnets, may be mentioned *The Faery Queen*, to the first three books of which seventeen sonnets were prefixed in 1590; and Gabriel Harvey's *Four Letters touching Robert Greene*, 1592, which was opened with no less than twenty-three. Chapman's *Homer*, in 1610, similarly contains fourteen dedicatory sonnets, later increased in number. Of a different type are the forty adulatory sonnets in form of a sequence addressed by Joshua Sylvester to Henry of Navarre "upon the late miraculous peace in France," in 1597. Although not sonnets in form, of similar adulatory character is *Astræa*, a series of octosyllabic acrostics eulogizing Queen Elizabeth which Sir John Davies devised in 1599. In this Davies followed the model of a like series, called the *Partheniads*, in *The Art of Poisy*, written twenty years earlier but now lost except for some fragments.

In the matter of conceit, the later sonneteers vied with each other to surpass in ingenuity both Sidney and his master Petrarch; and in the main they succeeded. Nor is it to be wondered that the conceit should develop most readily in the sonnet, where intensity of feeling, real or simulated, was compressed into a form and a mode of expression alike conventional and restricted. Among the sonneteers Daniel and Drayton, coming early, are less given to the conceit than their successors. From the excesses of the conceit Spenser's good taste largely preserved him; while Shakespeare, though by no means free either from the artificialities or even the trivialities of the sonneteering tribe, offers very few examples of "the elaborate inventional conceit," as it has been called. It is among the lesser men that we find the conceit in full blossom. Thus Constable declares that the basest notes of his Diana's voice exceed the trebles of angels; Giles Fletcher bids his mistress put down her fan from before her face and

put out the sun; and Tofte's Laura lays her handkercher to
dry snow white on quicksedge wrought with lovely eglantine.
The sun is slow, so she casts her glance upon it and dries the
cloth, but burns his heart. Lynche's thoughts reach out
beyond our planetary system to conceive of

> The tallest ship that cuts the angry wave
> And plows the seas in Saturn's second sun.

The anonymous author of *Zepheria* thus rings ingenious
change on an old theme:

> Let not Disdain (the hearse of virgin graces)
> The counterpoison of unchastity,
> The leaven that doth sour the sweetest faces,
> Stain thy new purchased immortality.
> 'Mongst Delian nymphs, in angels' university,
> Thou, my Zepheria, liv'st matriculated
> The Daughters of ethereal Jove, thy deity
> On holy hill have aye perpetuated.
> O then, retire thy brows artillery,
> Love more, and more bliss yet, shall honor thee.

The after-history of the sonnet is not long. In 1604
Sir William Alexander, the friend of Drummond, published
a series of a hundred or more sonnets under the title of *Aurora*.
The collection is interspersed with a few songs and elegies,
and formally inscribed to the Countess of Argyle. Alexander's
poetry is decorous and graceful, and clearly modeled on
French examples. The sequence was probably written
within the period of the sonnet. The sonnets of Drummond
are scattered through his poems and belong, like the few of
William Browne of Tavistock, to the first decade of the reign
of James. Of Davies of Hereford's large collection, *Wit's
Pilgrimage*, 1610, devoted, with even-handed justice, half to
love and half to religion, mention has already been made. A
few rare little volumes, not strictly of sonnets, but protracting the
impetus of the sonnet, are *Daïphantus or the Passions of Love*,
by Anthony Scoloker and Breton's *The Passionate Shepherd*,
both in 1604; *Dolarnys Primrose*, by John Reynolds, 1606; and
long after, George Wither's *Fidelia*, 1617, and *Fair Virtue,
the Mistress of Phil'Arete*, 1622. It is altogether likely that

the exquisite love poetry of these last two works of Wither was written early in the reign of King James and before Puritanism had acidulated the nature of that sweet singer. *Daïphantus* is memorable for one superlative serious poem, entitled "The Passionate Man's Pilgrimage," later printed as Sir Walter Raleigh's among his *Remains*. This poem is tuned to the high and insolent vein which his contemporaries ascribed to the Muse of Raleigh and deserves a place beside the equally vigorous indignation of his most popular poem, "The Lie." A tradition that "The Passionate Man's Pilgrimage" was written by Raleigh in the Tower in expectation of the immediate execution that threatened him in 1603, adds to the poignancy of his words. The poem is too long to quote here entire. These are some of the lines of it:

> Give me my scallop-shell of quiet,
>   My staff of faith to walk upon,
> My scrip of joy, immortal diet,
>   My bottle of salvation,
> My gown of glory, hope's true gage;
> And thus I'll take my pilgrimage.
>
> Blood must be my body's balmer,
>   No other balm will there be given;
> Whilst my soul, like quiet palmer,
>   Traveleth towards the land of heaven;
> Over the silver mountains,
> Where spring the nectar fountains:
>   There will I kiss
>   The bowl of bliss;
> And drink my everlasting fill
> Upon every milken hill:
> My soul will be a-dry before;
> But after, it will thirst no more.
>
>   .   .   .   .   .
>
> From thence to heaven's bribeless hall,
> Where no corrupted voices brawl;
> No conscience molten into gold,
> No forged accuser bought or sold,
> No cause deferred, no vain-spent journey:
> For there Christ is the King's Attorney.
>
>   .   .   .   .   .

Be thou my speaker, taintless pleader,
Unblotted lawyer, true proceeder!
Thou giv'st salvation even for alms;
Not with a bribèd lawyer's palms.
And this is mine eternal plea
To him that made heaven, earth and sea,
That, since my flesh must die so soon,
And want a head to dine next noon,
Just at the stroke, when my veins start and spread,
Set on my soul an everlasting head.
Then am I ready, like a palmer fit,
To tread those blest paths which before I writ.

To return to the sonnet sequences of amatory import,
five of them stand out distinct in poetical merit above the
rest: these are, in order of time, Sidney's *Astrophel*, Daniel's
Delia, Drayton's *Idea*, the *Amoretti* of Spenser, and the *Sonnets* of Shakespeare. Of the first two enough has been said
in this book. Michael Drayton's career in poetry was to be
a long and honorable one, for to him, as to the other poets
just mentioned, sonneteering was but the passing fashion
of the moment. In the longer reaches of his work, Drayton
is a Spenserian, as shown in his love of allegory and the pastoral mode, the sweet continuousness of his measures, his
natural felicity, even in his want of design and lengthy elab-
orateness. And for all these things in time Drayton's popularity came to equal almost that of his master. But the
earlier sonnets of Drayton preceded both Spenser and Shakespeare. Drayton's sonnets, judged as a whole, appear to
echo successively Daniel, Sidney, and Shakespeare Drayton's
Idea began with a few sonnets among several pastorals, published in 1593. In the next year, the sonnets were separated
from the pastorals, augmented to fifty-one, and called *Idea's
Mirror, Amours in Quartorzains*. With his sonnets, as with
his other work, Drayton practised constant revision, omission,
and addition, so that by the definitive edition of 1619, *Idea* had
come to contain many sonnets, written long after the sonnet-
craze, while other earlier ones had been suppressed. Indeed,
one sonnet of Drayton's (the one beginning "Since there's

no help, come, let us kiss and part") which impressionistic criticism has discovered to be "so fine that nobody but Shakespeare could have written it," appears for the first time in this edition of 1619, three years after Shakespeare's death. Drayton's sonnets in general have less of grace and art than those of Daniel; at times they are even somewhat harsh. Despite their "originals," they seem less Italianate than the earlier sequences, although their metrical facility and ease are prevailing, and two or three will maintain their place among the very best sonnets of their time. Many parallels have been found between the sonnets of Drayton and those of Shakespeare, and it would be difficult to prove Drayton always the borrower. The majority of such parallels, however, are easily referable to the conventional poetical furniture of the time with which it was imperative that every well-turned sonnet-sequence be equipped; and some of Drayton's sonnets must have followed Shakespeare's.

Drayton's *Idea* purports by its very title to be no more than an objective expression of the poet's ideal of womanhood. Yet here, as elsewhere, the ingenuity of scholarship has discovered, or thought that it has discovered, references of supposedly autobiographical import. On this whole topic of the subjective significance of these sonnet-sequences, suffice it to say that it is as easy to interpret mere lyrical hyperbole into a *chronique scandaleuse* as it is temporarily to etherialize real human passion into what Bagehot called, in a different connection, "evanescent mists of lyrical energy." It does not seem altogether reasonable to deny the existence of an actual person inspiring a poet to become a sonneteer simply because he may have translated from foreign poets and borrowed the conventional ideas of his time as to courtship. Artificiality does not always imply insincerity and, although a poet may write without any objective undercurrent, that kind of undercurrent is assuredly not so rare, as the world goes, as to make every translator and imitator a pretender in affairs of the heart. On the other hand it is impossible not to sympathize with the frankness of the preface to Giles Fletcher's sonnets to *Licia, or Poems of Love* "in honor of the admirable and singular virtues of his Lady," 1593, wherein he writes:

If thou muse what my Licia is? Take her to be some Diana, at the least chaste; or some Minerva: no Venus, fairer far. It may be she is learning's image, or some heavenly wonder: which the precisest may not mislike. Perhaps under that name I have shadowed [The Holy] Discipline. It may be, I mean that kind courtesy which I found at the patroness [Lady Mollineux] of these poems; it may be some college. It may be my conceit [i.e. fancy] and pretend nothing. Whatsoever it be; if thou like it, take it.

The *Amoretti* of Spenser, a sequence of eighty-eight sonnets, appeared in print with *Colin Clout's Come Home Again* and the *Epithalamion* in 1595. Spenser published no other edition of his sonnets and they were not reprinted until the collective edition of his works in 1611. The *Amoretti* must have been written during the years 1592 to 1594, and thus they correspond in time with the height of the vogue of the sonnet. It was in June of the latter year that Spenser married Elizabeth Boyle, the lady indubitably addressed in these poems. A critical analysis of the *Amoretti* discloses that the series falls naturally into two parts, the second beginning with the sixty-third sonnet. Up to that point the sonnets are concerned with Spenser's courtship. In the second part, the lofty celebration of love's victory is the poet's theme. It is characteristic of Spenser thus to have continued his sequence. It is also characteristic of him not to have stopped at the eighty-fifth sonnet which is the real conclusion of the sequence, but to have added several sonnets, doubtless written at other times. Though perhaps in this we are wronging Spenser, as this feature of an irrelevant gathering in of sonnets, not related to the sequence and sometimes not even by the author of it, is a familiar feature of many collections, among them Shakespeare's, and may be referable to the printer.

In the following sonnet there is less of the conceit and

convention of the species than we sometimes find even in
Spenser:

> More than most fair, full of the living fire
> Kindled above unto the Maker near;
> No eyes but joys, in which all powers conspire
> That to the world naught else be counted dear;
> Through your bright beams doth not the blinded guest
> Shoot out his darts to base affections wound;
> But angels come to lead frail minds to rest
> In chaste desires, on heavenly beauty bound.
> You frame my thoughts, and fashion me within;
> You stop my tongue, and teach my heart to speak;
> You calm the storm that passion did begin,
> Strong through your cause, but by your virtue weak.
> Dark is the world, where your light shinèd never;
> Well is he born that may behold you ever.

This other is closer to the spirit of Petrarch as interpreted by
his imitators of the later Renaissance; but is a no less favorable
specimen of Spenser's sonneteering art:

> Restore thy tresses to the golden ore,
> Yield Cytherea's son those arcs of love,
> Bequeath the heavens the stars that I adore,
> And to the orient do thy pearls remove,
> Yield thy hands' pride unto the ivory white,
> To Arabian odors give thy breathing sweet,
> Restore thy blush unto Aurora bright,
> To Thetis give the honor of thy feet;
> Let Venus have thy graces her resigned,
> And thy sweet voice give back unto the spheres;
> But yet restore thy fierce and cruel mind
> To Hyrcan tigers and to ruthless bears;
> Yield to the marble thy hard heart again:
> So shalt thou cease to plague, and I to pain.

As to Spenser's "own marriage hymn of thanksgiving" the
Epithalamion, beautiful if robust poem that it is, it has well
been said that had Spenser "been silent, he would have felt
that he wronged Hymen as well as the Muses." It was in
this spirit that Spenser wrote the *Amoretti* which, despite

their delicate art and their many points of contact with Italian and classical poetry, can hardly be regarded as other than the genuine outpourings of a lofty and chivalric nature and of a quality, as poetry, second to the best of the sonnets of Sidney and Shakespeare alone.

Despite some recent skepticism and scholarly Platonic suspicions we may reaffirm with confidence that *Astrophel and Stella* had its inspiration in a passion sufficiently real to take on a genuinely tragic tone to one of the ardent nature of Sidney. Spenser's *Amoretti*, too, won him the lady of his choice. What, then, of the sonnets of Shakespeare? Are they, too, based on experience in life or are they mere literary exercises, compounded of shreds and patches, filched from French and Italian concettists where they are not the mere figments of an imaginative mind?

The life of Shakespeare will be best considered with his dramatic work later in this book. Whatever the precise time of Shakespeare's coming up to London and the conditions of his earlier life there, he must soon have learned something more of the society of gentlemen and gentlewomen than could have fallen to the lot of one who saw such personages from the boards of the theater alone. We know that Shakespeare found an early patron in the young Earl of Southampton; for Shakespeare dedicated both *Venus and Adonis* and *Lucrece* to him. Recently the Earl of Rutland (like Southampton an intimate of Essex and to become involved with him in his ruin) has been discovered to have been also a patron of Shakespeare. And while the matter is not susceptible of proof, there is surely nothing irrational in supposing that William Herbert, Earl of Pembroke, was likewise at some time the poet's patron, the more especially when it is remembered that Shakespeare's fellow-actors, Heming and Condell, thought Pembroke the fit person with his brother, the Earl of Montgomery, to whom to dedicate the folio edition of the dramatist's works.

Shakespeare was imitative in his earlier work. *Titus Andronicus*, if conceivably his work, is a case in point. We shall see soon how he followed the lead of Lyly in comedy

and learned from Marlowe in tragedy and chronicle play.
In his sonnets, too, Shakespeare followed the fashion of his
time. And although they were first printed in a piratical
edition, as late as 1609, there is every reason to believe that
they coincided in point of the time of their composition with
the general vogue of the sonnet and were well known by circulation in manuscript "among his private friends," at least
as early as 1598. The Sonnets, like all other subjects connected
with Shakespeare's name, bristle with difficulties, though
most of them are of the commentators' own making. There
is question about their dedication, about the way in which
they came to be published, about the person or persons to
whom they may have been addressed, about their order, their
significance, and about the time when they were written. As
to this last, opinion has just been expressed. The publication
of Shakespeare's Sonnets is believed by some to have been
procured, like the publication of many other Elizabethan
books, by a personage who may be best described as a procurer of copy. It was the business of this personage to obtain
"for publication literary works which had been widely dis-
seminated in written copies and had thus passed beyond
their author's control." Nash thus procured the publication
of sonnets of Daniel, as we have seen above, much to that
poet's disgust; and an earlier striking example of the same
thing was Gascoigne's borrowing of the manuscript of Sir
Humphrey Gilbert's pamphlet, called A Discourse of a New
Passage to Cataia, and publication of it on his own account.
According to this view, the "procurer of copy" in the case
of Shakespeare's Sonnets was an humble person. A clerk or
copyist, who was none too scrupulous, might have opportunities
of acting in this jackal capacity that a more honest man would
miss. The dedication of the sonnets to "Mr. W. H." as
"the onelie begetter" is then regarded as referable merely to
this bookseller's matter; and the actual name of "Mr. W. H."
— whether William Hall, Hart, Hughes or anything else —
becomes a matter wholly negligible. The greatest difficulty
which this theory escapes is the necessity of considering "Mr.
W. H." to stand for "the Right Honorable William, Earl

of Pembroke, Lord Chamberlain to His Majesty, one of the
Privy Council and Knight of the most noble Order of the
Garter." So to have misaddressed a peer of the realm might
have been made a Star Chamber matter in Shakespeare's
day. There still continue, however, a few in the purlieus
of scholarship who insist that "Mr. W. H." is intended to
indicate the Earl of Pembroke and that he was alike the ded-
icatee of the *Sonnets* and their inspiring subject. That
Shakespeare should have made no effort to interfere with the
printing of his sonnets need excite no surprise. This whole
matter of sonnet writing was at least a dozen years old in
1609; and, with his greatest dramatic work behind him and on
the point of retiring from the stage, Shakespeare could well
afford to neglect these passages of his youth.

Some other questions about the sonnets are not so readily
disposed of. It will be remembered that the *Sonnets* of
Shakespeare consist of two series the first, to cxxvi, "addressed
to a young man"; the second, from cxxvii to clii, "addressed to
or referring to a woman." There is a greater connectedness
in the first series; but neither are arranged in consecutive
order and even this general division is not wholly justified
in every case. Moreover not a few of the sonnets, especially
towards the end, seem thrown in haphazard. By some,
among them the great poet Browning, Shakespeare's *Sonnets* have been thought to detail matters purely imaginative; by others to be dramatic exercises as free from
autobiographical allusions as the plays themselves, though
perhaps written to serve the purpose of some other lover than
Shakespeare, possibly the Earl of Southampton. Again,
several writers, mostly German, have discovered an allegorical
interpretation for the sonnets, making the "Mr. W. H."
of the dedication stand for "William Himself" and finding
nature, romanticism, Greek art, and what not, after the manner of the second part of Goethe's *Faust*, locked up in the
cabalistic lines of the poet. As the young man is fair and
the lady dark, it might as logically be suggested that we have
here a myth of the sun god and that the dark lady is the goddess of eclipse.

Without going into refinements and combinations of interpretations, the story of the sonnets is neither difficult nor involved; sonnet cxliv, published by Jaggard in *The Passionate Pilgrim*, in 1599, supplies us with the key.

> Two loves I have of comfort and despair;
> Which like two spirits do suggest [tempt] me still [ever];
> The better angel is a man right fair
> The worser spirit a woman, colored ill.

The poet has become the devoted friend of a youth much younger than himself and of a station in life above him. At much the same time he yields to a passionate infatuation for a dark lady who keeps both men in her toils to their undoing. The first group of sonnets details the growth and fluctuations of the poet's affection for his friend (which in the parlance of the time is continually called love), an affection which has endured three years, which has been menaced by favors bestowed upon another poet (variously identified with Daniel, Chapman, or Barnes), and by the circumstance that, in his absence, his friend has sought to become his rival in the favor of his mistress. The sequence ebbs and flows with the emotions of the poet, now exultingly promising immortality to the subject of his praise, at other moments reproaching him for sensuality or for patronage bestowed on his rivals, despairing of himself, his profession as actor, and of the age, and longing for death; again returning to protestations of unfaltering love and constancy in friendship. The second series deals more briefly with the poet's passion for his mistress whose "blackness" — to use the Elizabethan word — he extols above the lily fairness of other men's beloveds; whom he reproaches for her unfaithfulness and for the wreck which she finally makes of the devotion of his friend as well as of his own.

Without returning to the various identifications, if the sonnets be of autobiographical import, Southampton is the fairest claimant for the rôle of Shakespeare's friend and patron, as he is known to have been both. Some still prefer, however, as we have seen, the Earl of Pembroke. There are difficulties in both interpretations. As to sirens, the court or Elizabeth was fuller of them than was ever the Ægean; and for my part I should be sorry to have the mask of anonimity torn from the face of this immortal shadow.

In the autobiographical interpretation of the sonnets one thing is to be noted. The tale is a tragedy; and it could only be such because its chief actor recognized to the full the distinction between good and evil and shows them to us in mortal struggle. The outcome is not told us; that evil did not ultimately triumph to the hopeless corruption of that great spirit, we have the true and noble ethics of his later works to prove. Is our Shakespeare less that he was tested in the fiery furnace of temptation which consumes the heart of man like chaff, and came forth refined and chastened from the ordeal ? Must we always put aside our charity when we judge the great ? And is that which is imperishable and immortal impaired by sharing that mortality which is ever man's whether in greater or less degree ? These are some of the questions which we should ask ourselves and in the answers which we can give to them abide content with what we have before us and not seek to explain away what does not comport with our own preconceptions.

As a sequence the *Sonnets* of Shakespeare are not pleasing. The story is not attractive, nor the uncontrol with which it is told. It produces the effect of a vivid, terrible, and confused dream; its very beauties seem the flowers of a heated and overwrought imagination; and while it strikes one in only a few of its interpolated notes as unreal, there is a distortion about it. As a sequence *Astrophel and Stella* is preferable; and we can understand why Hallam said of the sonnets: "It is impossible not to wish that Shakespeare had never written them." But if we come to the consideration of individual sonnets, here is Shakespeare preëminent. Unequal as the sonnets are, considered together, — some of them on a level with Lynche or Barnes — there remains a collection, the poetic excellence, the masterly touch and truth of which no other poetry of the Elizabethan age can approach. Moreover their range is as various as their excellence is superlative,

now trifling with words or punning on his name, now play-
fully satirical, now rising to the impassioned strains of ecstatic
joy and confidence, now in the slough of despond or remorse
and fraught with that deep experience in life which makes
Shakespeare the greatest of all poets.

> When, in disgrace with fortune and men's eyes,
> I all alone beweep my outcast state,
> And trouble deaf heaven with my bootless cries,
> And look upon myself and curse my fate,
> Wishing me like to one more rich in hope,
> Featured like him, like him with friends possessed,
> Desiring this man's art and that man's scope,
> With what I most enjoy contented least;
> Yet in these thoughts myself almost despising,
> Haply I think on thee, and then my state,
> Like to the lark at break of day arising
> From sullen earth, sings hymns at heaven's gate;
> For thy sweet love remembered such wealth brings
> That then I scorn to change my state with kings.

> No longer mourn for me when I am dead
> Than you shall hear the surly sullen bell
> Give warning to the world that I am fled
> From this vile world, with vilest worms to dwell;
> Nay, if you read this line, remember not
> The hand that writ it; for I love you so
> That I in your sweet thoughts would be forgot,
> If thinking on me then should make you woe.
> O, if, I say, you look upon this verse
> When I perhaps compounded am with clay,
> Do not so much as my poor name rehearse,
> But let your love even with my life decay,
> Lest the wise world should look upon your moan,
> And mock you with me after I am gone.

The fervor, the music, the distinction of these lines, may be
equaled, though not surpassed, again and again among these
exquisite lyrics. Can poems such as these be conceived as
mere literary exercises, inspired in the passing fashion of the
moment and bearing no freight of an actual experience in life?
And yet could not the mind that fashioned, as from within,

alike the doubts and questionings of Hamlet and the unimaginative certainties of Henry V, the wicked egotism of Iago, and the benign magnanimity of Prospero, — and this though he was neither Prospero, Iago, Henry, nor yet Hamlet,— could not this man have written even these sonnets without once letting us into the veritable secrets of his great and mysterious soul? The question is insoluble; and it is better so. It is well that there should still remain some mysteries which the prying scrutiny of research must leave among the riddles of time.

CHAPTER IX

SHAKESPEARE IN COMEDY AND IN CHRONICLE HISTORY

I N two of the preceding chapters of this book the earlier history of the drama in Elizabeth's reign has been traced, first with Lyly at court and then with Marlowe and his fellows on the popular stage of London. We turn now to the often told story of Shakespeare, especially in what we may reasonably reconstruct concerning the earlier half of his life and career as a dramatist.

It is a commonplace of literary biography that the materials out of which to construct a life of Shakespeare are exceedingly scant; scantier, it is sometimes added, than similar data concerning other men, his associates and contemporaries. The statement is not borne out by the facts. The material as to Shakespeare's life, even unembellished, is not inconsiderable; and it is a mistake to suppose the subject closed. There are, for example, some one hundred and seventy-five separate and individual evidences of Shakespeare's private life in the shape of official records, documents, entries, notices, and allusions, all of them contemporary. Most of these, as might be expected, have reference to his dramatic and poetic works, but twenty documents which concern his life and contain his name might be cited in any court of record to-day for the facts that they witness. Of the total twenty-six relate to births, marriages, and deaths; and five are evidences of ownership in the precinct of Blackfriars. The rest concern suits at law, and include a tax assessment when Shakespeare lived in the neighborhood of Bishopsgate, (though this has of late been questioned), certain deeds and mortgages, and his will. Most recently of all, we hear of Shakespeare as a witness in a lawsuit among the papers of which turns up a deposition, signed by his own hand, adding a sixth to the slender total of his other five signatures. According to this, Shakespeare lived, from 1598 to 1604, as a "sojourner" or sub-tenant in the house of one Christopher Mountjoy, a French Huguenot and prosperous tiremaker, at the corner of Silver and Monkwell Streets, in the parish of St. Olave, not far from Cripplegate.[1] All this is a slenderer show of materials than that which we can scrape together concerning several of his contemporaries, statesmen, noblemen, and men of public service. We do not know as much about Shakespeare, for example, as we know about Sidney, Raleigh, Burleigh, or even Ben Jonson, who was much in the employ of the court; but we know far more of Shakespeare than we can glean of Marlowe, Webster, or Fletcher. In fact we know more of Shakespeare than we know of any other man of his time *similarly circumstanced;* and this is due not only to the industrious researches of the scholars and editors of three centuries, but to the indisputable fact that Shakespeare was interesting to his own age.

The recorded facts of Shakespeare's life are familiar to all; how he was baptized April 26, 1564, at Stratford, the son of a yeoman, John Shakespeare, and Mary, his wife; how he entered into a bond when scarcely nineteen to marry Ann Hathaway who was nine years his senior; how Susanna, their daughter, was born so soon as to explain the necessity of the irregularity of but once asking the bans; and how other children followed to increase the responsibilities of a husband not yet of age. There is record of young Shakespeare's consent in 1587 to the mortgage of property of his mother's at Ashby; and the scene then changes from Stratford to London. In 1592 comes Greene's allusion, in the *Groatsworth of Wit,* enviously attesting Shakespeare's success as a playwright, with Chettle's recognition, in his *Kind-Heart's Dream,* of Shakespeare's standing as a man and an actor; the dedications of *Venus and Adonis* and of *Lucrece* to the Earl of Southampton follow in the next two years. And now begin the entries of the Stationers' Register, first of plays, some doubtfully

[1] See C. W. Wallace, *New Shakespeare Discoveries, Harper's Magazine.* March, 1910.

Shakespeare's and as yet without his name. Later his name appears with the titles, and popular plays run into six and seven editions during his lifetime, while piratical printers not only publish works that are Shakespeare's own (commonly, we may believe, against his will), but affix his name to plays with which he had nothing to do. Within the lifetime of no Elizabethan dramatist were half so many plays printed as of Shakespeare; and of no other playwright can it be said that his work was so often pirated or his name so frequently misused. This points to but one thing, the name of Shakespeare was a name to conjure with in his day; people wanted to read what they had heard of his on the boards.

We know that this repute came in the first instance from the theater. In 1595 Shakespeare is mentioned in the accounts of the Office of the Revels; his membership in the leading theatrical company of the day, the Chamberlain's, is established by record in 1594; and he is named, especially as an actor in Jonson's *Every Man in His Humor* in 1598. Meanwhile there is evidence of his affiliation with his home and family in Stratford and of his increase in wealth and importance. His son Hamnet — strange variant of Hamlet — is buried at Stratford in 1596; and a draft of arms is granted, not to William, but to John Shakespeare, his father. In the next year the poet purchases the freehold of New Place, the finest house in his native town, and we hear of other purchases intended and consummated. There is correspondence as to the loan by Shakespeare of money and as to petty suits at law, brought and gained by him. Death comes to his family again, his father dying in 1601, his brother Edmund in 1607, his mother the following year. His first-born, Susanna, marries in the former year and Shakespeare becomes a grandfather. There is the purchase of more land, of property in Stratford and in London, and there are legacies of friendship left to Shakespeare. At last there is his will, executed March 25, 1616, and on April 23, traditionally considered Shakespeare's birthday, the man is no more. These are the facts in the main. Into the traditions we cannot here enter.

Books have been written on what Shakespeare learned at

school; he learned more out of doors. Jonson said that he had small Latin and less Greek, and Aubrey gossips that he knew Latin pretty well. The two opinions tally, as Jonson and Aubrey viewed Latin from different quarters. The late Churton Collins, in a scholarly essay on the learning of Shakespeare, has quite upset the old notion that Shakespeare was unacquainted with the classical authors; but it may be suspected that Shakespeare never read a foreign book if he could obtain the matter that he wanted in translation. Shakespeare was not so learned a man as Ben Jonson, to say nothing of Camden or Bacon; but it has now long been exploded that Shakespeare was "a rude, natural-born genius," a species of inspired idiot who knew not the wise things that he was uttering. As Bagehot so happily put it: "There is clear evidence that Shakespeare received the ordinary grammar-school education of his time and that he derived from the pain and suffering of several years, not exactly an acquaintance with Latin and Greek, but like Eton boys, a firm conviction that there are such languages." Moreover the stamp of genius is on Shakespeare's life. He was not the man to submit to any real inferiority and, whatever his early deficiencies, the plays attest how he corrected them. There is no proof that Shakespeare attended the Stratford grammar school. He could have attended no other. There is no copy of William Lilly's *Grammar* extant which bears Shakespeare's signature. It is unlikely that he studied any other, for this was the approved Latin book of his day and long after.

The happy and competent knowledge which Shakespeare exhibits of many subjects, some of them technical and professional, has led to a host of surmises as to his probable occupation after leaving school. He has been thought a farmer, a huntsman (which he certainly was), a lawyer, a printer, a soldier, an usher in a school, and a surgeon. Aubrey repeated an earlier tradition which made Shakespeare exercise his father's trade and added that "when he killed a calf he would do it in a high style and make a speech." We need not believe this story; indeed, we need not believe a word of Aubrey; but it has been well observed that this idle anecdote suggests at least the theatrical genius. Shakespeare used the picturesque Bible phrase of his time, not because he had studied for the Church, but because he was an Elizabethan with a memory for the phrase; he observed with marvelous accuracy the symptoms of insanity, not because he was an alienist but because he was observant of the psychology of man. As to his legal acquirements, Professor Raleigh remarks that "it was not for nothing that Shakespeare was his father's son": and besides, Shakespeare had lawsuits of his own. A late discovery concerning him discloses a suit in which he was the successful plaintiff in 1615.[1] As to all these surmises of Shakespeare's avocations, let them remain surmises. To him who laboriously acquires a petty barony in some little kingdom of knowledge, the grasp, the sweep, the accuracy of Shakespeare's perceptions must seem supernatural, if not based on diligent studies such as his own.

Before we leave Stratford and the youth of Shakespeare it may be observed that many books have treated Shakespeare's nature-lore, his knowledge of animals, his acquaintance with birds, his insects, even his fishes. A delightful book, *The Diary of Master William Silence*, has shown the completeness of Shakespeare's knowledge of the contemporary nomenclature of the popular sports of hunting and hawking and his devotion to the horse. But Professor Raleigh has set us straight as to the nature-lore of Shakespeare which was clearly that of the keen but superficial observer, not that of the modern scientific devotee of nature study. Shakespeare wasted no time observing the habits of animals when men were to observe. He makes plenty of mistakes in natural history and accepts the traditional qualities of the impossible beasts of the medieval bestiary, "the toad that wears a precious jewel in his head," "the unicorn that is betrayed with trees," "the basilisk that kills at sight"; but he makes no mistakes as to his men and women: there his touch is certain as his knowledge is profound.

[1] See *Englische Studien*, xxxvi, 1906, where this discovery of Professor Wallace is most conveniently consulted. It was first communicated to *The London Standard*, October, 18, 1905.

Why Shakespeare went up to London is perfectly clear; he was compelled to make a living for his family; a poaching expedition and threatened uncomfortable consequences may have hastened his departure. When he first arrived in the metropolis is not so certain. However it came about, Shakespeare was on the boards as an actor before 1590 and already done with his apprenticeship to the writing of plays. A year or two later he is one of the sharers or part owners in the most successful company of London.

When Shakespeare took his place in the lead of his profession he found the public prepared to welcome and appreciate theatrical entertainments by generations of familiarity with them; and he found, also, a secular drama already well advanced in a hardy vernacular growth, together with a stage which had passed beyond amateurishness into the beginnings of a recognized profession. Moreover, literature had all but shaken free of medievalism with its allegory and intent to instruct, to look at life steadily and yet to see that life, at need, in the transfiguring light of poetry. Shakespeare could have learned very little, except by way of warning, of Robert Wilson, who was active among the Earl of Leicester's players and the Queen's between 1574 and 1584; even although the scenes of Antonio's negotiations with Shylock have been regarded as "anticipated" in Wilson's morality, *The Three Ladies of London*, printed in the latter year. Equally slight for the coming master of the stage must have been Shakespeare's contact with the famous clown of his time, Richard Tarlton, whose name has been attached by way of surmise to an older play on subject-matter afterwards treated by Shakespeare in his histories on Henry IV and Henry V. And yet it was precisely stuff such as this that the young Shakespeare was set to revise. However, Shakespeare was not without examples worthy his young ambition, and in Lyly and Marlowe he found them.

Of the precise chronology of Shakespeare's plays, as of those of most of his contemporaries, we are far from certain. Except for *Titus Andronicus* and *Romeo and Juliet*, which in revision falls beyond, the plays of Shakespeare's imitative period are either romantic comedies or dramas based on the history of English kings. We have touched sufficiently on *Titus* already for the purposes of this book. Let us turn first here to the earlier romantic comedies. *Love's Labor's Lost* is usually assigned to the earliest place among the comedies of Shakespeare (not later than 1591), and, although not published in quarto form until 1598 and then possibly revised, several features confirm this position. This comedy, with all its originality, is pronouncedly Lylian in its personages, dialogue, and in type, in that it is, like *Midas* or *Endimion*, full of personal, political, and other satirical allusions. In this and in the peculiarity that it is the only plot of all Shakespeare's plays which he appears frankly to have invented, *Love's Labor's Lost* stands alone. Shakespeare's knowledge of the courtly society that he attempts to depict in this comedy can not be pronounced other than amateurish. This is high life as seen from without; and the frequently trivial badinage of the three courtiers and ladies, so evenly arrayed each against each, the absurdities of Holofernes, Nathaniel, and the rest, despite much promise, all serve to confirm this. Shakespeare never repeated this experiment in transplanting the allusive and satirical court drama of Lyly to the common stage. But he soon tried another experiment, in *The Comedy of Errors*. Here he had the example of old English plays such as *Ralph Roister Doister* and Gascoigne's *Supposes;* and it is impossible to credit him with ignorance of Plautus, whether he read the *Menæchmi* in some English version by William Warner or (if there are difficulties in this) in the original. *The Comedy of Errors* (written in 1591 if not even before), is a bustling and inventive farce of action. It redoubles the difficulties of the comedy of mistake, and produces as a result the most successful specimen of its class. It is worthy of note that among the many imitations of Roman comedy which Elizabethan drama affords, Shakespeare's *Comedy of Errors* should have outstripped all the efforts of the scholars. But Shakespeare never returned to Plautine comedy, though many comedies of the general type, mixed with that of disguise, followed him, developing in turn through the work of Chapman and Jonson into a favorite variety of the comedy of manners.

In his third extant experimental comedy, *The Two Gentlemen of Verona* (also first written about 1591), Shakespeare found a dramatic species to which he afterwards adhered. This was the romantic comedy of love and intrigue, based on Italian tales of the type made famous especially in Painter's *Palace of Pleasure*, 1566. The plot of *The Two Gentlemen of Verona* is that of the story of the shepherdess, Felismena, in Montemayor's Spanish romance, *Diana Enamorada*, with the possible intervention of a lost play. As to the romantic drama in general type, it first manifested itself successfully, as we have seen, in the tragical works of Kyd and Marlowe or in dramas of heroical type like Greene's *Orlando* and *Alphonsus*, which hark back to *Tamburlaine*. Save for translations of Italian comedies such as *Supposes* by Gascoigne, 1566, it is difficult to find examples of lighter Italian stories dramatized until we reach Shakespeare. Whetstone's *Promos and Cassandra*, 1578, fulfils the conditions of an English comedy modeled on an Italian tale, in this case a "novel" of Cinthio's *Gli Hecatommithi;* but the plot is all but tragic and, though free at least from Seneca, is far removed from that lightsome and buoyant tone which we habitually associate with the term romantic comedy. Perhaps the only claim of Whetstone's coarse and verbose play is based on the fact that Shakespeare's genius subsequently transformed it into *Measure for Measure*. *Mucedorus*, a sprightly if elemental little comedy of romantic tone, was published first in 1595, and, despite some notion that Shakespeare may have had hand in it, is best assigned to the authorship of Thomas Lodge. But the source of *Mucedorus* is Sydney's *Arcadia* and, although the play is undoubtedly very early, it is questionable if it preceded *The Two Gentlemen of Verona* on the stage. Returning then to this comedy, it becomes important in the history of the drama not only because in it Shakespeare first found his bent, but also because of its peculiar isolation as an early English comedy dealing romantically with love. As to the comedy itself, despite many faults, disclosing the continuance of the influence of Lyly, *The Two Gentlemen of Verona* gives promise in the decision and discrimination with which its principal figures are drawn — the faithful Valentine, the recreant Proteus, bright and generous Sylvia and steadfast, loving Julia — of the greater comedies to come. After these earliest comedies, Shakespeare applied himself to history and tragedy. Into neither need we follow him here; but rather look onward to the only two other comedies that are accepted as early by universal consent. *The Merchant of Venice* was on the stage by 1594, and, in all likelihood, modeled on an old play, mentioned by Gosson in 1579, in which apparently both the story of the Jew and that of the "Lady of Belmont" were already combined. By the time that Shakespeare turned to the writing of this play, he had already deserted the guidance of Lyly for that of Marlowe, as will appear more fully in our discussion of the chronicle plays. The influence of Marlowe's Barabas on Shakespeare's Shylock has often been pointed out; and it is patent, whether in reminiscence of individual traits and passages or, as has been lately argued, in the very contrast of each poet's conception of the Jew.[1] It is a mistake to suppose that the Jew was little known either to the literature of the time or by actual acquaintance with him in the London of Elizabeth. Aside from Gosson's mention, just alluded to, and the Geruntus of Wilson's *Three Ladies of London*, a just and honorable creditor, there was in actual life Roderigo Lopez, the queen's Jewish physician, the trial and execution of whom for alleged complicity in a plot against Elizabeth's life, early in 1594, excited much popular interest. Whether it was this that led Shakespeare to his subtle study of Shylock, as has been held, or not, certain it is that that famous character is conceived in a full realization of the grotesqueness bordering on laughter and the pathos bordering on tears which characterizes his strange personality and situation. The admirable conduct of this play in the successful intermingling of comedy with a serious motive which rises for a moment almost to the height

[1] *Shakespeare's Jew and Marlowe's Christians*, by William Poel, *Westminster Review*, 1909.

of tragedy, its pervading humor and altogether delightful personages, attest that in *The Merchant of Venice* Shakespeare had reached, to the full, the manhood of his genius.

A Midsummer-Night's Dream is usually dated 1595 and is thought by some to have been written to celebrate a noble marriage, a purpose for which its grace and gaiety well fitted it. No source has been found for the major plot, though either *The Knight's Tale* of Chaucer or Plutarch's *Life of Theseus* may have served for the parts concerning that modified ancient hero. Here Shakespeare has made a poet's use of the supernatural, creating out of hints in popular folk-lore a new order of beings in the enchanting and dainty fairyland of Oberon and Titania. With its forest glades, peopled with bewildered lovers and fairy folk, the grotesque histrionic attempts of the "base mechanicals," and its pseudo-classic background of ancient Athens, Theseus and his amazonian bride, *A Midsummer-Night's Dream* marks the very acme of the difficult Renaissance art of agglomeration; for only the richest fancy, the most exquisite sense of the music of words and the harmony between poetic expression and poetic thought could achieve such artistic unity in elements so repugnant.

Turning back for the nonce to the beginnings of Shakespeare's conversancy with the stage, the chronicle play (which, it may be interjected, is a drama dealing in epic wise with subjects derived from the history of England) is the most striking of the several forms of literature which resulted from the realization of the national idea. Pride in England's present greatness, in the success of Elizabeth's fleet against the Armada of the King of Spain, and her skill in preserving her throne despite the fulminations of Rome, begot an enthusiasm for the great deeds of Englishmen in the past such as had been unknown before. Of this literature in other forms an account has already been given in the first chapter of this book. It was inevitable both that the stage should share in this tide of patriotism and that the foremost writer for that stage should contribute most largely to the drama of this type. Shakespeare devoted literally a third of his dramatic activity to the writing of plays based on what was accepted at the time as English history, and he wrote many more such chronicle histories, as they were called, than any three of his competitors combined.   In these historical dramas, too, better than elsewhere, can we discern the probable steps in his apprenticeship to his art.

Three plays on the events of the long but unhappy reign of King Henry VI are to be found in collective editions of Shakespeare.   The first of these, we are told by Nash in an often quoted passage, achieved an unusual success in 1592, especially on account of certain vivid scenes in which the hero, Talbot, figured in his warfare against the French; and it is likely that the other two parts followed closely in consequence. But if we examine these three plays, we find that all show clear marks of revision and rewriting, and an earlier version of the second and the third parts of *Henry VI*, differing materially from Shakespeare's, is extant.   These two old plays may be called by a shortening of their cumbrous titles the first and second parts of *The Contention between the Two Noble Houses of York and Lancaster*, or shorter still, 1 and 2 *Contention*.   Part first of *Henry VI* seems to indicate revision chiefly in the interpolation of individual scenes; while the other two (2 *Henry VI* and 3 *Henry VI*), by a comparison with their earlier versions (1 and 2 *Contention*), show rewriting line for line, in which, however, a large proportion of the original lines are retained intact.   Some have held that, in these revisions, Shakespeare was only making over his own earlier work.   But none of this work was claimed by him or published in his lifetime as his.   Inasmuch, moreover, as Shakespeare was charged by Greene with plagiarism and a passage was parodied in proof from one of these very plays, it is better to believe that, in the three parts of *King Henry VI*, Shakespeare was refashioning the earlier material of others or at least work in which he had only shared with older fellow playwrights.   The internecine feuds of the Wars of the Roses, detailed so minutely in this trilogy, seem deficient to us in interest as we read them to-day.   To the Elizabethans the theme was an absorbing one, for it was thence that the stable Tudor monarchy under which they lived had been evolved.

As to the quality of these first ventures of Shakespeare into history, their promise is clear. Of a mere youth who could so revise the inchoate material of his predecessors almost anything might be predicted.

But no account of Shakespeare can be complete without a reference at this point to the notorious attack upon him of Robert Greene, in his *Groatsworth of Wit purchased with a Million of Repentance*, published late in 1592. This death-bed pamphlet of poor Greene has been quoted already in a passage describing the status of the contemporary actor. In an address to "His Quondam Acquaintance," in which he includes Marlowe, Peele, and Lodge, Greene bids them beware of "these puppets [the actors] that speak from our mouths" and of "antics garnished in our colors." And he continues:

> There is an upstart crow, beautified with our feathers, that in his *Tiger's heart wrapt in a player's hide* supposes he is as well able to bumbast out a blank-verse as the best of you; and being an absolute *Johannes factotum* is, in his own conceit, the only Shake-scene in a country . . . . Never more acquaint [those apes] with your admired inventions, for it is pity men of such rare wit should be subject to the pleasures of such rude grooms.

These allusions are clear to him who runs. The "Tiger's heart wrapt in a player's hide" is a parody on "Oh tiger's heart wrapt in a woman's hide," applied by the Duke of York to Queen Margaret, the "she-wolf of France," in the third part of *Henry VI*, and contained in that part of the play which Shakespeare took over from the 2 *Contention*. That Greene's rancorous opinion was not the prevalent one among Shakespeare's fellows in his profession, is proved by the ample apology which Chettle made soon after, in his *Kind-Heart's Dream*, for his part in the publication of Greene's unhappy tract.

To return to the chronicle play, Shakespeare soon followed up his success with a more independent effort, the condensation of two anonymous old chronicle plays, called *The Troublesome Reign of King John*, by rewriting into one effective tragedy. This must have been early in 1593. Shakespeare's

King John marks a decided advance, and this notwithstanding much fidelity to an original which is far from worthy of contempt. It is in such personages as Falconbridge, Hubert, the little prince, and the two wrangling queens that we find the distinctness of characterization, the mingling of humor and pathos that came later so much more fully to distinguish our greatest dramatic poet. And in the dastard John appears, too, suggestion of a deeper study of character. But Shakespeare was not content to stop here. He turned from revision to imitation, recognizing, as who could avoid it, the masterly passion of Marlowe and filled with ambition to emulate his triumphs. *Richard III*, which must soon have followed *King John*, in 1593, is Shakespeare's one thoroughly Marlowesque tragedy. And this is patent alike in the heroic proportions of the distorted hero, monster that he is of conscious wickedness and crafty design, and in the lyric quality of the emotion which pervades many scenes. *Richard III* must have been to Shakespeare a *tour de force* much like the earlier *Titus*. Both are splendid followings of another man's gait and manner. Indeed, if we would realize to the full what Shakespeare could do with a popular historical portrait, his Richard Crookback should be compared with the older *True Tragedy of Richard III*, to which gross if strongly written play he owed very little.

Marlowe's *Edward II* must have been written within a twelvemonth of the date of his death in May, 1593. Whether Shakespeare's *Richard III* preceded Marlowe's play or not, it may be taken as almost certain that *Richard II* was planned in direct and daring emulation of Marlowe's successful tragedy. The subject-matter of these two later plays is as nearly identical as English history can afford; for in each a monarch who is unworthy to rule is thrown, in the contrast of circumstances, against a group of rebellious barons, and in each his problematic character with his pitiful fall holds the center of the stage. But in *Richard II*, though he chose Marlowe's theme, Shakespeare enfranchised himself from Marlowe's method. It seems almost as if Shakespeare had determined to rival Marlowe on his own ground but in a manner of Shakespeare's own choosing. The conception of the wayward poetical-minded king, a *poseur* in fortune as well as in mischance, the contrast of his levity with the sagacity, unimaginativeness, and political effectiveness of Bolingbroke, the grasp and knowledge of the world which this tragedy presumes, and the sure touch and poetry with which it is written and embellished — all of these things place *Richard II* not only far above *King John* and *Richard III* but disclose Shakespeare as the triumphant rival of the now dead Marlowe, even though it be confessed that the closing scene of the latter's *Edward* remained, in its terror and pathos, as yet unequaled by the younger dramatist.

In dramas such as these of Shakespeare and of Marlowe the tragedy of a man at odds with fate transcended the accidental circumstance that the protagonist was an English sovereign. But the average type, that in which history was staged epically and continuously, remained high in the popular esteem. Not to go too far afield here in the mention of what can be no more than mere names in a work of this scope, Peele's inferior *Edward I*, 1590–1591, had been of this type; and so was Heywood's *Edward IV*, 1594, a play of no inconsiderable merit and dramatic excellence; Munday and Chettle's *Robin Hood, Earl of Huntington*, 1598, and several like productions. So that when Shakespeare put forth, in 1597, the first part of his *Henry IV*, with its history diversified by the humors of a group of irregular humorists, headed by immortal Falstaff, he was only returning to the epic type of the chronicle play which from the very first had admittted the element of comedy. The popularity of *Henry IV*, with its story of the wild life of Prince Hal, the contrasted heroic Hotspur and witty, godless Falstaff and his rout, took the town by storm, and a second part was almost immediately demanded. To this Shakespeare responded in *2 Henry IV*, and the following year witnessed the conclusion of the trilogy in *Henry V*, England's ideal king in action in triumphant warfare with England's hereditary enemy, France.

In these three dramas we have the height to which the English chronicle play attained. Shakespeare made as much of the undramatic elements of continuous history as was possible and he covered their inherent want of cohesion with his consummate art of portraiture, character thrown into contrast, and with the incessant play of his incomparable humor. The picture of the hero king, Henry V, when all has been said, is one of the most remarkable in Shakespeare. For it is the practical, unimaginative man of action, a conformist at heart despite his youthful escapades, who may be conceived to be the most difficult for the imaginative and poetical mind to appreciate and sympathetically reproduce. But Shakespeare himself was a confident and sagacious man of affairs; and there are no limits to the catholicity of his sympathies and affections. Shakespeare is as present in the stern and inevitable repudiation of Falstaff by the regenerate young king as he is in his revels and those of his pals, royal and common, at the Boar's Head Tavern in Eastcheap.

Falstaff is more frequently mentioned in contemporary allusion than any other character of Shakespeare; and the first part of *Henry IV* (with *Richard III*, for other reasons) reached a larger number of editions within the period of Shakespeare's lifetime than any other one of his plays. This popularity led also to imitation. Four poets in the employ of Henslowe — Munday, Drayton, Wilson the younger and Hathway — set to work on a hurry order to write a rival play and produced two plays on the life of Sir John Oldcastle, under which name Shakespeare seems at first to have figured Sir John Falstaff. Only one of these plays remains extant and it is far from deficient either in humor or dramatic spirit; although, it must be confessed, that the thievish hedge-priest, Sir John of Wrotham, is a petty and futile attempt to rival the unparalleled wit of Falstaff. A tradition relates that, delighted with these plays of *Henry IV*, Queen Elizabeth expressed a wish to see Falstaff depicted in love and that *The Merry Wives of Windsor*, 1598, was Shakespeare's reply. Clever and diverting comedy that it is, it is also notable as the only one of Shakespeare's frankly to accept an English scene. The buffeted and defeated Falstaff of the *Merry Wives* is but a shadow in silhouette in comparison with the robust lover of Doll Tearsheet in 2 *Henry IV*.

Although *Henry VIII* is a chronicle play, consideration

of it may be deferred for the present because of its affiliations, by reason of Fletcher's hand in it, with the later plays of Shakespeare. Of the chronicle play in general it may be sufficient to say that it flourished in great variety of combination with other dramatic elements especially throughout the last ten years of Elizabeth's reign. In tragedy it begot such productions as *Thomas of Woodstock*, 1591, an exceedingly able anonymous play on events in the reign of Richard II which preceded Shakespeare's tragedy of that sovereign; it mingled with drama of domestic type in Heywood's *Edward IV*, with comedy of disguise in *Look About You*, 1594, and the Robin Hood plays of Munday and Chettle; and continued in the dramatic biographies of lesser historical personages such as Sir Thomas More, Cromwell, Stukeley (ranging from 1590 to 1596), and many more. On the death of the queen a series of obituary plays were staged, detailing the principal events of her life, directly as in Heywood's *If You Know Me Not You Know Nobody;* allegorically in Dekker's *Whore of Babylon;* or dealing with the history of her immediate predecessors, as in *Sir Thomas Wyatt*, the scene of which is laid in the reign of Queen Mary; or in Rowley's *When You See Me You Know Me*, which describes events in the reign of Henry VIII. It is best to place Shakespeare's play on this monarch in this group, which falls within the first three years of James, whatever may have been its subsequent history.

Still another variation from the usual type of the chronicle play was that which dealt chronicle wise with the legendary history of England. Among Elizabethan annalists and writers of plays little distinction was drawn between the deeds of Brutus, legendary founder of Britain, Macbeth, and Henry V; for all were fish to the historical drag-nets of the time. *Gorboduc* and *Jocasta* first levied on material of the mythical historical type, although inspired primarily by Seneca. Peele apparently was the first to transfer this species of tragedy to the popular stage in *Locrine*, 1586, and the older *King Leir*, staged about 1594, and perhaps by Lodge, is another example. *The Birth of Merlin*, 1597, by William Rowley and several like productions soon followed. It was this type of drama in its tragic form that Shakespeare soon glorified in *Macbeth* and *King Lear*. The final absorption of the chronicle play was romantic and in this, too, Shakespeare shared in such a play as *Cymbeline*, the scene of which is legendary ancient Britain, although its interest is purely romantic.

In 1598 Francis Meres included in his *Palladis Tamia*, "A Comparative Discourse of our English Poets with the Greek, Latin and Italian Poets," recognizing Shakespeare therein as the greatest dramatist and poet of his day and declaring him "most excellent in both kinds [that is, comedy and tragedy] for the stage." His sonnets, as yet unpublished, his narrative poems, and twelve plays are mentioned by name; and the list includes all the plays named in this chapter except one, *Henry V*, which had not yet been staged. Meres further names a comedy under title of *Love's Labor's Won*. Some have thought this a lost play, others have identified it with *Much Ado About Nothing* or with *All's Well that Ends Well*. If (as still others have surmised), it was an earlier name for the *Taming of the Shrew*, that play, also, may have been among the experiments of Shakespeare in comedy, though its known derivation from two earlier plays, *The Taming of a Shrew* and Gascoigne's *Supposes*, leaves it not improbable that Shakespeare, whatever the period of his work, was only the reviser.

Six comedies of Shakespeare remain above those already mentioned to attest the height of his dramatic genius in this kind of play within the remaining years of Elizabeth's reign. Of these *Much Ado About Nothing* is usually supposed to have been staged soon after the appearance in print of Meres' "comparative discourse." The story of Hero and Claudio was derived by Shakespeare from a novel of Bandello, though probably not without the intervention of an English play. The delightful courtship of Beatrice and Benedick seems an amplification of the relations of Rosaline and Biron in *Love's Labor's Lost*, and in its sheer comedy affords a happy contrast to the somber elements of the major plot of Don John's machinations. Dogberry and Verges, though their originals might well have kept the peace in any hamlet in England, were discernible in all their unmitigated absurdity only by the eye of their creator. Lightsome and joyous *As You Like It*, on the stage by 1599, is an interesting example of Shakespeare's fortunate use of material near at hand. As a rule and especially in his earlier period, the great dramatist preferred the rewriting of a play to any other process. Some twenty of his plays are almost certainly so derived from former dramas, English or foreign. In *As You Like It*, Shakespeare's immediate source was the pleasing pastoral romance of Lodge, known as *Rosalynd or Euphues' Golden Legacy*. In turning Lodge's story into a play Shakespeare amended its Euphuistic manner, which was now a fashion of the past; and while he retained some of the pastoral spirit, he added to it the freshness that pervades the English conception of an out-door life of outlawry contained in the ballads of Robin Hood, and submitted the whole to much delicate raillery. The characters, too, as we compare them with Lodge's originals, are more subtly conceived and cast in a finer mold. Their motives are more elevated and they themselves far less conventionally pastoral. There is no more delightful love-making than that of Orlando and his Rosalind, and when we recall that the melancholy Jaques, Touchstone with all his quips, his Audrey, and other characters are Shakespeare's additions to the tale, we can see how he could better admirable material and make out of a pleasing tale a comedy of unmatchable wit, wisdom, and lyrical beauty.

Twelfth Night or What You Will, 1601, offers a tempting problem to the seekers after sources in which no less than five plays, Italian, Latin, and German, and three stories are involved. Although a good *prima facie* case has been made out for Shakespeare's acquaintance with a Latin comedy called *Lælia*, he doubtless found his chief material in the story of *Apolonius and Silla*, in *Barnabe Riche, his Farewell to the Military Profession*, and Malvolio's pretended madness may have been suggested in another story of the same volume. Once more, if we compare Shakespeare with his sources, we find how immeasurably he has refined his personages and the motives that guide their actions, how he has condensed, leaving out the irrelevant and repetitious, to create a whole group of characters — Malvolio, Sir Toby, Sir Andrew, Maria, and Feste, most fascinating of his clowns — and give coherence to one of the most delectable of his comedies.

What event happened in the life of Shakespeare to produce the revulsion from all that was bright and joyous as depicted in the comedies just enumerated to the more serious themes of *All's Well That Ends Well* and *Measure for Measure* and the gloom and misanthropy of *Troilus and Cressida* we can never know. Perhaps the sonnets — which with the last-named play are equally of the literature of disenchantment — paralleled these weightier dramatic works. Perhaps these were no more than the passing moods that may beget in the musical composer, for example, the composition of a *scherzo* or rhapsody on one day, and on the next a requiem. *All's Well That Ends Well* is commonly dated about 1602, although evidence has been found in the text to indicate that the comedy, as we have it, is the revision of earlier work, perhaps the play named by Meres in 1598 as *Love's Labor's Won*. The story of Helena, the physician's daughter, her cure of the king of France and her pursuit and winning in the end of her recreant husband, all is to be found in *The Palace of Pleasure*, borrowed thence from Bandello. But the Countess of Roussilon, most engaging picture of elderly womanhood, Lafeu the steward, and the cowardly boaster, Parolles, all are of Shakespeare's invention, as is the difficult handling of the character of the heroine in a situation little calculated under ordinary circumstances to inspire our admiration and consent. It has been held that Bertram's base associates, his hesitation, and plain lying in the dénouement (which is Shakespeare's entirely), come "perilously near overshooting the mark" in the effort to enlist our sympathies on the side of Helena; and the play has been more seriously impugned for the coarseness and the daring of Helena's device to trick her husband into her arms. But granting all this, Shakespeare's power over character and plot had not failed him in *All's Well*. Similarly, *Measure for Measure* has been submitted to criticism on the score of its coarseness of detail in certain scenes and for its frank and unhesitating treatment of a subject which modern daintiness affects to ignore.

Measure for Measure contains passages which seem to place its staging after the accession of James in 1603. If we are to judge this powerful and unpleasant play of Shakespeare justly, we must recognize how he has humanized the repellant qualities of Whetstone's *Promos and Cassandra*, his original in the tempted Puritan, Angelo, in peerless and immaculate Isabella, and her weak and erring brother, Claudio.

Among the many problems that the plays of Shakespeare raise, few are more nearly insoluble than those involved in the strange but in no wise inferior "comedy" of *Troilus and Cressida*. The work was registered in 1603, printed in quarto with two different title-pages but identical texts in 1609, and reprinted in the folio with many detailed differences. There are parts of *Troilus and Cressida* which seem the work of another hand, yet there are passages unmistakably Shakespeare's at his best. The tone of the play is not only unheroic but distinctly bitter and satirical at times; and it has been thought by some that in *Troilus and Cressida* we have Shakespeare's contribution to the war of the theaters, of which we shall hear more in the next chapter, and that the gross figure of Ajax is Shakespeare's attack on Ben Jonson. The story of Troilus and the faithless Cressida was a favorite subject not only in the Middle Ages (as Chaucer alone is sufficient to witness), but in the drama preceding Shakespeare. The dramatist may well have caught the spirit that converts the Trojan heroes into medieval knights, shivering lances for fair ladies, and the satirical tone in his treatment of antiquity from some one of the four or five plays on this subject, his predecessors, or from Greene's *Euphues his Censure to Philautus*, as has been surmised. Certain it is that vividly conceived as are Shakespeare's Cressida and Pandarus, bearing comparison with their originals in Chaucer, heroic as is Troilus, subtle and worldly wise as is Ulysses, the effect of this drama is disheartening, for here alone within the range of Shakespeare's dramatic activity do we feel that his faith in man has forsaken him and he has substituted for the nonce doubt, suspicion, and misanthropy for the larger traits of mind and heart that are prevailingly his.

Thus as the reign of the old queen was drawing to its close, we find Shakespeare established in a worldly prosperity and success in his art that drew the eyes of envy and admiration upon him. His thrift extended not only to personal investments in tithes and the purchase for his age of the best house in Stratford; it extended to a prudent foresight as to the future of his company when Elizabeth's successor should come to the throne. There is a well-known topical allusion to the departure of the young and popular Earl of Essex for Ireland in the prologue to the last act of *Henry V;* and a well-authenticated story tells of the acting, by men of Shakespeare's company, of *Richard II* before the conspirators at the time of the Essex rebellion, that their courage might be whetted and an example set them of the deposition of an English sovereign. Plainly Shakespeare looked forward hopefully to the new reign to come. He did more. With his company in disgrace in 1601 for these performances, he made a business alliance with one Laurence Fletcher, an actor who had already taken a troupe to Edinburgh and was known personally to King James; and the upshot of this alliance appeared in the circumstance that, on the accession of the king, the Chamberlain's men (Shakespeare's company), was the first to pass under the royal patronage, becoming the King's players.

But there are other things to contemplate in Shakespeare's rise within the reign of Queen Elizabeth. Without seeking as yet the heights of the greater tragedies, Shakespeare had traveled far from the trivialities of *Love's Labor 's Lost* to the consummate comedy of *Twelfth Night* and *As You Like It.* Books have been written on this absorbing theme; and the development of Shakespeare's genius has been traced in his verse and his style, his rhetoric and his taste, and in the larger influences of his experience and contact with men. Clearly even Shakespeare must once have been an apprentice to his art; and quite as certainly he soon transcended all the tricks and rules of the playwright's trade. An attempt to trace the poetical growth of Marlowe is frustrated at once by the brevity of his meteoric career. On the other hand, Ben Jonson was too much the conscious artist, despite the length of his life, too much the constructive mechanician of his own artistic development, to make it possible for us to observe in him those processes in the unfolding of genius which in their orderliness and their inevitability are as capable of prognostication as the processes of nature. Shakespeare's career as a dramatist was of at least twenty years' continuance. His openness to impressions was that of a field long lain fallow; and, save for certain storms that beset all life, his calm and benignity was that of nature and of the wide heavens. It is here that we can look for natural growth, for development as obvious and rational as the unfolding of a flower. It is not only that Shakespeare was imaginatively and creatively the most richly endowed of mankind; he was happy in suffering fewer lets and hindrances in his development than most men. He did not see life through learned and classical spectacles like Jonson, nor through the kaleidoscopic lenses of Italian romance and allegory as did Spenser. He was not hampered, like Sidney, by the necessity of experimentation in literature; nor led on by speculation to the overturning of the reasoning of a scholastic world like Bacon. It may be confidently affirmed that Shakespeare, better than most writers, yields to that analysis that discloses an orderly growth in all that goes to constitute the outward as well as the spiritual and inward qualities of genius.

And when this analysis is made, we find, to summarize, first a versification trending gradually from a certain degree of regularity and rigidity to the freedom of a master of his craft in the employment of pauses, redundancy, suppression or substitution of syllables, whereby Shakespeare's blank-verse becomes a thoroughly plastic medium in his hands, adaptable, as English verse had never been before, to the thousand moods that constitute the demands of the drama. Secondly, as to Shakespeare's style, we find it characterized by affluence in diction and vocabulary, by a lavish, at times extravagant, use of what he has, and by spontaneity, absolute ease and readiness, and as absolute an unrestraint. Let us take two passages in conclusion of this matter, the first from *A Midsummer-*

Night's Dream, the second (if we may look forward for the moment) from *Cymbeline*.

> These are the forgeries of jealousy:
> And never, since the middle summer's spring,
> Met we on hill, in dale, forest, or mead,
> By pavèd fountain or by rushy brook,
> Or in the beachèd margent of the sea,
> To dance our ringlets to the whistling wind
> But with thy brawls thou hast disturb'd our sport.
> Therefore the winds, piping to us in vain,
> As in revenge, have suck'd up from the sea
> Contagious fogs; which, falling in the land,
> Have every petty river made so proud,
> That they have overborne their continents:
> The ox hath therefore stretch'd his yoke in vain,
> The ploughman lost his sweat; and the green corn
> Hath rotted ere his youth attain'd a beard:
> The fold stands empty in the drownèd field,
> And crows are fatted with the murrain flock;
> The nine-men's morris is fill'd up with mud;
> And the quaint mazes in the wanton green,
> For lack of tread, are undistinguishable:
> The human mortals want their winter cheer;
> No night is now with hymn or carol blest: —
> Therefore the moon, the governess of floods,
> Pale in her anger, washes all the air,
> That rheumatic diseases do abound:
> And thorough this distemperature we see
> The seasons alter: hoary-headed frosts
> Fall in the fresh lap of the crimson rose;
> And on old Hiems' thin and icy crown
> An odorous chaplet of sweet summer buds
> Is, as in mockery, set: the spring, the summer,
> The childing autumn, angry winter, change
> Their wonted liveries; and the mazèd world,
> By their increase, now knows not which is which:
> And this same progeny of evils comes
> From our debate, from our dissension;
> We are their parents and original.

Away! — I do condemn mine ears that have
So long attended thee.   If thou wert honorable,
Thou wouldst have told this tale for virtue, not
For such an end thou seek'st, — as base as strange.
Thou wrong'st a gentleman who is as far
From thy report as thou from honor; and
Solicit'st here a lady that disdains
Thee and the devil alike. — What ho, Pisanio!
The king, my father, shall be made acquainted
Of thy assault: if he shall think it fit,
A saucy stranger in his court, to mart
As in a Romish stew, and to expound
His beastly mind to us, — he hath a court
He little cares for, and a daughter who
He not respects at all. — What ho, Pisanio!

In the former of these quotations it matters little that the embroidery runs a little less or more amply.   In Imogen's strong defiance of a treachery that only her innocence has made her dull to perceive, there is not a word too much.   Shakespeare seldom errs with a display of luxuriance in these supreme dramatic moments; but full restraint, like much else, came, even with Shakespeare, after years and trial.

Other things that mark the development of Shakespeare's genius concern his gradual improvement in taste, in dramatic technique, characterization, and in the attitude that he assumes towards the creatures of his brain.   Shakespeare never entirely freed himself of the tyranny of the word.   His age seems never to have wearied of puns, and verbal fence and quibble.   On the other hand and barring this, with time came power and grasp.   And nowhere in our literature is there to be found a more marvelous display of the ductility, the subtle music, the significance and associative force of English words, than these plays disclose in their finer passages.

This chapter has already exceeded its bounds.   To another, that on the heyday of tragedy, must be deferred the further discussion of Shakespeare's development in the dramatic technique and larger qualities of his art.

CHAPTER X

VERNACULAR DRAMA OF DEKKER, HEYWOOD, AND MIDDLETON

AS compared with that of Elizabeth, few ages in the world's history have accepted with such unaffected faith at once the hard inevitability of facts and the enchanting possibilities of fortune. And in few times was life in the coarse fiber of its daily routine so shot with bright threads of romantic experience and adventure. It is related that the queen, who had ardently expressed to the Scottish ambassador, Melville, her wish that she might see and speak with her dear sister, Queen Mary, was taken with Melville's proposal that, dressed as a page, her majesty accompany his train to Scotland; and that she dallied with the idea for days. As to the stage, so peculiarly the mirror of the time, few sorts of Elizabethan thought and action were left unrepresented thereon; and that representation, as often as not, mingled with what was familiar and at hand, things rare and strange, recognizing that the separation of these two, the visible and the invisible, the actual and the ideal, is more a habit of thinking than it is ever a feature of life itself.

It was this combination of a recognition of the actualities of life with a fine romantic spirit that raised the eclectic and somewhat slovenly art of Greene to a position of respect; and in Dekker, Greene's successor in certain forms of the drama as well as in the pamphlet, we find no dissimilar combination Of the life and extraction of Thomas Dekker little is known. He informs us in one of his pamphlets that he was born in London. Probably this was not far from 1570. The form of his name and his evident familiarity with the Dutch language suggest that his family came originally from the Low Countries. Dekker first appears as a dramatist in 1598, though it is not unlikely that by that time he had been for several years conversant with the stage. He continued to write plays, pamphlets, broadsides, anything, for forty years, and at one time prepared pageants for the city. Dekker's life was full of struggle and toil, he was much in prison for debt and received charity at the hands of Edward Alleyn, the actor. In the drama Dekker exhibits an art as mixed and varied as that of Greene himself. As to subject and general conduct, Dekker is governed almost completely by the taste and demands of the city, even though he rises occasionally into the regions of the truest poetry as in passages of *Old Fortunatus*. This comedy was on the stage by 1599. In plot it levies, as *Faustus* did before it, on the old romantic folk-lore of Germany; although Dekker also contrives to give to the whole that flavor of the English morality which we find so strong in Marlowe's tragedy. The story of Dekker's comedy deals with Fortunatus, an elderly native of Cyprus, who receives at the hands of the goddess of fortune the gift of an inexhaustible purse and steals from "the Soudan of Babylon" a cap which has the power to convey the wearer wherever he may desire. Fortunatus soon dies in his folly — for he has chosen wealth when he might have had better things — and the play proceeds to set forth the contrasted careers of his two sons, Ampedo, who is virtue, ignorant how practically to employ Fortune, and Andelocia, who lavishes her gifts in self-indulgence and vice. The extant version of *Old Fortunatus* has been adapted for court. This explains why Dekker has so lavished on it his delicate fancy and a power of poetical expression that will compare favorably with the best of his fellows in the drama. Of several beautiful lyrics that this play contains, none is more musical than the song contrasting Vice with Virtue:

> Virtue's branches wither, Virtue pines,
>   O pity, pity, and alack the time,
> Vice doth flourish, Vice in glory shines,
>   Her gilded boughs above the cedar climb.
> Vice hath golden cheeks, O pity, pity,
>   She in every land doth monarchize.

> Virtue is exiled from every city,
> Virtue is a fool, Vice only wise.
> O pity, pity, Virtue weeping dies:
> Vice laughs to see her faint; — alack the time.
> This sinks; with painted wings the other flies:
> Alack that best should fall, and bad should climb.
> O pity, pity, pity, mourn, not sing,
> Vice is a saint, Virtue an underling.
> Vice doth flourish, Vice in glory shines,
> Virtue's branches wither, Virtue pines.

At the conclusion of the comedy, the palm of victory is awarded to Virtue, who now turns to the queen with the words:

> All that they had or mortal men can have,
> Sends only but a shadow from the grave.
> Virtue alone still lives, and lives in you;
> I am a counterfeit, you are the true;
> I am a shadow; at your feet I fall,
> Begging for these, and these, myself and all.
> All these that thus do kneel before your eyes
> Are shadows like myself: dread Nymph, it lies
> In you to make us substance.

In *The Shoemakers' Holiday*, 1600, we have, as typically as delightfully, the bourgeois spirit of Elizabethan London. The disguise of high-born Lacy as a shoemaker's apprentice to win the love of Rose who is only a lord mayor's daughter; the faithful wife, Jane, who foils her rich and persistent suitor in her faith in the return of her cobbler husband, Ralph, who has been impressed for the wars; above all, the humors of Simon Eyre among his journeymen and apprentices, prince as he is of shoemakers and good fellows, with his elevation to the mayoralty and the friendship of his king — such is the subject-matter of this busy, delightful comedy, borrowed and bettered as it is from one of the prose tales of Thomas Deloney. *The Shoemakers' Holiday* is typical of one of the happiest groups of the comedy of contemporary life. Dekker presents the life about him frankly, merrily, and roundly, seeking neither the lesson of the moralist nor the distortion of him who scorns and satirizes. There were other Elizabethan examples of this type of comedy, such as the anonymous *Wily Beguiled*, Henry Porter's lively *Two Angry Women of Abington*, and William Haughton's *Englishmen for My Money*. Shakespeare's *Merry Wives of Windsor*, too, is of this type; and all were on the stage by 1598 and hence preceded Dekker's shoemakers. Another favorable specimen of lighter comedy is *The Merry Devil of Edmonton*, 1600, which has been ascribed to the authorship of Drayton and touches the supernatural in its introduction of the English Faustus, Peter Fabel. Indeed, should we seek for the roots of this sort of play, we should find them deep in morality times when the picturing of familiar everyday life on the stage rose into popularity as a means of enlivening the serious intent of the old drama to teach right living.

Dekker was much given to the practice of collaboration and wrote plays with at least half a dozen other authors. Such a play was *Patient Grissel*, 1598, in which Chettle and Haughton both had a share with Dekker. This dramatizing of a medieval story of the slavishly devoted wife, long since told by Chaucer, brings Dekker into touch — as does the story of Jane for that matter in *The Shoemakers' Holiday* — with a long series of domestic dramas in which the virtues of the faithful wife are set forth and extolled. This universal theme exhibits itself in almost every conceivable form in Elizabethan drama, in tragedy as well as comedy, in foreign as well as in English setting, now throwing into contrast the jealous or neglectful husband or exacting lover, and again placing beside the faithful wife the wanton or her less malignant contrast, the shrew. Between 1602 and 1607 some half-dozen dramas combine the subject of the faithful wife with that of the young spendthrift, for such *How a Man May Choose a Good Wife from a Bad*, by Joshua Cooke, the anonymous *London Prodigal*, Wilkins' *Miseries of Enforced Marriage*, and Marston's *Dutch Courtezan*, their very titles proclaim them. Of equally early origin in the drama are the lighter comedies of this class which throw into prominence the nature of the "shrew," beginning. as they do, with *The Taming of a Shrew*, before 1590, which Shakespeare revised in his *Taming of the Shrew*, later answered by Fletcher in *The Woman's Prize or the Tamer Tamed*, which may date as early as 1606. This story of the taming of Petruchio by a second wife who followed poor Katherine, who had become too tame to live long, enjoyed great popularity in the reign of King Charles, when it was often acted on alternate nights with Shakespeare's comedy. In *The Honest Whore*, printed in two parts, 1604 and 1630, Dekker collaborated with Middleton. Here the themes of the shrew and the submissive and virtuous wife are united in a new aspect into a serious drama which, save for one or two of Heywood's, rises well above the best of its class. Here is told the story of a fallen woman's regeneration by means of a passion inspired in her by one who takes her passing fancy but withstands her blandishments. And herein also is displayed in vivid realism her steadfastness in virtue when temptation returns to her at the hands of this very man, and she is compelled to endure want and ignominy for her refusal to return to a life of sin. The figure of Bellafront is admirably conceived and executed and remains, with that of Signor Frescobaldo her old father, who in disguise as her servant sustains her in her struggle to lead a virtuous life, the most effective and touching piece of character drawing in which Dekker had a hand.

Quotation in patch and fragment is always unsatisfactory, but never more so than when it seeks to suggest the large lines of a finished picture. Frescobaldo has long disowned his dishonored daughter and, assuming an air of hearty content, declares: "Though my head be like a leek, white, may not my heart be like the blade, green?" He continues:

May not old Frescobaldo, my Lord, be merry now, ha? I have a little, have all things, have nothing: I have no wife, I have no child, have no chick, and why should not I be in my jocundare?
Hipolito. Is your wife then departed?
Fresco. She's an old dweller in those high countries: yet not from me. Here, she 's here; a good couple are seldom parted.
Hipolito. You had a daughter too, sir, had you not?
Fresco. Oh, my Lord! this old tree had one branch, and but one branch growing out of it: it was young, it was fair, it was straight: I pruned it daily, drest it carefully, kept it from the wind, helped it

to the sun; yet for all my skill in planting, it grew crooked, it bore crabs: I hewed it down. What 's become of it, I neither know nor care.

Told that Bellafront is dead, he cries:

Dead! My last and best peace go with her! I see Death 's a good trencherman; he can eat coarse, homely meat as well as the daintiest. Is she dead?

Hipolito. She 's turned to earth.

Fresco. Would she were turned to heaven. Umh! Is she dead? I am glad the world has lost one of his idols . . . . In her grave sleep all my shame and her own: and all my sorrow and all her sin.

Hipolito. I 'm glad you are wax, not marble.

But later, undeceived and assured that Bellafront is not really dead, but poor, and her husband, who had first betrayed her, in jail for the killing of a man, Frescobaldo breaks out once more against his daughter, declaring:

I am sorry I wasted tears upon a harlot, ... I detest her, I defy both, she is not mine, she 's —

Hipolito. Hear her but speak.

Fresco. I love no mermaids. I 'll not be caught with a quail-pipe.

Hipolito. You 're now beyond all reason. Is 't dotage to relieve your child, being poor?

Fresco. 'T is foolery to relieve her. Were her cold limbs stretched out upon a bier, I would not sell this dirt under my nails to buy her an hour's breath nor give this hair, unless it were to choke her.

Hipolito. Fare you well, for I 'll trouble you no more.

Exit Hipolito.

Fresco. And fare you well, sir. Go thy ways; we have few lords of thy making that love wenches for their honesty. 'Las, my girl, art thou poor? Poverty dwells next door to despair; there 's but a wall between them. Despair is one of Hell's catchpoles; and lest that devil arrest her, I 'll to her. Yet she shall not know me. She shall drink of my wealth as beggars do of running water, freely, yet never know from what fountain's head it flows. Shall a silly bird pick her own breast to nourish her young ones: and can a father see his child starve? That were hard, the pelican does it, and shall not I?

Turning from Dekker, whose other plays from their affiliations in authorship and subject may be best considered elsewhere, we find in Heywood even a closer representative in the drama of the ideals of the city and of its preference for homely and domestic subjects. Thomas Heywood came of Lincolnshire and was both younger and somewhat better born than Dekker. Heywood's birth was about 1575. He was sometime fellow of Peterhouse, Cambridge, and, judged by his use of the classics, a good scholar. He became an actor about 1596, covenanting not to act for any other company save Henslowe's. He appears, however, both to have acted and written for several companies of players. Heywood was altogether the most fertile among the old dramatists, declaring himself that he was concerned, in whole or in part, with the composition of two hundred and twenty plays. Of these some thirty-five alone have survived; and their author interested himself as little as did Shakespeare in the preservation or publication of any of them. Like Dekker and Middleton after him, Heywood furnished pageants for the city; and he contributed largely in his later years to pamphlet literature. The two chronicle plays of Heywood have already received the brief mention which their relative merits deserve. The bias of Heywood's dramatic art towards domestic drama is patent in both these plays, *Edward IV* turning chiefly on that sovereign's relations to Mistress Jane Shore and her unhappy story, *If You Know Not Me*, lugging in much biographical matter concerning Sir Thomas Gresham and a somewhat apocryphal nephew of his to eke out the account, by way of obituary in 1604, of "the troubles of Queen Elizabeth." It is likely that between these two chronicle histories and about 1596, Heywood made his strange adventure into classical story, dramatizing ancient mythology as he found it in Ovid, the *Iliad*, and elsewhere. The novelty of this departure was justified by its success; for *The Golden, Silver, Brazen* and *Iron Ages*, as the published titles ran, comprise no less than five plays of disjointed and heterogeneous material, astonishingly well done when the conditions are considered. Another early venture of Heywood's links on to the heroical dramas such as Greene's *Orlando Furioso, Charlemagne*, and *The Thracian Wonder*. But here, as in the histories, the taste of the London citizen and his credulity as to romantic marvels ruled to produce, in *The Four Prentices of London*, a preposterous combination of knightly adventure with a glorification of civic pride. It was the absurdities of these London "prentices," sons to "the old Earl of Bulloigne," and the impossible adventures by means of which each carved out for himself a kingdom, that Beaumont later ridiculed in his noteworthy dramatic burlesque, *The Knight of the Burning Pestle*, 1607. But the citizens preferred their *Prentices*, and Beaumont's clever satire remained to be appreciated by a later and a more sophisticated generation.

However, the strength of Heywood lay not in these experiments. He contributed an admirable play to the series which contrasts the faithful wife with the prodigal son in *The Wise Woman of Hogsdon*, doubtless acted about 1604. And if he is the author of *The Fair Maid of the Exchange*, he added, in the valiant cripple of Fenchurch, a new and interesting figure to the drama. *A Woman Killed with Kindness*, first published in 1607, is Heywood's most distinctive work. In it two situations of ordinary domestic life are interwoven into a plot less straggling and careless than is usual with this author. I can not find these situations so improbable and contrary to experience as some of late have found them. A sister's honor offered in barter for the satisfaction of a supposed debt of honor incurred to an enemy, the seduction by an ingrate of his benefactor's wife, a woman of seeming sense and virtue, surely such are not situations of "naive unreality." This last, indeed, with its attendant plight of an honorable man, wronged by the woman he continues to love but with feelings chastened by the offense which he abhors, is Heywood's favorite situation. It is the story of Jane Shore, her honorable husband, and the king in *Edward IV;* of Frankford, his wife, and her betrayer in *A Woman Killed with Kindness;* and of Winifred, Young Geraldine, and his faithless friend in *The English Traveler*, a play of later date. In the supreme scene of *A Woman Killed with Kindness*, when, having suffered her paramour to escape, Frankford, the wronged husband, con-

fronts his guilty wife who has fallen groveling at his feet, we
have the following dialogue:

Mistress Frankford. Oh, by what word, what title, or what name,
Shall I entreat your pardon? Pardon! oh!
I am as far from hoping such sweet grace
As Lucifer from heaven. To call you husband —
O me, most wretched! I have lost that name,
I am no more your wife.

.   .   .   .

Frankford. Spare thou thy tears, for I will weep for thee:
And keep thy countenance, for I 'll blush for thee.
Now I protest, I think 't is I am tainted,
For I am most ashamed; and 't is more hard
For me to look upon thy guilty face,
Than on the sun's clear brow. What would'st thou speak?
Mist. Frank. I would I had no tongue, no ears, no eyes,
No apprehension, no capacity.
When do you spurn me like a dog? when tread me
Under your feet? when drag me by the hair?
Though I deserve a thousand thousand fold
More than you can inflict: yet, once my husband,
For womanhood, to which I am a shame,
Though once an ornament — even for his sake
That hath redeemed our souls, mark not my face,
Nor hack me with your sword; but let me go
Perfect and undeformèd to my tomb.

.   .   .   .

Frank. My God, with patience arm me! Rise, nay, rise,
.   .   .   .   . O Nan! O Nan!
If neither fear of shame, regard of honor,
The blemish of my house, nor my dear love
Could have withheld thee from so lewd a fact,
Yet for these infants, these young harmless souls,
On whose white brows thy shame is charactered,
And grows in greatness as they wax in years, —
Look but on them, and melt away in tears.
Away with them! lest, as her spotted body
Hath stained their names with stripe of bastardy,
So her adulterous breath may blast their spirits
With her infectious thoughts. Away with them.
Mist. Frank. In this one life I die ten thousand deaths.

And the scene ends with the husband's solemnly declared decision to banish his wife from his sight and that of their children forever, and to leave her, with every creature comfort about her, absolutely an exile from his life and love.

Such was not the usual fate, we may feel sure, of culprits like Mistress Frankford, who sufficiently declares her expectation of the customary brutal justice of the time. Heywood was a novel moralist for his age and preached — shall we call them without offense — the bourgeois virtues of charity, restraint, and self-control, alive to the superior quality of human pathos over mere terror and revenge. It is this directness, honesty, and the homely pathos that Heywood employs in the treatment of situations, such as these that caused that rare critic of our old drama, Charles Lamb, to dub him with no extravagance of phrase, a "prose Shakespeare," and to remark on his utter carelessness as to the preservation or publicity of his plays: "Posterity is bound to take care that a writer lose nothing by such a noble modesty." In his later and lesser plays: in *The Fair Maid of the West*, 1603, breezy comedy of adventure that it is; in *Fortune by Land and Sea*, 1607, which he wrote with Rowley; in the intrigue, classically derived, of *The Captives* (of doubtful date); even in the later *Challenge for Beauty* and *Royal King and Loyal Subject*, influenced as both of these last were by the new romantic sentimentality of Fletcher, we find ever recurring in Heywood's plays a charming unaffectedness of manner and a pathos that is born only of a true humanity of heart. Heywood long survived most of his fellow-dramatists, dying, it is believed, as late as 1648.

In estimating the value of literary work such as that of Dekker and Heywood, whatever the demands of absolute criticism, we can not but take into consideration the conditions under which much of that work was done. The little we know of Dekker spells improvidence and its consequent privation and suffering. The bookseller, Kirkman, relates of Heywood that he wrote something every day, filling at times the backs of tavern bills or other chance scraps of paper with his notes and scribblings: a sufficient glimpse into the Bohemianism of that playwright's surroundings. Both Heywood and Dekker lived for years in a kind of bondage (shared by many of their fellows) to Philip Henslowe, pawnbroker, manager, and exploiter of the theater; for, whatever the lack of specific proofs, there seems little reason to make out that a vulgar, illiterate man, who grew rich on the labor that kept others in beggary, was really a beneficent friend to actors and playwrights and an enlightened encourager of the drama. Fortunately for the modern historian of the drama, Henslowe kept a species of general memorandum and account book in which he recorded day by day his dealings with plays and playwrights. This work is known as *Henslowe's Diary.* It is still preserved in Dulwich College which was founded by Edward Alleyn, the actor, Henslowe's son-in-law, with money inherited at least in part from Henslowe. *Henslowe's Diary* has been published more than once and of late carefully edited and annotated,[1] so that we have, now easily at hand, much information as to the theatrical business of Elizabeth's day, at least so far as it was conducted by the most successful and aggressive of the rivals of Shakespeare.

Henslowe's Diary, the entries of which lie between 1592 and 1614, contains references by name to nearly every popular dramatist of his immediate time; and the signatures of a number of them appear subscribed to agreements, obligations, and other papers. Neither Shakespeare's name, nor Beaumont's, nor Fletcher's, appears in *Henslowe;* for the obvious reason, his dealings were not with them. But aside from Dekker and Heywood, the lesser names of Munday, Chettle, Haughton, Hathway, Drayton, Wilson, and others of the popular school recur again and again in his pages, attached not only to plays which remain to disclose the nature of the wares in which Henslowe dealt, but to many more which time has happily suffered to perish. Other men, some of them among the greatest in later times, began in apprenticeship to Henslowe and worked out into a larger field and a greater independence. Such were Middleton, Chapman, Marston, Webster, and Jonson, each one of whom devised, wrote, and mended plays for

[1] See the ed. by W. W. Greg, 1904–1908.

Henslowe, received advances in earnest for his promises, accepted obligations, and was bailed by him, on occasion, out of the debtors' prison. In the *Diary* may be found memoranda of Henslowe's returns from the several theaters — the Rose, the Swan, the Fortune and the playhouse at Newington — in which he was at various times interested; his expenditures for various companies — the Earl of Sussex's, Lord Strange's, the Queen's, and the Admiral's men; his loans to playwrights and agreements with actors, advances of money to property makers and costumers; and a large number of letters, more or less concerned with dramatic affairs. From these pages we learn that a new play cost Henslowe from six to eight pounds sterling, and that the price of plays more than doubled before the end of his life in 1616. With due allowance for the difference in the purchasing value of money, it is difficult to imagine how the dramatic writers of the day contrived to make even a modest living out of their vocation. This alone is enough to explain why they so frequently turned to acting, to pamphleteering, to pageant making, and such patronage as might be secured; and this is why the only men who acquired a competence out of their traffic with the stage were Alleyn, Burbage, and Shakespeare, each one of whom was a manager as well as an actor. Before we leave *Henslowe's Diary* one caution is necessary to the unwary. The picture which this book of accounts discloses is less an example of what we may assume to have been likewise the conditions of Shakespeare's authorship than a contrast of those conditions. Henslowe was a shrewd man of business who built theaters where and when they were wanted, catered to the taste of the moment, and exploited art and, in exploiting it, degraded it as his kind always does. The management of Shakespeare's company is not to be conceived as in every way ideal. Shakespeare and Burbage, too, were men of business; but each was possessed of the artist's temperament which admits the existence of ideals even if it does not always follow, much less attain them. Happily Shakespeare's age, with all its materialism, retained the Renaissance recognition and worship of art, and hence with his three or four companies and a score of poets, with readiness to do anything in art or in business that might be conceived of as popularly demanded, Henslowe battled for years in vain for leadership over the Chamberlain's men who employed, besides Shakespeare, not more than two or three other poets, and enjoyed some eighty per cent of the patronage of the court.

A long and forbidding group of domestic dramas are those most simply denominated the murder plays. They deal, for the most part, with actual tragedies frequently of recent occurrence, and may be regarded as among the productions of our old drama that performed one of the most popular functions of the modern newspaper. A larger proportion of plays of this class than of some others have perished and there is no need here to chronicle their forgotten titles. The first murder play in point of time that remains extant is *Arden of Feversham;* and it is, by universal consent, conceded to be the finest example of its type. *Arden* was in print by 1592, and has by some been dated back to a time prior to the Armada. The story is that of the sordid murder, after several abortive attempts, of Arden by his unfaithful wife, Alice, and her paramour, a base serving-man named Mosbie. The source in Holinshed is followed with close fidelity, and little attempt is made to order the material artfully, much less to ennoble the subject by flights of poetry or depths of moralizing. The force of the tragedy lies in its simple and vivid realism, in the unrelenting faithfulness with which the unknown author has contrived to produce an artistic effect by representing the blind infatuation of Arden's wife for a worthless, menial coward, and the weakness and fatalism of the husband's own nature, until inevitable tragedy overtakes all. In its robust and vigorous kind, it is not possible to find the equal among English plays of *Arden of Feversham;* and this excellence has led to the opinion — held by no less an authority than the late Mr. Swinburne — that we have in this tragedy early dramatic work of Shakespeare's. "Ease and restraint of style," a mastery of humor and irony, and a depth of insight into character and motive, these are some of the qualities indubitably possessed by the author of *Arden of Feversham.*

And all of these are Shakespeare's, if we judge him at large and especially in his later work. But Shakespeare was no such master of these maturer qualities of his art in 1590; and it is difficult to conceive of the unrestrained and poetical pen that wrote *Romeo and Juliet*, as capable of disclosing simultaneously the controlled, if coarser, art of *Arden of Feversham*. Thomas Kyd is much the likelier guess. Whoever the author of this remarkable play, the suggestion of an indigenous tragedy of everyday life, raised to a grade of artistic success and permanence less by the graces of poetry than by the force of uncompromising realism, was not realized in subsequent dramas of the type.

Among minor murder plays may be named *A Warning for Fair Women*, 1598, "containing the most tragical and lamentable murder of Master George Sanders of London, nigh Shooter's Hill, consented unto by his wife," and *Two Tragedies in One*, 1599, in which the contemporary killing of one Beech, a chandler in Thames Street, is detailed with a crude and rigid respect for the letter. A more important murder play is the one-act *Yorkshire Tragedy*, 1605, wherein the story of a young and well-born murderer, named Calverley, was placed on the boards while the matter was as yet fresh in the memories of the auditors, and in a kind of continuance of Wilkins' *Miseries of Enforced Marriage*, 1605, a domestic play already mentioned. The "Shakespearean manner" discovered by some in this brief dramatic sketch is due doubtless to a more or less successful imitation of the superficialities of the master's style rather than to any closer contact with him. It is fair, however, to add that *The Yorkshire Tragedy* was acted by the King's company. But Shakespeare was not its only poet. The later scattering murder plays of this bourgeois type fall beyond the period with which this book is concerned.

In the comedies that have thus far been described in this chapter and in the more serious plays, to a certain extent as well, the attitude of the author has been that of the simple chronicler of what he sees before him, except for the tinge of romance that enters into productions like *The Four Prentices of London, Old Fortunatus,* or *The Merry Devil of Edmonton.* This in general is the attitude of Heywood, and of Dekker in his earlier works. There is, however, another and very different aspect in which life may be presented successfully on the stage, and that is the satirical. In this method of presentation the thing seen is not nearly so important as the effect to be produced on the beholder; the essentials of life hold no such place as its conventions and accidental superficialities. In a word, with the advent of satire the drama becomes conscious. Sometimes the satirical dramatist is a moralist as we shall find in Jonson. At others, as in Middleton, he stops short of any intention to teach or improve, content with the mere transcript of life in its comic, contradictory, and scandalous departures from custom and convention.

Thomas Middleton was born in 1570 and received his education at Cambridge and Gray's Inn. His work, despite much coarseness, discloses a better bred man than either Dekker or Heywood; but his career differs little from theirs in the variety of his contributions to the drama, to civic pageantry, and to pamphleteering. The earliest plays of Middleton were written in conjunction with Munday, Dekker, or Webster in the workhouse of Henslowe, and they comprise refashionings of older plays of the chronicle type, such as *The Mayor of Queenborough,* 1597, and an *Entertainment to King James,* which he wrote with Dekker in 1604. Middleton later frequently collaborated with William Rowley, and some excellent work was the result. For the present we are concerned with Middleton's comedies of London life and manners which he wrote, for the most part, between 1604 and 1614. These begin in *Michaelmas Term* (which equals the modern phrase, London in the season, though it deals with a different grade of life), and extend through *A Trick to Catch the Old One, A Mad World my Masters, Your Five Gallants* to *A Chaste Maid in Cheapside* and *No Wit no Help Like a Woman's.* These titles are themselves descriptive of the subject-matter of these comedies and this enumeration by no means exhausts the list. In Middleton's comedies recur again and again the young spendthrift, going the pace, eternal

darling of those that delight in the theater; the usurious
money-lender whom we laugh to see hoist with his own petard;
uncles and fathers duped, trusting maids deceived but ever
faithful; braggarts beaten; fools despoiled and abused; and
wit forever triumphant. Middleton's intention, in a word,
was the presentation on the stage of a witty and satirical picture
of contemporary London life. He avoided any attempt at
romance, such as Greene and Dekker were prone to, and he
escaped the moralist's attitude of Jonson as well. Middleton's
search was not for the charm of the unusual, and he had no
uncommon insight into common things; nor did he, on the
other hand, paint his world to show how wicked it was. His
words might have been: "This is the London of my day;
come, let us laugh about it"; and, having amused you with
the truth as he saw it, he has done all. In the accomplishment of this result Middleton employed not only a discerning
eye and a wide if superficial experience in life, but the constructive arts of a consummate dramatist and a ready, fluent
style, in all respects adequate to his purpose. Middleton is
the truest of realists, but he is commonly disappointing; not
that we expect poetry here — it belongs little to his subjects
— but that there is a worldliness about him, a willingness to
extenuate moral turpitude and explain away moral upright-
ness that, however it be justified by human experience at
times, is displeasing in art.

This careless, witty, conscienceless, satirical comedy
became the most prevalent of its time and was imitated by
several of Middleton's contemporaries, whose ideas of life
were sounder than his own. Thus Dekker in collaboration
with John Webster (later to make so great a name in romantic
tragedy) wrote, between 1603 and 1606, two plays, *Westward
Hoe* and *Northward Hoe*, that mark the very depths of the
gross and vicious realism to which the comedy of the day occasionally descended: and lesser imitations, among which
David, Lord Barry's one comedy, *Ram Alley*, 1609, and Na-
than Field's *Woman is a Weathercock* and *Amends for Ladies*,
both 1611, are the best, followed in quick succession. Even
when plays were not wholly given up to this mode of comedy,

when the romantic ruled or their scene was translated to outlandish countries, an under plot or episode frequently maintained the favorite satirical picture of contemporary manners which no veil of Italian lawn nor Spanish domino could entirely disguise.

When all has been said, however, the greatest of the disciples of Middleton in the comedy of manners was John Fletcher, a dramatist destined to outstrip him in the multiplicity of his gifts, and this notwithstanding the fact that there is a greater Middleton than the Middleton of the comedy of manners. The best of Fletcher's comedies of London life, to which we shall return later in this book, only glorify, by means of a somewhat finer perception of its possibilities, the kind of drama that Middleton had rendered by his talents popular on the stage.

But, as already suggested, Middleton's dramatic activity was not confined to comedies of manners. The earliest play with which his name has been associated, *The Mayor of Queenborough*, 1597, is a chronicle history converted into a romantic drama; and *The Old Law*, 1599, a capital farce on what in our contemporary phrase we denominate "Oslerism"; *Blurt, Master Constable*, 1601, and *The Phœnix*, both have a like romantic cast. William Rowley, with whom Middleton was associated in many plays, was an actor as well as a playwright. Rowley was likewise the author of several pamphlets of the type made popular by Greene and Dekker, among which *A Search for Money*, 1609, descriptive of the low life of the city, is typical. In 1607 we find Rowley in collaboration with Day and Wilkins in the composition of a formless production for the stage called *The Travails of Three English Brothers;* and it is not unlikely that Rowley's unaided effort, *A Shoemaker a Gentleman*, followed within two or three years. This vigorous comedy is, like *The Four Prentices* of Heywood, a direct appeal to the bourgeois prejudices of the citizens of London; for therein is told of the apprenticeship of a Roman prince, Crispianus, to a London shoemaker and of much else, familiar as well as heroic and strange. At what time Rowley rewrote an earlier play, *Uter Pendragon*, into *The Birth of*

Merlin, first published in 1662 as "by Shakespeare and Rowley," it would be difficult to say. This play, like *The Shoemaker*, is far from devoid of merit, and though coarse to an extreme in parts, is characterized by a certain honesty of purpose and command of boisterous humor that give Rowley his place. Rowley's greatest drama, the tragedy *All's Lost by Lust*, belongs to a period beyond the limits of this book. His association as a collaborator with Middleton began about 1614 by the temporary union of the companies for which each had been previously writing and continued until the death of Middleton in 1627. The most noteworthy products of this joint authorship, *The Spanish Gipsy* and *The Changeling* (by all odds the greatest play in which Middleton had a hand), also fall beyond us. But in the very year of the death of Shakespeare these two playwrights produced *A Fair Quarrel*, raising and disposing of an interesting question in an age of dueling: dare a man fight in a quarrel unless he believes that he defends the truth? The Elizabethan age had its problems as we have ours. *The Honest Whore, A Woman Killed with Kindness, A Fair Quarrel*, are problem plays in the Elizabethan sense. This last is a fine serious drama of its class and deserves, in its virile directness, the praise that is evoked from Charles Lamb in contrast to "the inspid levelling morality" to which the modern stage of Lamb's time, if not of ours, was tied. "A Puritanical obtuseness of sentiment," continues the critic, "a stupid infantile goodness, is creeping among us instead of the vigorous passions, and virtues clad in flesh and blood, with which the old dramatists present us. Those noble and liberal casuists could discern in the differences, the quarrels, the animosities of man, a beauty and truth of moral feeling, no less than in the iterately inculcated duties of forgiveness and atonement. . . . To know the boundaries of honor, to be judiciously valiant, to have a temperance which shall beget a smoothness in the angry swellings of youth, to esteem life as nothing when the sacred reputation of a parent is to be defended, yet to shake and tremble under a pious cowardice when that ark of an honest confidence is found to be frail and tottering, to feel the true blows of a real disgrace blunting that sword which the imaginery strokes of a supposed false imputation had put so keen an edge upon but lately: to do, or to imagine this done in a feigned story, asks something more of a moral sense, somewhat a greater delicacy of perception in questions of right and wrong, than goes to the writing of two or three hackneyed sentences about the laws of honor as opposed to the laws of the land, or a commonplace against duelling." The main plot of *A Fair Quarrel* is alone enough to atone for all the moral lapses of Middleton's comedies of manners. To what degree the ruder but more generous nature of Rowley was responsible for the success of this excellent drama we need not here inquire.

Any further pursuit of the comedy of manners would lead us either into a wider consideration of Fletcher or into a contrast with the Jonsonian comedy of humors. Both topics will be best treated below. In the vernacular domestic drama discussed in this chapter, whether it display itself in the direct realism of Dekker, the homely pathos of Heywood, or the flippant actualism of Middleton, we may realize better than in the contemplation of the drama in its higher types how truly of the people the Elizabethan dramatists were. This is not where the poetry and the ideality of Elizabethan literature reside, but where a vigorous part of its truth is to be found: and art ceases to be art alike when tethered hand and foot to the actualities of the mundane world or when those bonds are wholly burst to leave it a disembodied ghost at the mercy of every unbeliever's incredulity.

CHAPTER XI

LATER ANTHOLOGIES AND LYRICS TO BE SET TO MUSIC

The miscellany made up of the work of several authors continued to be the accepted mode of publishing lyrical verse; and in most cases the fiction at least of reluctance on the part of the author to appear in print was sedulously maintained. *Britton's Bower of Delight*, 1591, was a pirated collection, trading on the well-known name of Nicholas Breton and including other work besides his own. *The Phœnix' Nest*, edited in 1593 by one "R. S. of the Inner Temple," whose identity is unrecoverable, contains much of the best poetry of Lodge as well as more of Breton; and *The Passionate Pilgrim*, 1599, is made up of poetry piratically culled from still more recent poets who were attracting the public eye. It is in this last anthology that Marlowe's "Come live with me" was first printed, besides two important sonnets of Shakespeare. And it was in *The Passionate Pilgrim* that several fine poems of Richard Barnfield (chief among them "As it fell upon a day") were attributed to Shakespeare, to cling to his name, despite proof to the contrary, and be often reprinted as his. *England's Helicon*, the richest of Elizabethan miscellanies, was published by John Bodenham, a general collector and editor, in 1600. The poetry that it gathered belonged to a somewhat earlier period than that of publication, so that it really precedes *The Passionate Pilgrim* as to the authors that it represents. Spenser, Sidney, Constable, Breton, Lodge, and Peele are the familiar names most frequently recurring in *England's Helicon*; and there is still about its many graceful Italianate poems not a little affectation of shepherds and shepherdesses. We may omit here more than a mention of certain irregular collections such as the several poems on the theme of "The Phœnix and the Turtle," including work by Shakespeare, Jonson,

Marston, and Chapman, affixed to that somewhat mysterious publication known as Chester's *Love's Martyr*, 1601; and mere gatherings of extracts like *Belvedere* (later called *The Garden of the Muses*) and *England's Parnassus*, both 1600. And it is unnecessary for us to be misled into confusing the fanciful titles which individual poets gave at times to their works — Munday's *Banquet of Dainty Conceits* or Breton's *Arbor of Amorous Devices* — with the titles of true anthologies.

The last important miscellany of lyrical verse in Elizabeth's reign is Davison's *Poetical Rhapsody*, published in 1602. Francis Davison was the eldest son of William Davison, Elizabeth's unfortunate privy councilor and secretary of state whom she disgraced for carrying her warrant for the execution of Mary Stuart to the Council. Francis was educated at Gray's Inn, where a masque of his was performed in 1594. Davison and his father were adherents of the Earl of Essex, like Southampton, Shakespeare's patron, and so many hopeful younger spirits of the time; and the young poet lost all chance of preferment in consequence. Francis made little of the law, and in 1602 turned his attention to publishing the poetry he had written and collected. There is no trace of him after 1608, when the will of his father was probated. He is supposed, however, to have lived until about 1618. As to his *Rhapsody*, it contains, besides his own poetry (which is distinguished for its erotic fervor and directness), that of his two brothers, some of Sir John Davies, of Donne, Sylvester, translator of Du Bartas, of Sir Henry Wotton, Thomas Campion, and much anonymous verse. *The Poetical Rhapsody* is full of sonnets and madrigals and represents poetry, mostly written at least a dozen years later than that contained in *England's Helicon*. A dozen years meant much in this age of peculiar literary quickening. Altogether this collection most fittingly opens a new period.

We have already traced in brief the history of the Elizabethan lyric and found it flourishing successively in pastoral form and in the sonnet. We have seen how general was the lyrical gift, how varied the nature of the poetry of this type, and how it was governed, in the main, by that sensuous delight in the beauty of the visible world that is the distinctive artistic note of the Renaissance. Upon the wavering of the sonnet fashion the attention of lyrists was directed chiefly to the writing of songs to be set to music. To these as they occur first in the song-books of the time and secondly in the dramas we now turn.

The early skill and prominence of the English in music has long been recognized. Indeed, the earliest period of modern music, that extending from 1400 to the uprise of Italian music with Palestrina in the latter half of the sixteenth century, has been designated by historians of music as the English period. Within this time the Flemings alone could hold their own with English musicians and composers, and it was not until Italian influence on literature had reached full flood that the corresponding influence in the sister art became at all important. From early times, too, in England the essential unity of poetry and song had received recognition. The poet and the musician frequently united in the same person, as in the case of King Henry VIII, to descend to no meaner example. Moreover, not only were poems of a distinctly lyrical nature habitually set to music, but narrative verses and ballads, often of considerable length, were actually sung. As to some of his lyrical *Posies*, Gascoigne remarks on the margin, "these have very sweet notes adapted unto them, the which I would you should enjoy as well as myself." Robert Southwell, the Jesuit father, proposed that his fervid religious poetry be sung; and so late as 1622, Patrick Hannay, a very obscure poetling, furnished the music for the first stanza of his poem, *Philomela*, with the unabashed intent that the remaining ninety or more stanzas be sung to the same tune.

The cultivation of music in the reign of Queen Elizabeth was universal. To play neither the lute nor the cithern, to prove unequal, whether young man or woman, to bearing your part at sight singing or to "running a discant," as the freer song was called, was to raise question of your nurture and gentle training. The very carters and tinkers caroled at their trades; and the weavers became proverbial for the excellence of their singing. Elizabeth prided herself on her technical

skill on the virginal, and was regaled when she dined in state
with kettle-drum and trumpets. The establishment of the
royal chapel was a considerable one, no less than sixty voices
being at times maintained therein at the royal expense. The
queen is said to have expended more than a thousand pounds
a year in the maintenance of the royal music; and positions,
such as those that we have already seen men like Edwards and
Hunnis occupying, were of dignity and of no small emolument.
The Elizabethan musician was a man of very special training.
Even a mere lutenist was often a university-bred man, and
no one could pretend to posts of importance in connection with
the queen's service, sacred or secular, who was not a doctor
of music of Oxford or Cambridge. The modern musician
who lives only by his dexterity of voice or skill on some one
instrument appears to have been little known to the time.
Where known at all, he was placed in the category of masters
of fencing or dancing. By the term musician, in the reign of
Elizabeth, a creative artist and composer was understood.

The Elizabethan song-book commonly supplied both music
and words, and was printed either in separate parts of alto,
basso, and so forth, or these parts were so arranged on the page
that three or four singers might sit on opposite sides of a table
and sing each his own part. The sacred song-book was of
course made up of hymns; the secular, usually of madrigals
and airs. These terms had very definite meanings which we
have lost in modern times. By a madrigal, in music, was
meant a polyphonic piece for several voices without accom-
paniment; while an air was acccompanied and, whether written
for one voice or for several, was not in counterpoint. As a
form of poetry, the Elizabethan madrigal is a poem of lyrical
or epigrammatic nature, integral like the sonnet, that is, not
composed of a succession of like stanzas. The madrigal,
metrically, is often made up of a system of tercets, followed
by a couplet or more; but none of these features are constant.
In length the madrigal ranges from half a dozen verses to
sixteen or even occasionally more; and the meter varies for
the most part independently of the rimes, and in verses of
differing lengths, most commonly lines of five and of three

stresses. Lastly, a preference is shown for feminine or double rimes over single ones, a trait derived from the madrigal's Italian original and referable to the English attempt to reproduce syllable for syllable for the meter's sake. A perfect little madrigal in nearly all the conditions of the species as well as in grace and in epigrammatic point is this, entitled "In Praise of Two," from Davison's *Poetical Rhapsody*, the author unknown.

> Faustina hath the fairer face,
> And Phyllida the feater grace;
>   Both have mine eye enriched:
> This sings full sweetly with her voice;
> Her fingers make as sweet a noise:
>   Both have mine ear bewitched.
> Ah me! sith Fates have so provided,
> My heart, alas, must be divided.

It is not to be supposed that composers, with the sudden popularity of madrigal singing, held with any degree of strictness in this matter of words, to any such rules as these of their Italian originals. The line between a short poem of nearly any meter and a madrigal was soon obliterated, and the quatrain and couplet asserted themselves (as in the sonnet) as the arrangements of rime peculiarly English. A responsible collection of *English Madrigals in the Time of Shakespeare* [1] discloses that the musicians of the age set everything to the fashionable part song: pastorals and experiments in foreign versification by Sidney, songs of Jonson's masques and of Shakespeare's plays, an occasional sonnet of lighter sentiment, and even several stanzas of *The Faery Queen*.

As to the introduction of the madrigal into England, it is related that the Earl of Arundel, visiting Italy in 1568, "employed Tarviso, an Italian musician, to compose a set for him. The word "madrigal," however, seems not to have been employed until the first song-book of the type, *Musa Transalpina*, collected by Nicholas Yonge, a London merchant, trading to Italy and enthusiastically fond of music. *Musa Transalpina* was published by William Byrd in 1588. In his preface

[1] By F. A. Cox, 1899; see pp. 13, 14.

Yonge writes: "I endeavored to get into my hands all such English songs as were praiseworthy, and amongst others I had the hap to find in the hands of some of my good friends certain Italian madrigals translated most of them five years ago by a gentleman for his private delight." Two years later Thomas Watson, the lyrist, published *The First Set of Italian Madrigals* "Englished not to the sense of the original ditty, but after the affection of the note." This statement of the title should dispose of the notion that Watson, who showed himself expert enough in Italian elsewhere, was ignorant or careless of his sources. He was after words that would set to the music whether sung in English or in the original. It is of interest to note that Watson's book was strictly contemporary, drawing on but four collections of Italian madrigals, none of them dating earlier than 1580.

From this point onward song-book after song-book issued from the press. A list of books of this kind, appearing between the time of the Armada and 1630, contains no less than ninety items, and discloses an equal number of composers. Sixty-six of these publications appeared between 1595 and 1615; and fifty, between 1600 and the year of Shakespeare's death. Hence the inference that the vogue of the song followed that of the sonnet, as the sonnet had followed the pastoral mode in popular estimation.

In turning to a consideration of those who were responsible for these song-books, we find, as a rule, only the names of the writers of the music given; at times it may be suspected that the name on the title-page is little more than that of the publisher or collector. For example, William Byrd, described as "the central musical figure of the Elizabethan age, celebrated early and living late," enjoyed for some years the monopoly of music publishing which he sold later or shared with Thomas Est and Thomas Morley. Byrd was certainly no more than the publisher of *Musa Transalpina;* but he was likewise a composer of note, as his *Psalms, Sonnets and Songs,* 1588, *Songs of Sundry Natures,* 1589, and several other collections attest. Once more, we have seen how the madrigal writers in their search for words set anything that they could lay their hands on to music. But when the song-books are examined, they disclose, nevertheless, a large proportion of lyrics, incapable of identification in the works of known poets, a matter that gives rise to the question how far the composers of the day may have been their own poets. On this point Mr. Bullen (who of all can best speak for the Elizabethan lyric) is of opinion that "as a rule composers are responsible only for the music"; while Mr. Davey, author of an excellent *History of Music*, says: "It appears to me that, as a rule, the poems and the music were simultaneously conceived; I ground this belief on the detailed parallelism in the matter of the successive stanzas in the airs through which the same music fits them all." A better argument might be founded on the uniformity of poetical style which at times accompanies the musical work of the same composer. Although, as to this, it has been affirmed that all the words of Morley's *First Book of Ballets*, 1595, are from the pen of Michael Drayton. In the works of the greatest man of this class, Thomas Campion, at least, we are certain that the two arts were fittingly and indissolubly wedded. And for this we may cite his own words "to the reader" prefixed to his *Third Book of Airs:* "In these English airs I have chiefly aimed to couple my words and notes lovingly together; which will be much for him to do that hath not power over both."

Among the several musicians who may thus not improperly be entitled to a place in the choir of Elizabethan lyrists, may be named John Wilbye, author of two sets of *Madrigals* in 1598 and 1609, and famed as "the greatest of English madrigalian composers"; Thomas Morley, the prolific author of no less than seven like works between his *Canzonets* of 1593 and his *First Book of Airs*, 1600; and John Dowland, the celebrated lutenist, author of four books of *Airs* before 1601. On the other hand these musicians often set the poetry of others to music. Thus Morley's *First Book* contains the original setting of Shakespeare's "It was a lover and his lass." And the songs which Richard Johnson composed for *The Tempest* are published in *Cheerful Airs and Ballads*, 1660. The memory of Dowland, likewise, has been associated with Shakespeare because of the fine sonnet, "In praise of music and sweet poetry," attributed by Jaggard, a piratical publisher, to the great dramatist and commonly republished since as his, though it is really Barnfield's. Dowland carried the fame of English musicians to the continent and was for years lutenist to the king of Denmark and to other great people abroad.

Other names of madrigalists there are: Orlando Gibbons, organist of Canterbury Cathedral; Philip Rossiter, associated with Campion and not without a place in the history of the drama; Thomas Weelkes, of whom we know little; Robert Jones, of whom we know nothing. Of Tobias Hume, we are only certain that he was a captain. The quality of the poetry in the song-books of these men occasionally reaches rare heights and lyric perfection. More commonly it rises little above the general level of the Elizabethan lyric. Take this one perfect stanza from Tobias Hume's *First Part of Airs, French, Polish and Others Together*, 1605, which Mr. Bullen picked out for the text, so to speak, of one of his collections of lyrics:

> O love! they wrong thee much
>   That say thy sweet is bitter,
> When thy rich fruit is such
>   As nothing can be sweeter;
> Fair house of joy and bliss,
> Where truest pleasure is,
>   I do adore thee:
> I know thee what thou art,
> I serve thee with my heart,
>   And fall before thee.

Quite as perfect for the music of their words are lines such as these: from *The Muses' Garden of Delights*, collected in 1601 by Robert Jones:

> The sea hath many thousand sands,
>   The sun hath motes as many,
> The sky is full of stars, and love
>   As full of woe as any:
> Believe me that do know the elf
> And make no trial for thyself;

or these lines, half whimsical yet deeply serious, from the same choice collection:

> How many new years have grown old
> Since first your servant old was new!
> How many long hours have I told
> Since first my love was vowed to you!
> And yet, alas! she doth not know
> Whether her servant love or no.

But when all has been said, in Thomas Campion we reach the prince of this tuneful realm of Elizabethan song. That so delightful a minor poet should have needed rediscovery towards the end of the nineteenth century is a matter all but inexplicable, for Campion's reputation was commensurate with his talents in his own age. The date of his birth is uncertain. He was educated at Cambridge and Gray's Inn, and published Latin *Epigrams* as early as 1594. His songbooks were printed between the years 1601 and 1619. In 1602 appeared his *Observations in the Art of English Poesy*, in which he attacked "the vulgar and inartistic custom of riming" and attempted to prove that English metrical composition was faulty in not following the classics. Campion was ably answered in the next year by Daniel, who expressed his wonder that such an attack should proceed from one whose "commendable rimes, albeit now himself an enemy to rime, have given to the world the best notice of his worth." Later in life Campion became a distinguished practitioner of medicine, and held, as well, an honorable place among contemporary musicians, alike for his compositions and for his excellent treatise, *A New Way to Make Four Parts in Counterpoint*, published in 1613. Although a conservative in theory as to versification, Campion was remarkably liberal as to music and wrote airs in preference to madrigals of set purpose. He says: "What epigrams are in poetry, the same are airs in music; then in their chief perfection when they are short and well seasoned."

The inspiration of Campion is more directly classical than that of almost any lyrist of his immediate time. Campion's limpidity of diction, his choice placing and selection of words, his perfect taste and melody, and his devotion to love, all are qualities which disclose how steeped he was in the poetry of Tibullus and Catullus. Unlike most of his fellow lyrists, Campion was practically uninfluenced by the contemporary poetry of Italy and France; at least his name appears not in the black lists of pilferers and plagiarists from these literatures in which our contemporary doctors' theses so revel and delight. But Campion's originality is not entirely confined to his aptness of expression. He keeps constantly before him his idea of the epigrammatic quality of such verse as he regards fit to set to airs. Take for example the following:

> Thou art not fair, for all thy red and white,
> For all those rosy ornaments in thee;
> Thou art not sweet, though made of mere delight,
> Nor fair nor sweet, unless thou pity me.
> I will not sooth thy fancies: thou shalt prove
> That beauty is no beauty without love.
>
> Yet love not me, nor seek thou to allure
> My thoughts with beauty, were it more divine.
> Thy smiles and kisses I can not endure,
> I 'll not be wrapt up in those arms of thine:
> Now show it, if thou be a woman right, —
> Embrace, and kiss, and love me in despite.

The turn here at the end almost equals that of the much praised sonnet of Drayton, "Since there's no help." Another distinguishing quality of Campion is the ease and ductility, so to speak, of his verse. What he does, he does so readily that it hardly seems difficult.

> Come, cheerful day, part of my life to me:
> For while thou view'st me with thy fading light,
> Part of my life doth still depart with thee,
> And I still onward haste to my last night.
> Time's fatal wings do ever forward fly:
> So every day we live a day we die.

Here not a word is inverted, unusual or turned to the slightest figurative use, and yet the effect is perfect of its kind. Campion, as this stanza suggests, was not quite wholly an amorist.

Among his poems will be found no inconsiderable number
possessed by a simple and quiet religious fervor; for the fashion of the song-book, like that of the sonnet and other lyrical
poetry, included divine as well as secular themes.

That the drama should have contained songs is as natural
as that the drama should have contained comedy; and the
origin of song and comedy is in the English drama referable
to much the same conditions, chief among them a desire to
amuse. If we turn back as far as the moralities and interludes
we shall find the few snatches of song, there indicated, commonly put into the mouth of the roisterer, the vice, or the devil;
though godly songs are not altogether wanting. The earliest
regular comedies are full of songs: there are some half-dozen
in *Ralph Roister Doister*, which the excellent old school-master,
Nicholas Udall, never found in his master Plautus; all are
sprightly, though of little value from a literary point of view.
Gammer Gurton's Needle, the other "earliest comedy," contains one famous bacchanal song, "Back and side go bare, go
bare," which alone is enough to immortalize that rude old
play. For genuine spirit and for the vividness of the medieval
tavern scene which it suggests, this song deserves a place beside "The Jolly Beggars" of Burns. In the tragedies and the
earlier histories there was little opportunity for the introduction
of songs; though there is at least one in Peele's *David and
Bethsabe* of merit. Marlowe has none in his plays, and Greene
lavished his lyrical gift upon his pamphlets. So far as we
know, the earliest English dramatist of note to appreciate to
the full the value of the incidental lyric in the drama and to
raise that species of song-writing to an art was John Lyly.
Epigrammatic though the songs of the Euphuist are, they deserve an honorable place in the poetry of their time; though
we may share in the late Mr. Henley's doubt if such poetry be
lyrical. Recall Lyly's best known song, "Cupid and my
Campaspe played at cards for kisses," and we can see how
artificial and witty this art of epigram really is. Then read
one of the few exquisite lyrics of Thomas Dekker, nearly all
of them contributed to plays, and we recognize the difference.
If asked to name one lyric and one only which should illustrate

to the full the music, the sincerity, and the spontaneity of Elizabethan poetry, I should choose neither the profound depth
of a Shakespearean sonnet nor the pastoral sweetness of Breton
or Greene, the haughty insolent vein of Raleigh nor the su-
premely original and at times contorted thought of Donne;
but Dekker's dainty lyrical sigh on " Sweet Content "

> Art thou poor, yet hast thou golden slumbers?
> O sweet content!
> Art thou rich, yet is thy mind perplexèd?
> O punishment!
> Dost thou laugh to see how fools are vexèd
> To add to golden numbers, golden numbers?
> O sweet content!   O sweet, O sweet content!
>> Work apace, apace, apace, apace;
>> Honest labor bears a lovely face;
> Then hey nonny nonny, hey nonny nonny!
>
> Can'st drink the waters of the crispèd spring?
> O sweet content!
> Swimm'st thou in wealth, yet sink'st in thine own tears?
> O punishment!
> Then he that patiently want's burden bears
> No burden bears, but is a king, a king!
> O sweet content!   O sweet, O sweet content!
>> Work apace, apace, apace, apace;
>> Honest labor bears a lovely face;
> Then hey nonny nonny, hey nonny nonny!

Almost equally beautiful though less musical is Dekker's
grave lyric, "O sorrow, sorrow, say where dost thou dwell,"
the more especially when we remember how the author spent
his days in unremittent drudgery, a slave to pawn-broking old
Henslowe, always in poverty and often in the debtor's prison.
There is something inexpressibly touching in the thought of
such a man singing of sweet content, and of the inequality of
fortune, the withering of virtue's fair branches, and the dwelling-
place of sorrow.   If it is the man beneath that is precious in
literature, we can spare many sweet sonnets and gay courtly
fopperies for a few poems such as these.   Closely allied to
Dekker in spirit is Nash, the writer of even fewer lyrics.   It

is in *Summer's Last Will*, Nash's one drama, that we find his lyrics, "Fading Summer" and "Death's Summons." These two poems assume to us a new and terrible import when we remember the grim and horrible visitant which was London's every few years, the plague. This play was written in a plague year and the refrain of "Death's Summons" consists of the very words of the official inscription, "Lord have mercy on us," which, with a cross, was affixed to the doors of what were called "visited houses."

The wider popularity on which the contemporary drama was based as compared with the choicer art of the musical composers results in the circumstance that lyrics incidental to plays are far less the reflection of foreign models. The latter, however, reflect passing fashions in English poetry with much faithfulness. The songs of Lyly and Peele are full of the pastoral and classical spirit preceding 1590. Shakespeare's earliest comedies exhibit the same tendency. The two gentlemen of Verona were, neither of them, shepherds, but a pretty song of that play asks:

> Who is Sylvia? what is she
> That all our swains commend her?

The succeeding sonnet humor is well illustrated in *Love's Labor 's Lost*, although none of the sonnets of that play are used for songs. The sonnet does not ordinarily set well to music, as the decasyllabic line is rather long for the average song-phrase, and the integral form cannot be split into short stanzas. None the less sonnets have been so set. Some of Campion's airs have words in this form.

The songs of Shakespeare are scattered through his plays and are of a lyrical beauty and variety which it is impossible to overpraise. More than twenty of them have been transmitted to us with music actually or traditionally known to have been used within the sixteenth and seventeenth centuries; and this number is materially raised by the circumstance that several of them exist in more than one contemporary version. Within the range of Shakespeare's own life Thomas Morley, Richard Johnson, Robert Jones, John Wilson, and other composers, unknown, set songs to music in *As You Like It, Much Ado About Nothing, Twelfth Night, The Winter's Tale, The Tempest* and other plays; whilst some of the poems of *The Passionate Pilgrim* were set by Thomas Weelkes and anonymous composers. As might be expected a large number of these songs must have been sung to melodies already well known. Whether some of them were set before the performance of the play and thus added to its attraction, or after, because of the popularity of the words, we can not say. The traditional tunes which have been handed down for generations have been more or less modernized in the process; but many of them contain enough of their probable original to support their claims. With the beautiful and to us old-fashioned settings of Shakespeare's songs by Dr. Purcell, by Hilton, Bannister, and others, in the generations after Shakespeare's death, we are not here concerned.

If the body of lyrics incidental to plays and masques be compared with an equal amount of lyrical verse of the period from Lyly to Ford, the dramatists will be found to hold their own in variety and originality of subject, in diversity and adaptability of meter, and to possess above all their contemporaries — not even excepting Campion and his group — the power of making words sing. Here as in everything that he touched Shakespeare is the greatest. There are no lyrics like his, from dainty little ditties such as "It was a lover and his lass" or the fairy music of Puck and Ariel, to the exquisite "Dirge" of *Cymbeline*: "Fear no more the heat o' the sun." If you are visited by doubts as to whether so ethereal a thing as you suppose a lyric to be, can be made to present a scene of homely realism and yet preserve its quality as a lyric, read the song, "When icicles hang by the wall," with which *Love's Labor's Lost* closes, and your doubts will be forever laid to rest. If you can withstand the gross temptations of "Back and side go bare, go bare," be careful not to get some of Shakespeare's lilting bacchanal rimes into your head, lest you fall into an undue appreciation of "cakes and ale."

All of the predecessors of Shakespeare were accomplished metrists and the diversity and inventiveness of their lyrical measures remain the admiration and delight of those who read their exquisite poetry. But here, too, as elsewhere, regal Shakespeare comes into his own, wielding an imperious scepter over all and claiming alike the vassalage of classical experiment, Italian importation, and sterling old English freedom in verse. It was Shakespeare who could manage the ripple of the redundant syllable and the *contretemps* of the substituted trochee. He compassed the mystery of that most difficult of English meters, trochaic octosyllables and, with the solitary exception of Campion, is the only Elizabethan lyrist who essayed the effect of a change within the stanza from one to another metrical system. The beautiful dirge of *Twelfth Night* is a much-quoted example of the kind in which the anapests slow down into iambics towards the close of each stanza:

> Come away, come away, death,
> And in sad cypress let me be laid;
> Fly away, fly away, breath,
> I am slain by a fair cruel maid.
> My shroud of white, stuck all with yew,
> O prepare it!
> My part of death, no one so true
> Did share it.

Equally felicitous is the change to the refrain of the famous song of *As You Like It:*

> Who doth ambition shun,
> And loves to live i' the sun,
> Seeking the food he eats,
> And pleased with what he gets,
> Come hither, come hither, come hither:
> Here shall he see
> No enemy
> But winter and rough weather.

With respect to choice and treatment of material, the lyrists of the age fall into three groups: those that modeled their work either on foreign or English literary models, the bookish poets, analogous to the bookish dramatists; those who, setting

great store on originality, gave to the world their own, such
as it was; and those who based their art on popular taste,
tradition, story, and balladry. Shakespeare belongs to the
last of these groups. Many of his songs are bits of folk-poetry,
crystallized into permanent artistic form by the interposition
of the poet's genius. The universality of that genius is more
largely due to the trait which makes Shakespeare, in drama
and lyric, the artistic form-giver to the popular spirit of his
race, than to any other one thing. The man who seeks to
raise popular appreciation to a standard which he has taken
beyond his age, has the sheer weight of the world to move
without a fulcrum. The man who rides on the crest of a wave
of popular advance or popular emotion receives his own impetus from that wave and, like the very spirit of the storm,
may come to lead whither he will. The dramatic require-
ments of certain situations demanded the singing of familiar
tunes, even if the words were somewhat adapted. Such are
the songs of the distraught Ophelia, and the grave-digger's
in the same play, the "ballads" of Autolycus and the catches
of Sir Toby and Sir Andrew Aguecheek. In plays such as
A Midsummer-Night's Dream and *The Tempest* there was
opportunity for greater originality. From the earliest times
an ability to sing must have been an essential of the actor's
profession. In the boy-companies everybody could sing, for
that was the chorister's first duty. We may infer that theatrical music in the reign of Elizabeth was of a far higher
general grade than now, both in its originality and in the excellence of its performance.

Excepting Shakespeare, the two greatest lyrists of this
class are Fletcher and Ben Jonson. Fletcher learned his
lyrical as he learned his dramatic art of Shakespeare; and in
his songs has caught much of the Shakespearean lightness
and winged delicacy. He displays the same facile grace and
ease of expression, the same mastery of effect combined with
a complete absence of effort that form distinctive traits of his
dramatic works. Shakespeare need not have been ashamed
of this dirge from *The Maid's Tragedy:*

Lay a garland on my hearse
Of the dismal yew;
Maidens, willow branches bear;
Say, I died true.

My love was false, but I was firm
From my hour of birth;
Upon my buried body lie
Lightly, gentle earth;

nor of the fine song in *The Two Noble Kinsmen*, and many
others. Fletcher, and more especially Beaumont, begin to
show a satirical and cynical strain in the lyric which was not
common to the earlier age. When Beaumont sings:

Never more will I protest
To love a woman but in jest:
For as they cannot be true,
So to give each man his due
When the wooing fit is past,
Their affection cannot last;

we may be sure that he has come under an influence not to be
found in the earlier lyrists, and matchable only in Donne in
one of his most characteristic moods.

Save for a few well-known poems of the very best lyrical
quality, Jonson's lyrics contributed to dramas and especially
to the masques lose much by excision from their context; and
yet his masques are full of beautiful poetry of this kind in
which the classicality of his style, his love of form and genuine
originality all show themselves to advantage. Discussion
of the poetry of Jonson may best be deferred for the treatment
of it in its larger aspects. In the masques, too, of Daniel,
Campion of course, and of minor writers may be found many
beautiful songs which the art of contemporary musicians rendered acceptable to the refined and fastidious taste of the courts
of Queen Elizabeth and King James.

Returning to the more popular drama, Heywood wrote
many songs, some of rare excellence, such as "Pack clouds
away" in *Lucrece*, and "Ye little birds that sit and sing" from

The Fair Maid of the Exchange. There is a freshness and genuine love of nature in Heywood that saves his lyrics from the effect of artifice which belongs to some of the best work of more polished poets. Heywood is also responsible for many mock-songs, as they were called; they do not add to his fame, but they enjoyed great popularity in their day. Among the other great dramatists, Chapman and Marston alone are devoid of song. Chapman because, like Spenser, he needed a larger vehicle in which to convey his poetical freight; Marston, possibly because the lyric vein was not in him. Middleton's songs are, the best of them, of incantation, as in *The Witch*, or of the mock type. Lastly, Webster, our master-poet in the domain of the terrible, has left us at least one lyric which deserves a place with Shakespeare's best. That is his immortal dirge from *Vittoria Corombona*, with which this chapter may fittingly close:

> Call for the robin-redbreast and the wren,
>   Since o'er shady groves they hover,
>   And with leaves and flowers do cover
> The friendless bodies of unburied men.
>   Call unto his funeral dole
>   The ant, the field-mouse, and the mole,
> To rear him hillocks that shall keep him warm,
> And, when gay tombs are robbed, sustain no harm;
> But keep the wolf far thence, that 's foe to men,
> For with his nails he 'll dig them up again.

It is of this poem that Charles Lamb wrote: "I never saw anything like this funeral dirge, except the ditty which reminds Ferdinand of his drowned father in *The Tempest*. As that is of the water, watery; so this is of the earth, earthy. Both have that intenseness of feeling, which seems to resolve itself into the element which it contemplates."

CHAPTER XII

EPIC, NARRATIVE, AND PASTORAL VERSE

SAVE for the broken torso of that beautiful triumph of romantic art and mingled medieval allegory, *The Faery Queen*, the age of Elizabeth produced no great epic; and even *The Faery Queen* fulfils the conditions of a world epic only partially, as its inspirations, *Jerusalem Delivered* and *Orlando Furioso*, fulfil them, and belongs, with all its merits, its charm, and its luxuriance of beauty, to its age and not with the *Iliad*, the *Divina Comedia*, and *Paradise Lost* to all time. But however the epic, defined in its strictness, may have fallen short in the dramatic and lyrical age that gave the world Shakespeare's plays and his sonnets, narrative poetry in the wider sense was neither neglected nor unpopular.

In the first chapter of this book our subject was the literature of fact, that extraordinary literary outburst that followed on the rebirth of national consciousness, an outburst which reached its height with the repulse of the Armada and fell off into mere echoes of the sonorous past in the reign of King James. This literature was couched not alone in prose chronicles and historical dramas but from the very first was wont to find an almost equally popular expression in narrative verse. *The Mirror for Magistrates*, that strange composite, the work of some fifteen authors and the growth of fifty years, is elegiac rather than narrative, reminiscent of the fates of fallen princes rather than descriptive of their actual careers; and yet *The Mirror* begot a numerous progeny. Except for Churchyard's narrative of *Shore's Wife*, the first historical poem modeled on the separate "legends," as they were called, of *The Mirror for Magistrates* was *The Complaint of Rosamund* which Daniel published in 1592. Samuel Daniel was a Taunton man, the son of a music-master. He received his education, as we have seen, at Oxford, leaving, however, before receiving his degree. He became a tutor to the Herberts and other noble families and doubtless traveled in this capacity into Italy whence he brought back the Italianate practice of sonneteering. He was of the Sidneian circle, and later of Queen Anne of Denmark's household; and he was early encouraged by the friendship and praise, in his *Colin Clout*, of Spenser himself. Even Nash approved Daniel's *Rosamund*, which the author soon republished "augmented." Like its models in *The Mirror*, *The Complaint of Rosamund* is elegiac in character and full of moralizing of no very original kind. But it is gracefully and well written as is all Daniel's poetry. In the next year no less than five poems of this sort appeared, treating, besides other topics, of the well-known historical figures of Robert of Normandy, Piers Gaveston, and Richard II, the work of men like Lodge, Drayton, and Giles Fletcher. The composition of such poems continues far into the reign of King James in the works of obscure as well as of better known writers and in poems discoursing of Queen Matilda, Owen Tudor, and Queen Katherine, of Edward IV and his courtship of Lady Gray, of the Lollard, Oldcastle, of Humphrey of Gloucester, and above all in the favorite theme of the age, the rise and fall of Richard III and "the preservation of King Henry VII."

But Daniel had long since attempted more ambitious historical poetry than this. In 1595 first appeared his *Civil Wars*, enlarged to eight books in the final edition of 1609. *The History of the Civil Wars* details, in an easy and graceful stanza of eight riming lines, the principal events in the history of England from the misrule of Richard II to the marriage of Edward IV, thus covering the same ground as Shakespeare's *Richard II*, the two plays on Henry IV, that on Henry V, and the three on Henry VI. It was Daniel's purpose to complete his epic up to the accession of Henry VII, the first Tudor king. But as the work lagged on, despite its popularity, into the reign of King James, there was no reason to carry out the original plan. Daniel ambitiously took for his model no less a work than the *Pharsalia* of Lucan; and it can not be denied that the English poet is animated throughout by a true patriotism of heart and a fine sustaining faith in the greatness of his country. But the Wars of the Roses offer no such theme as the struggles of Pompey and Cæsar; nor was Daniel a match for the clever Roman. The *Civil Wars* is not without grace and merit as a poem; but with all his rhetoric and sedulous deliberation, Daniel never reaches a true epic height, and the rapid changes from one to another historical figure and episode are destructive of the least semblance of unity.

This want Daniel's rival in the historical epic, Michael Drayton, sought to supply by taking Roger Mortimer for the hero of his poem, entitled on its first appearance in 1596 *Mortimeriados*, later, on its completion and rewriting in *ottava rima* in 1603, *The Barons' Wars*. Drayton's is an abler poem than Daniel's. Its characters, Edward II, Isabella, and Mortimer, are those already immortalized in Marlowe's fine drama on that unfortunate monarch. Drayton maintains, too, throughout an heroic pitch, alike in the events of war and statecraft and in the passionate love of his hero for Queen Isabella. This was not Drayton's first attempt at historical verse, as his *Legend of Piers Gaveston* had been printed in 1593. In 1597 Drayton essayed another variety of historical poetry. *England's Heroical Epistles* is a series of imaginary letters in couplets, supposedly exchanged between royal and other historical lovers; and, though from its plan wanting in anything like real unity, is characterized by much dignity and beauty. In 1607 Drayton published his *Legend of the Great Cromwell* in a volume with the "legends" of *Queen Matilda* and *Robert, Duke of Normandy*, already written some years since. Though incessantly adapting his poetry to changed conditions, remodeling it, and revising, Drayton continued remarkably constant to early influences. His latest work in the "historical legend" by no means betters *The Barons' Wars*. And yet the finest single literary expression of Elizabethan national spirit found utterance in a poem of Michael Drayton. But this is not his tedious narrative of *The Battle of Agincourt*, which he published late in the reign of King James when the martial fire that had animated Elizabethan England had long since faded into a memory, but in a single lyric that first saw the light in the *Poems* of 1605 and which Drayton included among his "Odes," and quaintly addressed "To my friends the Cambro-Britons and their Harp, his Ballad of Agincourt."

> Fair stood the wind for France,
> When we our sails advance,
> And now to prove our chance
>   Longer not tarry,
> But put unto the main,
> At Caux, the mouth of Seine,
> With all his warlike train,
>   Landed King Harry.
>
> .   .   .   .   .
>
> And, turning to his men
> Quoth famous Henry then,
> "Though they to one be ten,
>   Be not amazèd;
> Yet have we well begun,
> Battles so bravely won
> Evermore to the sun
>   By fame are raisèd."
>
> .   .   .   .   .
>
> And ready to be gone,
> Armor on armor shone,
> Drum unto drum did groan,
>   To hear was wonder;
> That with the cries they make
> The very earth did shake,
> Trumpet to trumpet spake,
>   Thunder to thunder.

The very tread of armies rings in lines like these, and later poets, in feebler ages than Drayton's, have not disdained to borrow both ideas and meter of the patriotic Elizabethan.

As to the man, Michael Drayton was born in Warwickshire in 1563. He apparently went to neither university, but was educated in the household of Sir Henry Goodere and enjoyed the patronage of Lucy, Countess of Bedford, one of the most liberal and universal patrons of poets and learned men of her day. To her he dedicated his *Mortimeriados*, although he characteristically withdrew this dedication on revision. Drayton began the cultivation of poetry in early youth and remained throughout a long life more undividedly attached to his art than almost any man among his contemporaries. Aside from a trivial attempt in 1590, called *The Harmony of the Church*, Drayton's first publication was a series of nine eclogues, closely following the manner of Spenser, to which he gave the title *Idea, the Shepherd's Garland*, in 1593. This word "*Idea*" he transferred to the title of his series of sonnets, *Idea's Mirror*, in the following year, not without a reference (if precisians will have it so) to a contemporary French title which has been already noticed. Of these sonnets and their writing we have already sufficiently heard in this book, and his later pastorals, the *Polyolbion*, and other works will claim our later attention. Drayton lived on to 1631 highly honored and intimate, as we know from two or three anecdotes, with his fellow country man, Shakespeare. Drayton received the honor of burial in Westminster Abbey.

We are apt to forget, if the number of editions of a man's work be any criterion, that next to Spenser Drayton, and then Daniel, enjoyed the greatest contemporary reputation as general poets during the lifetime of Shakespeare. But we must recall that besides these, their epic labors, both were notable lyrists and both dabbled in the drama,— Daniel with Senecan tragedies and exotic pastorals, Drayton on the popular stage in Henslowe's mart, concealing his traffic with the stage in later time and feeling with Shakespeare the degradation of making himself a motley to the view of groundlings and common fellows.

A third notable historical epic of the time was William Warner's *Albion's England*. Warner, who was a London attorney, wrote earlier than either Daniel or Drayton, his book appearing in 1586; and he is remarkable even at that date for his imperviousness to contemporary influences. Like Southwell, though in a very different field, Warner wrote in the manner of Gascoigne, Googe, and Turberville long after those earlier worthies were dead, employing habitually the long fourteeners for his epic verse. *Albion's England* is an episodic narrative poem professing for its general theme the history of England from "the division of the world after the flood to the coming of the Normans." It is full of incident and digression, and it may be suspected was more prized at times for its romantic stories — such as that of Argentile and Curan — than for its "history." *Albion's England* enjoyed, none the less, an immediate and deserved popularity from its patriotic sentiment and its homely and unpretentious style. Warner continued his chronicle to the accession of Queen Elizabeth in the edition of 1592; and a final, sixth, edition was printed in 1612 after the author's death, still further enlarged to include some of the events of the reign of James. In 1604 an unsuccessful variation on the rimed chronicle was attempted by Sir William Harbert, in his *Prophecy of Cadwallader,* "containing a comparison of the English Kings with many worthy Romans, from William Rufus to Henry V." This work has more merit than has usually been accorded it. Thomas Deloney's *Crown Garland of Roses,* 1613, is a collection of ballads on stories derived from English history, and of no particular merit. A further degeneration of historical verse is represented in scattered broadsides and ballads of which it is unnecessary here to speak. Taylor, "the Water Poet's" illustrated doggerel chronicle of English kings represents the final absorption of this sort of verse chronicling: and Taylor falls without our period.

Another group of narrative poems, distinctively of the Renaissance, and many of them of exquisite beauty, are those which describe, and in describing, extol the ecstasies of earthly love. The age was franker in its speech and art than we, and dared openly to admire not only the cold and chiseled beauties of the Venus de Milo, but likewise the warm flesh tints of the same goddess of beauty as depicted by the florid brush of Correggio. Marlowe, translator of the *Amores* of Ovid when a lad at college, at a time when he should have been engaged with more modest classics, was the first among the greater English poets thus to celebrate the glories of corporal passion. In this Marlowe stands in striking contrast with Spenser who, as the poet of chivalry, finds in restraint of passion and in a service devoted to beauty, his ideal of true love, as he finds in the metaphyscial discussions of the Platonic philosophy, love's truest expression. Marlowe's *Hero and Leander* is really an amplification of a classical poem attributed to Musæus. It was first printed in 1598 as a fragment, and appeared later in the same year, completed by the strenuous hand of George Chapman. This lovers' tale of Hero and Leander is a poem of rich and varied beauty and finer in theme than either *Venus and Adonis* or *Lucrece.* Sensuousness is the note of Marlowe as it is of Keats; and reticence was not a quality of Elizabethan times. But this is not the only characteristic of Marlowe's part in *Hero and Leander.* Marlowe's diction flows with limpid clearness; his imagery is exquisite and the story, in its simple outspokenness, as spontaneous and natural as the loves of Romeo and Juliet themselves. Whether for its descriptive energy and eloquence or for its vivid and highly poetical portrayal of the effects of absorbing youthful passion on man and maid, *Hero and Leander* must remain one of the most astonishing poems in the language. In this passage we have Marlowe's ease, limpidity, and sufficiency of phrase. His music, in its larger cadence, and the full glory and color of his poetical style must be sought in the poem itself.

> On this feast-day — O cursèd day and hour! —
> Went Hero thorough Sestos, from her tower
> To Venus' temple, where unhappily,
> As after chanc'd, they did each other spy.
> So fair a church as this had Venus none:
> The walls were of discolor'd jasper-stone,
> Wherein was Proteus carved; and overhead
> A lively vine of green sea-agate spread,
> Where by one hand light-headed Bacchus hung,
> And with the other wine from grapes out-wrung.
>
> .   .   .   .
>
> And in the midst a silver altar stood:
> There Hero, sacrificing turtles' blood,
> Veiled to the ground, veiling her eyelids close;
> And modestly they opened as she rose:

Thence flew Love's arrow with the golden head;
And thus Leander was enamourèd.
Stone-still he stood, and evermore he gazed,
Till with the fire, that from his countenance blaz'd,
Relenting Hero's gentle heart was strook:
Such force and virtue hath an amorous look.
It lies not in our power to love or hate,
For will in us is overruled by fate.
When two are stript, long ere the course begin,
We wish that one would lose, the other win,
And one especially do we affect,
Of two gold ingots, like in each respect:
The reason no man knows; let it suffice,
What we behold is censured by our eyes.
When both deliberate, the love is slight:
Whoever loved that loved not at first sight?

Chapman's continuation which takes up the story from the moment of the height of the lovers' joy, is no unworthy one; though we miss, in his full and sometimes difficult and labored lines, the clear sweetness of the earlier poet.

The next poem of this type, if indeed it may not have preceded Marlowe's, is Thomas Lodge's *Glaucus and Scilla* in the story of which a nymph courts an unwilling swain much as Venus courts Adonis in Shakespeare's poem, and with words and imagery of a honied sweetness that match the earliest Shakespearean manner. When we note that the meter of the two poems is also the same (a stanza of six lines, the first four alternately riming, the last two a couplet), and further recall how invariably in all his work Shakespeare followed whither others led, the conclusion is complete that Lodge's poem was the model of Shakespeare's. *Venus and Adonis* is termed in the dedication to his patron, the Earl of Southampton, "the first heir of my invention," and its erotic uncontrol confirms the statement. The poem was printed in 1593, the year of Marlowe's death, and enjoyed an immediate repute, running through seven editions before the conclusion of Elizabeth's reign. Nor was *The Rape of Lucrece*, which appeared in 1594, much less popular, although the theme is more serious and its treatment more dramatic and earnest. Neither of these love tales is frivolous in Shakespeare's hands   The one, as it has been described, is, "of the innocence of early manhood that is proof against the blandishments of Venus; the other of the innocence of womanhood, outraged by man's lust, and choosing death to set the pure soul free from the prison of a tainted body." Coleridge dilated on the promise and immaturity of these two poems of Shakespeare. The latter quality needs no illustration; their promise Coleridge finds in the consummate sweetness of their versification and the remoteness of their subject-matter from the poet's own life and emotions; for it is the second-rate man, not the truly great, who thrusts forward his own experiences and emotions to the uninterested gaze of strangers. Coleridge likewise found here that minute and faithful imagery which is everywhere Shakespeare's and, in *Lucrece*, a full promise of that true philosophy of life that enables Shakespeare so invariably to see things in large, so little unsteadied by the unessentials that surround them. In Coleridge's own words, "Shakespeare possessed the chief, if not every, requisite of a poet,— deep feeling and exquisite sense of beauty, both as exhibited to the eye in the combinations of form, and to the ear in sweet and appropriate melody; that these feelings were under the command of his own will; that in his very first productions he projected his mind out of his own particular being, and felt, and made others feel, on subjects no way connected with himself, except by force of contemplation and that sublime faculty by which a great mind becomes that on which it meditates. To this must be added that affectionate love of nature and natural objects, without which no man could have observed so steadily, or painted so truly and passionately, the very minutest beauties of the external world."

Of the other poems of this class it is not needful to say much. Marston the dramatist's first work, *The Metamorphosis of Pigmalion's Image*, 1598, deserved the order of the Archbishop of Canterbury that it be burned wherever found, and Marston's subsequent excuse that he wrote it to turn ridicule on amatory poetry is a piece of Marstonian impertinence. *Salmacis and Hermaphroditus*, 1602, has been attributed to Francis Beaumont, but is unworthy alike of his taste and his genius. For its exquisite lusciousness *Britain's Ida*, which treats of the loves of Venus and Anchises, was attributed to Spenser on the title-page of the edition of 1628, but must be referred to his disciple, Phineas Fletcher. The others of the class are negligible until we reach *Narcissus* of James Shirley, published two years after Shakespeare's death, and a poem of unusual merit and beauty.

The unexampled versatility of this extraordinary age did not even stop short of poetry on philosophy, statecraft, and topography, and extended Spenserian allegory diversely to religion and to human anatomy. Sir John Davies, of whom we have already heard as the author of a set of *Gulling Sonnets*, attained distinction in the law. In his youth he had written a series of *Hymns to Astræa*, 1599, each an acrostic constructed on the words "Elizabeta Regina," and surprisingly good considering such limitations. Davies likewise wrote a clever *jeu d'esprit* in verse called *Orchestra or a Poem on Dancing*, 1596, in which he represents Antinous, chief of the suitors of Penelope, arguing with that constant lady to prove the art of Terpsichore the move-all and be-all of the world. In 1599 appeared Davies' interesting philosophical poem, *Nosce Teipsum*, "a discourse in two elegies," so runs the title, "first of humane knowledge, secondly, of the soul of man and the immortality thereof." Davies' work has been well described as "a popular exposition of current ideas by a man who has no distinctive opinions." He maintains "with the agreeable assurance of a ready dialectician" that "all learning is uncertain and vain except knowledge of self and God"; and he has contrived to set forth these metaphysical commonplaces in language absolutely simple and direct, adorned with graceful and fitting illustration, and expressed in admirably competent verse. *Nosce Teipsum* is as typical a representative of Elizabethan popular philosophy as the *Essay on Man* is typical of the popular thought of the time of Queen Anne; nor can Davies' work be esteemed a less successful piece of that hybrid, metaphysical poetry. In reading some of its smooth and even stanzas we can not but wonder whether Pope did not know

more of it than he might have been willing to confess.   And
we note with interest that Davies' stanza — which is that of
Gray's *Elegy*, a quatrain of decasyllabic verse alternately
riming — is also the same which Dryden used and so praised
Davenant for "inventing" thirty years after the death of
Davies.

Fulke Greville, the early friend of Sidney, is the author of
no less than five poetical "*Treatises*," as he called them, on
*Human Learning, Fame and Honor, War, Monarchy and
Religion*, first printed posthumously in 1633 in *Certain Learned
and Elegant Works*.   It is doubtful whether they may not
have been written at least in part within the reign of Queen
Elizabeth.   On their political side these abstract and often
difficult poems deal in a spirit of mingled frankness and irony
with their great themes, paralleling the counsels of Macchiavelli in his *Prince* in parts but maintaining throughout that
strange Calvinistic stoicism which is characteristic elsewhere
of their exceedingly interesting author.   Greville's *Treastise
of Human Learning* not only links on to Davies' *Nosce Teipsum*, with which it agrees as to the limitations and vanities
of human knowledge, but comes into contact as well with
Bacon's manifesto of the new science, *The Advancement
of Learning*, printed in 1605.   It falls, too, into contrast with
Daniel's fine poem *Musophilus, or a General Defence of all
Learning*, 1599, which in a dialogue between Musophilus, the
lover of the Muses, and Philocosmus, the worldly man, enthusiastically upholds the "holy skill" of letters and stands
opposed alike to the popular agnosticism of Davies, to the
"practical utility" of Bacon, and to the "moral utility of
Greville."   Daniel has well been considered one of the last
of the humanists; for in him was combined, to the full, the
love of learning and the appreciation of the dignity of the
scholar, with a fine loyalty to England and faith in the great
destiny of the English tongue.   The following apostrophe
to "heavenly Eloquence," recently quoted by Mr. Courthope, deserves transcription for its truly "imperial" prophecy
of that spread and potency of our language which we have
come now in part to know.

Thou, that cans't do much more with one poor pen
Than all the powers of princes can effect:
And draw, divert, dispose, and fashion men
Better than force or rigor can direct.
Should we this instrument of glory then
As th' unmaterial fruit of shades neglect?
Or should we careless come behind the rest
In power of words that go before in worth,
Whereas our accents, equal to the best,
Is able greater wonders to bring forth,
Where all that ever hotter spirits exprest
Comes bettered by the patience of the north.
And who in time knows whither we may vent
The treasure of our tongue, to what strange shores
This gain of our best glory shall be sent,
T' enrich unknowing nations with our stores?
What worlds in the yet unformèd occident
May come refined with th' accents that are ours?
Or who can tell for what great work in hand
The greatness of our style is now ordained,
What powers it shall bring in, what spirits command,
What thoughts let out, what humors keep restrained,
What mischief it may powerfully withstand,
And what fair ends may thereby be attained?

Returning to the honorable name of Michael Drayton, as
early as 1598 he is reported to have been engaged on a work
called *Polyolbion*, printed in part in 1613, and completed in
thirty "songs" in 1622. The title describes this truly surprising work as "a chorographical description of all the tracts,
rivers, mountains, forests and other parts of this renowned
isle of Great Britain, with intermixture of the most remarkable
stories, antiquities, wonders, rareties, pleasures, and com-
modities of the same . . . digested into a poem by Michael
Drayton." It is amazing in a work of such stupendous
length and with subject-matter by its nature so monotonous,
how uniformly poetical the author has contrived to be. *Polyolbion* is truly a production without parallel in the annals of
any literature; for as Lamb said, Drayton "has not left a
rivulet so narrow that it may be stepped over without honor-

able mention, and has associated hills and streams with life and passion beyond the dreams of old mythology." This grand and patriotic theme, the celebration of his fatherland, Drayton must have derived from the unfulfilled dreams of the old antiquary Leland. Selden, the famous scholar and publicist, did not disdain to adorn the earlier part of Draytons' work with learned notes and commentary, and the original editions are illustrated with quaint maps in which the personified geniuses of town and country are represented bodily to the view. Ridiculous as it may seem thus to personify every hill and metamorphose every stream into a classical nymph or river god, and alien as is Drayton's old alexandrine verse to our modern tastes, no one reading in the *Polyolbion* can fail to recognize the poet in Drayton and to treat with becoming respect these labors of a by-gone time that stand like huge Pelasgian walls, inexplicable from the hands of men as men are now.

Despite the many other poetical influences that give to the age of Elizabeth a variety in quality and kind not surpassed in Victorian times, the dominant concord of Spenser's sweet verse was heard strong and constant in the poetical concert that continued for a generation after his death. Spenser's allegory, his continuousness, his delight leisurely to dwell on beautiful details, his diffuseness and carelessness as to design or as to ultimately landing from the crystal flood of his on-flowing verse anywhere: all of these qualities were perpetuated in his kind, though no one of the Spenserians reaches a place beside his master.

Allusion has already been made to the poetical Fletchers. Besides John, the great dramatist, and Giles the elder, his uncle, who wrote sonnets in the sonnet time and traveled into Muscovy, there were the two Spenserians, sons of Giles, named Phineas and Giles the younger; and there was likewise, somewhat later, a religious poet Joseph Fletcher, who does not, however, concern us. Phineas Fletcher was born in 1582; Giles, his brother, some three or four years after. Both were educated at Cambridge and both entered the church, leading useful if uneventful lives. Giles the younger died early, in 1623; Phineas was alive in 1649. The frequent allusions in their poetry, each to the other, disclose the warm brotherly affection between them, and their poetical kinship is as close as that of their blood.

Christ's Victory and Triumph by Giles Fletcher the younger was published at Cambridge in 1610. It is an ambitious epic poem in the manner of Spenser, treating of Christ's victory in heaven, on earth, his triumph over death, and his triumph after death. The subject is overlaid with an exuberance of allegory, typifying and personifying the emotions and passions, and is full of passages of exquisite poetical imagery. Giles Fletcher attempts a variation on the famous Spenserian stanza, reducing it to eight lines by the omission of the sixth. *Christ's Victory and Triumph* is a beautiful poem of its type and throbs at times with the true religious fervor which distinguishes the rapturous religious poetry of Richard Crashaw. Phineas Fletcher's contribution to the poetry of this class is almost equally successful, if more curious in kind. *The Purple Island* was first printed in 1633. It is the opinion of Dr. Grosart, Fletcher's editor, that the poem was substantially written as we have it early in the days of King James, an opinion true in the main, if perhaps questionable as to those passages which show a grasp and understanding of Harvey's famous discovery of the circulation of the blood, a first announcement of which was made by him in a lecture in the year of the death of Shakespeare. *The Purple Island* is "an elaborate allegorical description of the human body and of the vices and virtues to which man is subject." The body is figured as an island, the bones its foundation, the veins its streams, and so on into a multiplicity of minute detail, though it is fair to state that the poem has a wider scope and rises in the later cantos to an allegory of man's intellectual processes, his emotions, and even of his religious ideas. The whole is framed in a pastoral setting and many are the passages which for truth to picturesque nature, poetic beauty of expression, and musical flow of verse are worthy the inspiration of their great master, Spenser. It seems hardly fair to quote from so fine a poem a passage which emphasizes its chief defect.   Yet the following is alone enough to show what Spenserian allegory could become when ingenuity triumphed, as it did only too often in long, uninspired reaches of the Spenserians, over poetic inspiration.   The poet — or rather the allegorist — has been describing the human mouth as an "arched cave."   He continues:

> At that cave's mouth twice sixteen porters stand,
>   Receivers of the customary rent;
> Of each side four — the foremost of the band —
>   Whose office to divide what in is sent:
> Straight other four break it in pieces small;
> And at each hand twice five, which grinding all,
> Fit it for convoy and this city's arsenal.

In *The Purple Island* and in *Christ's Victory and Triumph* we have Spenserian allegory, Spenserian epic continuity, even an imitation of Spenserian stanza, for *The Purple Island* is written in the meter of *Christ's Victory*, which we have seen was a variation — not an improvement — on the stanza of *The Faery Queen*.   But the influence of Spenser in the pastoral was even more pervasive and lasting.   A list of English eclogues following *The Shepherds' Calendar* and running not beyond the lifetime of Shakespeare, includes the names of Peele, Watson, Barnfield, Lodge, Sabbie, Drayton, William Browne, George Wither, and Christopher Brooke.   Of these an unimportant *Eclogue Gratulatory*, addressed to the Earl of Essex, was published by Peele in 1589.   Thomas Watson's *Melibœus*, an elegy on the death of the queen's secretary, Sir Francis Walsingham, was written first in Latin and translated by the author in the following year.   Watson was the author of other Latin eclogues.   Barnfield's *Affectionate Shepherd*, four years later, is a free following of the Vergilian eclogue, and the work of a rare young poet of whom it may be said that he deserved the confusion which long existed between some of his lyrics and Shakespeare's.   Lodge wrote both eclogues of an amatory and of a meditative cast. The first are found in *Phillis honored with Pastoral Sonnets*, 1593; the second form part of his little volume entitled *A Fig for Momus*, and appeared two years later.   In these latter Lodge displays his literary relations to Spenser, Drayton, and Daniel, whom he celebrates under guise of pastoral names, and shows, like Spenser before him, that he had read the popular eclogues of Mantuan. Lodge is always a sweet poet and a master of musical effect; but he is happier in the lyric pastoral than in the eclogue. *Pan's Pipe* by Francis Sabbie of the same date is described in the title as "three pastoral eclogues in English hexameters." It is a less notable work and equally referable to previous models. William Basse's three pastoral elegies, published in 1602, really form a short pastoral romance. Like his later work, beyond our period, they are possessed of little merit.

The most important of Spenser's followers in the reign of Queen Elizabeth was Drayton, whose industry and genuine poetic gift once more inspire and hold our esteem. It was in 1593 that Drayton published his *Idea, the Shepherd's Garland fashioned into Nine Eclogues;* a tenth with much revision of the rest appeared in 1606; and towards the end of his career the poet returned to the pastoral mode in his *Muses' Elizium* as he had still practised it as occasion arose throughout the *Polyolbion* and elsewhere. *The Shepherds' Calendar* was undoubtedly the model of the young poet, although *The Shepherd's Garland* is knit in no such close continuity as Spenser's poem. Drayton's pastorals, too, are less weighted with serious matter moral and religious and freer from veiled satire. Like Spenser's they sound the full gamut of the oaten reed, treating of love requited and unrequited, eulogizing the queen in a fine ode, and meditating "in higher strains." Drayton uses a great variety of meters, is full of genuine touches of nature, and musical with the choice lyrical gift of his time.

We may pass such a production of mixed verse and prose as *England's Mourning Garment Worn by Plain Shepherds*, wherein Henry Chettle, memorable as the editor of Greene's *Groatsworth of Wit*, lamented the death of "Elizabeth, queen of virtue, while she lived, and theme of sorrow, being dead." It is chiefly interesting for his arraignment of the poets Warner, Chapman, Jonson, Shakespeare, Drayton, and others for not singing threnodies to her deceased majesty. Shakespeare, especially, under the pastoral name of Melicert, is adjured to

> Drop from his honied Muse one sable tear,
> To mourn her death that gracèd his desert,
> And to his lays opened her royal ear.

There is record of the writing of twelve eclogues about this time by Edward Fairfax, the translator of Tasso. But only two of them and the fragment of a third are now extant. They are said to concern chiefly contemporary affairs, to deal with abuses in the church and in a panegyric of English maritime adventure. Minor pastoralists of the earlier years of King James were Sir George Buc, Master of the Revels from 1608 to 1622, and Lewis Machin, a very small dramatist. The first used the eclogue form to celebrate the Plantagenet succession in a curious poem entitled *Daphnis Polystephanos*, printed in 1605. Machin's three ecolgues, in easy but no very distinguished verse, touch on erotic themes of the class of *Hero and Leander* and appeared affixed to a like production by William Barkstead, the actor, called *Mirrha the Mother of Adonis*, bearing date 1607. Needless to say, neither Fairfax, Buc, nor Machin write in the manner of Spenser.

The last group of Spenserians, all of them pastoralists, cluster about the closing years of Shakespeare's life. William Browne of Tavistock is chief among them, an amiable retiring man, possessed of a simplicity of character and heartfelt love of nature that remind us somewhat of Wordsworth, remote though Browne is from any trace of Wordsworth's power of spiritual insight. Browne lived between 1591 and 1643. He received his education at Exeter College, Oxford, Clifford's Inn, and the Inner Temple, for which last he wrote a beautiful masque. Like so many of the poets before him, Browne enjoyed the patronage and encouragement of the Herbert family, and his poetical impulse comes direct from the pastoral poetry of Drayton, his acknowledged friend and sponsor. Besides Browne, there was Christopher Brooke, son of a wealthy tradesman who had been thrice mayor of his native town of York, and a friend and intimate of Donne.

George Wither, most voluminous of later pamphleteers, in whom the acid of satire spoiled one of the sweetest of poets, was the third; and John Davies of Hereford, the writing-master and author of many books in verse and prose, seems likewise to have been of their counsels. In 1613 appeared Browne's *Britannia's Pastorals;* in 1614, his *Shepherd's Pipe,* to which were added eclogues by the other three. In 1615 Wither wrote his *Shepherd's Hunting* while a prisoner for libel in the Marshelsea, and in 1616 Browne issued a second instalment of *Britannia's Pastorals,* a third part remaining until the last century in manuscript. In this group of pastoral poems we have by far the most important contribution of its kind to English literature and it is suprising to find how single an influence pervades this by no means inconsiderable body of poetry. Wither's *Shepherd's Hunting* conceals an allegory of his own imprisonment for "hunting" with his many hounds of satire (in his *Abuses Stript and Whipt,* 1611) the monsters of the country-side. Otherwise these eclogues are without ulterior allusion save to the pleasant poetical friendship of the little brotherhood. Story in these poems there is none, and their diffuseness far exceeds that of Spenser. But the readers of Browne and his fellows may feel sure that "at whatever page they open, they have not far to travel before they find entertainment."

Browne is essentially a descriptive poet, his "mood is generally calm and quiet, like the painter of actual scenery." There is little movement in his poetry, a broken and meandering thread of story, and next to no human interest. Even his lyric moods, which are often graceful, have almost none of that glow and fervor which is characteristic of many of his contemporaries. The strongest trait of Browne, as of Drayton, is his devoted love of country; but where Drayton with impartial loyalty celebrates all England in particularizing each part, Browne, strong in his local affections, never strays far from his native Tavistock and realizes the dreams of Arcadia in the familiar features of his native Devonshire. Thus it is that Browne expresses himself in terms of this amiable provincialism:

Hail, thou, my native soil! thou blessed plot,
Whose equal all the world affordeth not!
Show me who can so many crystal rills;
Such sweet-clothed valleys or aspiring hills;
Such wood-ground pastures, quarries, wealthy mines;
Such rocks in whom the diamond fairly shines;
And if the earth can show the like again,
Yet will she fail in her sea-ruling men.
Time never can produce men to o'ertake
The fames of Grenville, Davies, Gilbert, Drake,
Of worthy Hawkins, or of thousands more
That by their power made the Devonian shore
Mock the proud Tagus; for whose richest spoil
The boasting Spaniard left the Indian soil
Bankrupt of store, knowing it would quit cost
By winning this, though all the rest were lost.

In conclusion of these paragraphs on the pastoralists that
followed Spenser I shall quote not Drayton, most poetical and
resourceful in this kind of poetry, nor Browne, who approached
most nearly our modern conception of the touch with nature;
but make some amends to excellent Phineas Fletcher, for
having gibbeted his ingenious allegory, by choosing two or
three stanzas from several of equal merit in his *Purple Island*,
that express to perfection this outworn ideal of the golden age.

Thrice, oh thrice happy shepherd's life and state,
    When courts are happiness' unhappy pawns!
His cottage low and safely humble gate
    Shuts out proud Fortune with her scorns and fawns;
No fearèd treason breaks his quiet sleep:
Singing all day, his flocks he learns to keep;
Himself as innocent as are his simple sheep.

.   .   .   .

Instead of music and base flattering tongues,
    Which wait to first-salute my lord's uprise;
The cheerful lark wakes him with early songs,
    And birds' sweet whistling notes unlock his eyes:
In country plays is all the strife he uses,
Or sing, or dance unto the rural Muses;
And but in music's sports, all differences refuses.

His certain life that never can deceive him,
  Is full of thousand sweets and rich content:
The smooth-leav'd beeches in the field receive him
  With coolest shades, till noon-tide rage is spent:
His life is neither tost in boist'rous seas
Of troublous world, nor lost in slothful ease;
Pleased and full blest he lives, when he his God can please.

His bed of wool yields safe and quiet sleeps,
  While by his side his faithful spouse hath place:
His little son into his bosom creeps,
  The lively picture of his father's face:
Never his humble house or state torment him;
Less he could like, if less his God had sent him:
And when he dies, green turfs with grassy tomb content him.

CHAPTER XIII

JONSON AND THE CLASSICAL REACTION

THE greatest of Shakespeare's contemporaries in the drama, a man historically even more important than Shakespeare himself, was Ben Jonson, poet, playwright, critic, satirist, laureate, and dictator of his time. Jonson was born in the year 1573, of a border family of Annandale, and was the posthumous son of a minister who had lost his estate by forfeiture in the reign of Queen Mary. His widow marrying again and beneath her, Jonson was "brought up poorly," but "put to school" at Westminster, and there befriended by the learned antiquary, Camden. Fuller states that from Westminster Jonson went to [St. John's College] Cambridge. If so, he remained but a short time; for he afterwards told Drummond that "he was Master of Arts in both universities by their favor, not his study." The trade of his step-father, that of bricklaying, proving distasteful, Jonson enlisted as a soldier and relates that "in his service in the Low Countries," he had, "in the face of both the camps, killed an enemy and taken *opima spolia* from him." Jonson returned to London in 1592, married, and began writing for the stage, probably about 1595. In 1597 he was in the employ of Henslowe and acting as one of the Admiral's men; and in the following year he is included in Meres' roll of honor as one of the best contemporary writers of comedy. It was in that year that Jonson killed "in duel" a fellow actor, named Gabriel Spencer, for which offense he was tried at Old Bailey and found guilty. He escaped the gallows by pleading the benefit of clergy, but remained some time in prison. It was under the stress of these experiences that Jonson became a Roman Catholic; but he returned to the faith of the Church of England after some ten or a dozen years. A pleasing tradition of this period relates that on his release Jonson sought employment for his pen with Henslowe's rivals, the Lord Chamberlain's company, in which Shakespeare had already become a prominent shareholder; and that *Every Man in his Humor* was accepted by that company through the good offices of Shakespeare who, we know, acted a part. This was the corner-stone of Jonson's success, though in all likelihood by no means the first of his dramatic efforts.

Every Man in his Humor, acted in 1598, is a satirical comedy of London life, skilfully constructed on the recognition of two principles: the necessity of sketching direct from life and the desirability of drawing your picture in a manner already accepted as in accord with good art and a recognized method. The comedy runs on an exceedingly slender story, the mistake of a father as to the real character of his son, his following to observe him, and the consequences to both and to the little group of personages by whom they are surrounded. The general intermeddling of a man-servant, named Brainworm, possessed of a mania for fooling everybody, precipitates several situations; the rest are the results of some dominant trait of each character. In a word, in *Every Man in his Humor* we have an example of a new kind of comedy, consciously developed by Jonson on the basis of a very definite theory of life and art, and known as the comedy of humors. The word "humor" in the parlance of the day signified a superficial tendency or bias of disposition that so ruled a person, permanently or for the moment, that one could say, this man affects gravity, this is a disconsolate lover, this third is a braggart or an affected fop. Jonson did not invent the word "humor"; and characters, thus conceived, were not only known to the stage before his time but were devised as made up of "humors" by Chapman a little before *Every Man in his Humor*. Jonson, extending this popular idea, held that a "humor" should be some overwhelming passion or unmistakable warp in character, such as Brainworm's passion for gulling everybody, Bobadil's mania of boasting though he is a coward at heart, or Downright, described in his name; and he avoided making his personages turn (as did some of his imitators) on petty affectations or mannerisms of speech.

Moreover, he constructed his play out of this clash of incongruous humors, and was concerned less with a picture, much less a story, of actual life than with the opportunity which this method afforded him for devising ridiculous situations, witty dialogue, and unlooked-for outcomes. Life is not much like such a succession of the clever unexpected; though Jonson's scenes can not be pronounced absolutely untrue to human nature. The characters of men in the world are not built up on such impossibly simple lines; yet the attention may not unfairly be directed to the ruling passion of a given personage, and personages, so possessed for the nonce, be chosen legitimately as subjects for the persons of comedy. In *Every Man in his Humor* Jonson succeeded surprisingly well in picturing, in vivid realism, the absurdities, the eccentricities and predicaments, so to speak, of Elizabethan life in terms of a glorified adaptation of the technique of Plautus.

This new variety of the comedy of manners leaped into immediate acceptance and popularity. It was imitated by everybody, at times by those not fitted for it; it was parodied and misunderstood. It was used for single characters or groups of them, as an underplot or episode; and this conception of stage character, degenerating frequently into caricature, continued to tinge the drama onward to the days of Sheridan, if not beyond. But we are not concerned with these wide influences. Among immediate effects, the word "humor" became current in colloquial speech and in titles of other plays: for example, Jonson himself reëmployed it in *Every Man out of his Humor* and, later, in *The Magnetic Lady or Humors Reconciled*. There was an anonymous and inferior comedy called *Every Woman in her Humor*, 1600, imitating more than Jonson's title; and, besides Chapman's *Humorous Day's Mirth* in 1599, Day wrote a sprightly comedy entitled *Humor out of Breath*, printed in 1608. As to Chapman, he was, in comedy at least, wholly of Jonson's school and method, as his admirable *All Fools*, 1599, and *May Day*, two years later, attest. Field was literally Jonson's scholar in the drama. But Jonson in this example of his comedy of humors was not even without his influence on the catholic and adaptable spirit of Shakespeare. It seems not irrational to refer such a group of humorists as Falstaff and his rout — Bardolph of the carbuncled nose, Pistol with his bombast scraps of plays, Falstaff himself of unmeasured girth, and that "minnow," his contrasted page — to this Jonsonian attempt to conceive theatrical personages on lines of definite simplicity and salient quality. Dr. Caius and his group in *The Merry Wives*, and the typical Scotch, Welsh, and Irish soldiers of *Henry V*, are similiar examples. All these plays correspond in point of time with the new rage of the Jonsonian humor, as did many others by lesser men such, for example, as *Oldcastle* and *The Merry Devil of Edmonton*, in both of which like groups of humorists recur.

During the next three years, from 1599 to 1602, Jonson was engaged in a theatrical struggle conducted by means of satirical dramas which is known to the history of the stage as the war of the theaters. Throughout the latter years of the reign of Queen Elizabeth the Chamberlain's company, acting continuously at the Globe, maintained its lead in the dramatic profession. Its principal rivals were the Admiral's men who occupied the Rose and moved, on its completion in 1600, to Alleyn's new Fortune Theater in Golding Lane, Cripplegate. In these years the companies of boy actors assumed an extraordinary importance. These were the Children of the Chapel Royal who occupied the private theater which Burbage had built in Blackfriars from the time of its erection, in 1596, and the Children of Paul's who appear to have acted in their singing-school attached to the cathedral. It has recently been argued, as we have seen above, that the prominence of the former company was due directly to royal patronage and that these boys, under the aggressive leadership of Nathaniel Giles, Master of the Queen's Chapel, were really maintained as actors, as well as singers for the Royal Chapel, out of the royal purse. At any rate, save for Shakespeare, they commanded the best pens of the moment, Jonson's among them; and they enjoyed, for two or three years, an unusual vogue because of the emphasis which they laid, in the plays written for them, on a general satire of the times and even on personal attack and lampoon.

To be sure, satire was no new thing in the drama and there is reason to believe that individual and personal attack had been employed on the stage not only privately, as at the universities, but publicly also and especially in the Martin Marprelate controversy, an account of which has been given in a previous chapter. The Marprelate plays have perished. Lyly and Nash were the dramatists chiefly concerned in them. As to the war of the theaters, or the "poetomachia," as Dekker called it, its origin is not certainly known. Some have referred it to allusions of a satirical nature to Jonson, contained in a satire by John Marston entitled *The Scourge of Villainy.* Jonson himself declared that "he had many quarrels with Marston, beat him, and took his pistol from him, wrote his *Poetaster* on him; the beginning of them were that Marston represented him on the stage." The "war" assumed two aspects from the first, the critical, in which Jonson arrogated to himself the censorship of poetry and the stage, and the personal, wherein he vigorously lampooned his enemies. We are certain that the principals were Jonson and Marston. Concerning the seconds and other aiders and abettors, much is dubious. Marston was two or three years the junior of Jonson, and was the son of a lawyer, sometime lecturer of the Inner Temple. He received his education at Brasenose College, Oxford, and his position among writers of non-dramatic satire in verse will receive our later consideration. Marston made a distinguished place for himself as a dramatist within the first decade of the century and, entering the church, lived on until 1634. He was an opinionated and self-satisfied young man of twenty-two in 1598, fresh from his classics at the university, and possessed of a conversancy with Italian which he had from his mother. Jonson, as the new writer of comedies of humors, just come into vogue, was as opinionated and self-complaisant in his success as was ever Marston. It is likely that Jonson's hands were by no means clean when he was attacked by Marston. In *The Case is Altered,* a quasi-romantic comedy written before *Every Man in his Humor* but which Jonson never acknowledged, he had gibbeted several of his contemporaries satirically, among them

Anthony Munday. In *Every Man in his Humor* he had quite as certainly satirized in Master Matthew the poet Daniel, against whom Jonson bore a continual grudge. Daniel had already been the butt of dramatic satire at the hands of Chettle and Dekker in one of the personages of *Patient Grissel*. It seems likely that *Histriomastix*, a play revised by Marston in 1598, contained in the character Chrisogonus, a poet, satirist, and translator, poor but contemptuous of the ignoble crowd, a picture of Jonson and one by no means discreditable to him. If this was intended by Marston as amends, Jonson refused so to construe it. It has even been surmised that this is the representation of Jonson on the stage to which the poet refers as the beginning of the quarrel.[1]

The first of Jonson's three great satires in dramatic form is *Every Man out of his Humor*, acted by the Chamberlain's company in 1599. Whatever differences may arise among students of the drama as to individual identifications, there can be no question that in this play Jonson lampooned several of his fellow poets, although the front of the satire is directed against citizen follies. Munday, Lodge, Daniel as Fastidious Brisk, " a spruce, affecting courtier," all have been thought to be the subject of Jonson's wit and scorn; whilst Carlo Buffone, "a public scurrilous and profane jester," was formerly supposed to be Marston (author of *The Scourge of Villainy*), especially because Carlo is pointedly alluded to as "the grand scourge or second untruss (that is satirist) of the time" (Joseph Hall having boasted himself the first). Of late, however, there has been a return to an old identification of Carlo Buffone with a notorious person named Charles Chester in the following passage from gossipy and notoriously inaccurate John Aubrey. He relates that Chester was "a bold importunate fellow . . . a perpetual talker, and made a noise like a drum in a room. So one time at a tavern Sir Walter Raleigh beats him and seals up his mouth (that is his

[1] On this whole topic, see the excellent work of J. H. Penniman, *The War of the Theatres, Publications of the University of Pennsylvania*, 1897, and his ed. of *Poetaster* and *Satiromastix*, 1913.

upper and nether beard) with hard wax. From him Ben
Jonson takes his Carlo Buffone (i.e. jester), in *Every Man in
his Humor*." Is it conceivable that after all Jonson was
ridiculing Marston and that the point of the satire consisted
in part at least in an intentional confusion of the "grand
scourge or second untruss" with "the scurrilous and profane"
Chester?

Asper-Macilente is Jonson's complaisant picture of himself, the calm, just, learned poet, carrying his brow high and
unruffled in the midst of a pack of the yelping curs of detraction. In 1600 followed Jonson's more elaborate satire,
Cynthia's Revels or the Fountain of Self-Love, this time acted
by the Children of the Queen's Chapel, and still further
advancing against his foes with the direct attack of his biting
and galling satire. Here Marston is certainly ridiculed in
the character Anaides, with Daniel, Lodge, and Munday as
before. His personages Jonson designates characteristically
under abstract names of Greek origin. Thus, Anaides
(Impudence), Hedon (Pleasure), and Asotus (the Prodigal)
— each accompanied by an appropriate female abstraction,
Moria (Folly), Philautia (Self-Love), and Argurion (Money)
— appear on the stage in brilliant and caustic dialogue, full
of allusions, personal, social, local, everything but political,
most of them lost to us (despite our most searching scholarship) but evidently affording an entertainment to the audiences
of the day, equaled only by what we learn of Aristophanes in
ancient Athens. Jonson himself figures as the righteous and
judicious Crites. The reversion of Jonson here, as again
in his latest plays, to the abstractions of the old morality and
to the method of allegory is a striking characteristic of his
strong English personality. It has been held that *Jack
Drum's Entertainment*, another unavowed comedy of Marston,
dating 1600, contains a second dramatic attack on Jonson in
the character of a ridiculous Frenchman of licentious habits,
Monsieur Fo de King; but this is questionable to say the
least. A satirical scene of Marston's *Antonio and Mellida*,
acted also in 1600, between Balurdo and a painter, has
been regarded a parody of a similar scene between Hieronimo

and a painter which occurs in that part of *The Spanish Tragedy* which we know that Jonson added by way of revision of Kyd's old work. But this assumes an earlier date for Jonson's revision than has yet been proved.

Jonson's third and final dramatic satire was *Poetaster*, acted (once more by the Chapel Children) in 1601. Here his avowed quarry was the inferior poets of the time who, he declares, had provoked him with "their petulant styles" for years "on the stage." In a parable of the poetasters of ancient Rome, Crispinus and Demetrius, Jonson contrasts their spleen, stupidity, habits of literary theft, and their envy of Vergil and Horace, with the virtue, moral righteousness, and impeccability of these two, in the latter of whom we recognize, once more, Jonson's favorite portrait of himself. Jonson was answered soon after by Dekker in his *Satiromastix*, 1602, which he seems to have been engaged by others to write. Dekker thus really comes into the quarrel near to its conclusion and the circumstance that *Satiromastix* is clearly an unfinished play — really of chronicle type and evidently altered in haste for this specific purpose — makes this the more likely. From a literary point of view, *Satiromastix* can not be pronounced a good play, though clever and pointed enough. But the arrogance of Jonson and his outrageous self-righteousness caused the time to award the palm to his opponents; and this despite Jonson's tremendous superiority in every quality that goes to make up effective dramatic satire. The arrogance of Jonson reaches its height in *An Apologetical Dialogue* which he affixed to *Poetaster*, on its publication in 1602 and which he declares was "only once spoken on the stage." Here the poet represents himself in conversation with two obsequious and admiring friends concerning his dramatic and other opinions and in contemptuous, but only too mindful, neglect of his enemies. It adds to our wonder at the sublimity of Jonson's arrogant self-esteem to learn that he acted himself, in this *Dialogue*, *in propria persona*. No lawsuits, however, appear to have resulted from these vituperative libels of the stage. And we find Jonson in friendship and collaboration with both Marston and Dekker a short time after. Hence we may infer that there was no small amount of playing to the gallery in all this dramatic warfare. As a specimen of Jonson's swift satirical dialogue in its lighter vein, let us take the following. Fastidious Brisk, "a neat, spruce, affecting courtier, one that wears clothes well, and in fashion," and Puntarvolo, "a vain-glorious knight, wholly consecrated to singularity," are the chief interlocutors. Carlo Buffone, described as "a good feast-hound or banquet-beagle," bears a minor part.

Fast. Good faith, signior, now you speak of a quarrel, I 'll acquaint you with a difference that happened between a gallant and myself; Sir Puntarvolo, you know him if I should name him, Signior Luculento.

Punt. Luculento! What inauspicious chance interposed itself to your two loves?

Fast. Faith, sir, the same that sundered Agamemnon and great Thetis' son; but let the cause escape, sir: he sent me a challenge mixed with some few braves, which I restored and in fine we met. Now, indeed, sir, I must tell you he did offer at first very desperately but without judgment: for, look you, sir, I cast myself into this figure; now he comes violently on, and withal advancing his rapier to strike, I thought to have took his arm, for he had left his whole body to my election, and I was sure he could not recover his guard. Sir, I missed my purpose in his arm, rashed his doublet-sleeve, ran him close by the left cheek, and through his hair. He again lights me here, — I had on a gold cable hatband, then new come up, which I wore about a murrey French hat I had, — cuts my hatband, and yet it was massy goldsmith's work, cuts my brims, which, by good fortune, being thick embroidered with gold twist and spangles, disappointed the force of the blow: nevertheless, it grazed on my shoulder, takes me away six purls of an Italian cut-work band I wore, cost me three pound in the Exchange but three days before.

Punt. This was a strange encounter.

Fast. Nay, you shall hear, sir: with this we both fell out and breathed. Now, upon the second sign of his assault, I betook me to the former manner of my defence; he, on the other side, abandoned his body to the same danger as before, and follows me still with blows: but I being loth to take the deadly advantage that lay before me of his left side, made a kind of stramazoun, ran him up to the hilts through the doublet, through the shirt, and yet missed the skin.

He, making a reverse blow, falls upon my embossed girdle — I had thrown off the hangers before, — strikes off a skirt of a thick-laced satin doublet I had, lined with some four taffetas, cuts off two panes embroidered with pearl, rends through the drawings-out of tissue, enters the linings, and skips the flesh.

Car. I wonder he speaks not of his wrought shirt.

Fast. Here, in the opinion of mutual damage, we paused; but ere I proceed I must tell you, segnior, that in this last encounter not having leisure to put off my silver spurs, one of the rowels catched hold of the ruffle of my boot, and being Spanish leather and subject to tear, overthrows me, rends me two pair of silk stockings that I put on, being somewhat a raw morning, a peach color and another, and strikes me some half-inch deep into the side of the calf; he, seeing the blood come, presently takes horse and away; I, having bound up my wound with a piece of my wrought shirt —

Car. O! comes it in there?

Fast. Rid after him, and, lighting at the court gate, both together embraced, and marched hand in hand up into the presence. Was not this business well carried?

A natural question arises here: where was Shakespeare during all this fuss and fury? especially as we know by a clear passage in *Hamlet* that he was neither ignorant of the matter nor without an opinion about it. There is moreover an allusion to the quarrel in an academic play called *The Return from Parnassus* in which Shakespeare is not only suggested as having taken a part in the quarrel but is spoken of as having gained the better of Jonson in it. Still further, some have thought that *Troilus and Cressida*, from its bitter and satirical spirit (so unlike the Shakespeare of earlier and later work) was the particular play in which the great dramatist took his part in these petty broils. However, in view of the circumstance that Dekker's *Satiromastix* was acted by Shakespeare's company in answer to Jonson's two satires, just performed by the Children of the Chapel, it seems not impossible to suppose this play, rather than *Troilus*, the one in which Shakespeare triumphed, vicariously to be sure, over the satire of the truculent Jonson. The passage in *Hamlet* referring to "the war" and constantly quoted, runs as follows. Hamlet has heard of the arrival of players at Elsinore and is in conversation with

Rosencrantz about them. He asks: "What players are they?" And Rosencrantz replies:

Even those you were wont to take delight in, the tragedians of the city.

Ham. How chances it they travel? Their residence, both in reputation and profit, was better both ways.

Ros. I think their inhibition comes by the means of the late innovation.

Ham. Do they hold the same estimation they did when I was in the city? Are they so followed?

Ros. No, indeed they are not.

Ham. How comes it? Do they grow rusty?

Ros. Nay, their endeavor keeps in the wonted pace: but there is, sir, an aery of children, little eyases, that cry out on the top of question, and are most tyrannically clapped for 't: these are now in fashion, and so berattle the common stages, — so they call them, — that many wearing rapiers are afraid of goose-quills, and dare scarce come hither.

Ham. What! are they children? who maintains 'em? how are they escoted? Will they pursue the quality no longer than they can sing? will they not say afterwards, if they should grow themselves to common players, — as it is most like, if their means are no better, — their writers do them wrong, to make them exclaim against their own succession?

Ros. Faith, there has been much to do on both sides; and the nation holds it no sin to tarre them to controversy: there was, for a while, no money bid for argument, unless the poet and the player went to cuffs in the question.

Hamlet learns that the regular troupes of the city have suffered what amounts to an inhibition or order to cease playing, because of the extraordinary popularity of an aery of children, that is company of boy actors, who are tremendously applauded by the public for performing satirical plays in which people are lampooned on the boards. And Hamlet's question —that is, Shakespeare's — is not, Who are the parties to the quarrel? or, How cleverly have the poets lashed each other? His thought is for the little actors, and the pity that they should thus be "tarred," or set on, to tear and worry, in such a rivalry, their older fellows in the profession, when it is likely that they, in time, must succeed the very men they are now attacking. It may be questioned if Shakespeare's personal contribution to the war of the theaters was more than this kindly admonition.

Even a cursory examination of Elizabethan plays discovers them occurring as to kind and subject in groups wherein some popular success is emulated by rival dramatists and the same or like topic exploited until the public calls for something new. Subjects derived from classical history or myth had been popular on the stage almost from the beginning. The direct suggestion came from Seneca; and from Sackville to Kyd the academic Senecan line was continued, by Daniel, Greville, and the coterie that preserved the traditions of Sidney, to Sir William Alexander and his *Monarchic Tragedies*, in the early years of King James. Except for Daniel's *Cleopatra* and *Philotas*, both of them graceful and dignified tragedies, none of these plays were intended for the stage. The whole group appears to have been influenced directly by the French Senecan, Robert Garnier, and the best of them are the remarkable closet dramas, *Alaham* and *Mustapha*, strange yet attractive product of the philosophic ponderings of Sir Fulke Greville, written perhaps before the death of Elizabeth. On the popular stage, aside from such old productions as Lodge's *Wounds of Civil War* and the anonymous *Wars of Cyrus*, which date about the time of the Armada, Marlowe's *Dido, Queen of Carthage*, printed in 1594, was one of the more important dramas levying on classical subjects, a tragedy in which Nash is alleged to have had a hand and one which, while far from ranking with Marlowe's greatest work, is no discredit to either author. A year or two later came Heywood's mythology dramatized in the sundry plays on the four ages, already mentioned; and about 1600, Shakespeare's *Julius Cæsar*.

It has been observed that Shakespeare's *Julius Cæsar* is one of the most regularly constructed of his plays. In it he seems to have caught more nearly than elsewhere the restraint of the classical spirit, though great as this tragedy is and full of the poetry, the wisdom, and the power of characterization that mark Shakespeare's plays everywhere more or less, *Julius*

Cæsar can not be declared, from the antiquarian's point of view, an accurate or an informing picture of ancient Roman life and history. Scholar and antiquarian that he was, the faults of such a production must have impressed themselves on a man like Jonson; and his *Sejanus*, first acted in 1603, was, if not exactly a reply, at least an expression of his own position. It seems from words of Jonson on the publication of *Sejanus* two years later that he had had in its first version a collaborator. And he is careful to have the reader know that, in printing, he has "rather chosen to put weaker and, no doubt, less pleasing [work] of mine own, than to defraud so happy a genius of his right by my loathed usurpation." Some have thought the "second pen" Shakespeare's. At any rate we know from Jonson's folio that Shakespeare was one of "the principal actors" in *Sejanus* and that, whatever its exact circumstances, the rivalry of these great spirits could not have been other than a generous one. In this tragedy of *Sejanus*, as to a lesser degree in his other tragedy dealing with classical history, *Catiline, his Conspiracy*, Jonson shows himself true to the classical ideals and theories that had always animated him. The earlier play was printed with elaborate scholarly references to authorities used in working up his material. The poet was not unjustly criticized for this pedantry, Marston slyly remarking in the preface to his *Sophonisba* (another able tragedy of this general type), that "to transcribe authors, quote authorities, and translate Latin prose orations into English blank-verse, hath, in this subject, been the least aim of my studies." *Sejanus*, with its admirable portrait study of Tiberius, derived from Tacitus, and *Catiline*, using as Jonson does in it the materials of Sallust's succinct account of that conspiracy, are splendid examples of Jonson's power practically to apply his just and reasonable classical theories about tragedy and literary art to current English conditions. It is not enough to say that if Jonson's figures are the truer Romans, Shakespeare's are the truer men. The art of the two is less opposed than to be contrasted. To the academician the free art of genius must always seem amazing and inexplicable, as it remains, for any rules that he can apply. But the art of the

academician has its place and deserves its praise. It is a credit
to these men of natures so diverse that they should have esteemed each other and worked thus together to produce an
artistic result. And it is an equal credit to the age that it
appreciated both, although it made Jonson honored and famous
and added riches only to the more popular success of Shakespeare.

In 1605 Jonson produced, with the help of Chapman and
Marston, to whom he was now fully reconciled, one of the best
comedies of London life in the language. This was *Eastward
Hoe*, a vivid picture of the tradesman's life presented in the
eternal contrast of the good and the evil-lived apprentice.
Here the authors succeeded in hitting the happy mean between purposeless art and moralizing, even though this comedy
does mark the climax of the parable of the prodigal son in
English drama. Neither preaching, allegory, nor abstraction
enter into this comedy to mar its effect; and yet its personages
are sufficiently typical to have appealed to its citizen auditors as they appeal for their truth, humor, and vivacity to the
reader to-day. The play, too, is so well knit and its plan is
so logically carried out that it is impossible to determine the
conditions of this fortunate collaboration. A passage containing satirical allusions to the Scotch was excised by order
of the royal council; but as passages were retained reflecting
on the country of the king's birth, Jonson and Chapman were
arrested and sent to prison for a time. In consequence of this
and of the popularity of *Eastward Hoe* on the stage, it was
printed three times in the year of its first presentation.

Volpone, often regarded as the most characteristic of the
comedies of Jonson, was acted for the first time in 1606 It
marks in tone a transition from the dramatic satires to the purer
comedies of contemporary life that follow a year or so later.
Volpone is the story of a Venetian grandee and his servant
Mosca, two scoundrels without a redeeming trait. They are
surrounded by a group of parasites and self-seekers whose
discomfiture at the hands of cleverer rascals than themselves,
with the final overthrow of these two, alone justifies the ethics
of the play. The cynical tone of *Volpone* and its attitude of

doubt as to the existence of virtue in the world raise the question as to whether such a play is comedy at all. Indeed, its method and tone are wholly tragic, although imprisonment, not death, overtakes the evil-doers. Jonson's view of comedy was derived from the ancients. To him the proper material for comedy is to be found in those departures from ordinary conditions, whether moral, social, or other, that rouse the phlegm of the satirist and moralist. The world to Jonson was made up for the most part of two classes, the fools and the knaves. And fools have been fair game for the knave time out of mind. There is such a thing, to be sure, as virtue; but unaccompanied by the protection of brains, it is likely to be little better than folly. Jonson can forgive anything but stupidity; and hence, Surley, the only respectable man in *The Alchemist* is discomfited, and that graceless scamp, Face, forgiven for his wit and success. It is somewhat strange that a man like Jonson, whose whole nature was grounded in a rigorous conception of moral ideas, should thus fail where Shakespeare and Dekker, careless observers of life as it is, succeed by an unerring instinct. But Shakespeare's appeal is almost always to the heart; Jonson's to the head and the critical understanding. Shakespeare's plots are made up of events generally beyond the control or even guidance of those whom they concern; and they involve in consequence an ebb and flow of passion with a resulting development or degeneracy in character. Jonson's plots on the contrary are a fabric of contrivances and devices, controlled by the cleverness and ingenuity of the characters of the play. In place of an ebb and flow of emotion, we have a struggle of wit, a play of mind against mind; and the characteristics of a personage once determined, he remains the same to the end.

After *Volpone*, Jonson gave up foreign scene for comedy. He even transferred the *locale* of *Every Man in his Humor*, in his revision of that play for his folio, from Florence to London, transforming Signior Lorenzo di Pazzi to Old Know'ell, Prospero to Master Welborn, Biancha to Mistress Bridget and Hesperida to Dame Kitely, dwelling "i' the Old Jewry." *The Silent Woman* and *The Alchemist*, 1609 and 1610 with

Bartholomew Fair, 1614, represent Jonson at his very best in comedies of the life of his native town. Jonson knew his London as well as his namesake, Dr. Johnson, in the age of the Georges; for satirist and moralist that the elder author was, he never forgot that the material for the drama is obtained primarily in the actual characteristics of people about you. *The Alchemist* details the doings of three sharpers who set up in a house, vacated for the time by reason of the plague, an alchemical furnace and by this and other means fool and cheat as many gulls as they can decoy thither. Their victims are, for the most part, contributary to their own undoing by their folly and wickedness and, in the dénouement, Face, the clever servant, prime mover of all villainy, is forgiven and a widow married out of hand after a manner known only to Roman comedy. *The Silent Woman* turns on the trick of Delphine, a knavish nephew, to regain his position as heir to his uncle, in the process of which his uncle, who detests noise, is driven almost frantic and a marriage (that he has planned to disinherit his nephew) is frustrated by the discovery that the wife is neither "silent" nor a woman, but an exceedingly noisy boy. Even slighter is the general fabric of the visit of Zeal-of-the-Land Busy, immortal Puritan, with his companions, to Bartholomew Fair, with the adventures that there befell them. Yet for clever plotting, for ingenuity of situation, sustained wit of dialogue, and humor in the conception of character and incident these comedies of Jonson have never been surpassed. Their age acclaimed them and imitated them again and again; and they held the stage as long as the comedies of Shakespeare and Fletcher, and after.

The rest of the plays of Jonson, except for a comedy called *The Devil is an Ass*, that failed on the stage in the year of Shakespeare's death, were not written until after the accession of King Charles in 1625. They were called by Dryden "Jonson's dotages," which is not fair; none the less *The Staple of News*, *The New Inn*, and *The Magnetic Lady* are certainly vastly inferior to his dramatic satires, his comedies, or the two Roman tragedies. But, great as was Jonson's activity in the composition of his score of originally devised and closely written dramas for the popular stage, this represents only one side of his busy career. Of his masques, their inventiveness and poetic beauty, we must write in a later chapter. He was the acknowledged leader, as poet laureate, of those who found their livelihood in entertaining the court of King James. And this primacy of his extended into the next reign. In criticism, Jonson was easily the first, and what he taught by precept he exemplified in a wide and various practice. Jonson's non-dramatic poetry includes lyrics, among them a few sonnets (though he did not love the form), satirical verse, chiefly in the shape of epigrams and mock poems, and a large amount of occasional verse for the most part made up of epistles, epitaphs, and dedicatory poems; for Jonson was on terms of intimacy with all the authors and half the nobility of his time. The author grouped these works under the headings *Epigrams* and *The Forest* and published both in the folio of 1616 to which he gave his careful personal attention. A third group (of miscellaneous poems) doubtless also of his making, appears in print for the first time in the posthumous second volume of his collected works, bearing date 1640, and is there designated *Underwoods*.

In turning to the non-dramatic poetry of Jonson, especially to his lyrical poetry, the first thing that we note is a sense of form, not merely detail and transition, like the "links, bright and even" of *The Faery Queen*, but a sense of the entire poem in its relation to its parts. This sense involves brevity and condensity of expression, a feeling on the part of the poet that the effect may be spoiled by a word too much, a feeling notably in contrast with the diffuseness, the continuousness and want of concentration characteristic of the Spenserian mode of the day. Jonson is writing in courtly compliment to his patroness Lucy, Countess of Bedford:

> This morning timely rapt with holy fire,
> I thought to form unto my zealous Muse,
> What kind of creature I should most desire,
> To honor, serve, and love, as poets use.

I meant to make her fair, and free, and wise,
Of greatest blood, and yet more good than great;
I meant the day-star should not brighter rise,
Nor lend like influence from his lucent seat.
I meant she should be courteous, facile, sweet,
Hating that solemn vice of greatness, pride;
I meant each softest virtue there should meet,
Fit in that softer bosom to reside.
Only a learnèd and a manly soul
I purposed her; that should, with even powers,
The rock, the spindle, and the shears control
Of Destiny, and spin her own free hours.
Such when I meant to feign and wished to see,
My Muse bade Bedford write, and that was she.

About such poetry as this there is a sense of finish rather than of elaboration. It is less continuous than complete; more concentrated, less diffuse; chaste rather than florid; controlled, and yet not always less spontaneous; reserved, and yet not always less natural. There are other things in the Jonsonian manner. It retained classical allusion less for the sake of embellishment than as an atmosphere — to borrow a term from the nomenclature of art. Its drafts on ancient mythology become allusive, and the effects produced by Horace, Catullus, or Anacreon are essayed in reproduction under English conditions. Not less eager in the pursuit of beauty than the Spenserian, the manner of Jonson seeks to realize her perfections by means of constructive excellence, not by entranced passion. It concerns itself with choiceness of diction, selectiveness in style, with the repression of wandering ideas and loosely conceived figures, — in a word, the manner of Jonson involves classicality. Sidney's return to the ancients has been called empirical; the classicism of Jonson may be termed assimilative.

It is thus that Jonson turns a lyric:

Still to be neat, still to be drest,
As you were going to a feast;
Still to be powdered, still perfumed:
Lady, it is to be presumed,

Though art's hid causes are not found,
All is not sweet, all is not sound.

Give me a look, give me a face,
That makes simplicity a grace;
Robes loosely flowing, hair as free:
Such sweet neglect more taketh me
Than all th' adulteries of art;
They strike mine eyes, but not my heart.

And in this wise he fashions two stanzas of an "Ode," one of the noblest of his many fine poems addressed to his notable friends of the day:

He stood a soldier to the last right end,
A perfect patriot and a noble friend,
        But most a virtuous son.
        All offices were done
By him so ample, full, and round,
In weight, in measure, number, sound,
As, though his age imperfect might appear,
His life was of humanity the sphere.

    .   .   .   .

        It is not growing like a tree
        In bulk, doth make men better be;
Or standing long an oak, three hundred year,
To fall a log at last, dry, bald, and sear:
            A lily of a day
            Is fairer far in May,
        Although it fall and die that night;
        It was the plant and flower of light.
In small proportions we just beauties see;
And in short measures life may perfect be.

In gnomic thought and moralizing, such as this or the noble *Epode* beginning, "Not to know vice at all," we have Jonson lyrically at his best, if such passages be strictly lyrical and not rather epigrammatic in the larger classical sense. The *Epigrams* of Jonson are full of cleverness and agile wit, and several playful poems, such as "A Fit of Rime against Rime" or "The Execration against Vulcan," are possessed of a lightsomeness and raillery, as his epitaphs declare a humane tenderness, such as we could hardly expect of the trenchant author of *Poetaster*.

We have seen how classical were Jonson's ideas as to the drama. This was only the most conspicuous example of the wider tenets that he held concerning literature at large. From his works and especially from his avowed opinions, expressed in his *Conversations with Drummond* and carefully noted down by that poet at the time, we learn that Jonson believed in the criticism of Horace and in the rhetoric of Quintilian; in the sanction of classical usage for history, oratory, and poetry; and that an English ode should be modeled faithfully on the structural niceties of Pindar. Despite all this, Jonson's theories about literature were not only, in the main, reasonable and consistent, they were often surprisingly liberal. Thus he could laugh, as he did, in a well-known passage of the prologue to *Every Man in his Humor*, at the absurdities of contemporary stage realism which,

> with three rusty swords,
> And help of some few foot-and-half-foot words,
> Fight over York and Lancaster's long jars;
> And in the tiring-house bring wounds to scars;

and yet declare, as to that fetish of the supine classicist, the three unities, that "we [English playwrights] should enjoy the same licence or free power to illustrate and heighten our invention as they [the ancients] did; and not be tied to those strict and regular forms which the niceness of a few, who are nothing but form, would thrust upon us." He could affirm that "Spenser's stanzas pleased him not, nor his matter"; and yet tell Drummond that "for a heroic poem there was no such ground as King Arthur's fiction." He censured the pastoralists for their unreality, and yet he had by heart passages of the *Shepherds' Calendar* and showed how he thought that a true pastoral drama should be written in the *Sad Shepherd;* he mocked the sonneteers, especially Daniel, in his satirical plays, for their sugared sweetness and frivolity; but wrote himself some of the finest lyrics of his age. The catholicity of Jonson's taste in its sympathy included the philosophy and eloquence of Lord Bacon, the divinity of Hooker, the historical and anti-quarian inquiries of Camden and Selden, the classical scholar-ship of Chapman, and the poetry of such diverse men as Spenser, Father Southwell, Donne, Sandys, Herrick, Carew, and his lesser "sons."

With consistent theories such as these applied with liber-ality, with catholicity of taste, and the force of a strong and confident nature such as was his, we can not wonder at Jon-son's influence on his time, the more particularly that the wild and inconsiderate spirit of much Elizabethan poetry laid itself only too readily open to criticism for its amateurishness and apparent want of any serious purpose in art. Further into the qualities that distinguish Jonson as a classicist — his habitual practice of occasional verse, his trend towards a pre-cise, pointed, and antithetical diction, his Latinized vocabu-lary, and his preference for the decasyllablic couplet over all other kinds of verse, we need not look further here. To Jon-son must be granted the credit of setting a standard of literary excellence, not recognized before his time; and of assuming, in so doing, an attitude of independence towards the public. Jonson developed the masque, as we shall see, and devised a species of Roman tragedy, conceived historically and freed alike from the restrictions of Senecan models and the improb-abilities of romantic treatment. He added the comedy of humors to the forms of the English drama. And it was this satirically heightened picture of contemporary life, handled with a restraint and finish ultimately traceable to classical example, that survived on the stage after the Restoration in the comedies of Davenant, Dryden, Etheridge and Vanbrugh. Thus it was that Jonson gave to the later drama one of its two permanent types; and, displaying the tastes and ideals that came, in still more restricted form, to rule English literature in the age of Dryden and Pope, set the channel in which Eng-lish poetry was to run for three generations as the founder of what is known as the classical school of English poetry.

CHAPTER XIV

SHAKESPEARE, WEBSTER, AND THE HEYDAY
OF ROMANTIC TRAGEDY

THE range and variety of Elizabethan tragedy is almost that of the entire drama itself; for religious, historical, and classical subjects, all find place among the tragic plays of the age, as well as the romantic biography and fiction that are levied on as their more usual sources. In previous pages of this book the beginnings of tragedy have been traced from its earliest examples in regular form, derived as they were from Seneca, to its realization in *The Spanish Tragedy* and in the greater works of Marlowe. The murder play, too, has been described; and its cruelty and crass realism found to have developed in *Arden of Feversham* into one example, at least, deserving a place beside the triumphs of contrasted romantic art. But these were not all the varieties of earlier Elizabethan tragedy; even the chronicle play, epic and often dramatically formless that it was, developed in the hands of Marlowe and Shakespeare into tragedy of a higer type and rose, in *Edward II*, in *Richard II*, and elsewhere, to a place beside romantic tragedy at its best.

There is no one influence in English tragedy so abiding and pervasive as that of the Roman poet Seneca. Without repeating what has already been suggested, it may be remarked that the early selection of Seneca, rather than the superior examples of ancient tragedy which Æschylus, Sophocles, and Euripides offer, was due to several considerations. First, Seneca was nearer to hand and he wrote in Latin, the universal language of the learning and diplomacy of the age. Secondly, Seneca's moral purpose, or at least his love of gnomic moralizing and putting the commonplace of obvious comment into the mouths of his personages, fell in well with the ideas of a time that had not yet learned to accept poetry and the drama as things properly existent without an ulterior moral end.

Lastly, Seneca was the most modern of the ancients and the most romantic of the classics; and his blood and revenge, his ghosts, furies, and horrors, were dear to an age which, however nice its appreciation of the more spiritual qualities of art, clung none the less to the robust, the virile, and the actual quite as tenaciously as the times that went before and those that have come after.

The earliest influences on Shakespeare in tragedy were those of Kyd and Marlowe. We may not like to think of Shakespeare as the author or even the reviser of *Titus Andronicus;* for the subject is horrible, the treatment often uninspired and blatant. But this tragedy is neither wanting in promise nor devoid of many touches that suggest the hand and heart of Shakespeare. If we are to seek for any solution of the enigma of Shakespeare's genius, we must expect just such crudity, such unawakened sensibilities, such want of taste as we find in *Titus* of the inexperienced Stratford lad. *Titus Andronicus* is precisely the kind of a play that a young dramatist of talent might write in his imitative period, overdoing the lust, the cruelty, and the blood of his subject in his endeavor to succeed, and from the very circumstance that these things were so remote from his own intellectual preoccupations. That the style and the manner of Greene, Peele, Kyd, and other authors have been found in it scarcely weakens the probability of its writing by Shakespeare; and the circumstance that the subject was popular (recurring in *Henslowe* under variations of title in 1591 and 1593, in a German version derived from a contemporary English play, and later in a Dutch version) merely adds to the likelihood of Shakespeare's choice of it. *Titus* is a horrible and tasteless tragedy, showing none the less in the quality of its diction and in its powerful conception of such personages as Aaron and Tamora unusual dramatic promise.

Titus must certainly have been on the stage before 1594, in February of which year the recently rediscovered first quarto was registered for publication.[1] *Romeo and Juliet,*

[1] The only exemplar of this quarto was discovered among the books of a Swedish gentleman of Scottish descent, named Robson, at Lund, Sweden, in 1905.

whether dated back to 1591 or left at 1596 or 1597, must not only have followed *Titus*, but, if taste, growth of power and restraint, and grasp of dramatic situation mean anything, some time must have elapsed between the two tragedies. Whatever Shakespeare's actual source for *Romeo and Juliet*, the subject had long been popular on the stage and in current poetry and fiction; so that here, as so often, Shakespeare becomes the artistic form-giver to a theme already well known and accepted. Inevitable tragedy though it is, *Romeo and Juliet* is written in the exuberant and poetical spirit that animates *A Midsummer-Night's Dream* and *The Merchant of Venice;* and youthful and untamed though this spirit is, we have in it abundant promise of much that was to come. In this great tragedy of adolescence, especially as we compare it with other examples of plays the theme of which is love, we are struck by Shakespeare's naturalness, the simple adequacy of his art, the poetry and clearness of his picture of human passion, and the genial play of his humor about a theme easily capable of degeneration into sentimentality in the hands of a less skilful artist. In Juliet we have for the first time to the full Shakespeare's unparalleled insight into womanhood and his recognition of the glory of her love. The true theme is Juliet's passion; Romeo's is paltry in comparison. Love clears Juliet's vision as to all things and, left to her prudence, her daring, her devotion, all had gone well. It is Romeo's eyes that are blind, and it is he that plunges distracted to the catastrophe.

By the time that Shakespeare again turned his attention to tragedy, he had completed, save for *Henry VIII*, his list of chronicle plays and now chose a subject from ancient history in a sense kindred to them. *The Tragedy of Julius Cæsar* has been variously placed as to date of composition between 1599 and 1601. Whether he used some now lost play or not, the dramatist's immediate source was the latter part of North's *Plutarch*, which alone accounts for the unheroic character given to the dictator, as Cæsar's greatness and his exploits belong to his earlier career. The play, indeed, is less the tragedy of Cæsar than that of Brutus, whom Shakespeare did not hesitate to present in a light far more favorable to his honesty, his disinterestedness, and kindness of heart than appears in the pages of *Plutarch*. In choosing thus the story of the fall of the greatest man of antiquity Shakespeare was attempting nothing novel. The subject had been treated on the stage by Gosson, by henchmen of Henslowe more than once, and at Oxford; and the source had been long since broached for other purposes, by Lodge for example in his *Wounds of Civil War*, as far back as 1588. The suggestion of a regulative example in Jonson for this play of Shakespeare's on Julius Cæsar has been made above. But it must be remembered that Jonson's own labors in this kind followed Shakespeare's tragedy. Whatever their relation, nothing could be greater than their contrast, for in Shakespeare the dramatist ruled, in Jonson the scholar. Neither of these great authors treated ancient history after the melodramatic manner of Seneca, for even Jonson, with all his veneration of the ancients, never tied — save in the fiction of text-books — to the strict laws that governed their art. But Jonson was solicitous of historical, biographical, and archæological truth. Hence he studied his originals with care and followed them with the scholar's fidelity. Shakespeare sought for a higher truth than these; and as artistic truth — not historical, biographical, or archæologic — is the truth of the drama, his work abides the touch of time as Jonson's never could. Shakespeare's *Julius Cæsar*, which was an immediate success, revived an interest in classical topics and not only did Jonson's *Sejanus* follow in 1603, but Marston's *Sophonisba*, Heywood's *Rape of Lucrece*, and Gwinne's Latin tragedy *Nero*, all belong to the same year. The first of these is a romantic drama of conglomerate type of no small merit; Heywood's play adds little to his credit; Dr. Matthew Gwinne's *Nero* is an ambitious work dedicated to the queen and true to all the theories cherished by Jonson.

Although Shakespeare turned to subjects for tragedy more truly romantic in the interim, he was drawn into other plays of this type a few years later by a second revival of interest in ancient story. To the year 1607 belong two plays on Cæsar and Pompey, the one anonymous, the other by Chapman, and likewise an English college play on Nero. And this year, or one or two thereafter, saw *Timon of Athens*, *Antony and Cleopatra*, *Pericles*, and *Coriolanus* as well. These plays group naturally together from their setting in ancient times. Their general source (save for *Pericles*) is Plutrach's *Lives*. But they differ widely in their minor sources, in the terms of their authorship, and in their relative qualities and excellence. *Pericles* is a romance of adventure and belongs elsewhere. *Timon*, even more than *Pericles*, is a work of great inequality and inconceivable as wholly from the hand of Shakespeare. In this story of hopeless misanthropy the dialogue of Lucian concerning Timon, and perhaps an earlier academic play, may have served for suggestions. It has even been doubted whether *Timon of Athens* was ever staged, and its place in the folio and the corruption of the text in places cast further suspicion upon it. With *Antony and Cleopatra* and with *Coriolanus* we are on firmer ground. The latter, on the stage by 1609, is a clearly conceived tragedy turning on a definite theme, the arrogant pride of Coriolanus, and developed with an artist's sense of the effectiveness of a single tone. It adds to our appreciation of this emphasis of effect to learn that the characteristics of Coriolanus are merely suggested in Plutarch's narrative. Shakespeare's misinterpretation of history in making "the dignified secession of the *plebs*" a turbulent mob, is thus justified by the dramatic demands of his subject as he conceives it. It is difficult to sympathize with the criticism that objects to Shakespeare's contemptuous representation of the mob in this tragedy and in *Julius Cæsar*. The drift and average of mankind in leaderless fluxion has always been fickle, stupid, and disorderly; and it requires more than seeing things as they are to wax eloquent on the virtues and prudence of men when they herd in the streets. Shakespeare, though country born, saw countrymen, rustic and the populace of London, ignorant and uncleanly; and he sacrificed no jot or tittle of the concrete truth to lofty generalizations on that figment of the imagination, the average man.

Just as we found Shakespeare raising the chronicle history

out of its species into a tragedy of world significance, so in this matter of ancient history he rises above the trammels of his sources in *Julius Cæsar* and in *Antony and Cleopatra*. This last remarkable tragedy is less an historical drama on the days of ancient Rome than a glorification of the time-worn fable which has converted the infatuation of an elderly debauchee for a royal light-o'-love into one of the supreme love stories of all time. In Shakespeare's hands Cleopatra holds our sympathy and, what is more, our respect. It is only necessary to compare this impetuous, variable, and fascinating serpent of the Nile with the Senecan frigidity of Daniel's picture of the Egyptian queen in his *Cleopatra*, 1593, or the painted meretrix that Fletcher later made of her in *The False One*, to realize to the full the strength of Shakespeare's portrait. Dryden, too, attempted a dramatic portrait of Cleopatra in his *All for Love;* and in emulating Shakespeare, surpassed himself; but he did no more. Depth, fullness of thought and impetuous imagery, all are qualities of Shakespeare's *Antony and Cleopatra* and it matters little that the scene is changed at will (fifteen times in the fourth act) and that constructively the drama straggles almost to the degree of a chronicle play. *Julius Cæsar* and *Coriolanus* are better constructed tragedies; but Shakespeare is seldom at his best under restraint and there is a larger utterance, a wider horizon in *Antony and Cleopatra* than in these earlier tragedies dealing with classical story.

In our endeavor to keep the tragedies of similar subject together we have advanced beyond the heyday of romantic tragedy. Let us return to the later years of Queen Elizabeth and to another topic. When Marlowe died he left behind him a play called *The Massacre at Paris* in which the consequences, rather than the terrible event, of the massacre of St. Bartholomew are set forth for the stage, and the Duke of Guise is gibbeted as a monster of wickedness. This lead, thus apparently for the first time pointed out, Chapman followed in some five dramas of tragic import and, although unequal, of a very real merit. Of Chapman we shall hear more fully in the next chapter when we reach a consideration of his famous translation of Homer. For the present it is enough to recall that Chapman's beginnings as a dramatist date at least as far back as those of Jonson and that his earliest plays were comedies of disguise, intrigue, and humors in the Jonsonian sense. In 1607 *Bussy D'Ambois* was printed for the first time, though certainly much earlier written. This tragedy tells the story of an impoverished bravo who became a favorite of Henry III, and sets forth at large the tangled intrigues and dissolute life of the court of that despicable monarch. This play was doubtless written far earlier, if it does not link even more closely on to *The Massacre at Paris* and *The Civil Wars in France*, three plays of 1598 by Dekker and others, long since lost. In 1604 Chapman wrote and staged, under influence of the popularity of the tragedy of revenge, a continuation of *Bussy*, entitled *The Revenge of Bussy D'Ambois*, wherein that worthy's brother Cleremont, "a Senecal man," as the author calls him, of misanthropic Hamlet type, figures as hero and avenger. Four years later appeared a more extensive work, *The Conspiracy and Tragedy of Charles Duke of Byron*, a drama in two parts, on French history almost contemporary. On complaint of the French ambassador that his royal master was represented on the stage in this production, the performance of it was stopped, and the author driven into hiding to escape arrest. When all was done, Chapman failed to secure permission to publish his work in its completeness, and it remains, a testimony of the efficacy of the censorship of its day. Byron's story is that of the treason of an arrogant and self-sufficient noble, whose contumacy when the royal clemency is offered him brings about his deserved fall. *Chabot, Admiral of France*, licensed only in the reign of King Charles, is the fifth of these French histories of Chapman; and though by far the best as a play, from its revision if not complete rewriting by Shirley, is beyond the range of our period. In the other four plays we have the most characteristic contribution of Chapman to the drama of his time. These French histories are full of poetry, thought, and a certain power of moralizing in verse for which their author is justly memorable. But they are, save for *Chabot*, formless and chaotic; though it is remarkable that Chapman's personages are none the less discoverable in so much detail and stand out often so dinstinctly. In these dramas, as in nearly everything he wrote, we feel that Chapman strives too hard. Ease and naturalness he seems never to have compassed; all is effort and strenuous endeavor, with not quite complete success. These were by no means the only plays levying on foreign contemporary history and after Shakespeare's death came several such, as Fletcher's *Barnavelt*, *The Noble Spanish Soldier* by Dekker, and William Rowley and Middleton's *Game at Chess*, which were close upon the heels of the events that they depict. A background of French "history" serves for two early anonymous romantic dramas, *The Trial of Chivalry*, 1597, and *The Weakest Goeth to the Wall*, 1600; the Faust-like biographical *Tragedy of Pope Alexander*, 1606, by the lyric poet Barnabe Barnes, is one of many quasi-historical tragedies of Italian scene. Other plays, such as *A Larum for London*, 1602, and *The Hector of Germany*, 1615, lay their scene in the last-named country. Among them is *Alphonsus of Germany*, an historical tragedy of no little force, of doubtful date, and even more doubtfully attributed by some to Chapman.

Let us turn back to our point of departure once more. Few plays enjoyed the popularity of *The Spanish Tragedy*, and few begot as time went on so large and vigorous a progeny. This popular work of Kyd is a tragedy of revenge and we have seen above how closely its story parallels that of Hamlet, an early version of which may be confidently attributed to Kyd also. It was in 1599 that young John Marston, fresh from the university and from penning sundry satires and unrestrained erotic poems, placed on the stage his *Antonio and Mellida* and *Antonio's Revenge*, two dramas of vital if unequal power and promise. The former is a serious drama, arrested just short of tragedy; the latter a tragedy of revenge following closely the method and even the details of *The Spanish Tragedy* and *Hamlet*. Thus Antonio's revenge is for a father slain, that vengeance is invoked by his father's ghost, Antonio is driven nearly mad by his grief and horror, and hesitates to kill his enemy, as does Hamlet, when in his power; while, as in *The Spanish Tragedy*, the catastrophe is brought about by a play within a play. But *Antonio's Revenge* is no mere copy; it is full of real and original horrors of its own and, with all its stridency and melodrama, an effective piece of work. Whether Marston started the revival or an earlier revival than we know inspired Marston, certain it is that a couple of years later *The Spanish Tragedy* was revived on the stage with great success and that no less a man than Ben Jonson was paid for additions, chiefly to the psychology (as we should call it) of the protagonist Hieronimo, the distracted father who seeks where to apply his vengeance for the murder of his innocent son. By 1603 the earliest quarto of *The Revenge of Hamlet Prince of Denmark* was printed. It was enlarged and revised in the following year, and a third version, differing in important particulars, appeared in the folio, seven years after Shakespeare's death. The rewriting of Kyd's old *Hamlet* by a rival company so soon after the revival and revision of *The Spanish Tragedy*, with *Antonio's Revenge* still holding the stage, makes all but irresistible the inference that these two old plays of Kyd were rewritten and revised in emulation the one with the other by the two greatest dramatists of their time. The problem that confronts the student as to this most notable of all the plays of Shakespeare is complex and difficult, and with the data at hand quite insoluble. Nor is the matter helped by the loss of any trace of Kyd's old *Hamlet* or the existence of a German version of the play derived from England, but whether before or after the Shakespearean quartos is doubtful. What was the nature of Kyd's original *Hamlet?* What parts have been retained by Shakespeare, and what are his changes and departures? What is the true relation of all these versions? Such are some of the questions we should like definitely answered but which seem, despite all the scholarship lavished upon them, likely to remain "in the backward and abysm of time."

Fortunately for the enjoyment of this world tragedy we need none of these extraneous matters. To the understanding of Shakespeare's depth of thought and wisdom we may

bring all the native wit and the added learning we may have
acquired and it will be none too much; but for these plays,
as works of fiction, verily he who runs may read, though he
must often content himself with *a* meaning rather than *the*
meaning. Therefore the madness or soundness of Hamlet,
the degree of his mother's guilt, was Ophelia frail or only
faulty, or Polonius the tedious old fool that Hamlet called him
— these are matters unimportant in view of the truth to life,
the insight into the depths of the human heart, and the larger
philosophy of life which this great drama gives us. We may
outlive the form of these dramas and find conventional and
stale the measured words and cadenced melody of their
rhetoric (if Mr. Shaw will so have it), but the sanity of Shakespeare's outlook on life is imperishable, and when we have
degenerately ceased to respond to his poetry we must remain
the subjects of his wit and of that incomparable wisdon that
flashes impartially on all and illumines whatever it touches.

But our tale of the tragedy of revenge is not yet complete.
In 1602 Henry Chettle put forth his melodramatic *Tragedy
of Hoffman or a Revenge for a Father*, which it is impossible
to believe was not written at least after the revival of the older
Hamlet if not subsequent to the appearance on the stage of
the earlier Shakespearean version of that play. Chettle
heaped several additional horrors on those already invented
by Marston and is especially ingenious in the variety of dread-
ful deaths by which his characters depart from this life.
About this time was staged *The Atheist's Tragedy* by Cyril
Tourneur, as appears by the title-page. Tourneur lived
much abroad, chiefly in the Low Countries; and his slender
literary work is negligible except for this play and a second,
The Revenger's Tragedy, printed without his name in 1607.
Both are powerful and effective dramas full of action and
inventive device although they differ materially in atmosphere
and design, the first assuming the moralist's attitude towards
life and crime, *The Revenger's Tragedy* flaunting a bitterly
cynical outlook on the world and all its doings. This contrast has raised a question as to whether both plays can be by
the same hand. Whatever the truth of this matter, in terrible

realism of effect, in mastery of horror and poetry, *The Revenger's Tragedy* takes its place in our drama as second only to Webster himself in these high qualities of tragic art. With the intervention between the two plays just named of Chapman's *Revenge of Bussy D'Ambois* already mentioned, we complete the list of tragedies of revenge, at least of the type strictly so called. The tragedy of revenge from its very nature deals with crime, conscience, and remorse. These plays make potent use of the supernatural and other terrors. Chapman is the clumsiest in the use of such devices; Marston and Tourneur are more successfully inventive. Shakespeare's ghosts trascend their disembodied fellows as his men and women excel the characters of other dramatists. And this is not because he was less willing to obscure in his art the line that marks what most men feel that they do know from that which they mistrust, as because the Shakespearean ghost is always true to the seat of his origin in the psychology of man.

To classify the subjects of Jacobean tragedy would be to run the gamut of human passion: love, jealousy, revenge, ambition, pride, all are there, as Shakespeare alone is enough to disclose. A powerful if forbidding group of tragedies is that which deals with womanhood in that deadly perversion by which woman exists but for the destruction of man. Such figures were Tamora in *Titus Andronicus* and the "lascivious queen" of *Lust's Dominion*, mistakenly attributed to Marlowe. Middleton, Marston, and Webster each contributed a drama of unusual reputation to this class and all three fall close to the year 1612. Middleton's *Women Beware Women* relates in its major plot the career of Bianca Capello, who is represented as at first the innocent victim of a lady-procuress, Livia, to the Duke de' Medici's lust, but sinks by steps to murder. A still more revolting underplot makes up an intricate but clearly constructed piece of realism, terrible in its truth as it is superlative in its art. *The Insatiate Countess* of Marston (though his authorship has sometimes been questioned) tells of the headlong career of a petulant wanton and the havoc that was wrought by her beauty and her crimes. Marston had treated the same theme, less luridly though

scarcely with less effect, in *The Dutch Courtesan*, described
as a comedy and linking, in the contrast that it sustains, with
the domestic dramas of the good wife and the wanton. The
third of these tragedies is Webster's *Vittoria Corombona* otherwise known as *The White Devil*.

John Webster, concerning the details of whose life we
know next to nothing, appears first in the history of the drama
as a co-worker, especially with Dekker, in Henslowe's mart
of plays. This collaboration begot the chronicle play *Sir
Thomas Wyatt* and the Middletonian comedies of manners,
Westward Hoe and *Nortward Hoe*, all on the stage by 1604
or 1605. Webster's hand in other plays does not concern us
as his authorship is doubtful. His unaided extant work
comprises four plays, *The White Devil*, *The Duchess of Malfi*.
The Devil's Law Case, and *Appius and Virginia*, published
variously in 1612, 1623, and 1654 and written it is difficult to
say precisely when. *The Devil's Law Case* is a romantic
comedy of no very striking excellence; *Appius and Virginia*,
a tragedy on the well-known classical story of very genuine
merit, though restrained and self-contained in great contrast
to the robust romanticism of Webster's most characteristic
work. It is on the two romantic tragedies that remain that
the reputation of Webster, as our greatest dramatist in the
domain of the terrible, rests secure, for there are no tragedies
of their kind that surpass them.

The White Devil purports to be the actual life-history of
"Vittoria Corombona, the famous Venetian courtesan." It
deals with the profligate Duke of Brachiano's infatuation for
Vittoria and the resulting tragedy to them both. But no
description can make clear the brilliant and fascinating personality of this "innocent-seeming white devil" of decadent
Italy, and the vivid group of personages — the cynical Fla-
mineo, her brother, her helpless and distracted mother, the
politic brothers Medici and Monticelso — that surround her.
The White Devil, because it departs both in general intent and
in many details from the facts of the celebrated case of the real
Vittoria Accoramboni, has been thought to have been derived
from the hearsay of some Italian traveler returned. The

story of *The Duchess of Malfi*, on the other hand, represents an embarassment of sources, though Webster unquestionably found the version that he used in the old quarry for Elizabethan playwrights, Painter's *Palace of Pleasure*. Webster's tragedy has been customarily dated after Shakespeare's death. It now appears that an actor, Willam Osteler, who took a part in *The Duchess of Malfi*, died towards the close of the year 1614. Indeed, it has been well argued that the likeness of Webster's two tragedies should place their composition close together. Perhaps 1610 for *The White Devil* and 1612 for *The Duchess of Malfi* is as near as need be. The latter tragedy tells of the vengeance which two brothers took on the duchess, their sister, for marrying without their knowledge or consent, a man in every respect worthy of her love, save for his rank. The refinements of their cruelty, carried out with inexorable precision to the bitter end, by a creature of their making, named Bosola; the steadfast, heroic fatalism of the duchess; the contrasted wickedness of the brothers, especially the remorse of Ferdinand, are among the finest things in the whole range of tragic literature and compare in the gnomic wisdom, the brilliant diction, and admirable poetry in which the drama is set with Shakespeare himself when all but at his greatest. Attention has been called to the success with which Webster creates an atmosphere of ominous gloom in these masterful tragedies, and how he works at times, in a manner familiar to Shakespeare, by means of instantaneous dramatic moments charged with revealing passion. The influence of the masterpoet on Webster has thus been happily called not literary but dramatic, and it is conceivable that it may have been derived less from a reading of Shakespeare's plays than from a study of them on the boards as acted.[1] As an example of the Websterian atmosphere take his transfigured use of the familiar lyrists' device of an echo in *The Duchess of Malfi*. Antonio, whose beloved duchess lies dead with her children, although he does not know it, is on his way with a friend to meet his

[1] See M. W. Sampson, *Webster, Belles Lettres Series*, Introduction, p. xix.

own death. The scene, as so often with Shakespeare, is vividly suggested in the dialogue.

> *Delio.* This fortification
> Grew from the ruins of an ancient abbey:
> And to yond side o' th' river, lies a wall,
> Piece of a cloister, which in my opinion
> Gives the best echo that you ever heard;
> So hollow and so dismal, and withal
> So plain in the distinction of our words,
> That many have supposed it is a spirit
> That answers.
> *Antonio.* I do love these ancient ruins.
> We never tread upon them but we set
> Our foot upon some reverend history;
> And questionless, here in this open court,
> Which now lies naked to the injuries
> Of stormy weather, some men lie interred
> Loved the church so well, and gave so largely to 't,
> They thought it should have canopied their bones
> Till doomsday.   But all things have their end:
> Churches and cities (which have diseases like to men)
> Must have like death that we have.
> *Echo.* *Like death that we have.*
> *Delio.* Now the echo hath caught you.
> *Ant.* It groaned, me thought, and gave
> A very deadly accent?
> *Echo.* *Deadly accent.*
> *Delio.* I told you 'twas a pretty one.   You may make it
> A huntsman, or a falconer, a musician,
> Or a thing of sorrow.
> *Echo.* *A thing of sorrow.*
> *Ant.* Aye, sure: that suits it best.
> *Echo.* *That suits it best.*
> *Ant.* 'Tis very like my wife's voice.
> *Echo.* *Aye, wife's voice.*
> *Delio.* Come: let's us walk farther from 't.
> I would not have you go to th' cardinal's to-night:
> Do not.
> *Echo.* *Do not.*

. . . .

Ant.   Necessity compels me:
Make scrutiny throughout the passages
Of your own life; you 'll find it impossible
To fly your fate.
   Echo.   *O fly your fate.*
   Delio.   Hark: the dead stones seem to have pity on you
And give you good counsel.
   Ant.   Echo, I will not talk with thee;
For thou art a dead thing.
   Echo.   *Thou art a dead thing.*
   Ant.   My duchess is asleep now,
And her little ones, I hope sweetly: oh heaven,
Shall I never see her more?
   Echo.   *Never see her more.*

As to the instantaneous dramatic moments, charged with revealing passion, such are the much quoted:

I am the Duchess of Malfi still,

and Ferdinand's words, as his sister lies dead before him:

Cover her face.   Mine eyes dazzle: she died young.

Of almost equal intensity is the last cry of Vittoria:

My soul, like to a ship in a black storm
Is driven I know not whither.

Returning to the tragedies of Shakespeare, *Titus, Romeo and Juliet,* the Roman plays, with *Timon* and *Hamlet,* each has received from us thus far that modicum of attention which a book of this plan can give it.   There remain *Othello, Lear,* and *Macbeth.   Othello* is the master tragedy on the passion of jealousy which Shakespeare had already touched in comedy in Ford of *The Merry Wives of Windsor,* and which he was to treat so much more fully in King Leontes of *The Winter's Tale* and Leonatus Posthumus in *Cymbeline.*   Just as Shakespeare raised the theme of man's love for woman to an idealized beauty in *Romeo and Juliet* and yet left it of the earth that engenders it earthy, so he ennobled, while in no wise emasculating its strength and terror, the venomous passion of jealousy.   There is scarcely anything in which Shakespeare is so in contrast with his competitors in the drama of

his time, for none has so contrived to preserve the dignity of
human character in the midst of the infirmities of passion
that beset it. *Othello* is usually dated 1604, after *Hamlet*
and immediately preceding *King Lear*. The barest hints in
a novel of Cinthio's *Hecatommithi* served for the framing of
Othello, Desdemona, and Iago; and Cassio's drunkenness,
Emilia's theft of the handkerchief, and the whole handling of
the catastrophe with much else are altogether Shakespeare's
invention. With his entire lurid brotherhood from the
tragedy of revenge about him — Vindici, Hoffman, Antonio,
D'Amville, and the rest — Iago remains the arch villain of all
literature. All of these "revengers" have a real impetus for
their crimes except D'Amville, and he dies mad. De Flores
in *The Changeling* is no more than a masterful voluptuary,
willing to face death with unutterable crimes that he may
enjoy and drag down with him the woman he has singled out
for his victim. Webster's Bosola, who resembles Iago in his
outspoken "honesty," is a connoisseur in crime, satiating a
morbid curiosity in the tortures of his victims and yet revert-
ing to his better self momentarily in the end. In Iago alone
is villainy wanton and gratuitous and the monstrous fruit of
petty and serpentine envy. And yet with all his malignity,
subtlety, and venomous spite, the most terrible thing about
Iago is that he remains human.

King Lear is best dated 1605; for in that year the old play,
King Leir and his Three Daughters (on which Shakespeare's
tragedy is founded), was entered in the Stationers' Register
and published, a thing unaccountable except on the assumption that the subject had been revived on the stage or elsewhere. From the point of view of ultimate source, *King
Lear* is a chronicle play; as the story, told in Geoffrey of
Monmouth, recurs in Holinshed, *The Mirror for Magistrates*,
and elsewhere, and was accepted, with other such "history,"
in its day. The underplot of Gloster and his blinding, with
his contrasted faithful and wicked son, skilfully parallels the
main story and is derived, in its essentials, from an episode
of Sidney's *Arcadia*. But here, as in *Macbeth*, Shakespeare
has not only glorified his material, he has transmuted it into

a something so entirely new that the accident of its origin — like the origin of the sad-eyed clown — is a matter of no moment. *Lear* is a tragedy of overpowering force and torrential swiftness. In no work of Shakespeare's are his personages so intensely conceived and nowhere does he more poignantly reach the heart than in this pitiful tale of hapless Cordelia and her distracted father.

With *Macbeth* — another chronicle play from its source in Holinshed but equally glorified above its type — we bring this enumeration of Shakespeare's tragedies to a close. *Macbeth* was written in 1605 or 1606, and doubtless after *King Lear*. It appeared in print for the first time in the folio, and it has been supposed suffered some mutilation of text and interpolation in a couple of scenes, found likewise in Middleton's *Witch*, a comedy of uncertain date. The opening scenes between Macbeth and his wife, the knocking at the gate, the appearance of Banquo's ghost, the prophecies of the witches in Macbeth's second interview with them, and the sleepwalking of Lady Macbeth, these are some of the things not found in the chronicle but found in the play. But little does this indicate the welding into a complete dramatic organism of this story of inordinate but halting ambition, steadied by marvelous constancy and wifely devotion in evil, and lured on to inevitable overthrow by the supernatural agency of "the weird sisters."

Were we to look for a prodigy in letters, where could we find the equal of *Julius Cæsar*, *Hamlet*, *Othello*, *King Lear*, *Macbeth* and *Antony and Cleopatra*, six master tragedies of all time, written in little more than the same number of years with the several serious comedies that accompanied them as well? The range of feeling, the depth of wisdom and understanding, to say nothing of the dramatic art and the sheer poetry of these great tragedies, stand out and beyond the achievements in literature of all other men in other times. And we read and study them, finding new truth and beauty in them as perennially as in nature and the return of spring. It is a great tribute to Shakespeare's genius that we disagree, as we do, about his people. Ordinary art produces much the same effect on each and every reader. We see the same object and agree about it. About real persons, historical or of our acquaintance, there is room for greater difference of opinion. It is because Shakespeare's characters are so real that we interpret them so variously, that we fall out about the sanity of Hamlet or the sincerity of HenryV. But Shakespeare's realism is far from all. Equally with Sophocles does Shakespeare in these great tragedies uphold the nobility and poetic elevation of the tragic art. His personages and their doings are absorbing above the interest that we feel in actual men because their innate qualities and capabilities, the things they do, they feel, and suffer, are resolved for us by the poet's energy into a finer, more logical and dignified reality than are ever these things in life.

We have traced above — as it is customary to trace them — some of the characteristics that marked the strengthening and ripening of Shakespeare's genius in his verse and style, his rhetoric and his taste. The technique of his dramatic art also grew strong with use and maturing genius. There is *Love's Labor's Lost* with its King of Navarre and the Princess of France, each attended respectively by three lords and three ladies who speak in strict alternation and, save for Biron, with as little to distinguish them as the three kings of Brentford. In *Romeo and Juliet* when the Montagues and Capulets assemble in the opening scene, the scene is built up like an arch: serving man of Montague, serving man of Capulet; Montague, Capulet; kinsman of Montague, kinsman of Capulet; Montague, Capulet, Lady Montague and Lady Capulet, with the prince for a cap-stone. This is not much better than *Gorboduc*. Such is not the daring structure at large of *King Lear*, with the plot of the king and his good and evil daughters paralleled and enforced with the story of Gloster and his good and evil sons, and the daring contrast, in that supreme scene of the storm, of senile dementia, congenital imbecility, and feigned madness. Much has been written of late on Shakespeare as a constructive artist, some wisely, some not so well. It has been thought that virtue lies in discovering "the climax" of Macbeth; and the precise point at which "the tragic force" of Othello arises is a thing to be argued with zeal and defended with might. A few years ago quite a new science of dramatic structure arose, founded on Freitag's interpretation of certain lecture notes of one of the students of Aristotle entitled the *Poetics*, and on other peoples' improvements and additions to Freitag. Moreover this new science, after the manner of new sciences, begot a horrid and numerous progeny of technical terms such as "motivation," "enveloping, counter and main action," "passion-movement," "derationalization," and "shock of Nemesis," with many things to learn and more to ponder. Now there is surely no more harm in charts of dramatic structure or diagrams of character-contact than in charts of the force of the wind or prognostications of temperature. But the last are no more the cause of good weather than the first are any real helps to our understanding of the genius of Shakespeare. We may admit that, if the truth be told and all the plays considered, Shakespeare is not conspicuous as a merely constructive dramatist. Jonson could write a more ingenious play, and one better able, in Ascham's quaint phrase, "to abide the precepts of Aristotle." Shakespeare had before him something better than elaborate and clever structure in which the mind is directed from the subject in hand to admiration for the cleverness of the artist or the difficulty of the problem. Shakespeare was seeking the dramatic and poetic picturing of life; for the rest he cared not a jot or tittle. Hence his carelessness at times and his indifference where lesser men would show anxiety; though, none the less, in tragedy where rigor of cause and effect is most demanded, there is little surplusage in Shakespeare's method and he rarely deviates from the direct course of his story. In this whole matter of dramatic structure it would be well to consider less the standard rule, whatever its learned derivation, and more the individual organic structure. It is of less importance to know that Shakespeare habitually reaches the turning-point of his action in the middle of the third act than to recognize that the organism of *Hamlet* is not that of *Macbeth* or *Othello*. *Antony and Cleopatra* is straggling and well drawn out in structure, for the events were long preparing that brought about the fall of these royal infatuated lovers. *Hamlet*, too, is lengthy and slow of development in harmony with the doubt and hesitancy that paralyzed the " revenger's " purpose and in accord with his introspective and pondering nature. *Othello* progresses gradually with the sinuous glides of serpentine Iago, to rush to immediate and overwhelming catastrophe when the passion of Othello breaks from Iago's guidance and suggestion. *Macbeth* is swift and accelerated as crime begets crime and remorse follows hard on the heels of ambition. Finally, *Lear* is of a torrential swiftness, bearing innocent and guilty alike to destruction, for the decree that carelessly dismembered a kingdom and banished Cordelia was the decree of a madman.

It is easy to see, as we read Shakespeare's plays in the general order of their writing, that Shakespeare viewed the world as mirrored in them from the changing points of vantage that mark his own growth from youth to the sager attitude of middle life. It was a young man that depicted the fire and passion of the lovers, Romeo and Juliet, and it was a younger man who was contented with the badinage and occasional silliness of *Love's Labor's Lost*. Shakespeare's attitude towards older people in the earlier plays also shows his youth. The elder Capulet is viewed solely from the lovers' point of view. Much might be said for the prudence and respectability of that old gentleman. Friar Laurence, too, talks exactly as a young man thinks that he has observed old men to talk. It was not for nothing that Shakespeare went through the Slough of Despond, depicted in the gloomier comedies of disillusion; for in the later tragedies is disclosed that fuller power that comes with years to sound the deeps of human crime and passion, till, in the latest plays we find Shakespeare again and again assuming the attitude of the older and wiser man who lives over again in recollection the past that once was his and seeks his real happiness in the joy and hopefulness of those who are shortly to succeed him.

The variety of Elizabethan tragedies as to subject, nature, and treatment calls for no further word. As a whole this drama is realistic and outspoken, unrestrained, and often melodramatic. Such men as Marston, Webster, and Tourneur loved to pile horror on horror. Less legitimate are the devices, later to be more lawlessly employed, whereby tragic themes are further heightened by making their motives abnormal: thus the ungodly become atheistic or at least cynically abandoned, and lust is supplanted by the horrible motive of incest. In contrast with his fellows in the drama, Shakespeare is always true to the normal mainsprings of human action and passion, however he may heighten his effects by a momentary fidelity to the coarser actualities of life. Shakespeare is always frankly realistic, where realism seems to him to be demanded by the nature of his subject. Moreover, Shakespeare's age frequently looked for realism where the usage of our time demands reticence or at least periphrasis. No two things are more commonly confused by most of us in our daily colloquial judgments of conduct than manners and morals. Manners are parochial, morals cosmopolitan. The manners of Shakespeare's day were not ours. Our manners might equally have shocked Shakespeare; for they are temporary as his were temporary. The moral atmosphere pervading Shakespeare's plays in large calls for few apologies to our age, although our speech is more refined. Shakespeare never confounds right and wrong; he never leaves you in doubt as to his attitude on important questions. Lear was half crazed and scarcely responsible for his folly, Cordelia had much to excuse her momentary stubbornness and unwillingness to humor her father's dotage with a few kind words, yet both are overwhelmed in expiation. Never was man more practised on by diabolical cunning and malice than was Othello, yet his doubt quite as much as his crime deserved the logic of his death.

In few things does Shakespeare differ more completely from the majority of the dramatists of his age than in his attitude towards woman. In the fine words of Ruskin: "Shakespeare has no heroes;— he has only heroines. . . . The catastrophe of every play is caused always by the folly or fault of a man; the redemption, if there be any, is by the wisdom and virtue of a woman, and failing that, there is none."

There is no cheap gallantry in these words nor in the dramatist whose deep insight into the manner of this world they celebrate. Indeed, for the flippancy and heartlessness of contemporary gallantry we must consult, not the works of Shakespeare, but those of Fletcher and Middleton. Except for those monsters of wickedness, Tamora, the two daughters of Lear, and wretched, trivial Cressida —a preposterous little trull for a fair youth like Troilus to trouble his heart about— there is scarcely a woman wholly bad in all Shakespeare. As to Cleopatra, in the romantic glory of her abandon to love as the all of the world, Shakespeare's Cleopatra is as distinguishable from the several frigid portraits of the Egyptian queen in Shakespeare's age as she is immeasureably above Mr. Shaw's ridiculous hoyden or Signor Ferrero's dainty and heartless Parisian with a genius for politics

But enough; in Shakespeare and Webster, English tragedy touched the elevation and dignity of the drama of Æschylus and Sophocles. Thereafter it declined and was superseded in popularity by a novel variety of play variously known as tragicomedy or "romance." This last stage of the drama in Shakespeare's lifetime claims a later and separate treatment, and to that place we here defer it.

CHAPTER XV

TRANSLATION IN VERSE AND PROSE

WE are apt to think of the age of Elizabeth as the age of Shakespeare and therefore the age of the drama; or as the time when the new inductive system was proposed as a substitute for outworn medieval methods of thought, and therefore as the age of Bacon. Remembering how the lyric flourished until England was a veritable "nest of singing birds," we dub Elizabeth's the age of the lyric; or recalling who first circled the globe and rifled the wealth of Spain in the cradle of its birth, we call Elizabeth's the age of discovery. Look where we will on that incomparable time we behold men physically, mentally, and spiritually active with the indefatigable buoyancy of youth which like each returning spring is always a new wonder. When the extraordinary interest which the sixteenth century took in the classics, in modern foreign literatures, French, Spanish, and especially Italian is considered, when we add, too, to all this the fact that it was within this period that the greatest of translations, our English Bible, was wrought by successive recastings to its perfection, the age of translation must seem no misnomer. Some years since an industrious scholar attempted an appraisement of Elizabethan translations from the Italian in three or four successive contributions. I say "attempted," not because the work was not well done, but because such a work could scarcely be pronounced complete except after exhaustive research quite disproportionate to its results. In the first paper there is mention of one hundred and sixty translations from the Italian within the hundred and ten years from 1550 to 1660 "made by ninety or more translators including nearly every well-known Elizabethan author except Shakespeare and Bacon": Jonson and Donne might likewise have been excepted. When the last of these researches was complete,

the total had risen to two hundred and eighteen English translations of one hundred and twenty-three Italian authors in
general literature and poetry, this not including more than
as many more that Lamb would have called "books in sheep's
clothing." A more recent appraisement of Spanish books
printed in Tudor England, including translations from the
Castilian tongue, mounts up to one hundred and sixty titles.
And a similar appraisement for France shows, only within
the lifetime of Shakespeare, the surprising total of nearly four
hundred titles. Though in this last list there are many cases,
such as North's translations of Amyot's French version of
Plutarch's Lives, in which French is simply the intermediary
language between the English translation and a classical,
Spanish, or Italian original. We await appraisements such
as these for the Dutch and Flemish books that found their
way into Elizabethan England in their native garb or translated. Even they could not have been inconsiderable; and
they were certainly more in number and in influence than the
few scattered books printed in the language of High Almaine,
as Germany was then called, that came into England for the
most part through some other foreign channel.[1] Now, if we
add to this mass of translation from modern foreign languages
the numerous English translations of the classics, from Bellen-
den's *Livy*, 1536, one of the earliest if not the first translation
of a Latin classic in England, to Chapman's *Homer*, completed
in the year of Shakespeare's death, remembering that the list
includes Horace, Juvenal, Vergil by three translators, Ovid,
at least in part, by four or five, Cæsar, Seneca, the dramas
and the prose, Lucan's *Pharsalia*, Apuleius, Heliodorus, Suetonius, parts of Plautus and Terence, with Hesiod, and
Musæus, parts of Theocritus, besides Homer, at one extreme
and Tacitus, Plutarch, and Josephus at the other, no question
can possibly remain as to the activity of the age in this placing
of foreign words in English dress.

[1] As to these appraisements see the work of Miss M. A. Scott in
the *Publications of the Modern Language Association*, 1895-1899; and
the monographs of Einstein, Underhill, and Upham in *Columbia
University Studies in English*, 1902-1908.

With such a mass of material before us, it is plain that it will be better to pick and choose a few typical translations which for one or another reason have most deeply affected the literature of their time rather than to attempt anything like an appraisement in mass of this largely forgotten material. In the time of the experiments in classical meters it was but natural that attempts should have been made to cloak the English version in a garb supposedly representing the ancient form. Surrey tried two books of the *Æneid* in blank-verse in 1557. In 1582, Richard Stanihurst, the Irish scholar and contributor to Holinshed's *Chronicles*, turned four books of the same great epic into hexameters, expressed in an eccentricity of vocabulary and grotesque homeliness of speech which excite new wonder whenever read. Thomas Drant, another like experimenter, theorized on hexameters, but translated the *Satires* of Horace and his *Ars Poetica* as well as parts of the *Iliad* into English rime. Arthur Golding had adequately, if diffusely, translated the *Metamorphoses* of Ovid, with Cæsar and Seneca's prose also, in the sixties and seventies, and the young Marlowe was drawn to the *Amores* of Ovid as he was drawn to reconstruct the fragment of Musæus on *Hero and Leander* by the warmth of the Renaissance imagination which begot as well the luscious sensuousness of Shakespeare's *Venus and Adonis*. Marlowe's translation of the *Amores* is that of a poet.

We do not know precisely the relations of Chapman to Marlowe; they must certainly have been intimate, for Chapman followed closely in Marlowe's footsteps, not only in the drama, but in translation, first Englishing Ovid's *Banquet of Sense*, and then completing, as we have already seen, Marlowe's unfinished *Hero and Leander*. George Chapman was an older man than Jonson and Marston, with both of whom we have already found him in association in the writing of *Eastward Hoe*. Chapman was born in 1559 at Hitchin in Hertfordshire, and was educated at Oxford, leaving, however, without a degree. He was late in turning to literature; at least there is no record of any publication by him before *The Shadow of the Night*, two poetical hymns, in 1594. The translation from Ovid, just mentioned, followed immediately after. It has been thought that Chapman wrote plays only under protest and for a livelihood. Allusions in *Henslowe's Diary* place his probable beginnings in comedy as far back as 1596, and plays of his were in print — witness *The Blind Beggar of Alexandria* and *A Humorous Day's Mirth* — by 1598 and 1599. Chapman's repute in the drama is referable to his romantic comedies, such as *The Gentleman Usher*, acted in 1602, and *Monsieur D'Olive*, 1605, as well as to his comedies of humor and intrigue and to his several dramas dealing with all but contemporary French history, of both of which we have heard. But Chapman was, besides, an original poet of repute, although his poems of this class are for the most part occasional. Among them may be named his *Tears of Peace*, 1609, an *Epicede or Funeral Song* on the death of his patron, Prince Henry, and *Andromeda Liberata*, 1614. This last celebrates in most unfitting allegory the infamous marriage of the notorious Somerset with the divorced Countess of Essex; and was a mistake characteristic of a scholar immersed in his studies and myopic as to the significance of passing events. This must have destroyed once and for all any chances of preferment that the poet may have had. In all his poetry Chapman is strenuous, intellectual, not emotional, with a large sense for the phrase, but often wanting in taste and plunging in the mazes of a contorted, difficult, and obscure style. It has often been remarked that no poet of his own time so resembled Ben Jonson. And this is true save for clarity of diction, sense of proportion, and restraint, none of which are among the virtues of Chapman. On the other hand, of no poet of the age, outside of Shakespeare, can it be said that he has left us so many poetical passages, moralizing wisely and memorably on life, and quotable alike for their significance and the beauty of their diction.

Chapman's famous translation of Homer was by no means the first attempt to English the father of Greek poetry. Aside from Drant's unpublished fragments of the *Iliad*, written before 1580, Arthur Hall had published in the following year *Ten Books of Homer's Iliads*, translated out of French in old-fashioned, fourteen-line, riming measure, a clumsy and inaccurate version. Chapman must have begun his Homeric studies well back in the reign of Queen Elizabeth, for the first instalment of his work, *Seven Books of the Iliads*, appeared in print in 1598, dedicated to the popular hero of the moment, the young Earl of Essex. A second instalment dedicated to Prince Henry followed in 1609; the *Iliad* was complete in 1611, the *Odyssey* in 1616. Chapman, always in poverty and holding the common world in lofty disdain, was encouraged by the prince in his translation and with the prince's untimely death all hope of reward for the poet's years of toil was at an end. Few translations have been more enthusiastically admired than Chapman's, even although his learning has been impugned by those who could never have translated anything into a poetical line. The unflagging and devoted zeal which Chapman brought to the prosecution of this great undertaking is only exceeded by the genuine poetic spirit that pervades it all. Nor can we say that either his zeal, his learning, or his poetry deserted Chapman in his other translations, of *Hesiod*, of parts of *Juvenal*, of the *Homeric Hymns*, and *The Battle of the Frogs and Mice* which his diligence also achieved. As a specimen of Chapman's translation let us take these lines from the famous speech in which Hector, departing for his fatal combat with Achilles, replies to the entreaties of Andromache:

Be well assured, wife, all these things in my kind cares are weighted.
But what a shame and fear it is to think how Troy would scorn
(Both in her husbands and her wives, whom long-trained gowns
    adorn)
That I should cowardly fly off! The spirit I first did breathe
Did never teach me that; much less, since the contempt of death
Was settled in me, *and my mind knew what a worthy was,*
Whose office is to lead in fight and give no danger pass
Without improvement. In this fire must Hector's trial shine;
Here must his country, father, friends, be in him, made divine.
And such a *stormy* day shall come (in mind and soul I know)
When sacred Troy *shall shed her towers, for tears of overthrow;*
When Priam, all his birth and power, shall in those tears be drowned.
But neither Troy's posterity so much my soul doth wound,

Priam, nor Hecuba herself, nor all my brothers' woes,
(Who though so many and so good must all be food for foes)
As thy sad state; when some rude Greek shall lead thee weeping
    hence,
These free days clouded, and a night of captive violence
Loading thy temples, out of which thine eyes must never see,
But spin the Greek wives' webs of task and their fetch-water be
To Argos, from Messeides, or clear Hyperia's spring;
Which howsoever thou abhorr'st, Fate's such a shrewish thing
She will be mistress.[1]

Well may Matthew Arnold have remarked, "How ingeniously Homer's plain strength is *tormented*"; for the words in this passage italicized by Arnold mark amplifications on the original which are wholly Elizabethan and only to an Elizabethan an improvement. And yet no translator of Homer who has followed Chapman has surpassed him in poetic spirit and none dare leave his version unconsulted. Well may Coleridge have said that Chapman's *Homer* is as truly an original poem as *The Faery Queen*. Indeed it is precisely on this score of originality, which was not to be had except in these very definite departures from the spirit and the letter of his text, that Chapman has been most severely criticized. When all has been said, however, concerning Chapman's

[1] For comparison, here is the same passage in the version of Lang, Leaf and Myers: "Then great Hector of the glancing helm answered her: Surely I take thought for all these things, my wife; but I have very sore shame of the Trojans and Trojan dames with trailing robes, if like a coward I shrink away from battle. Moreover mine own soul forbiddeth me, seeing I have learnt ever to be valiant and fight in the forefront of the Trojans, winning my father's great glory and mine own. Yea of a surety I know this in heart and soul; the day shall come for holy Ilios to be laid low, and Priam and the folk of Priam of the good ashen spear. Yet doth the anguish of the Trojans hereafter not so much trouble me, neither Hekabe's own, neither King Priam's, neither my brethren's, the many and brave that shall fall in the dust before their foemen, as doth thine anguish in the day when some mail-clad Achaian shall lead thee weeping and rob thee of the light of freedom. So shalt thou abide in Argos and ply the loom at another woman's bidding, and bear water from fount Messeis or Hypereia, being grievously entreated, and sore constraint shall be laid upon thee."

"barbarizing of Homer" and transmuting with a high Teutonic hand the *Iliad* into a species of *Niebelungen Lied*, it may be doubted if the age of Shakespeare could have produced a poet better fitted for the work. Jonson, or possibly Drayton, alone combined the scholarship, the industry, and the poetic instinct for such a task; but Jonson wanted the generous heroic spirit that sustains the pages of Chapman; and Drayton, with all that he might have gained in clarity of diction over Chapman, is as little likely as Spenser himself to have escaped (even to the degree to which Chapman escaped it) the fantasticality of thought and ornateness of treatment that must have kept every true Elizabethan at arm's length from the simple brevity and severe sufficiency of Homeric art.

No other poetical translation of the classics in this age is comparable to Chapman's work, although two excellent prose translations, North's *Plutarch* and Holland's *Natural History of Pliny*, deserve places beside it. Fuller styled Philemon Holland "the translator general of his age, so that those books alone of his turning into English will make a country gentleman a competent library." Holland lived between 1552 and 1637, was educated at Cambridge, and became a school-master at Coventry. His translations began in 1600 with Livy's *Roman History*, and included, besides others, Plutarch's *Morals*, the *Twelve Cæsars* of Suetonius, and Xenophon's *Cyropædia*. Holland also translated Camden's *Britannia* into English in 1610, and enjoyed the popularity to which his industry and faculty of cursive and graphic writing entitled him. Sir Thomas North was an older man, possibly born as early as 1535. He did not survive into the reign of King James. As a younger son of Roger, the second Lord North, Sir Thomas enjoyed many advantages; he published his translation of *Plutarch's Lives* in 1579. This famous work was not translated directly out of the Greek, but, as the title-page declares, "out of the French" of Jaques Amyot, which had appeared in 1559. North had the advantage, while on an embassy with his father, of meeting Amyot who was then Bishop of Auxerre, so that his undertaking was well advised. With the advantage of a scholarly and in the main remarkably accurate version of an incomparable original, North contrived to produce a truly great translation. To this a kindliness of spirit and an artless directness of speech, combined with a fine command of idiomatic but far from inelegant English, contributed in no small degree. North's *Plutarch* went through six editions before the Restoration and remains of especial interest as the source whence Shakespeare derived his ancient history. The amount of Shakespeare's obligation extended not only to the subjects of his well-known plays, *Coriolanus*, *Cæsar*, and *Antony and Cleopatra*, but likewise to suggestions, classical names for his dramatis personæ, and innumerable allusions scattered up and down the dramatist's works. Moreover, in following no one of his other sources has Shakespeare changed so little the thought and borrowed, so often in long passages, the verbal raiment of another's ideas. Not only does he take over bodily North's picturesque and effective vocabulary, but he reproduces his turns of phrase and peculiarities of idiom, his arguments and figurative illustrations. How many of the pictured details of Enobarbus' glowing speech describing Cleopatra's pageant on the river Cydnus, Shakespeare had from North's translation of the *Life of Antonius*, the following passage will disclose:

She disdained to set forward otherwise, but to take her barge in the river of Cydnus; the poop whereof was of gold, the sails of purple, and the oars of silver, which kept stroke in rowing after the sound of the music of flutes, howboys, cithernes, viols, and such other instruments as they played upon in the barge. And now for the person of herself, she was laid under a pavilion of cloth of gold of tissue, apparelled and attired like the goddess Venus commonly drawn in picture: and hard by her, on either hand of her, pretty, fair boys apparelled as painters do set forth god Cupid, with little fans in their hands, with the which they fanned wind upon her. Her ladies and gentlewomen also, the fairest of them, were apparelled like the nymphs, Nereids (which are the mermaids of the waters) and like the graces; some steering the helm, others tending the tackle and ropes of the barge, out of the which there came a wonderful passing sweet savor of perfumes, that perfumed the wharf-side pestered with innumerable multitudes of people. Some of them followed the barge all along the river-side: others also ran out of the city to see her coming in. So that in the end, there ran such multitudes of people one after another to see her, that Antonius was left post alone in the market-place, in his imperial seat, to give audience: and there went a rumor in the peoples' mouths, that the goddess Venus was come to play with the god Bacchus, for the general good of Asia.

It has been well said that in North alone among his sources Shakespeare met his match; and there are passages — such as the famous one describing the death of Cleopatra — in which Shakespeare has not succeeded in bettering his original. North's *Lives of the Noble Grecians and Romans*, "compared together by that grave, learned philosopher and historiographer, Plutarch of Chæronea," as the title runs, is a noble monument of simple and dignified old English and a quarry well worthy the use of the master-poet.

Let us now turn to some of the translations from modern tongues. Among the Italians the *Eclogues* of Mantuan seem earliest to have attracted the Elizabethan translator Turberville, in 1567, as they later attracted Spenser to imitation in *The Shepherds' Calendar*. With the eighties came the influx of the lyric, especially the sonnet, which was more frequently imitated than translated, and the song which was often turned literally into the northern tongue, syllable for syllable, that it might be sung to the original Italian tune. But by far the most important poetical translations of the age from the Italian were those of the epics of Tasso and Ariosto. The story is related how young Sir John Harington, court wit and privileged, from the queen's having stood sponsor to him at his christening, had the impertinence to translate and pass from hand to hand one of the cantos of the *Orlando Furioso*, to which Ariosto had prefixed the warning that it should be avoided "by ladies and those who valued ladies." Brought to the ears of Queen Elizabeth, she bade Harington to take himself home and not dare to come into the royal presence until he could bring back with him a complete translation of the *Orlando*. This the clever young rascal accomplished in haste and with ease and thus regained his royal god-mother's favor. Readiness and facility rather than any great poetic power characterize Harington's *Orlando Furioso*, which was printed in 1591 and enjoyed no little fame. Harington preserves the *ottava rima* of the original, but makes coarser the irony and humor of the Italian poet. A witty and capable preface, called *An Apology for Poetry*, precedes the translation. Here Harington discourses in justification of epics such as the *Orlando*, and upholds his brief for poetry at large with arguments against the Philistines which, as has well been said, men of Sidney's and Harington's intellectual caliber do not waste their time in employing to-day. The *Orlando Inamorata* of Boiardo was indifferently translated by Robert Tofte in 1598. It has been described as "singularly unequal" but not without "dexterity of versification." Tofte also translated *Two Tales from Ariosto* and other Italian works. As to Tasso, a faithful if rather unpoetical version of the first five cantos of *La Gerusalemne Liberata* was made by Richard Carew, a Cornish gentleman in 1594, to be followed six years later by the famous and enduring rendering of the entire work by Edward Fairfax. With Tasso's pastoral *Aminta*, translated by Abraham Fraunce in 1587, *Il Pastor Fido* of Guarini by one Dymock in 1602, and the *Satires of Ariosto* done into English by the pamphleteer Gervais Markham, we complete an enumeration of the more important translations from Italian poets.

Elizabethan translation of Italian prose began earlier and is far bulkier. It may be said that English translations, adaptations, and imitations of the Italian *novellieri* constituted by far the most popular reading of the period of Shakespeare's childhood, contributing sources, it has been estimated, to practically a third of the drama, and furnishing an inexhaustible model and inspiration for English fiction and poetry. The typical Elizabethan example of a collection of Italian *novelle* is *The Palace of Pleasure*, "beautified, adorned and well furnished with pleasant histories and excellent novels selected out of divers good and commendable authors," by William Painter, 1566. Painter was a school-master at Sevenoaks and had first projected his book in 1562. A later completed edition of this popular work contains one hundred and one tales, "partly translations and partly imitations of Italian *novelle*," and this is generally the character of these collections of stories. There were upwards of a dozen such, imitated and, in the quaint phrase of the day, "forged only for delight," up to the time when Shakespeare began his dramatic career; and they were, of course, his natural sources. Among the more important were *Certain Tragical Discourses*, the work of Sir Geoffrey Fenton, 1567; *The Forest or Collection of Histories*, by Thomas Fortescue, and *The Rock of Regard*, by George Whetstone, both in 1571; *A Pettie Palace of [George] Pettie his Pleasure*, 1576; *A Courtly Controversy of Cupid's Cautels*, containing five tragical histories, by Henry Wotton; also Barnabe Riche his *Farewell to the Military Profession* in eight novels, 1581, and Whetstone's *Heptameron of Civil Discourses*, 1582. Turberville's *Tragical Tales* are in verse. Single stories were many and gradually developed from mere translations such as Arthur Brooke's poetical version of *Romeus and Juliet*, 1562, or the *Excellent History of Euryalus and Lucretia*, 1567, to original stories purporting to be translations like Gascoigne's *Adventures of Master Ferdinando Jeronimi*, 1572, originally *Freeman Jones*, and more accurately Gascoigne himself.

The Italian authors whose work appears in these English translations and imitations are many. Thus Whetstone derives his *Heptameron* mainly from the *Hecatommithi* of Cinthio; Barnabe Riche draws chiefly on Bandello; while Painter harks back to Boccaccio as well as Bandello, although both he and Fenton appear to have derived most of their material through the intermediary of similar collections in French by Belleforest and Boisteau. In tracing a play through its foregoing versions as they appear in these collections, English, French, and Italian, it is not always an easy matter to discover which was the probable original. In the case of Shakespeare, fortunately, such is his customary fidelity to his source, that he is more readily followed than almost any dramatist of his day. For example, the tragical tale of the ill-starred lovers, Romeo and Juliet, had been told first to Western Europe by Masuccio di Salerno, soon after 1470; by Luigi da Porto, in his story, *La Giulietta*, in 1535; and by Bandello, in his *Novelle* in 1554. From the last, it was translated into French by Boisteau to form one of the stories of François de Belleforest's *Histoires Tragiques*, 1559. Three years later, Arthur Brooke translated the story into English verse; and, in 1567, it appeared in Painter's *Palace of Pleasure*. The essentials of the story have been found in a Greek romance of the second century, *Abrocomas and Anthia*, by Xenophon of Ephesus. But all this learning is to little purpose: Shakespeare's source was, as usual with him, the nearest and most obvious, Brooke's English poem, not without a knowledge, however, of the tale as related by Painter and Bandello. Thus it is that Painter garrulously straggles through the beginnings of a well-known story:

The family of the Capellets . . . was at variance with the Montesches which was the cause that none of that family repaired to that banquet but only the young gentleman, Romeo, who came in a mask after supper with certain other young gentlemen. And after they had remained a certain space with their vizards on, at length they did put off the same. . . . But by means of the torches which burned very bright, he was by and by known and looked upon of the whole company, but especially of the ladies, for besides his native beauty wherewith nature had adorned him, they marvelled at his audacity, how he durst presume to enter so secretly into the house of that family which had so little cause to do him any good. Notwithstanding the Capellets, dissembling their malice, either for the honor of the company or else for respect of his youth, did not misuse him either in word or deed: by means whereof with free liberty he beheld and viewed the ladies at his pleasure, which he did so well and with grace so good as there was none but did very well like the presence of his person. And after he had particularly given judgment upon the excellency of each one according to his affection, he saw one gentlewoman amongst the rest of surpassing beauty who (although he had never seen her before) pleased him above the rest; and [he] attributed unto her in heart the chiefest place for all perfection and beauty, and feasting her incessantly with piteous looks, the love which he bare to his first gentlewoman [the "unexpressive" Rosaline] was overcomen with this new fire that took such nourishment and vigor in his heart as he was not able ever to quench the same but by death only.

But poetry and fiction by no means represent the sole varieties of Italian literature translated by Elizabethans. A list of "miscellanea," after mention of these, includes nearly four hundred numbers and is subdivided into "theology, science and the arts, grammars and dictionaries, voyages, history and politics, manners and morals." It represents works as diverse as Sir Thomas Hoby's excellent translation of *The Courtier* of Castiglione and trifles innumerable, such as *A Treatise* "concerning the use and abuse of dancing," and *A Joyful Jewel* "containing preservatives for the plague." Most notable among other Elizabethan translations from Italian prose works of importance may be named Fenton's version of Guicciardini's *Wars of Italy*, 1579; Macchiavelli's *Art of War*, by Peter Whitehorne, 1573; and the same author's *Florentine History*, translated by Thomas Bedingfield in 1595. *The Prince*, most famous and influential of Macchiavelli's works, seems not to have been translated in Shakespeare's time.

As to Spanish, after the early vogue of Guevara (whose *Golden Book of Marcus Aurelius* was translated by Lord Berners in the reign of Henry VIII), and after the personal influence of the Spanish humanist Vives, exerted during his residence at Oxford in the same reign, the earliest influence of the peninsula upon England was exercised in the translations, by such men as Frampton, Thomas, and Nichols, of Spanish accounts of exploration and discovery in new lands; material in short of the kind later to be arranged and codified by Hakluyt himself. A considerable number of Spanish religious books were translated too, chiefly of a type heretical in their own land. Nor were the mystics and Catholics without their translator of the devotional tracts of Fray Luis de Granada, the famous Dominican, in Richard Hopkins. Sidney and his circle were interested in Spanish; though only a couple of the lyrics of the *Arcadia* are directly traceable to the *Diana* of Montemayor, the story at large shows an acquaintance with the Spanish pastoral romance. Translations of various romances of chivalry, the *Amadis de Gaule*, *Palmerin d'Oliva*, and *Palmerin of England*, were made by Anthony Munday, with other help, to regale the humbler readers of English fiction. These date between 1588, when his *Palladino of England* appeared, and 1619, when *Primaleon of Greece*, "son to Palmerin d'Oliva," concluded the series. But by far the most important translation from the Spanish was the vigorous and able version of Cervantes' masterpiece published by Thomas Shelton in 1612 under the title *The Delightful History of the Witty Knight, Don Quixote*. This admirable work, though begun in 1607, was not actually completed until 1620. It has received high praise, alike for the author's extraordinary grasp of the difficult original and for his employment of idiomatic English.

Turning to France, we find Arthur Hall translating Homer from the French in 1581, as North had Englished his *Plutarch's Lives*. Spenser translated Du Bellay and incorporated passages derived from the pastorals of Marot in his *Shepherds' Calendar;* Lodge was a notorious borrower from Ronsard, Phillipe des Portes, and other French lyrists; while in the drama, Lady Pembroke and Thomas Kyd translated the *Antoine* and the *Cornélie* of the French Senecan, Robert Garnier. But most of these things have already found record and need not further delay us. An important, though forgotten, work is Edward Grimestone's *General Inventory of the History of France*, a compendium of De Serres, Matthieu, Cayet, and others, published in 1607. Grimestone, whose works are now of the greatest scarcity, was a busy translator and compiler, publishing besides other works a *History of the Netherlands* in 1608 and a *History of Spain* four years later. But if contemporary popularity were always the measure of worth, the fame of Joshua Sylvester might stand beside that of Spenser, where many of his contemporaries placed it, for his translation of the scriptural narrative poem, *La Semaine*, of the Huguenot poet Du Bartas. This, Sylvester entitled *Du Bartas his Divine Week*. It appeared in completion in 1606. Sylvester emulated the manner of Spenser and was not without his influence on William Browne and even on Milton. The translator of Du Bartas was a ready versifier, something of a concettist, and sustained at all times by a genuine religious enthusiasm. He belongs to the tribe later represented by Quarles, and Wither in the uninspired stretches of his religious verse.

Among Elizabethan translations from the French, the most famous is Florio's *Montaigne*. Florio's father was a Florentine Protestant who fled from Italy on account of his religion. His son John, who was about the age of Spenser, was educated at Oxford, enjoyed, like Shakespeare, the literary patronage of Southampton, and married a sister of the poet Daniel. In the reign of James, Florio became reader in Italian to Queen Anne. Florio's Translation of the *Essais* of Montaigne was published in 1603; and while not so accurate as that of Charles Cotton, 1686, has qualities of individuality that will insure it a place among the great translations of a translating age. The authenticity of the signature of Shakespeare in the copy of Florio's *Montaigne* in the British Museum has been called into question. But we may still feel sure, from the well-known passage in *The Tempest* (that in which Gonzalo describes an ideal republic), that this was one of the books that Shakespeare read.

But when all has been said, the richest prose product of the Elizabethan age, indeed of any age or language, is the *Authorized Version of the Bible in English*. Among the thousands of volumes of commentary — religious, antiquarian, and philological,— that have been written upon this cornerstone of Christianity, but little comparatively has been said until of late of its transcedent position as an English classic or of the deep and abiding effect which it has worked, whether directly or indirectly, upon English prose style; and a feeling, far from improper, of awe and reverence has conspired to deter many from a treatment of this book as we treat others, although the reasonablenss of such a proceeding must be plain to any student of history. The thirty-nine distinct parts of the *Old Testament* and the twenty-seven of the *New*, form the extant literature of a whole people during a period of over a thousand years. As such we need not be surprised to find no family likeness of parts, either in style, matter, or mode of treatment. The Bible contains legend, history, biography, poetry, proverbs, parables, philosophy, and ethical and political injunctions. Many of the books are exclusively theological or religious, others are purely narrative or lyrical. *The Book of Job* is dramatic, at least in form. With all this diversity of subject-matter, the first thing that strikes one in the style of the English Bible is the extraordinary quality of its diction "remarkable," as it is, "for clearness, simplicity and strength." Homely, plain, and Saxon and yet endowed with a dignity, a grace and sweetness which may be imitated but never approached. So widely is this admirable quality of diction acknowledged that the late Cardinal Newman, most eminent of Anglican converts to Roman Catholicism, is reputed to have once asked, "Who will say that the uncommon beauty and marvellous English of the Protestant Bible is not one of the greatest strongholds of heresy in this country?"

It is a mistake to consider the *Authorized Version* as mainly the work of the King James translators in 1611. As a matter of fact the *Version* was gradually perfected during the greater part of the century by a succession of eminent theologians. The first of these was William Tyndale, a student of Greek under Colet and Grocyn at Oxford, later a pupil of Erasmus at Cambridge. Tyndale was a man with one idea — the translation of the Bible — to the end that the people might know Christ from the pure fountain-head. Animated with the spirit of Wyclif, he endured "poverty, exile, bitter absence from friends and innumerable other hard and sharp fightings," and finally martyrdom for this great end; for he was burned at the stake for his opinions, at Antwerp in 1536. Tyndale's *New Testament*, which differed from all previous translations in being made not from the Latin *Vulgate* but from the original Greek, was published in 1525. It was immediately ordered suppressed and burned by Archbishop Warham; orders very effectively carried out. But Tyndale continued his labors, translating parts of the *Old Testament* which were variously published and making a definitive revision of his *New Testament* in 1534. It has been said of Tyndale that he fixed the literary style of the Bible.

In this very year the convocation petitioned the king to

authorize a translation of the Bible into English, and Cranmer suggested a board of bishops and other learned men to superintend the undertaking.   This came to nothing, but Thomas Cromwell, then secretary of state, urged Miles Coverdale to print a translation on which he had long been engaged, and this appeared in 1535, the first complete English Bible, and the first to obtain the right of circulation in England.   Coverdale was neither the scholar nor the extreme Protestant that Tyndale had been; his work was chiefly editorial and supervisory, and it was based on "sundry translations not only Latin, but also of the Dutch [German] interpreters" and on Tyndale.   Two revised editions of Coverdale's Bible appeared in 1537.   In the same year appeared a completion of Tyndale's work, known as the *Matthews' Bible* from the name which stands at the end of the dedication, but apparently the work of one John Rogers.   This work, like Coverdale's, was dedicated to King Henry VIII, and furnished with marginal comments of a somewhat contentious nature.   It was allowed. Cromwell again commissioned Coverdale to revise the Bible and in 1539 appeared the *Great Bible*, as it was called, from the large size of the volume and its sumptuous character.   The edition of 1540 contains an Introduction by Cranmer and is sometimes known as *Cranmer's Bible*.   Copies of this Bible were set up in every church and the services even were deserted at times by those eager to read for themselves the word of God. Numerous editions of the *Great Bible* followed in the next two years (there were six in 1540 and 1541 alone); and from its appearance must be dated that familiar acquaintance with the Bible and love of its very word which has since especially characterized English speaking people.   Another Bible precisely contemporary with the *Great Bible* was the work of an Oxford scholar named Richard Taverner, who made some valuable corrections in the *New Testament*, but revised the *Old* mainly by reference to the *Vulgate*.

In the reactionary years towards the close of Henry's reign the reading of the Bible was forbidden; all Bibles bearing Tyndale's name were ordered to be destroyed, and Coverdale's *New Testament* was added to this condemnation.   The reign of Edward removed these restrictions and revived the publication of the Bible. Though no new version appeared in this reign, there were thirteen editions of the Bible complete, and thirty-five of the *New Testament*. With the accession of Mary, the reaction set in again. Rogers and Cranmer were executed; and Coverdale, now Bishop of Exeter, escaped with difficulty overseas, settling at last with other English fugitives in Geneva, where Calvin and Beza were holding Protestant sway. There Coverdale proceeded with his life work of Bible revision. But the greater part of the labor fell to younger hands, William Whittingham (who was married to Calvin's sister), in collaboration with other English scholars completed the work, publishing the *Geneva Bible* in 1560. These revisers were especially aided in their labors by the Latin translation of Theodore Beza, the most eminent Biblical scholar then living and, as might be expected, their marginal commentary was Calvinistic in tone. The *Geneva Version* long remained the popular Bible for home reading and exerted no inconsiderable influence on the *Authorized Version*.

With the accession of Elizabeth a new official Bible was needed; and Archbishop Parker with a group of learned men, for the most part dignitaries of the English Church, set about a revision of the *Great Bible*. This was accomplished by 1568 and is known as the *Bishops' Bible:* it at once superseded the *Great Bible* in the churches, but was, owing to the method of its revision, wanting in uniformity and somewhat uneven in execution. The *Bishops' Bible* by no means supplanted the *Geneva Version* in popular, and especially in Puritan, esteem.

Although the Romanist's point of view did not favor a popular reading of the Scriptures, such was the contemporary interest in a knowledge of the book of books that an English Bible, neither the work of English bishops nor of Calvinistic divines, became a demand of the moment. The preparation of this version was naturally given to the English scholars of the seminary which had been founded, first at Douay and continued later at Rheims (though it returned to Douay) by the Jesuits, for the ostensible purpose of bringing about the reconversion of England to the Roman faith. The *New Testa-*

ment of the *Douay Bible* appeared in 1582; but the work was not complete until the year 1609. Gregory Martin and other Oxford scholars, members of the Society of Jesus, were, in the main, responsible for it. This translation was made not from the Hebrew and Greek of the original, but from the Latin *Vulgate* on the ground that this was the Bible of Jerome and Augustine and therefore the true version of the Roman Church.

Lastly we reach the *Authorized Version* of 1611, the Bible which served all English speaking Christians (save communicants of the Church of Rome), until the *Revised Version* of 1881. The scheme of revision, for much of which King James must be held personally responsible, included a board of some fifty revisers of Oxford, Cambridge, and London, and involved not only independent work, but frequent consultation and comparison. The revisers were instructed that the *Bishops' Bible* was "to be followed, and as little altered as the original will permit;" though other versions might be used "when they agree better with the text than the *Bishops' Bible*." As a matter of fact the King James revisers had as little liberty assigned them as our own recent revisers, and they took less. Two features of the *Authorized Version* were its omission of all marginal commentary, and its adoption from the *Geneva Version* of the division of the chapters into verses. Another feature was its retention of the ecclesiastical terms which Tyndale had violently banished. The superiority of the *Authorized Version* over all others in literality, in its freedom from sectarian or party zeal, and in literary style is beyond dispute or cavil, and no words could exaggerate its potent and marvelous influence on English religion and literature alike.

If the question be asked How could such a perfect result be brought about under such circumstances? several reasons may be assigned. First, the nature of the original, offering not only a subject-matter involving the most interesting of all topics but a style in many parts for the equal of which we may look in vain through the literatures of the world. Secondly, the real piety of the translators and revisers, infusing into them a wholesome awe in the prosecution of their great task and a painstaking care, lest they should impair the truth and beauty of the word of God. Third, the state of the English language,—that of a vigorous adolescence, alike removed from the stuttering childhood of multiform Anglo-Saxon and from the conventional and somewhat trite phraseology that marks every highly-lettered tongue. And finally, the character of the age that produced Shakespeare, Bacon, Jonson, and Spenser, all writers, be it remembered, of superlative prose. To expatiate upon this last point would be to tell the history of the whole century; suffice it to say, that it is the age that has not yet ceased to believe nor yet begun to conceive itself possessed of all knowledge which alone could have produced this inimitable translation of an inimitable work.

CHAPTER XVI

HISTORY, DIVINITY, AND OTHER PROSE OF CONTEMPORARY COMMENT

THE opening chapter of this book treated of the literature of fact, that more or less literary reflection of past tradition that we call history, and present exploit, especially in the way of maritime and its attendant military adventure. The Elizabethan conception of history as exemplified in the pages of Holinshed or Stow is crude in the extreme. It neither discriminates nor chooses, but takes whatever has been chronicled before, without hesitancy or question; and it knows no ordering of material save the chronological sequence of events. But no age could scrutinize and study the past, alike of England and of foreign and ancient nations, as did this age, and remain blind to the fatuousness of so childish a handling of historical material. Sir Thomas More had already presaged better things in his *History of Richard III*; and Cavendish's *Life of Wolsey*, though more in the nature of memoirs than of actual history, is the work of an observer, with his heart in his subject and a natural aptitude for direct narrative. Towards the end of Elizabeth's reign a conception of history superior to that of mere chronicles and annals began to obtain. The learned antiquary, William Camden, patron of Ben Jonson, had already written his *Britannia*, 1586, in Latin, although it was not Englished until Holland's version of 1610. Camden's *Britannia* is not history, but an antiquarian topography of Britain. But the ideal of research which such a work involved (an ideal which it has been affirmed that Camden derived from a brief personal acquaintance with the famous Flemish geographer, Abraham Ortelius, who visited England in 1577) was something obviously applicable to the pursuit and writing of history. Camden's *Britannia* enjoyed an immediate success, reaching a third edition in 1590 and being reprinted

abroad. His later *Annals of Queen Elizabeth*, 1615, exemplified his method, satisfactorily applied to the history of his own
time, and forms with his *Remains concerning Britain*, 1605
(alone of his works first published in English) an honorable
memorial of one of the most learned and respected scholars
of his age. As to the method of documentary research in the
early years of King James, Fulke Greville relates in his *Life
of Sidney* that he purposed writing a history of the reign of
his late queen, Elizabeth, and "adventured to move the secretary (Sir Robert Cecil) that I might have his favor to peruse
all obsolete records of the council-chest from those times down
as near to these as he in his wisdom should think fit." Cecil
asked this inquirer after historical material to come again in
three weeks' time, and on this second visit he condescended
"to question me":

> Why I would dream out any time in writing a story, being as likely
> to rise in this time as any man he knew; then in a more serious and
> friendly manner examining me, how I could clearly deliver many
> things done in that time which may perchance be construed to the
> prejudice of this.   I shortly made answer that I conceived a historian
> was bound to tell nothing but the truth, but to tell all truths were both
> justly to wrong and offend not only princes and states, but to blemish
> and stir up against himself the frailty and tenderness, not only of
> particular men but of many families with the spirit of an Athenian
> Timon; and therefore showed myself to be so far from being dis-
> couraged with that objection as I took upon me freely to adventure
> all my own goods in this ship, which was to be of mine own build-
> ing.   Immediately this noble secretary . . . seriously assured
> me, that upon second thoughts, he durst not presume to let the council-
> chest lie open to any man living.

John Hayward, afterwards knighted by King James, was
born the same year with Shakespeare, dying in 1627, one year
after Bacon. Educated at Pembroke College, Cambridge,
Hayward rose to a certain distinction as a lawyer and was
patronized and encouraged in his historical labors by the king.
His works begin with a *History of the First Year of Henry
IV*, 1599, which sent him to the Tower for some ill-timed
flattery of Essex. He wrote, later, the lives of William I,

William II, Henry I, and Edward VI, besides *Annals* (of the earlier years) *of Queen Elizabeth.* Hayward was at one time associated as a colleague with Camden in Chelsea College, which James had founded. He seems to have caught somewhat Camden's idea of research and makes in his writings a brave show of learning; but from a want of any sense of proportion or of criticism, his efforts serve to little purpose. Hayward, however, set himself the definite task of rising out of the slough of the annalists and chroniclers into something like the literary history practised by the ancients. Livy and Tacitus thus became his models and he imitates them often in that wherein they are least defensible, their rhetoric and their formal imaginary oratorical passages. Bacon records that Queen Elizabeth inquired of him as to Hayward's "unlucky first attempt" at history, "whether there were no treason contained in it." To which Bacon replied: "For treason I can not deliver opinion that there is any, but very much felony." And when her majesty asked hastily, "How and wherein? I told her the author had committed very apparent theft; for he had stolen many of his sentences and conceits out of Cornelius Tacitus."

A minor historian of England was John Speed, the continuator of Stow's *Chronicle* down to the accession of James. His *History of Great Britain* dates 1611. Daniel, the poet, was likewise the author of a lengthy *History of England from the Conquest to the Reign of Edward III.* But despite his abilities as a stylist, Daniel contributed nothing to the advancement of the art of historical writing. The greatest piece of historical composition of the reigns of Elizabeth and James is Bacon's *History of Henry VII.* In this short essay — for it is not much more — the writing of history in English leaps with a bound to a place beside Tacitus and Thucydides himself.[1] But this was the work of Bacon's latest years and, printed in 1621, falls beyond us.

Among Elizabethan histories of foreign countries it is somewhat difficult to distinguish between translators and those whose compilations have a greater claim to originality. A

[1] See Spedding, *Works of Bacon*, vii, 4, 5.

busy historian, not without a homely merit of his own, was Edward Grimestone, already mentioned among translators for his compilation of French annals into a portentous volume entitled a *General Inventory of the History of France*, 1607. Whether Grimestone's *History of the Netherlands, of Spain*, and other later works that followed, were less completely compilations, we are not at present in possession of the facts to tell. A more famous work in its day was *The General History of the Ottoman Turks* by Richard Knolles, fellow of Lincoln College, Oxford, and later Master of the Grammar School at Sandwich. This history was the labor of ten years and appeared, elaborately printed with a dedication to the king and embellished with "portraits" of the sultans, in 1603. Knolles is said to have drawn largely on "a Latin history of the Turks published at Frankfort in 1596." His relations to a translation of Georgievitz's *De Turcarum Moribus* by H[enry] Gough in 1570, entitled *The Offspring of the House of the Ottomans*, might be worthy of inquiry.

Scarcely less a compilation, but in literary standing and quality far above these works, is Sir Walter Raleigh's *History of the World*, published in 1614. Written during his twelve years' imprisonment in the Tower with a sentence of death suspended over his head, this stupendous work is yet conceived in a spirit of leisure and pervaded with an absorbed interest in matters of detail that is simply astounding considering the circumstances. Sir Walter Raleigh was born about 1552, and was thus the same age precisely as Spenser whose early friend he was. Handsome in person, daring, brilliant, and unscrupulous as to the means of attaining success, Raleigh became a favorite of the queen, grew rich on monopolies, and was spoiled and petted by fortune. He came of the old Devonshire stock of sea-dogs and martial heroes. The famous navigator, Sir Humphrey Gilbert, was his half-brother, Sir Richard Grenville his cousin. Raleigh had fought by land against Spain in Ireland and in the Netherlands; and he had fought with the Huguenots in France. He had sailed with his brother Gilbert in one of his voyages against the commerce of Spain, and had helped the Earl of Essex "to singe the Spanish king's beard" at Cadiz. He had fitted out ships for the Armada and searched for fabulous El Dorado, burning Spanish towns by the way. Imprudence in espousing the claim of the Lady Arabella Stuart to the crown brought about the fall of this enemy of Spain early in the reign of James; and his conviction of high treason and long imprisonment led to the block at last in 1619. Raleigh's was certainly a strangely romantic career; and better perhaps than in greater historic figures can we discern in him the contradictions and contrasts that make the age of Elizabeth and James so fascinating and inexplicable at times. Raleigh was deeply interested in the exploitation of England, to his own advantage as well as the empire's. But he was likewise a poet possessed of a "lofty and insolent vein," scorning the world, its snares and vanities. Raleigh had been a friend of Marlowe, and reputed a member of a club of atheists, or at least free-thinkers, in his youth; yet it was to him that Spenser confided the ethical scheme of his ideal of a moral world in *The Faery Queen;* and *The History of the World* is imbued throughout with a spirit of piety which no unbeliever could affect. Raleigh's *History* has been called a stupendous work; it is such not only because of its bulk (for there are bulkier Elizabethan works), but because of the extraordinary scope of its plan and range of its subject-matter. Indeed, the book is less a history than "a series of dissertations on law, theology, mythology, magic, war and the ideal form of government," illustrated by an exceedingly diffuse account of the rise and fall of several of the great empires of the world. Raleigh must have had the help of many scholars in the assembling of the material at least for this huge mass; and Jonson informs us that he had his share in the portion dealing with the Punic Wars. But the work, however unequal in parts, is governed by the imperative spirit of Raleigh throughout, whose eloquence (more particularly in the preface and in the celebrated apostrophe to death with which the book ends), rises to court comparisons with the best Elizabethan and later English prose.

Into the many admirable prose writings of the age devoted

to antiquarian studies on the one hand and statecraft, either historically considered or in criticism, on the other, it is impossible to enter here. These topics belong from their contemporary conditions less to the domain of the literature of power than to that of the literature of knowledge, and although often conceived in a spirit of broad and philosophical generalization, are limited none the less by the occasions that produced them. During the latter half of the reign of Elizabeth an informal society of antiquarians existed, founded by Archbishop Parker; its ruling spirits were Camden, Speed, Selden, and Cotton. Of the first two we have just heard; John Selden, born in 1584, was the most learned of legal antiquaries. His great work was *The History of Tithes*, published in 1618. Selden was also a noted wit; but his *Table Talk* was mostly the gathering of his later years. It was in 1598 that Sir Thomas Bodley, a diplomat of note, made his offer to found a library in the University of Oxford; this was accepted and the library formally opened in 1602. Sir Robert Bruce Cotton was an enthusiast in the collection of old manuscripts. He published no more than a history of *The Reign of Henry III*, and this in 1627. But most of his extraordinary hoard of old documents were acquired during the later years of Elizabeth's reign and the earlier of James. There are no more imperishable memorials of the love of learning in the age of Shakespeare than the Bodleian Library at Oxford and the Cottonian Manuscripts of the British Museum. Among Elizabethan antiquaries none has maintained so popular a reputation and one so thoroughly deserved in his local field as John Stow, the chronicler and the antiquarian of old London. Stow was originally a tailor, but was led by a passion for his subject to minute and personal research among the antiquities and monuments of London and to write a book, absolutely unparalleled in its kind. Stow's *Survey of London* was first printed in 1598 and is the starting-point of all inquiry into the subject of Elizabethan and earlier London. Stow is so intent on his subject that he tells it well, unconscious of his force and directness. Like his fellow chroniclers Stow takes whatever is to his hand in the work of his predecessors, content that he be meted a like measure by those that come after. Stow has been pillaged assuredly for far more than he ever borrowed.

Singularly gifted and versatile was Sir Henry Wotton, a Kentish gentleman, younger kinsman of Bacon and a personal friend of Donne whom he met at New College, Oxford. Wotton was much abroad in the service of the state and his breadth of spirit in politics as in religion made him at once capable of intimacy with scholars such as Isaac Casaubon, with whom he lived at Geneva, and with Cardinals Bellarmine and Allen at Rome. Wotton was esteemed and trusted by King James; and his devoted attachment to the service of his sovereign's daughter, the beautiful and unhappy Elizabeth, Queen of Bohemia, was the romance of his life. On his retirement from diplomatic life in 1624, Wotton became Provost of Eton. His literary work embraces a *History of the Republic of Venice*, a *Life of Donne*, and a *Treatise on Angling*, all of these only projected however, although the last two were carried out by Wotton's friend and biographer, Izaak Walton. Wotton's most important work in his day was his treatise on *The State of Christendom*, printed in 1637, towards the close of his life. The *Reliquiæ Wottonianæ*, published in 1651, includes topics as various as *The Elements of Architecture*, *A Survey of Education*, the "Characters" of two or three historical personages, *Letters*, *Aphorisms*, and a few poems, two or three of which — among them the fine lines to the Princess Elizabeth beginning "You meaner beauties of the night" — gained a lasting and deserved celebrity. Wotton, like Selden and Bacon, had the gift of putting things. He was possessed, too, of a delicate critical taste for poetry. It was Wotton who first enthusiastically approved *Comus;* and it is fitting that this chivalrous, scholarly, and capable man should live forever in Walton's fine biography.

Such writings as these of Wotton and many like them of less conspicuous literary merit are best described under a generic title such as the prose of contemporary comment; for the conditions of the moment begot them and, while they rise in dignity of subject-matter and in care of composition above the grade of mere pamphleteering, their interest to us must remain curious and historical rather than strictly literary. Thus Richard Mulcaster, first Master of the Merchant Tailors' School, wrote originally and eloquently in his *Positions concerning the Training up of Children*, in 1581, and showed himself a worthy successor of Ascham and Elyot in a subject which we now call pedagogy and dignify with many technical and professional difficulties. In Mulcaster's book and in John Brinsley's *Ludus Literarius*, 1612, will be found many a new idea, grown old to be rediscovered by the historically uninformed of our own discovering age. The education of the young has always been an absorbing theme to pedagogues and parents. Even the great Lord Burleigh turned aside from the cares of practical statecraft to pen, in admirably phrased and unadorned English, *Ten Precepts to his Son* wherein such apothegms as "Marry thy daughters in time lest they marry themselves," and "He that payeth another man's debts seeketh his own decay" disclose his kinship in blood, as in worldly sagacity, to his great nephew, Francis Bacon. It was in the year of the Armada, before any certain work of Shakespeare's, that Dr. Timothy Bright, physician to St. Bartholomew's Hospital, set forth a little book called *Charactery: An Art of Short, Swift and Secret Writing by Character*, and thus founded the modern art of stenography. Many a "spurious quarto" of Shakespeare's and others' plays doubtless owes much to the art of Dr. Timothy Bright. A more professional work of the same author was his *Treatise on Melancholy*, 1586, by some supposed to have suggested Robert Burton's famous *Anatomy of Melancholy* published in 1621.

Attention has been specifically called of late to a remarkable series of state documents concerning Ireland, among them Sidney's defense of his father's administration as viceroy, Spenser's dialogue, and later papers and reports by Bacon, Sir John Davies, Fynes Moryson, and Sir Thomas Stafford. It is interesting to think of some of these men whom we remember chiefly for their poetry, as taking their part in government and practising, often with consummate success, the difficult art of statecraft. Spenser's work is written in dialogue form and is entitled *A View of the State of Ireland*. It was licensed in 1598, and is a clear and direct piece of prose writing based upon knowledge and remarkably well arranged and handled. In *Certain Considerations touching the Plantation in Ireland*, 1609, Bacon is critical of the administration of the time. Sir John Davies, in his *Discovery of the State of Ireland*, 1613, contributes a history of the country, which he supplemented, in 1617, with an account of the Tyrone rebellion. More personal in nature and for the most part well below the literary level are the several diarists, among them the celebrated astrologer, Dr. John Dee, who calculated an auspicious day for Queen Elizabeth's coronation and long outlived her; Sir Robert Naunton, who racily sketched in his *Fragmenta Regalia*, her favorites; and Robert Carey, later Earl of Monmouth, who tells in lively narrative how he carried the news of the old queen's death to her eagerly expectant successor. To two diaries, that of John Manningham of the Middle Temple and that of the quack physician and astrologer, Dr. Simon Forman, a peculiar interest attaches, as each affords us contemporary record of the performances of plays of Shakespeare. The notes which the Scottish poet, William Drummond of Hawthornden, made concerning the life, opinions, and literary gossip of Ben Jonson, who visited him in 1619, offer us the best contemporary picture of Shakespeare's greatest literary competitor. It is fair to remember that these *Notes of Conversations of Ben Jonson* were neither published nor intended for publication by Drummond; but were rescued from oblivion generations after the Scottish poet's death. *The Autobiography of Sir James Melville*, the diplomat, deals at large with the history of Scotland as the *Diary* of his namesake, the reformer, deals with the Scottish church in his time. Both works were published posthumously and are of greater literary pretensions than the fragments just enumerated.

Several controversies, more or less literary in nature, have found mention above. Besides the Marprelate dispute, so drastically suppressed, and the personal literary duel between Harvey and Nash, there was the old academic question of classical verse as the vehicle of English poetry, and the long

Puritan attack on the stage and on social abuses. Another controversy, involving more serious consequences than any matter of opinion, was the semi-religious question involved in the Elizabethan belief in witches. In 1584 Reginald Scott put forth an elaborate and learned work entitled *The Discovery of Witchcraft*. Scott was a Kentish esquire and justice of the peace, and left behind him a practical little treatise on the staple of Kent, entitled *The Hop Garden*, 1574. It was in the exercise of his official duties that Scott was drawn into an appreciation of the enormities and injustice that frequently resulted from the popular notions concerning witchcraft; and he entered heart and soul into the question on this impetus, and with a large mass of writings on the subject (such as those of Bodin and Weier) before him. But Scott was ahead of his time. He was denounced with singular unanimity by the clergy; and King James, who was something of a connoisseur in witches himself, so far condescended in his zeal as to answer this heretic with his royal hand in his *Demonology*, 1597, wherein he pronounced the opinions of Scott "damnable." This excursion of King James into demonology was by no means his only publication. He had taken part, when a lad and still under the supervision of his tutors, in the discussions about poetry that belonged to the days of Sidney, in his *Essays of a Prentice in the Divine Art of Poetry*, 1584. And a few years later, in 1589, he displayed the interest in theology that he maintained throughout his life in *Meditations on Revelations*. The *Basilikon Doron*, 1599, is a book of advice to his son, crowded with marginal references to the classics and the Bible, for James was nothing if not pedantic. Although it is fair to add that even in this James was not conspicuous according to the learned fashion of his day — or of ours, if the truth be confessed. As to the wise saws and modern instances of this book, it has been remarked that they might have come with better grace from a monarch less a victim to favoritism. But few authors can stand the test of judgment by the conduct of their lives. Two opinions of this royal author stand forth in relief: his absolute faith in the divine right of kings, set forth in several treatises; and his hatred of the new-fangled habit of smoking, denounced in *A Counterblast to Tobacco*, 1604. As to his controversy with Scott, on his accession to the throne James took a thorough means of silencing his adversary by ordering every copy of *The Discovery of Witchcraft* to be burnt. Happily for Scott, he died a subject of Queen Elizabeth.

Still another class of books based on contemporary experiences, and of the greatest possible interest to the student of manners and of the past, is that reported in the several records which Elizabethan travelers by land into foreign parts have left of their journeys and observations. The earliest of these travelers was Fynes Moryson, a gentleman of Lincolnshire and student at Cambridge, who obtained a license to travel in 1589; and, two years later, started on a series of journeys that took him not only through the more important parts of western Europe but to Copenhagen, Danzig, and Cracow, and then to Cyprus, Jerusalem, and Constantinople. Moryson was an observant and leisurely traveler. It was his custom to reside in a place to become acquainted with it. He thus lived at one time, a student at the University of Leyden, sojourned for months in Rome, studying antiquities under the protection of the English Cardinal Allen; while so long was his stay in Constantinople, he tells us, that he had contracted the habit — necessary for his protection among the Turks — of keeping his eyes fixed upon the ground and never looking a man in the face. Like a true traveler, Moryson was interested in everything: polity, manners, national traits, methods of transportation, architecture, diet, apparel, and foreign coinages. And he was possessed of the industry, requisite to a careful chronicling of all that he saw, and a homely clarity and directness of expression, not unillumined at times with an appreciative sense of humor. Moryson wrote up his *Itinerary* (as it was finally called on publication in 1617) no less than three times; first in Latin, secondly translated, and lastly abbreviated. The work is, from its mass of detail, of enormous length and the last of its three parts remains unreprinted and partly even now in manuscript. Earlier therefore in print was Thomas Coryate with his *Crudities Hastily Gobbled Up*,

1611, the account of the author's travels a year or two previous, mainly in France and Italy. Coryate, after failure to obtain his degree at Oxford, became a species of privileged buffoon at court where he affected whimsicality of appearance, speech, and manner, and rivaled in repute "Archie" Armstrong whom Jonson called "the principal fool of the state." From Coryate's character and from the enormous mass of semi-ironical prefatory matter in commendation of the author and his work which he procured at the hands of his many friends, *Coryate's Crudities* might be supposed to be wholly a book of fictitious foolery. Such however is far from the case. Coryate tells, for the most part, a plain unvarnished tale, by no means wanting in interest, despite the fact that his ways have been so much traveled since his time. Coryate started on a second tour in 1612, visiting Constantinople, Damascus, and Aleppo and going thence by caravan to Ispahan and Lahore, and visiting the Great Mogul, by whom he was kindly received. But of this journey we know only by a brief report of Purchas. Coryate lost his life by fever at Surat in 1617. Of less interest is the narrative entitled *The Total Discourse of the Rare Adventures and Painful Perigrinations* of William Lithgow first published in 1614 and detailing an extension of Coryate's first journey to Jerusalem and Cairo. Lithgow likewise went abroad again and, although his life was saved by the intervention of an English consul, it was not until he had endured torture on the rack at the hands of the Inquisition in Spain for his Protestantism. Lithgow's style, like that of Coryate is, at times, affected and absurdly precious. But to speak of either of these writers as Euphuistic is to obscure the significance of words. The last of the travelers to write within the lifetime of Shakespeare was George Sandys, paraphraser in verse of parts of the Bible and translator of Ovid at a later time when he was secretary to the governor of the colony of Virginia. Sandys' *Relation of a Journey begun A. D.* 1610 was published in 1615 and is the clear and unaffected narrative of a man of breeding who traveled neither in the adventurous spirit of Coryate nor as the vagabond that Lithgow was compelled to become. Sandys enjoyed peculiar advantages while in Jerusalem, seeing many things denied to other travelers, among them "the dwelling of Zebedee, the sycamore on which Judas hanged himself, the 'Castle of Lazarus,' and the vault from which he was raised,the house of Simon the Leper, the fount where Bathsheba bathed her feet, the palace of Pilate, and the convent to which the Magdalen retired from the vanities of the world." With the tomb of Juliet still on view at Verona and the many curiosities of "Shakespeare"— to mention none other — to be seen at Stratford and elsewhere, let no one cast a stone at the credulity of either Sandys or other of these Elizabethan "sight-seers."

Two examples of the prose of contemporary comment, very diverse in their natures, have been reserved for a somewhat fuller treatment. These are Greville's *Life of Sidney* and Jonson's *Timber or Discoveries*. Both were posthumous publications, and both these men have already been considered elsewhere and in other connections. Sir Fulke Greville, who received from James at his coronation Warwick Castle and was years afterwards raised to the peerage as Lord Brooke, is best remembered as the early friend of Sidney and the one among the "favorites" of Queen Elizabeth who (doubtless due to his own prudence) suffered least from the royal changes of temper. Greville's literary repute is at least three-fold; for his lyrics of intellectualized emotion, for his singularly difficult Senecan dramas, and for his poetical treatises on statecraft. To these we must add his writings in prose, chiefly represented in the *Life of Sidney* and in *A Letter to an Honorable Lady*. The latter is really a disquisition in the abstract on marriage for love. It was never sent, nor indeed addressed, to any real person; but is deeply interesting and full of profundity of thought. The *Life of Sidney* is not a biography at all, but appears to have been intended as a species of autobiographical preface to Greville's collected works, illustrating less the outward happenings of his life than his relations to the two beings whom he most loved and revered, Sidney, the friend of his youth, and his "incomparable queen," Elizabeth. In the course of a narrative that wanders whither the author will, guided by associations and recollections often

irrecoverable to-day, Greville expresses himself on many subjects on which he had pondered in the course of a long and ac-
tively useful public life. His reading must have been wide, yet
he is strangley unaffected either by the erudition or the literature of his time. A more completely metaphysical mind than
Greville's it would be difficult to discover. He was a Stoic
in an age of Platonism, a theorist in statecraft among poli-
ticians. He is full of Macchiavelian subtlety and insight, but
stands aloof from argument, controversy, and all practical
applications. Consciousness of the gauds and ornaments of
rhetoric as such he knows not at all; and yet the very essence
of poetry and of beauty of expression is his at times, not only in
his verse but in his prose as well. Fluency is the quality that
is furthest from the thought as from the style of Greville.
What he says, he says with gravity, with a certain hesitant
difficulty; and he abounds in indirections of speech and sentences in which we wander with him as in a maze. But there
is certainly (if we will but seek it) a significance, depth, and
beauty in the thought of Greville that make it worth the labor
of attainment and that come to exercise on him who learns
to know him a peculiar fascination. The comparison which
has been made of Greville to Polonius, with his pedantic
parade of shallow, hackneyed truisms, and his incessant bab-
ling to no purpose, seems peculiarly unhappy. King James
with his *Basilikon Doron* — the advice of Polonius to his son
written in large and in all seriousness — King James is Polonius; not Greville, whose lofty preoccupation with abstract
truth and search therefor, together with a certain awkwardness
of style, despite his power to express a beautiful thought in apt
and fitting raiment, seem qualities more in common with our
American Emerson.

Ben Jonson's *Timber or Discoveries made upon Men and
Matter* was gathered with other material at the end of the
second folio of the poet's collected works, 1641. The book
has been called a "species of commonplace book of aphorisms
flowing out of the poet's daily reading." But it is also much
more. For although many passages are all but literal translations, culled from the classics or from medieval or contem-

porary Latin and other authors, every note is stamped with the powerful personality of Jonson and penned with the utmost care as to details of expression and style. Moreover, other entries are not literary but allusive to Jonson's contemporaries or expressions of his estimate of them. Such are the famous passages concerning "Shakespeare *nostrati*" (our country-man), as Jonson calls him in pride, and the one on Bacon and his eloquence. Jonson esteemed both men and noted his regard in unaffected terms. Of Bacon his words are:

My conceit of his person was never increased towards him by place or honors. But I have and do reverence him for the greatness that was only proper to himself, in that he seemed to me ever, by his work, one of the greatest men, and most worthy of admiration, that had been in many ages.

As to Shakespeare, Jonson draws nearer the man himself in the memorable words: "For I loved the man, and do honor his memory on this side idolatry as much as any."

Religious and devotional writings form a very considerable proportion of the total output of the Elizabethan and Jacobean press. Apart from the revision and innumerable editions of the Bible and the various adaptations, translations, and para-phrases into which it was wrought in parts by the devout, apart too, from the *English Prayer Book* and other manuals and rituals of devotion, the mass of controversial "literature" which was begotten first of the break with Rome, and secondly by the schism that arrayed Anglican and Puritan in two hostile camps, was legion, even if now as dead as the herd of swine, possessed of devils, that cast themselves into the sea at Gad-arene. Divinity, employing literary art, as it must only for an ulterior purpose, is all but wholly of the literature of knowl-edge, however it may wing its words with poetry or glow with the passion of faith. Moreover, theological writing more completely than any other form of prose is contemporary in its purpose and tethered to the conditions of the moment. For even when the religious principles involved are of the widest significance and application, the theology of one age needs commonly to be translated in terms of the next, and issues that have once seemed momentous, creeds for which men laid down their lives, are no more to generations that come after than remote, jagged rocks that break the monotony of a level horizon.

The battle royal of new and militant English Protestantism against the Church of Rome in matters ceremonial and dogmatic had been fought out mostly by those who survived, if at all, not far into the reign of Elizabeth. Sir Thomas More and Erasmus were agreed with the reformers as to the existence of abuses within the church; but the controversy of the former with Tyndale pivoted on the question, could the church be reformed from within and survive. It is better to think of Tyndale as the first of the devoted scholars that gave their time to the translation of our English Bible than to recall in him the bitter controversialist, attacking *The Practices of Prelates*. And it is better to remember Cranmer, first Protestant Archbishop of Canterbury, as the artistic form-giver to the beautiful diction of the *Book of Common Prayer*, than for his voluminous and now forgotten writings on the eucharistic and other controversies that shook the theological structures of the time.

We may pass over the intervening decades of minor controversy in which figured the once potent names of Whitgift, Rainolds, Featley, Andrews, and Field. Towards the close of Elizabeth's reign the religious equilibrium which she had so long contrived to maintain was rendered unstable, first by the activities of the Jesuits in their endeavors to win back England to the faith of Rome; and secondly, by the militant attitude of Puritanism. Among the many Roman Catholics of English birth who took their part in the pamphlet warfare of the time may be named Thomas Stapleton, prominent during the nineties in the counsels of the English college, founded by the Jesuits at Douay, and the author, amongst much else, of a *History of the English Church* and an *Apology for Philip II* as against Elizabeth. A more notable man in the England of his time was Robert Parsons, who came back to his native country, about 1580, an accredited missionary from the Vatican to carry on innumerable intrigues and to write innumerable pamphlets in the cause of his church. His little volume of

Christian exercises, entitled *A Christian Directory*, enjoyed an extraordinary vogue. Among many, perhaps the most conspicuous reply to the Roman Catholic position in later Elizabethan years was John Rainolds' *De Romanæ Ecclesiæ Idolatria*, 1596.

Although the attack on Rome and Romish "practices" continued almost unabated, long before the time when such men as Rainolds began to write, Puritanism had arisen and with it new issues and contentions. The Renaissance had stood for individualism, and individualism fostered the ideals of nationality; the Protestant idea went further to give to each people its national church. But it was felt that the world had lost something in thus sacrificing the ambitious ideal of Rome: a world united in a universally accepted faith, under one supreme and apostolic head, who stood in spiritual power above princes as princes stood temporally above common men. It was at this juncture that John Calvin conceived his ingenious plan of a Christian republic which a happy train of circumstances enabled him to put into practice with triumphant success at Geneva. Calvin's reorganization of the church in relation to the state found its basis in the Christian man "elected and called of God, preserved by his grace from the power of sin, predestinate to eternal life." "Every such Christian man is in himself a priest, and every group of such men is a church, self-governing, independent of all save God, supreme in its authority over all matters ecclesiastical and spiritual." Without entering into the details of Calvin's nice balance of power, by which administration, election, interpretation of Scripture, decision of doctrine, discipline, and even excommunication, all are provided for within the congregation, it is sufficient to note this most important corollary: "To this discipline princes as well as common men are alike subject; princes as well as common men must take their doctrine from the ministers of the church." Calvin was at one with the Church of Rome in thus setting up a spiritual and ecclesiastical supremacy over all political and national claims. But "the Pope of Geneva" was not the same as the Pope of Rome. On the other hand, Calvin was at variance with the political and social systems of every nation of Europe in placing the ultimate source of power neither in prince, parliament, nor people, but in the individual Christian man; for, however despotic might seem the Calvinistic idea of the authority of pastor and elder, both alike were subject, in the last resort, to the vote of the congregation. How deeply the "exiles" from England drank of the Calvinistic font must be clear to the most careless reader of history. The new Puritan idea was alike counter to the ideals of a national and established church and to any monarchical form of government. That this idea should ultimately have led to armed conflict with both church and state was in the very nature of things. But with these larger issues we are not here concerned. One service Calvinism assuredly rendered mankind in its recognition of the individual man and his place as a political and social unit at the basis of modern democracy.

It was these essential doctrines of Puritanism, with the innumerable other points in which the Calvinistic interpretation of Christianity fell into variance with the tenets of the Church of England, that Richard Hooker set himself to refute in *The Laws of Ecclesiastical Polity*, four books of which appeared in 1594, the other three posthumously in 1648 and 1662. The literary attacks of Martin Marprelate on the bishops and on what, from the Puritan point of view, was regarded as a usurpation of power, preceded Hooker; and they have already received attention above in our consideration of the popular pamphlet literature. Hooker substituted, in this warfare between the opposing forces of Puritan and Anglican, coolness and circumspection for passion and abuse, a consideration of the question on the basis of principle and general law for personality, recrimination, and scurrility, and in so doing definitively stated the position of the Church of England at the end of Elizabeth's reign.

Richard Hooker was humbly born at Heavitree, near Exeter, in 1554. He was from the first a student of extraordinary precocity and industry; and, attracting the attention of Jewell, Bishop of Salisbury, went up to Oxford where, as one of the fellows of Corpus Christi College, he gained an unusual repute for his learning and piety. Hooker took orders in 1581; and four years after was appointed, through the influence of Archbishop Whitgift, Master of the Temple. It was here that Hooker, much against his will, was drawn into a theological controversy with Walter Travers, who was afternoon lecturer in the Temple, and who maintained Presbyterian views concerning church government with great ardor. As Fuller put it, the pulpit of the Temple "spake pure Canterbury in the morning and Geneva in the afternoon," — a condition of affairs that soon became intolerable. Hereupon the archbishop intervened and, on a technicality, forbade Travers to preach, a move that helped neither the bishops' cause nor improved the temper of Travers, who continued the controversy (now become hopelessly personal) in print. Hooker replied, defending himself especially against the charge of latitudinarianism. But he was heartily sick of controversy and besought his patron to remove him from the Temple to a quiet retreat in the country. This he at length found in the living of Boscombe, near Salisbury, and it was there that, pondering in peace on the questions so raised in the heat of controversy, Hooker projected and wrote his life-work, *The Laws of Ecclesiastical Polity*. In 1595 Hooker was translated to the better living of Bishopsbourne in the neighborhood of Canterbury, where he died towards the close of the year 1600.

In person Hooker has been described by Walton as mean in stature, insignificant in appearance and address, and conducting himself at all times "so as to give no occasion of evil, but . . . in much patience in afflictions, in anguishes, in necessities, in poverty and no doubt in long suffering; yet troubling no man with his discontents and wants." While it has been suspected that Walton, like the true literary artist that he was, overrated the insignificance of the personality of Hooker that he might heighten the contrast with his brilliancy of mind and argumentative power, it is certain that Hooker was a man of impoverished vitality, shrinking from an active contact with life, and singularly dependent on the good offices of others — which seem to have been offered him unsought — in the ordinary affairs of life. According to the often related story of Walton, on the suggestion made by a kindly-disposed matron that he needed a wife, Hooker commissioned her to find him one. And the matron provided for him "her daughter Joan, who brought him neither beauty nor portion; for her conditions," continues Walton, "they were too like that wife's which is by Solomon compared to a dripping house; so that the good man had no reason to rejoice in the wife of his youth." Walton completes his picture with a description of a visit paid Hooker by two of his pupils. They found him "with a book in his hand" tending "his small allotment of sheep in a common field; which he told his pupils he was forced to do then, for that his servant was gone home to dine and assist his wife to do some necessary household duties. But when his servant returned and released him, then his two pupils attended him unto his house, where their best entertainment was his quiet company which was presently denied them; for Richard was called to rock the cradle."

The Laws of Ecclesiastical Polity comprehends an exhaustive explanation and justification of the theological position of the Church of England, between the Puritan who claimed the Bible for his sole and exclusive authority, and the Roman Catholic to whom the authority of the church stood above all. In the first book Hooker endeavored to explain the philosophical position of the Church of England and to make clear its place as an institution in the universal scheme. The second book takes issue with the Puritan assumption that the Bible contains all the law and all guidance in things spiritual and temporal that can be needed by the Christian man; while the third denies the Calvinistic assumption that a form of church government is prescribed in the Scriptures or is even discoverable in them. The fourth book contests the charge that the ceremonies of the Church of England are in any wise popish; and the fifth is concerned with an exhaustive vindication of that church as to the minuter attacks of the Puritans. In the sixth book Hooker turns from defense to attack the Presbyterian system of church government; the seventh correspondingly attempts a vindication of Episcopacy; while the last explains and defends the doctrine of royal supremacy in the church.

Whatever Hooker's suggested debts to the theological system of the Spanish theologian, Suarez, or to Thomas Aquinas, for comprehensiveness of design and admirable quality of detail the *Ecclesiastical Polity* must be pronounced a work deserving the highest praise.   Despite much dialectic skill and an unquestionable integrity of purpose, it can not be said that Hooker is either a clear or an accurate reasoner. His fairness of attitude and moderation of spirit, however, make him peculiarly the man to have set forth the position of the church of compromise.   Hooker is above all things scholarly and literary, but singularly free, with all his learning, from the slightest trace of pedantry and the scholar's darling sin in his age, the overplus of quotation.   Hooker's style, too, is devoid of literary affectations or the slightest strife after rhetorical effect; and yet he is again and again effectively eloquent where the current of his argument hurries him into the rapids of similitude.   Attention has been called to the purely bookish nature of Hooker's figures and illustrations. It may be doubted if a figure drawn from nature or a personal observation of man can be found from cover to cover of the *Ecclesiastical Polity*, as it may be doubted if this meek and shrinking scholar ever made an independent observation on the visible things of this world in his life.   And yet there is something estimable about both the man and his work.   We do not, it is true, return to *The Laws of Ecclesiastical Polity* — unless we be churchmen — with the pleasure which attracts us to the witching phrase and sly humor of Hooker's biographer, worthy Isaak Walton; but we feel that Hooker has written a surprisingly permanent book when we consider his theme, and one alike an honor to his wide theological learning, his integrity of mind, and his power to compel language into the artistic mold of thought.   Hooker is one of the great English prose stylists, fortunate that in his lifetime his vine-like nature, that needed always the prop of patronage to sustain it, was so sustained as to produce a great book. Hooker has been even more fortunate posthumously, as few authors have been more constantly and consistently overpraised.   The familiar grouping of his name with Spenser's,

Shakespeare's, and Bacon's is preposterous, because Hooker's talents are reconstructive and, in no primary sense, creative; and because the field which he tilled so fruitfully was, after all, but a little plot of ground.

It is difficult to quote from a work such as Hooker's; but perhaps this passage will disclose, as well as an extract can, the unaffectedness of his diction, its impersonality and effective rhetoric.

The bounds of wisdom are large, and within them much is contained. Wisdom was Adam's instructor in Paradise; wisdom endued the fathers, who lived before the law, with the knowledge of holy things; by the wisdom of the law of God, David attained to excel others in understanding; and Solomon likewise to excel David by the selfsame wisdom of God — teaching him many things besides the law. The ways of well-doing are, in number, even as many as are the kinds of voluntary actions, so that whatsoever we do in this world and may do it ill, we show ourselves therein by well-doing to be wise. Now, if wisdom did teach men by Scripture not only all the ways that are right and good in some certain kind, according to that of St. Paul concerning the use of Scripture, but did simply, without any manner of exception, restraint, or distinction, teach every way of doing well, there is no art but Scripture should teach it, because every art doth teach the way how to do something or other well. To teach men therefore wisdom professeth, and to teach them every good way, but not every good way by one way of teaching. Whatsoever either man on earth or the angels of heaven do know, it is as a drop of that unemptiable fountain of wisdom; which widsom hath diversely imparted her treasures unto the world. As her ways are of sundry kinds, so her manner of teaching is not merely one and the same. Some things she openeth by the sacred books of Scripture, some things by the glorious works of nature; with some things she inspireth them from above by spiritual influence, in some things she leadeth and traineth them only by worldly experience and practice. We may not so in any one special kind admire her, that we disgrace her in any other, but let all her ways be according unto their place and degree adored.

Vastly in contrast with a style such as this is the personal note, with which the following passage from one of Donne's sermons opens, and the vivid and ingenious imagery that succeeds:

If I should inquire upon what occasion God elected me, and writ my name in the book of life, I should sooner be afraid that it were not so, than find a reason why it should be so. God made sun and moon to distinguish seasons, and day and night, and we cannot have the fruits of the earth but in their seasons; but God hath made no decree to distinguish the seasons of his mercies; in Paradise, the fruits were ripe the first minute, and in heaven it is always autumn, his mercies are ever in their maturity. We ask our daily bread, and God never says you should have come yesterday. He never says you must come again to-morrow, but to-day if ye will hear his voice, to-day he will hear you. If some king of the earth have so large an extent of dominion in north and south, as that he hath winter and summer together in his dominions, so large an extent east and west as that he hath day and night together in his dominions, much more hath God mercy and judgment together; he brought light out of darkness, not out of a lesser light; he can bring thy summer out of winter, though thou have no spring; though in the ways of fortune, or understanding, or conscience, thou have been benighted till now, wintered and frozen, clouded and eclipsed, damped and benumbed, smothered and stupi-fied till now, now God comes to thee, not as the dawning of the day, not as in the bud of the spring, but as the sun at noon, to illustrate all shadows, as the sheaves in harvest, to fill all penuries: all occasions invite his mercies, and all times are his seasons.

Donne, the man and the poet, will claim us in a chapter to come. He had been much engaged in theological studies and writing before he took orders in 1615. As reader in divinity at Lincoln's Inn up to 1619, and as Dean of St. Paul's between 1621 and ten years later, Donne became a famous preacher and nearly two hundred sermons, some of them more like treatises for their length and elaboration, attest his zeal, his extensive learning and eloquence in this field of his final choice. The originality, the subtlety, intellectuality, and fanciful wit of the poet Donne, all are present in these remark-able discourses, transfigured by the steady light of a passionate religious conviction such as only those who have once travailed in the ways of the world can truly feel. But the *Sermons* of Donne, like the voluminous *Contemplations* of Hall (begun in 1612), fall for the most part beyond our period, and find mention here only because they complete our story of the literary careers of two of Shakespeare's notable contemporaries. Hall, to receive attention in the next chapter, is better remembered in the history of literature for his claim to be "the first English satirist" than as the Bishop of Norwich, with whom Milton disdained not to measure controversial swords. Among other famous pulpiters, Henry Smith was described in his time as "silver-tongued Smith"; Daniel Featley was valiant especially against Anabaptists; and eloquent Lancelot Andrews, active among the translators of the *Authorized Version* of the Bible, defended his sovereign, King James, when the latter was fallen in controversial battle under the spear of the redoubtable Cardinal Bellarmine. Richard Sibbes, too, was lauded for his pulpit oratory in King James' time; and Thomas Adams was dubbed by no less an authority than Southey "the prose Shakespeare of Puritan theologians," whatever these words may convey to those who can understand. Of all these notable pulpiters, with their sermons, their meditations, works of edification, and manuals of devotion, the outer fringe of a great literature, and as such the soonest dispensed with — it is enough to have mentioned each with honor in his place.

CHAPTER XVII

ELIZABETHAN SATIRE, THE EPIGRAM AND THE "CHARACTER"

SATIRE is alike a mode and a form. As a mode it is constant to practically all literature, verse, drama, prose fiction, and the essay. So considered there is among the Elizabethans one superlative satirist, and that is Ben Jonson of whose dramatic satires — chief among them *Every Man Out of his Humor, Cynthia's Revels,* and *Poetaster* — an account has already been given above. Formal satire, on the other hand, is a different thing. It came comparatively late in English as into other literatures. It is derived, in all the literatures of modern Western Europe, direct from the Romans and is one of the most self-conscious, as it is one of the most easily distinguishable, of literary forms. Although the satire of any given age must commonly be read with notes in the next, as the conditions on which its allusions are founded have lapsed into a half-forgotten past, its elements are remarkably constant and its subject-matter changes very little from age to age. "Satire," according to Heinsius (quoted by Dryden in his *Dissertation on Horace*), "is a kind of poetry, without a series of action, invented for the purging of our minds; in which human vices, ignorance, and errors, and all things besides, which are produced from them in every man, are severely reprehended; partly dramatically, partly simply, and sometimes in both kinds of speaking; but, for the most part, figuratively, and occultly; consisting in a low familiar way, chiefly in a sharp and pungent manner of speech; but partly also, in a facetious and civil way of jesting; by which either hatred, or laughter, or indignation is moved."

It was in the nature of things that so self-conscious a literary form as satire should flourish for the first time in the first literary epoch of England which had learned to know

itself and criticize its surroundings. Such an age was that of
Elizabeth which, with all its love of novel and romantic ideas,
had none the less within it that conservative force of reaction
which we have already seen exerted to the full in the ideals and
practices of Jonson.

Older English satire was altogether informal; its source
was not Horace or Juvenal, but contemporary life. It was
likely to take either the form of burlesque or invective and
was often political as well as social in its aim. The details of
the satire of earlier Tudor times do not concern us here;
suffice it to say that Barclay's celebrated *Ship of Fools*, Erasmus' *Praise of Folly*, and the vigorous satires of the redoubtable Skelton, though all show acquaintance with classical
satirists, are of irregular medieval type, though freed in a
measure from that leisurely and incessant allegorical quality
which makes medieval satire so insupportable to the modern
reader.

But three Roman satirists survived the wreck of time.
These were Horace, Persius, and Juvenal; and all were known,
at least in part, while Juvenal was dear to the medieval understanding. All three were printed among the earliest printed
books. The *Satires* of Horace were translated by Thomas
Drant, an experimenter in classical meters for English, as early
as 1566; but Persius was Englished by Holyday only in the
year of Shakespeare's death, and Juvenal not until much later.
The eighteen satires of Horace and the twenty odd epistles
which are very much like them, are the humorous narratives
of personal experiences, with witty comment and reflections
upon them of a kindly natured man of the world. Horace
says: "Come let us laugh together at the follies of men; ourselves included." The sixteen satires of Juvenal, on the other
hand, with which may be included the six of Persius, differ in
pursuing the method of direct rebuke. They are the deeper
and severer thoughts of the moralist and the philosopher, and
they are as pessimistic in tone as they are bitter and ironical
of speech. These were the men whom the Elizabethan writers
of regular satire set themselves to imitate. But a curious
error in the origin of the word, or confusion at the least, had

much to do with affecting their practice of this art of the ancients. As all know, the Latin word *satura* signified a mixture of fruits, as Dryden translated it, a hotchpotch. Most of the Elizabethans thought of a satire as a "satyrus," a "mixed kind of animal who was imagined to bring the rude observations of his simple life to bear upon the faults of humanity." Even *Every Man out of his Humor* was registered in 1600 as "a comical satyre." Nor were the satires written in Italy and France in imitation of the Roman satirists — the satires of Ariosto, of Alamanni, of Fresnayne, and Régnier — unknown to the writers of England, although it may be suspected that contemporary foreign authors exercised less influence in satire than in some other forms of literature.

Sir Thomas Wyatt is, as Warton called him, "the first polished English satirist," and his three poems of this type — which however he did not call satires — are taken almost direct from Horace not without traces of an acquaintance with the other Roman satirists and more especially with the Italian Alamanni. At the same time they deserve much praise for their English quality in detail, for their poetic and ideal spirit, and for the humane character of their reflective mood which was caught from Horace and perhaps was never so well repeated by any subsequent English satirist. Wyatt's meter is the *terza rima* of Italy. In the same meter is Surrey's "*Satire against the Citizens of London*," a serious moral poem in no sense a true satire. It has been remarked, as to this subject, that "there is an interesting contrast between Wyatt and Surrey — the former borrowing the spirit [of satire from Italy] without the name, and the latter the name without the spirit."

The earliest Elizabethan satirist is Edward Hake, a lawyer and *protégé* of the Earl of Leicester, whose *News out of Paul's Churchyard* was registered in 1568. Hake is a follower of old English satire and is little affected either by classical example or classical urbanity. His outlook on life is pessimistic and his picture of his "sottish sinful brittle age," as he terms it, while full of observation, is neither of any unusual merit nor very original. The most important of the early satirists is George Gascoigne, whose *Steel Glass* long enjoyed a deserved popularity. This earnest moral poem has the distinction of being one of the earliest non-dramatic poems of any length to be written in English blank verse. It was printed in 1576 and is based on the conception that most human wrongs are due to the defective, if beautiful, visions reflected by flattery in glasses of crystal or beryl, while the poet in contrast holds up the true mirror of burnished steel to the commonwealth, reflecting therein all manner of men in their just proportions. *The Steel Glass*, though eloquent, is scarcely more a satire in the classical sense than Spenser's *Mother Hubberd's Tale*, printed in 1591 but written far earlier, in which is related the prosperous adventures of two scoundrels, the fox and the ape, in a manner suggestive of Chaucer and its probable original, the fable of *Reynard the Fox*. It is of interest to note that *Mother Hubberd's Tale* is the first satirical poem to appear in the familiar decasyllabic rimed couplet. Nor is the regularity with which Spenser here practised that popular measure less worthy of note.

The life of that interesting man and genuine poet, John Donne, must be deferred for the present, as he is here to claim our attention merely as a satirist in regular form. To Donne the penning of his six or seven satires was as incidental to a career of celebrity in prose, poetry, and divinity as was the writing of *Venus and Adonis* to Shakespeare. Donne's *Satires*, like most of his other verse, saw print only after his death, five appearing in 1633, a sixth in 1635, the seventh, the authenticity of which has been not unreasonably questioned, not until 1669. The actual date of their writing is difficult to ascertain; but there seems much reason to believe several of them already written by 1593 and well known, like Donne's lyrical poetry, in manuscript. Donne's *Satires* are written in decasyllabic couplets, the measure universally followed by regular satire in later times. But Donne's verse, here even more than elsewhere, is rough, irregular, and careless of the graces of versification. Donne's style, too, like his verse, is rugged and conversational, yet concise and compact in thought and at times obscure from the use of a Latinized construction;

but ever vigorous, true to the object seen and observed at an angle of the author's own. The subjects of Donne's *Satires* and their method, combine the narrative and reflective satire of Horace with the spirit of direct rebuke. While prevailingly pessimistic in tone, they by no means assume the Juvenalian attitude of authority to castigate vice and patronize virtue. The first satire of Donne describes how a young gallant of the time took the scholar from his books to walk abroad, the gallant's estimate of passing acquaintances, and his flight from his friend at sight of a pretty face at a window. The second attacks the vices and chicanery of lawyers, as the fifth lays bare the abuses and delays of justice; the fourth describes, in Horatian manner, that ubiquitous habitant of civilized places, the bore; whilst the last and doubtful one makes sport of the new carpet-knights of King James' creation, a stock theme for the ridicule of the age, and concludes with some references, more free spoken than courteous, to Essex, the late queen, and the new king. By far the best of these *Satires* is the third, which deals in a serious tone, rising to momentary eloquence, in an unwonted theme for satire of classical type, religion. Donne hits off in capital manner those who seek variously for true religion, telling how one,

> Thinking her unhous'd here, and fled from us,
> Seeks her at Rome, there, because he doth know
> That she was there a thousand years ago;

a second seeker,

> to such brave loves will not be enthrall'd,
> But loves her only who at Geneva is call'd
> Religion — plain, simple, sullen, young,
> Contemptuous, yet unhandsome.

Still another "stays still [that is, always] at home here," and that

> because
> Some preachers . . . . . .
> . . . bid him think that she
> Which dwells with us is only perfect.

Whilst a fourth
                                    doth abhor
    All, because all can not be good; as one,
    Knowing some women false, dares marry none.

Then rising to a higher strain he sings:
        Though truth and falsehood be
    Near twins, yet truth a little elder is.
    Be busy to seek her; believe me this,
    He 's not of none, nor worst, that seeks the best:
    To adore, or scorn an image or protest,
    May all be bad. Doubt wisely, in strange way
    To stand inquiring right, is not to stray;
    To sleep or run wrong, is. On a huge hill,
    Cragg'd and steep, Truth stands, and he that will
    Reach her, about must, and about must go
    And what the hill's suddenness resists, win so;
    Yet strive so, that before age, Death's twilight,
    Thy soul rest, for none can work in the night.

This passage marks the height of Elizabethan satire and
Donne stands for his sincerity, for the new light that his
original mind casts upon what he sees, as for the steadiness
of his vision and honest outspokenness, foremost among Elizabethan satirists.

In 1595 Thomas Lodge, long fledged to literature of almost
every type, printed his *Fig for Momus*.   These satires, like
Donne's, were written in decasyllabic couplets, but Lodge's
regularity and smoothness of versification deserve the name
of heroic couplet as Donne's verses never could.   It is a moot
question as to whether Donne, Lodge, or Joseph Hall is to
be credited with the choice of this meter as the fitting raiment
for satirical verse.   Hall certainly wrote decasyllabics more
nearly approaching the compactness and regularity of those
of Dryden and his time than any other man of early days.
But the whole question is wrapped up with another, who was
the first English satirist, an honor which Hall claimed for
himself.   Donne seems the best claimant, although his work
was published long after Lodge's and Hall's, which latter was
in print by 1597.   Donne was widely read in manuscript;

Hall was most generally popular. Lodge seems to have been with some justice neglected, as the four satires which constitute his *Fig for Momus* are alike wanting in "the Horatian urbanity and the Juvenalian vigor." The latter Roman poet is plainly Lodge's model, not Horace as is sometimes said. But the English satirist shows many touches with both Horace and Persius, while maintaining an earnest and optimistic English spirit. Lodge's *Fig for Momus* is singularly free from local color and contemporary allusion and, while avoiding the affectation of a Roman atmosphere, is satire in the abstract and wide of the concreteness of Donne's allusions.

Joseph Hall, later successively Bishop of Exeter and of Norwich, was by far the most generally read of Elizabethan satirists. Born as far back as 1574 and a Cambridge man, he lived to show his loyalty to church and state in now forgotten writings and died a very old man shortly before the restoration of King Charles. Hall's *Satires* amount to some thirty-five in number. The entire work is called *Virgidemiarum, Six Books*, of buffetings; the earlier books are described as "*Toothless Satyrs*," and subdivided into three books, respectively, poetical, academical, and moral, 1597; while the other three appeared in the following year under title *Three Last Books of Biting Satyrs*. These distinctions, however, are not vital. It was Milton who years after, in the heat of religious controversy in which the episcopal satirist held the opposite side, attacked Hall in a passage negligible for its personalities but not for the view of contemporary satire which it discloses. "A satire," writes the great poet, "as it was born out of tragedy, so ought to resemble his parentage, to strike high and adventure dangerously at the most eminent vices among the greatest persons and not to creep into every blind tap-house, that fears a constable more than a satire. But that such a poem should be toothless, I still affirm it to be a bull, taking away the essence of that which it calls itself. For if it bite neither the persons nor the vices, how is it a satire? And if it bite either, how is it toothless? So that toothless satires are as much as if he had said toothless teeth."

The compactness and regularity of Hall's meter has

already been referred to; his style was scarcely less suggestive and prophetic of the age to come, in its hardness, brilliancy, wit, and restraint.   Concerning his obscurity, his fondness for unfamiliar allusions and a certain remoteness of phraseology, the last has been referred to Hall's avowed admiration for Spenser and imitation of him, his fondness for unfamiliar allusions, to his following of the Roman satirists.   Hall's vocabulary is not barbarous, as has sometimes been charged, and as to the other faults of obscurity they belonged in a measure to the contemporary conception of satire whence they have descended into the critical opinions of modern times.   Indeed, it is quite notable that the first of the "biting satires" is the best imitation of Juvenal as it is likewise the most difficult to understand.

The subject of obscurity in poetry is of a wider interest than the satires of Hall and I can not forebear the quotation of two fine passages of our Elizabethan poets on the topic.   The first is from Daniel's *Musophilos* and reads:

> For not discreetly to compose our parts,
>   Unto the frame of men (which we must be)
> Is to put off ourselves and make our arts
>   Rebels to nature and society,
> Whereby we come to bury our desarts
>   In the obscure grave of singularity.

A very becoming opinion is this for "well languaged Daniel," true poet if somewhat conventional man that he was.   But it should be read with this weightier passage of Chapman, *Homeri Metaphrastes* as he delighted to call himself.   "Obscurity in affection of words and indigested conceits is pedantical and childish; but where it shroudeth itself in the heart of his subject, uttered with fitness of figure and expressive epithets, with that darkness I will still labor to be shrouded."

To return to Hall, in his *Satires* "poetical," he declares that "the nine Muses are turned harlots" in his degenerate age, inveighs against the "huff-cap terms and thundering threats" of tragedies like *Tamburlaine*, the license of the stage clown, the absurdities of experiments in classical versification in

English, the affectations and warmth of amatory poetry, and other like matters. There is wealth of allusion to contemporary literature in these and in the "academical satires" where the bad poetry of one Labeo and the folly of writing for money are especially attacked. But all is so obscurely phrased that, save the mention of *Tamburlaine* and enthusiastic praise of Spenser, most of Hall's allusions remain problematic. The interesting thing about the satirist's literary criticism is the consciousness of his attack on the prevailing romantic spirit of his age: and this at its very height. Without here going further into the subject-matter of Hall's *Satires* it may be noted that the remainder is of the conventional Roman type alike for its subject and its treatment. Hall was frankly imitative and while his attitude has much of the assumption of the professed moralist, there was clearly in this young man of twenty-three the making of the serious and militant bishop that he afterward became.

As much can not be said for John Marston, the dramatist, although he, too, died a clergymen of the Established Church. Marston, who was of Hall's age, followed up the publication of Hall's *Satires*, with five *Satires* and his *Metamorphosis of Pigmalion's Image*, published together in 1598. Later in the same year his *Scourge of Villainy* appeared, made up of eleven more satires. The author signed both works with a pseudonym, W. Kinsader; and they enjoyed for a time a popularity almost equal to the *Satires* of Hall. Marston followed Donne and Hall in the now finally approved decasyllabic couplet, but with far less ease, compactness, and smoothness than the latter, and with a corresponding want of epigrammatic effect though not without a gain in vigor. Marston is intentionally crabbed and grotesque and his vocabulary of "new minted epithets," so ridiculed by Jonson, has justly been described as monstrous though he only employs such terms in his more conscious moments. Marston is no more obscure than the other satirists of his time. The range of Marston's topics includes the usual "satirical" material—hypocrites, flatterers, the foolish lover, lust and luxury, procrastination, effeminacy, affectations, and personal foibles. Hall's

work was evidently their immediate inspiration, although
evidences of the author's familiarity with Roman satire are
not wanting, and *Satire IV* of the earlier set contains a direct
answer to some of Hall's strictures upon contemporary literature. *The Scourge of Villainy* sounds a note of conscious
literary coxcombry which is one of the peculiar characteristics
of Marston. The second edition, that of 1599, is dedicated
"To his most esteemed and best beloved Self." Then follows
a series of impertinent stanzas headed: "To Detraction I
present my Poesy"; and the work concludes with an address
to "Everlasting Oblivion":

> Thou mighty gulf, insatiate cormorant!
> Deride me not, though I seem petulant
> To fall into thy chops. Let others pray
> Forever their fair poems flourish may:
> But as for me, hungry Oblivion,
> Devour me quick, accept my orison,
> My earnest prayers which do importune thee,
> With gloomy shade of thy still empery,
> To veil both me and my rude poesy.

On all of which it has been sagaciously observed that "oblivion is too easily had ever to be loudly demanded." None
the less there is merit in these vigorous if not quite always,
honest verses of Marston, nor are they wanting in a sense of
design. Thus in the "Cynic Satire," as he calls it, his theme
(in which we recognize a parody on the desperate exclamation
of Shakespeare's Richard III) is "A man, a man, my kingdom for a man!" and creature after creature, all but seeming
men, parade before the satirist, to be anatomized under the
eye of Lynceus who, it will be remembered, of all the Argo-
nauts was keenest of sight.

Elizabethan satire, in the restrictive sense and as compared
with that of other ages, can not be rated very high. The misanthropy of Marston and Hall's judicial cynicism hardly ring
quite true. Indeed, these worldly-wise satirists were sated
with the gauds and snares of life at two or three and twenty.
But for any deep-seated convictions on moral issues, any real

detestation and revolt against evil, such as distinguished Jonson's dramatic satires despite his self-poise and arrogance, we may look through the easy going pages of these young literary triflers in vain.

If we turn from the field of formal and more or less extended satire in the manner of the ancients to the many epigrammatists and writers of irregular satirical verses, we find the species holding its own with the many satirical pamphlets of the prose pamphleteers. Thus we have, in 1598, the year of Marston's *Scourge of Villainy*, Thomas Bastard's *Chrestoleros*, a collection of two hundred and ninety epigrams; Edward Guilpin's vernacular and interesting *Skialetheia*, "a Shadow of Truth in Certain Epigrams and Satires"; and William Rankins' *Satires* in seven-line stanzas, ridiculing the absurdities of contemporary fashions. Rankins had previously trespassed in this field with his more notorious prose satires, *The Mirror of Monsters* and *The English Ape*, in the former of which he attacked especially "the spotted enormities of players." In 1599 appeared John Weever's *Epigrams in the Oldest Cut and Newest Fashion*, and also *Microcynicon*, the latter unnecessarily attributed to the dramatist Thomas Middleton. The prose pamphlets of Nash and Harvey, the last in their notorious war of personal abuse, were but a year or two old in 1599. Hall's satires had come out in the previous year, and Dr. Rainolds was thundering from Oxford his total *Overthrow of Stage Plays*. Evidently this plain and bitter speaking was overdone; for, towards the end of 1599, an order was issued by the ecclesiastical authorities, commanding that Hall's and Marston's satires, the *Microcynicon*, and certain other books, among them those of the Nash-Harvey controversy, should "be brought to the Bishop of London to be burnt," and that "no satires or epigrams be printed hereafter." This order was duly executed as to most of these works; it was "staid" as to Hall, by what influence or for what reason is to us unknown.

But satire and epigram were not thus to be put down. Other epigrams were those of the courtier and author of *Nosce Teipsum*, Sir John Davies, of various date and writing;

those of his namesake, John Davies of Hereford, writing-master, entitled *The Scourge of Folly*, 1611; and George Wither's *Abuses Whipt and Stript*, of the same date. Fitz-geoffrey and Owen penned epigrams of classical flavor in Latin; at the other extreme, Samuel Rowlands, general pamphleteer and hack-writer, put forth, between 1600 and twenty years later, a series of quaintly named satirical book-lets in verse, among them *The Letting of Humor's Blood in the Head Vein*, *'Tis Merry When Gossips Meet*, *Diogenes Lanthorn*, and the like. In the very last years of Shakespeare's lifetime, and after some subsidence, the epigram revived into a sudden brief lease of life. For in 1613 Sir John Harington published the first of his *Epigrams Pleasant and Serious*, and Richard Braithwaite, in 1615, his *Strappado for the Devil;* while in the next year, that of Shakespeare's death, appeared Robert Anton's rare volume of literary epigrams called *Vice's Anatomy Scourged* and, most important of all, Ben Jonson's *Epigrams*, which form one of the divisions of the collective edition of his works, 1616.

The Elizabethan epigram can not be considered as of much higher general merit than was the more formal satirical verse of the day. The word, epigram, was employed with great looseness to signify almost any brief non-lyrical poem not involving a narrative; and much occasional verse was in-cluded in the mass. Of the English epigrammatists, Jonson is easily the first, though there is wit and merit of its kind both in Bastard's *Chrestoleros* and in the *Epigrams* of Sir John Harington. These lines of Jonson, for example, "On Some-thing that Walks Somewhere," are epigram in the restrictive sense, and an excellent specimen of Jonson's satirical wit:

> At court I met it, in clothes brave enough
> To be a courtier; and looks grave enough
> To seem a statesman: as I near it came,
> It made me a great face; I asked the name.
> A Lord, it cried, buried in flesh and blood,
> And such from whom let no man hope least good,
> For I will do none; and as little ill,
> For I will dare none: Good Lord, walk dead still.

But Jonson considered this fine epitaph on his friend, Sir John Roe, likewise an epigram.

In place of 'scutcheons that should deck thy hearse,
Take better ornaments, my tears and verse.
If any sword could save from Fates, Roe's could;
    If any muse outlive their spite, his can;
If any friends' tears could restore, his would;
    If any pious life e'er lifted man
To heaven, his hath: O happy state! wherein
We, sad for him, may glory, and not sin.

However, the real interest in verse of this kind lies in its allusiveness and in the illustrations that it offers of the customs and manners of its time. Though even here, such was the force of precedent and example in an age of classically educated men, that many of the topics as well as the treatment at large of both satire and epigram must be sought, not in contemporary Elizabethan life, but in the pages of Horace, Juvenal, and Martial.

If we turn now from satire and epigram in verse to its kindred prose, we trespass into an even larger field, and one in which division and classification become well-nigh impossible. In the previous chapter of this book devoted to the pamphlet and the prose of controversy much of the earlier material, generically to be designated satire in prose, has already found its proper place of mention. Nash and Dekker in their prose are nothing if not satirical, whether the satire is incidental to fiction as in *Jack Wilton*, or to personal or political controversy. Such work as Dekker's *Gulls' Hornbook* is of course wholly and delightfully humorous and satirical, and it links in its origin and association not only with the wider continental satire, of which *Grobianus* is the type, but also with the interesting series of English pamphlets in which the nature and the shifts of contemporary vagabonds and sharpers are unmasked and, in unmasking, satirized. As early as 1565, John Awdeley put forth his *Fraternity of Vagabonds*, and two years later Thomas Harman followed with his *Caveat for Common Cursetors*. Both describe the various types of thieves, sharpers, and beggars that infested the streets of

London, Harman dealing even with their slang. These earlier works, however, are less satirical than seriously descriptive. Greene was not without his knowledge of them when he turned his ready pen to depicting the life of their successors in his series of five pamphlets on the haunts, characters, and subterfuges of the conycatchers, as he called the rogues, confidence men, and their like of the metropolis. These pamphlets begin with *A Notable Discovery of Cosenage*, registered as *The Art of Conycatching* in 1591, and extend through several additional parts of similar title to *The Black Book's Messenger* in the following year. In them Greene drew not only on previous writers but on his own experiences, writing up his material precisely as a modern reporter might do, with considerably less regard for mere facts than for a lively and effective presentation of his subject. The like series of Dekker, which was published early in the reign of James, while borrowing much from his predecessors, is more humorous and satirical in character. This pamphlet work of Dekker's begins with *The Batchelors' Banquet*, in 1603, and extends through *The Dead Term*, *The Bellman of London*, *Lanthorn and Candlelight* to *The Gulls' Hornbook*, in 1609. Samuel Rowlands was Dekker's immediate rival in this exploitation of low life. But his many booklets, such as *Greene's Ghost*, 1602, and *Martin Markall*, 1610, show neither Dekker's genial humor, literary aptitude, nor powers of observation.

Into the smaller satirical pamphlet literature at large it is unnecesssary for us to go far. It descends to mere broadside and catchpenny, now laughing at folly with Robert Armin, a professional stage clown, in his *Fool upon Fool or Seven Sorts of Sots*, 1605, and *Nest of Ninnies*, 1608; now lampooning contemporary fashion in Rankins' *English Ape*, 1588; attacking the stage as in the same truculent writer's *Mirror of Monsters*, of the previous year, or Dr. Rainolds' *Overthrow of Stage Palys*, 1599; or deriding the vanities of feminine attire, as in Gosson's *Pleasant Quips for Upstart New-Fangled Gentlewomen*, 1595. A later attack of this kind, entitled *The Arraignment of Lewd, Idle, Forward and Inconstant Women*, by Joseph Swetnam, 1615, called forth a number of retorts, some of them as violent and irrational as their cause and, among them, an anonymous satirical comedy, called *Swetnam, the Woman Hater Arraigned by Women*, 1620, a very curious production. This small prose of satirical contemporary comment shades off into religious as well as social satire and controversy; for these satirists, objectors, and reformers were often, like Gosson, Stubbes, Wither, and Prynne somewhat later, Puritans and biased in their attitude towards life and the habits of their fellow men by a creed the rigor of which discomforted not only its professors but those who had the misfortune to differ with them as well. The typical social satirist of this type of strictly Elizabethan times is Philip Stubbes, the writer of several religious pamphlets in the eighties and early nineties. It was in 1583 that he published his *Anatomy of Abuse*, "containing a discovery or brief survey of such notable vices and imperfections as now reign in many Christian countries of the world; but especially in a very famous island called Ailgna (anagram for Anglia), together with most fearful examples of God's judgment executed upon the wicked for the same." Stubbes' book is quaint and diverting in parts; and it is not without a certain force for its plain speaking, honesty, and homely humor. But the last is for the most part unconscious; for Stubbes was terribly in earnest, and trivial follies and pastimes, harmless in themselves, are borne down in common overthrow with the seven, and other deadly Puritan sins in his trenchant anathemas as things accurst. The following is one of Stubbes' "fearful examples," somewhat curtailed in its diffusive eloquence:

A gentlewoman of Eprautna (that is Antwerp) of late . . . being a very rich merchantman's daughter, upon a time was invited to a bridal or wedding, against which day she made great preparation for the pluming of herself in gorgeous array, that as her body was most beautiful, fair, and proper, so her attire in every respect might be correspondent to the same. For the accomplishment whereof she curled her hair, she dyed her locks, and laid them out after the best manner. She colored her face with waters and ointments. But in no case could she get any (so curious and dainty she was) that could starch and set her ruffs and neckerchers to her mind . . .

Then fell she to swear and tear, to curse and ban, casting the ruffs under her feet and wishing that the devil might take her when she wear any of those neckerchers again. In the mean time (through the sufferance of God)the devil, transforming himself into the form of a young man . . . came in. . . .and, seeing her thus agonized and in such a pelting chafe, he took in hand the setting of her ruffs, which he performed to her great contentation and liking. This doen, the young man kissed her, in the doing whereof he writhe her neck in sunder, so she died miserably, her body being metamorphosed into black and blue colors, most ugglesome to behold. Preparance was made for her burial, a rich coffin provided, and her fearful body was laid there in, and it covered very sumptuously. Four men immediately assayed to lift up the corpse, but could not move it; then six attempted the like, but could not once stir it from the place where it stood. Whereat the standers by marvelling, caused the coffin to be opened, to see the cause thereof. Where they found the body to be taken away; and a black cat, very lean and deformed, sitting in the coffin, setting of great ruffs, and frizzling of hair, to the great fear and wonder of all beholders.

What the epigram is, as contrasted with the great variety of satirical verse that surrounds it, the "character" is in its own group of prose satires. "To square out a character by our English level," says Sir Thomas Overbury, "it is a picture, real or personal, quaintly drawn in various colors, all of them heightened by one shadowing ": in words less figurative, a "character" is a brief descriptive sketch of a personage, involving a ruling quality, or of a moral quality, exemplified in a typical personage. The remote origin of this species of essay, (for it is clearly such), is traceable to Plato's disciple, Tyrtamus of Lesbos, generally known by the name that his master bestowed on him for his eloquence as Theophrastus, the divine speaker. In 1592 appeared Isaac Casaubon's Latin translation of the twenty-nine extant *Characters* of Theophrastus, and to this may be confidently attributed the vogue of this peculiar *genre* in English literature a short time after. Despite some suggestive forerunners such as Harman's descriptions of the rogues of his earlier time, already mentioned, and further back (if we must turn to poetry) Chaucer's inimitable personages of the "Prologue" to *The Canterbury Tales*, to Ben

Jonson, who read everything, must be assigned the first step towards a popularization of the "character." Thus the dramatis personæ of *Every Man out of his Humor* discloses after the name of each person a brief satirical description, designating his salient traits or "humor."

Puntarvolo. A vainglorious knight, over-Englishing his travels, and wholly consecrated to singularity; the very Jacob's staff of compliment; a sir that hath lived to see the revolution of time in most of his apparel. Of presence good enough, but so palpably affected in his own praise, that for want of flatterers he commends himself, to the floutage of his own family. He deals upon returns, and strange performances, resolving, in despite of public derision, to stick to his own particular fashion, phrase, and gesture.

In the text of *Cynthia's Revels* there are several passages in which personages are thus wittily and succinctly described. Indeed it might be worthy some consideration whether Jonson's whole notion of character portrayed by ruling trait or "humor" may not have been originally suggested by the Theophrastian "character."

These plays of Jonson preceded *Characters of Vices and Virtues* by Joseph Hall, the satirist, by some nine or ten years; but it is specifically to Hall and not to Jonson that the "character" in its stricter Theophrastian form owed its popularity. Jonson, as a dramatist, had emphasized the sketch of a personage involving a ruling quality, and to this point of approach later "characterism," as it was called in its time, returned. Hall, on the other hand, as a moralist, conceived of the character as a moral quality exemplified in a typical personage. Between his English, *Virgidemiarum, Six Books*, 1597, and his *Characters*, printed in 1609, Hall had published a witty Latin satire entitled *Mundus Alter et Idem*, 1605, translated as *The Discovery of a New World*, three years later. Hall's *Characters* fall into "characterisms" of virtues and, secondly, of vices. Individual essays treat of the wise man, the valiant man, the truly noble, the good magistrate; the hypocrite, the busybody, the malcontent. It is thus that the last, a favorite of the age in life as in the drama, is in part described:

He is neither well full nor fasting; and though he abound with complaints, yet nothing dislikes him but the present; for what he condemned while it was, once past he magnifies, and strives to recall it out of the jaws of time. What he hath he seeth not, his eyes are so taken up with what he wants; and what he sees he cares not for, because he cares so much for that which is not. . . . Every blessing hath somewhat to disparage and distaste it; children bring cares, single life is wild and solitary, eminency is envious, retiredness obscure, fasting painful, satiety unwieldly, religion nicely severe, liberty is lawless, wealth burdensome, mediocrity contemptible. Everything faulteth, either in too much or too little. This man is ever headstrong and self-willed, neither is he always tied to esteem or pronounce according to reason; some things he must dislike he knows not wherefore, but he likes them not; and otherwhere, rather than not censure, he will accuse a man of virtue.

Hall's *Characters* are exceedingly well written, full of worldly wisdom and animated by a sound average philosophy of life. They are often wittily expressed. His shortcomings are incessant contrast and antithesis. We weary soon of his neatness of phrase, and his literary tidiness; and we breathe uneasily before long in this atmosphere of admirable moral abstraction.

It is not unlikely that the famous *Characters* of Sir Thomas Overbury were written much about the time of Hall's, of which however they were far from a mere imitation. Their extraordinary popularity — six editions in a single year and sixteen in less than a generation — is referable in part to their merit, but mainly to the notorious murder of Overbury, which grew out of the greatest scandal of the court of King James. Sir Thomas Overbury was born in Gloucestershire in 1581 and educated at Queen's College, Oxford and the Middle Temple. He became an intimate associate and adviser of the king's favorite, Sir Robert Carr, later Viscount Rochester, and was knighted by King James in 1608. Rochester had been carrying on a flirtation with the frivolous young Countess of Essex whose boy husband (worthy of a better wife) had been traveling extensively abroad. Upon his return, although compelled to live with him, his countess showed for the earl, her husband, nothing but repugnance and contempt. After two or three years of this life, a project was formed by which the countess was to sue, on what could only have been false pretences, for a divorce, thus to make a way for a marriage with Rochester. Her father and uncle were won over to this plan, and King James unquestionably connived at the designs and intrigues of his favorite. Overbury, as the friend and adviser of Rochester, strongly opposed from the first both the policy of a divorce and a marriage for his patron with a woman such as Lady Essex. Moreover he had not been silent in this disapproval; but had written, and perhaps circulated, a poem called *The Wife*, published after his death, to dissuade Rochester from a step so ill advised. For this Lady Essex took a terrible revenge. On Overbury's refusal to accept a foreign mission which the king was induced to tender him, he was committed by the king's council to the Tower for contempt of the royal commands and, after a number of abortive practices against his life, was finally poisoned by an apothecary's assistant, Lady Essex's creature, some ten days before the judgment granting her her wished-for divorce. The sumptuous marriage of Lady Essex, Christmas of the same year, to Rochester, now raised to the earldom of Somerset that her ladyship might retain her rank, and the trial and conviction, three years later, of the guilty pair with their several accessories for the murder of Overbury, completed one of the blackest pages in the annals of the Stuarts. It was these events that gave a notoriety to Overbury's poem, *The Character of a Wife*, first published separately in 1614, and later in the same year with some twenty-nine other "characters" in prose. In the following editions the number of characters "by Sir Thomas Overbury and his friends," grew by accretion until, in the last of the old editions, that of 1638, they numbered eighty, the work thus having grown into an anthology, so to speak, of this species of essay.

In such a collection the quality is of course far from equal. Overbury's own work is literary in its aim rather than moral. His characters, to speak of them at large, disclose no very deep observation of individual traits; nor are they typical in any such sense as the "humors" of Jonson or the "characterisms" of Hall. But they are certainly clever, epigrammatic, and both brightly and quaintly written. Occasionally, as in "The Good Wife," "The Happy Milkmaid," or "A Worthy Commander in the Wars," the author (whoever he was) rises above mere smartness to a touch of sincerity and even of tenderness. The following famous description is somewhat condensed to conform to the plan of this book, not that diffuseness in the character as it was written demands it:

A fair and happy milkmaid is a country wench, that is so far from making herself beautiful by art, that one look of hers is able to put all face physic out of countenance. . . . All her excellences stand in her so silently, as if they had stolen upon her without her knowledge. The lining of her apparel (which is herself) is far better than outsides of tissue; for though she be not arrayed in the spoil of the silk-worm, she is decked in innocency, a far better wearing. . . . She rises therefore with chanticleer, her dame's cock, and at night makes lamb her curfew. In milking a cow and straining the teats through her fingers, it seems that so sweet a milk-press makes the milk the whiter or sweeter; for never came almond glove or aromatic ointment off her palm to taint it. The golden ears of corn fall and kiss her feet when she reaps them, as if they wished to be bound and led prisoners by the same hand that felled them. Her breath is her own, which scents all the year long of June, like a new-made haycock. She makes her hand hard with labor, and soft with pity; and when winter's evenings fall early (sitting at her merry wheel), she sings a defiance to the giddy wheel of fortune. . . . Thus lives she, and all her care is that she may die in the spring-time, to have store of flowers stuck upon her winding-sheet.

On the success of Overbury's work, the character became the rage of the moment. Nicholas Breton was earliest in the field with his *Characters upon Essays Moral and Divine*, 1615, in which the influence of Bacon's *Essays* is acknowledged and more patent than the example of Hall or Overbury. In 1616 appeared *The Good and the Bad* by the same author. Here the characters are presented in pairs, as the worthy judge and the unworthy, the honest man and the knave. These are true characters and are not wanting in the grace and lightness of touch that distinguish their clever and adaptable author. Through subsequent essays and characters of Geoffrey Minshull, Henry Parrot, and others the species reached its height in literary excellence and perfection of form in John Earle's *Microsmography or a Piece of the World Characterized*, first printed in 1628, and all but as popular in its time as Overbury's had been. But these latter works fall beyond our period.

CHAPTER XVIII

BACON, JURIST, PHILOSOPHER, AND ESSAYIST

MANY reasons conspire to give to Francis Bacon a position of peculiar prominence in any consideration of English literature. A notable lawyer under Elizabeth, he attained to the woolsack and the chancellorship in the reign of King James. A philosopher of great, if questioned reputation, an orator of approved eloquence, an able historian, and our earliest English essayist — all these phases of a distinguished career must claim our attention, together with the great intrinsic worth of most of his writings, the excellence and variety of his style, the stimulating quality of his aphorisms, and lastly, the mingling of his name with Shakespeare's, strange fruit of the ignorance, singularity, and perversity of the last generation and our own.

Francis Bacon was born in January, 1561, the son of Nicholas Bacon, Queen Elizabeth's first Lord Keeper, and his second wife, Anne Cooke, who was sister to the wife of Lord Burleigh, the famous chancellor of Elizabeth. Bacon passed through the usual education of a gentleman of the day at Trinity College, Cambridge, and Gray's Inn, going abroad with an embassy when but sixteen years of age, and finding himself fatherless with but small fortune in 1579. Destined from the first for the law, he was admitted an utter barrister in 1582; becoming a member of Parliament in 1584, through the interest of his uncle Burleigh, and two years later a bencher of his Inn. Bacon's mother was described in her time as "exquisitely skilled in the Greek and Latin tongues"; she was also austerely religious, and avowed and practised a Puritanism of opinion from which her son Francis must soon have become estranged. Indeed, his earliest work is a letter of advice to the queen in which he deals wisely and moderately with one of the most difficult of her political problems, the treatment of her own Roman Catholic subjects. In these early days Bacon was needy, extravagant, careless of practical affairs, compelled to labor at his profession for bread, wait in chargeable attendance at court for advancement, in ill health and neglected by his family. As to Burleigh and his cousin Cecil, Bacon was assiduous in his cultivation of both, and incessant in seeking through them for advancement. Burleigh could not have doubted Bacon's abilities or his subserviency to the family interests. He may have been suspicious of his talents and have mistrusted his philosophic ambitions. Burleigh certainly remained unsympathic. Cecil's apathy towards the interests of his brilliant cousin continued into the next reign. But Bacon could not be long in any assemblage of men without making felt the power and sublety of his mind; and his employment on public business was not infrequent during the ensuing years, though not in any matters of great moment or in posts of emolument. He was heard towards the last of the long and violent Marprelate quarrel in an able paper on *Controversies in the Church* in which he opposed alike the factious temper of the Puritans and the government's unwise rigidity as to conformity.

About this time Bacon formed a warm friendship with the Earl of Essex, one of the most remarkable men of his age, highly favored of the queen, and apparently destined to a career of power and splendor. Essex seems to have been drawn to Bacon by a genuine appreciation of his larger and higher ambitions; for Essex was an intelligent patron of learning, and an accomplished and cultivated man himself, possessed of a generosity of temper and liberality in friendship that account for his popularity and the hosts of his friends. In 1593 the attorney-general's place fell vacant, and Essex, now a privy councilor, at once sought the post for Bacon. Bacon was young for such advancement, and better known for his pursuits of philosophy and literature than for his learning in the law. Besides, Sir Edward Coke, nearly ten years his senior, already solicitor-general and famed for his technical knowledge of the law, wanted the post for himself. The Cecils suggested a compromise, by which Coke should be promoted to the attorney-generalship and Bacon become his successor as solicitor. But Essex refused compromise, and the queen appointed Coke attorney. Then Essex pressed for the solicitorship for Bacon; but he was passed over for an inferior man. Essex could do most things with the queen, but he could not promote Bacon; and Bacon suffered the added mortification of seeing the rich young widow of Sir Christopher Hatton, to whom he had made his addresses on the advice of Essex, accept the hand of Coke, his rival.

Various reasons have been assigned to explain why so able a man as Bacon should not have received during the lifetime of Elizabeth that recognition to which his talents entitled him. One biographer states that it was Bacon's "fate through life to give good advice only to be rejected, and yet to impress those who received it with a sufficiently good opinion of his intellectual capacity to gain employment in work which hundreds of others could have done as well." With Bacon a settlement in life was only the means to a larger end. In 1592, when thirty years of age, we find sure indications of the ambitious philosophical designs that were to make him famous. In one of his many letters of appeal to Burleigh, he disclosed his hopes and aspirations, declaring "I have taken all knowledge to be my province," and this less in the spirit of a boaster than in a fervid conviction, born of days of meditation and self-questioning. Bacon took the world about him as it was, accepted with cynical indifference its moral standards, and strove to thrive, as others thrived, by the world's methods. In the interest of worldly success he enlisted his keen intellect and his supple understanding; but he failed, for the most part, to make men his counters because he neither reached nor sought to reach their affections. If there was one thing in which Queen Elizabeth exceeded most monarchs, it was in a certain feminine intuition into character that enabled her to keep herself surrounded alike by the ablest and the most trustworthy of counselors. Elizabeth's tardy recognition of Bacon is one of the evidences of this. However willing she might have been to joke with the clever youth and call him "her little Lord Chancellor," she must have felt from the first that Bacon was an unsafe man; and it was reserved for her pedantic successor to be deceived by qualities of intellectual brilliancy, unsupported by the homelier, safer virtues that might well have misled a deeper man than the author of *A Counterblast to Tobacco*. It was in the reign of James that Bacon's honors crowded upon him; and it was in that reign that his memorable fall came.

Essex continued the friend and patron of Bacon, impetuously bestowing an estate valued at £1800 upon him, and gained for him at last the post of one of the queen's counsel in 1596. No greater contrast could be conceived than that between Essex, ardent, masterful, inprudent, and headstrong, whom the old queen doted on and spoiled only to punish him for the presumption that she had invited, and Bacon, cool, intellectual, and subtle, working sinuously and circumspectly to personal ends, but stumbling at times among the gins and snares of that corruption and intrigue that was to bring about his ultimate fall. Bacon became the earl's adviser in the handling of his affairs, especially the management of his difficult royal mistress, seeking (there can be little question) to rise in the rise of the favorite. Whether an instance of the basest ingratitude in the annals of history or one of those cases in which the law of self-preservation may be pled in extenuation of an act outrageous in itself, it is certain that when the difficulties of the reckless career of Essex came to their logical conclusion, an impeachment for high treason, Bacon repudiated and explained away their intimacy, appeared of counsel against his benefactor, and was among the most powerful influences that brought about the earl's conviction and execution.

With the accession of James, the lets and hindrances to the career of Bacon were no more. He was first knighted, became in time an intimate of the king, and rose through the place of king's counsel in 1604, to Keeper of the Privy Seal in 1617, Lord Chancellor under the title Lord Verulam in 1619, and Viscount St. Albans two years later. Among the many trials that Bacon conducted as Lord Chancellor was that of Sir Walter Raleigh, the splendid adventurer and favorite of Elizabeth, who had long languished in the Tower under the displeasure of King James. To Bacon, in his judicial capacity, Raleigh was no more than "an unscrupulous pirate and peculator," and he did not concern himself with the circumstance that the charge was an old one, trumped up to serve the reëstablishment of the cordial relations between the King of England and the King of Spain. Into the circumstances by which the enemies of Bacon made head against him and convicted him of bribery we need not enter. Coke was brutally jubilant among them. We may feel sure that Bacon's conduct in the case of Essex was now remembered against him, not only by Southampton (who had been ruined and in prison for years for his part in the rebellion of Essex), but by many more. In a general movement against the abuses and corruption of the courts, Bacon was thus singled out and, from his exalted position and personal distinction, became the center of attack. Brought to trial, the verdict of his peers of the House of Lords found Bacon guilty in all the charges brought against him, and punished him with a fine of £40,000, imprisonment in the Tower during the king's pleasure, banishment from the court, and a deprivation of any right to serve the commonwealth in Parliament or otherwise. Southampton's desire that the chancellor be degraded from the peerage was the only extremity at which the verdict paused. And yet one thing was even more remarkable than this sudden overthrow in two months' time of the foremost judge of the realm; this was Bacon's complete and servile submission. It does not appear when the evidence is carefully sifted, as was not done in his time, that Bacon actually took bribes for the perversion of justice. His decisions were in accord with the evidence and the law, but he fell in only too readily with a system which, accepting large gifts from suitors pending the decision of their cases, and on the decision of cases in the suitor's favor, mingled payment for services with gifts of a questionable nature to the intolerable corruption of the administration of justice. Bacon's confession that "in the points charged upon me, although they should be taken as myself have declared them, there is a great deal of corruption and neglect, for which I am heartily and penitently sorry," should be accepted sorrowfully and without comment as conclusive, by all lovers of the truth. Bacon survived his disgrace but four years, although the king, in recognition of his long services to the state, tempered the fine and penalty, and preserved him in his dignities, his honors, and his titles. Bacon's life is a subject on which it is painful to dwell; and this when all has been said in extenuation. His is a glaring example that the highest intellectual gifts are consistent with self-seeking, servility, ingratitude, and corruption. And it is no mitigation that the conduct of politics and even of justice in his day were far from free of any of these traits. The high-sounding aphorisms of the Baconian philosophy have in them ever the ring of hollowness and mockery, and as we read them we forget the learning of the chancellor and the wisdom of the philosopher in the servility of the courtier and the littleness of meanness rebuked.

The works of Bacon are conveniently considered in three classes, his professional, philosophical, and literary writings. With the first we need not concern ourselves. None of them were published in the author's lifetime, although he prepared four *Arguments of Law* for the press. It is the opinion of the editor of Bacon's professional works that they exercised comparatively small influence on the progress of English law. They are distinguished, however, like his other work, by an intellectual clearness of vision beyond his age. In 1605 Bacon published *The Advancement of Learning*, which has been called "a careful and balanced report on the existing stock and deficiencies of human knowledge." This work was not conceived at first as a part of his *Instauratio Magna* or *Great Instauration* (or *Restoration*), but was subsequently arranged to precede or form a part of the *Novum Organum*. It was fifteen years later, in 1620, when at the height of his prosperity, that Bacon published this most important part of his philosophical system, setting forth "the new instrument of thought and discovery," which he believed would prove the key to the command over nature. But the intervening years, with all his outer distractions, had been years of assiduous industry and labor in his great task. The rejected projects of Bacon would stock a dozen average men with ideas for their combined lifetimes. "Experimental essays and discarded beginnings," treatises, matter biographical so far as it concerned his hopes and philosophical aspirations, mythology in *The Wisdom of the Ancients* as allegorically shadowing forth later truth, a fanciful philosophical tale, *The New Atlantis* — such were some of the chips and materials of experiment that lay to one side in that busy intellectual workshop in the center of which stood, when all was at an end, the incompleted colossus of *The Great Instauration*.

"The *Instauratio*, as he planned the work, is to be divided," says Ellis, the notable editor of Bacon, "into six portions, of which the first is to contain a general survey of the present state of knowledge. In the second, men are to be taught how to use their understanding aright in the investigation of nature. In the third, all the phenomena of the universe are to be stored up in a treasure-house, as the materials on which the new method is to be employed. In the fourth, examples are to be given of its operation and of the results to which it leads. The fifth is to contain what Bacon had accomplished in natural philosophy, 'not however according to the true rules and methods of interpretation, but by the ordinary use of the understanding in inquiring and discovering.' It is therefore less important than the rest, and Bacon declares that he will not bind himself to the conclusions which it contains. Moreover, its value will altogether cease when the sixth part can be completed, wherein will be set forth the new philosophy — the result of the application of the new method to all the phenomena of the universe. But to complete this, the last part of the *Instauratio*, Bacon does not hope: he speaks of it as 'a thing both above my strength and beyond my hopes.'" [1]

As we have it not only the *Instauratio* but the *Novum Organum* itself is only a fragment. It was published in 1620 (as we have seen), and in Latin. *The Advancement of Learning*

[1] *Bacon's Works*, ed. Ellis and Spedding, i, 71. The two quotations of Bacon's Latin words, as quoted by Ellis, I have transcribed in the translation by Spedding.

appeared first in English. Other parts of the *Instauratio* and "works on subjects connected with the *Instauratio* but not intended to be included in it," are in English and Latin or, as more frequently, only in Latin. Such are the *Historia Vitæ et Mortis*, printed in 1622, often quoted by Izaak Walton; and *De Dignitate et Augmentis Scientiarum*, the enlarged and Latinized version of *The Advancement of Learning*. In 1627, the year after Bacon's death, appeared *Sylva Sylvarum or a Natural History* in English, a collection of observations and experiments in the nature of things, remarkably wide in its range and often accute in discernment, but hopelessly antiquated long since not only to the physicist but to the average man. How impossible it is for even the sagest of men to escape his age is discernible in such a passage as this:

There is a stone which they call the blood-stone, which worn, is thought to be good for them that bleed at the nose: which (no doubt) is by astriction and cooling of the spirits. *Quære*, if the stone taken out of the toad's head be not of the like virtue; for the toad loveth shade and coolness.

Elsewhere Bacon recounts, with apparent acceptance and approval, that "the heart of an ape, worn near the heart, comforteth the heart and increaseth audacity." But surely he who in Jonson's words could not "spare or pass a jest," is less the philosopher than the wit when he adds: "It may be the heart of a man would do more, but that it is more against men's minds to use it; except it be in such as wear the relics of saints."

Many an educated man, asked who was Francis Bacon, might describe him as the inventor of philosophic induction. This is of course absurd. The method of scientific inquiry in the Middle Ages was deductive, that is, the generalization was applied to the particular case. This method is apt to result in an examination of only those facts which are previously supposed to be likely to sustain a preconceived theory or opinion, or at least to waste much time in ingeniously devised syllogisms, arguments, and explanations without a sufficient critical examination of the premises on which they may be founded. It was to right this that Bacon wrote the *Novum Organum*. And the method he advocated was that of inductive logic, the procedure of which was generalization with the purpose of establishing the principle only after an exhaustive gathering and consideration of the particular facts involved. It was a "systematic analysis and arrangement of inductive evidence, as distinct from the natural deduction which all men practise" that Bacon proposed; in his own happy illustration:

The men of experiment are like the ant; they only collect and use: the reasoners resemble spiders, who make cobwebs out of their own substance. But the bee takes a middle course; it gathers its material from the flowers of the garden and of the field, but transforms and digests it by a power of its own. Not unlike this is the true business of philosophy; for it neither relies solely or chiefly on the powers of the mind, nor does it take the matter which it gathers from natural history and mechanical experiments and lay it up in the memory whole, as it finds it; but lays it up in the understanding altered and digested.

Bacon's noble, if somewhat utilitarian, ideal, thus, of the office of philosophy was its mastery of the secrets of nature "to extend more widely the limits of the power and greatness of man." Bacon's criticism of past error was just and needful, his separation of science from religion valuable in itself and for its consequences; his enlistment of physical experiment in application for the benefit of mankind most suggestive and in time fruitful. But we learn with amazement that this great and novel philosophy rejected the Copernican system of astronomy, held mathematics in undisguised contempt, and yet disdained not to discuss and accept current fallacies of popular lore such as the trivialities quoted above, some of them as old as Pliny's *Natural History* and disprovable by far less cumbrous methods than those of inductive logic.

In short the position of Bacon as a philosopher is by no means the assured one that ignorance is apt to suppose it. His place at the dawn of modern science was that of one who points the true direction though he follow it not himself. Bacon was not a partaker in any actual scientific discovery of his day, nor a leader to any discovery that came after. He was not even in sympathy with the science of his time. For he disparaged Copernicus and criticized adversely Gilbert's treatise *On the Magnet*. While Bacon was condemning all investigation into final causes, Harvey completed his deductions as to the circulation of the blood; while Bacon was questioning the advantage of any use of optical instruments, Galileo was scanning the heavens with his telescope and adding star to star. Moreover, as to the Baconian system, practical workers, like the anatomist Harvey, like Liebig the chemist, or Bernard the physiologist, "say that they can find nothing to help them in Bacon's method." And Spedding, most appreciative of the editors of Bacon, declares: "Of this philosophy we can make nothing . . . . We regard it as a curious piece of machinery, very subtle, elaborate and ingenious, but not worth constructing, because all the work it could do may be done another way." Induction is not a method fruitful in results. However valuable Bacon's philosophical works may be in inspiration, for any value as an instrument or practical method of work — much less one that was to revolutionize the intellectual processes of mankind — this gigantic project must be pronounced a failure.

Of the literary work of Bacon the chief is the well-known *Essays or Counsels Civil and Moral*. This famous book appeared first in a very small octavo volume, in 1597, with the title, *Essays, Religious Meditations, Places of Persuasion and Dissuasion*. The two latter items of this three-fold title refer to two other works, *Meditationes Sacræ* in Latin, and *Of the Colors of Good and Evil*, a fragment in English. Neither was afterwards reprinted with the *Essays;* and the *Essays* themselves were but ten in number. It is of interest, in view of the man that Bacon planned to be and inevitably became, that the topics of these earliest essays should have been of study, discourse, ceremonies and respect, followers and friends; of suitors, expense; regiment of health, of honor and reputation, of faction, and of negotiating. The work was immediately recognized and, like most popular Elizabethan books, soon pirated. In 1612 Bacon himself brought out a new edition, enlarged to thirty-eight essays under the simpler title, *The Essays of Sir Francis Bacon;* and in 1625 *The Essays or Counsels Civil and Moral of Francis Lord Verulam,* now augmented to fifty-eight in number, represents the final state of the work. From the epistle of the first edition, dedicated to his brother, Anthony Bacon, it appears that the nucleus of the ten original essays had "passed long ago from my pen," that is, were written at a time well prior to their publication in 1597. It also appears that they were printed by the author to stay unauthorized publication; for such seems the meaning of the words: "I do now like some that have an orchard ill-neighbored, that gather their fruit before it is ripe to prevent stealing." In a later dedication to Prince Henry, suppressed however owing to his death, Bacon speaks of his purpose: "The want of leisure hath made me choose to write certain brief notes, set down rather significantly than curiously which I have called *essays.* The word," he continues, "is late, but the thing is ancient. For Seneca's *Epistles* to Lucilius, if one mark them well, are but essays, that is dispersed meditations, though conveyed in the form of epistles." That Bacon had another besides this ancient model is not to be questioned, although he quotes Montaigne but once. The *Essais* of Michel de Montaigne had appeared first in 1580, and by the time that Bacon wrote had reached at least a dozen editions in France. His title — *essay,* attempt, endeavor, modest enough in its day — Bacon had, beyond doubt, of Montaigne. Except for this and the genius of both, there is little in common between the two authors; for the gossipy self-portrayal of the French epicurean is at the opposite pole to the worldly wisdom, the abstract philosophy, and the glittering apothegm of the English lawyer.

The first things that strike the reader of Bacon's *Essays* are their brilliancy, their polish, and their disconnectedness. As we read further, we appreciate more fully their practical sagacity, their wealth of pertinent illustration and quotation (after the manner of the time), and their extreme condensity, both of thought and of expression. The subjects of these *Essays* are, for the most part, abstractions,— truth, love, ambition, vainglory; but some relate to social and human relations, as parents and children, and the essay on marriage, and more to politics, social conditions, and conduct in life. Not least interesting are they at large in that they reveal the man habituated to thought on all things, now great with the larger issues of human existence, again minutely particular in the minor things and even the trivialities of life. Of subject-matter less momentous are the essays "of Building," "of Masques and Triumphs," "or the Regiment of Health," and the delightful paragraphs "of Plantations," and "of Gardens." While partaking largely of the quaintness which, to us at least, seems a pervasive quality of Elizabethan literature, Bacon's is a remarkably modern tone, and his short, crisp sentences and sureness of statement enhance his modernness of diction. Bacon's analogy and illustration is exhaustless, and he shines at times with the brilliancy of epigram and the gorgeousness of a magnificently rhetorical imagination. But however prismatic the colors, Bacon is absolutely devoid of any warmth of passion. Such a man must have been a great orator from the power of his mind, if not from the eloquence of his heart. And we read for the first time, with positive expectation that it is to be found somewhere, the celebrated passage of Ben Jonson as to the eloquence of the Lord Chancellor:

There happened in my time one noble speaker who was full of gravity in his speaking; his language, when he could spare or pass a jest, was nobly censorious. No man ever spake more neatly, more pressly, more weightily, or suffered less emptiness, less idleness, in what he uttered. No member of his speech but consisted of his own graces. His hearers could not cough or look aside from him without loss. He commanded where he spoke, and had his judges [i. e. those before whom he was pleading] angry and pleased at his devotion. No man had their affections [i. e. emotions] more in his power. The fear of every man who heard him was lest he should make an end.

Returning for a moment to the style of the *Essays*, sententiousness, condensity, and pregnancy of thought have seldom been carried to such a degree. And these things were compassed, as we know by reference to the successive versions, only by the most assiduous and painstaking revision. Indeed, outside of the pages of the great Roman historian, Tacitus, it may be doubted if a more complete success has ever been attained in a like terse and difficult style. Yet it is a mistake to think of Bacon as a man possessed of a single literary style, however excellent. *The Advancement of Learning* exhibits the philosopher's evidences of design, and the whole treatise is written with the continuity and copious flow which is suitable to so stately a topic. In *The History of Henry VII*, and especially in the interesting fragment, *The New Atlantis*, the narrative is handled with a directness and steady progress that must surprise the reader who knows his Bacon, as too many of us do, only by the *Essays*.

So as marvel you not at the thin population of America, nor at the rudeness and ignorance of the people; for you must account your inhabitants of America as a young people; younger a thousand years, at the least, than the rest of the world; for there was so much time between the universal flood and their particular inundation. For the poor remnant of human seed which remained in their mountains peopled the country again slowly, by little and little; and being a simple and savage people, (not like Noah and his sons, which was the chief family of the earth), they were not able to leave letters, arts, and civility to their posterity.

Very different in style and structure are the familiar words:

Read not to contradict, nor to believe, but to weigh and consider. Some books are to be tasted, others to be swallowed, and some few to be chewed and digested: that is, some books are to be read only in parts; others to be read, but cursorily, and some few to be read wholly and with diligence. Reading maketh a full man, conference a ready man, and writing an exact man.

And yet with all this literary excellence, and with a reputation to endure while English literature shall last, few great men have so little deserved a place of literary eminence by their own act. Bacon, unlike many of his great contemporaries — Sidney, Spenser, Raleigh, Hooker, and Jonson — held his mother tongue in undisguised contempt, and spent much time in translating his works into Latin that they might endure to posterity. In his own words, often quoted, from a letter to his friend, Sir Toby Matthew:

My labors are now most set to have those works, which I have formerly published, as that of *Advancement of Learning*, that of *Henry VII*, that of the *Essays*, being retractate and made more perfect, well translated into Latin by the help of some good pens which forsake me not. For these modern languages will at one time or other play the bankrupts with books: and since I have lost much time with this age, I would be glad, as God shall give me leave, to recover it with posterity.

Bacon was, in all probability, insensible of the glorious wealth of literature that was springing up around him; or if sensible, too pusillanimous to trust his fame in the same vehicle with that of low-born playwrights and Bohemian pamphleteers. He preferred the passionless rhetoric of a dead tongue to this living carriage of animate speech; and as a penance, much of his work lies as in the tomb, the resort of the enthusiastic metaphysician or the curious historian of speculative thought.

It would ill have become the philosopher who "took all learning for his province" to have remained wholly unconversant with the poetical and the theatrical activities of his age. And despite the Baconian insensibility noticed above, of these "toys," too, the great man took a condescending cognisance. As early as 1587 we find Bacon one of some half-dozen young gentlemen, members of Gray's Inn, engaged in devising dumb shows (such as those in *Gorboduc*) for "*Certain Devices*," acted before her majesty. In 1592 Bacon wrote "speeches" for a device presented to the queen when entertained by Essex. Bacon also contributed similarly to the *Gesta Grayorum* in the protracted festivities of his Inn, in 1595. Far later, in 1613, on the occasion of the celebrations incident to the marriage of the king's daughter Elizabeth to the Prince Palatine, Bacon is described as "the chief contriver" of Beaumont's excellent masque. Lastly, in the following year, Bacon was designated, "the chief encourager" of the anonymous *Masque of Flowers*, on which he is said to have expended no less than £2,000. Yet if we would know Bacon's attitude as to these matters, we must turn to the well-known *essay*, "of Masques and Triumphs." There it is that he writes:

These things are but toys to come amongst such serious observations. But yet since princes will have such things, it is better they should be graced with elegancy than daubed with cost. Dancing to song is a thing of great state and pleasure. . . . Acting in song, especially in dialogues, hath an extreme good grace: I say acting, not dancing, for that is a mean and vulgar thing. And the voices of the dialogue would be strong and manly: a base, and a tenor, no treble; and the ditty high and tragical, not nice or dainty. Several choirs, placed one over against another, and taking the voice by catches, anthem-wise, give great pleasure. Turning dances into figure is a childish curiosity. And generally let it be noted that those things, which I here set down, are such as do naturally take the sense and not respect petty wonderments. It is true, the alterations of scenes, so it be quietly and without noise, are things of great beauty and pleasure: for they feed and relieve the eye before it be full of the same object. Let the scenes abound with light, especially colored and varied, and let the masquers or any other that are to come down from the scene, have some motions, upon the scene itself before their coming down: for it draws the eye strangely and makes it with great pleasure to desire to see that it can not perfectly discern.

And after another page of this patronizing, he abruptly breaks off: "But enough of these toys." Elsewhere Bacon speaks with similar disdain of "the transcendence of poesy"; advises that we "leave the goodly fabrics of houses for beauty only, to the enchanted palaces of the poets; who," he adds, "build them with small cost"; and quotes with approval St. Jerome's designation of poetry as *vinum daemonum* (*i. e.* wine of devils) "because it filleth the imagination . . . but with the shadow of a lie."

The late Dr. Grosart, an indefatigable editor and gleaner in the well-reaped fields of our old literature, has collected "The Poems of Francis Bacon." The collection includes *The Translation of Certain Psalms*, six or seven in number, which curiously enough his lordship published himself, in 1625, with a dedication to George Herbert; and two other pieces. As to the psalms, Bacon translated them, as who did not in that age from Sir Philip Sidney and Queen Elizabeth herself, to Bishop Parker, and Sternhold and Hopkins? As to their merit as poetry, Spedding remarks: "An unpractised versifier who will not take time and trouble about the work, must of course leave many bad verses: for poetic feeling and imagination, though they will dislike a wrong word, will not of themselves suggest a right one that will suit meter and rime: and it would be easy to quote from the few pages that follow not only many bad lines, but many poor stanzas." Dr. Grosart, on the other hand, whose enthusiasm for the particular author that he happened at the moment to be editing commonly outstripped his judgment, declares himself able to make "fresh discoveries of beauty, ineffable scintillations of true 'Promethean heat'" in these psalms, whenever he "returns" to them. Of the other two poems, one beginning:

> The man of life upright whose guiltless heart is free
> From all dishonest deeds and thoughts of vanity,

is attributed by somebody to Bacon in the manuscript in which it occurs, and is verily such "as might very well have been written by Bacon, or by a hundred other people." Lastly, "the expansion of a Greek epigram," as the remaining "poem" attributed to Bacon is entitled, is a production calling for more attention. It is superior in workmanship to any of his psalms, and it is less a translation, or even a paraphrase, of its original (an epigram from the *Florilegium*, attributed to Poseidippus), than a new poem on the suggested theme. These lines run as follows:

> The world's a bubble, and the life of man
>   Less than a span;
> In his conception wretched, from the womb,
>   So to the tomb;
> Cursed from his cradle and brought up to years
>   With cares and fears:
> Who then to frail mortality shall trust,
> But limns on water or but writes in dust?
>
> Yet, whilst with sorrow here we live opprest,
>   What life is best?
> Courts are but only superficial schools
>   To dandle fools;

The rural part is turned into a den
    Of savage men;
And where 's a city from foul vice so free
But may be termed the worst of all the three ?

Domestic cares afflict the husband's bed,
    Or pains his head:
Those that live single take it for a curse,
    Or do things worse;
These would have children; those that have them moan
    Or wish them gone:
What is it, then, to have or have no wife,
But single thraldom or a double strife ?

Our own affections still at home to please
    Is a disease;
To cross the seas to any foreign soil,
    Peril and toil;
Wars with their noise affright us, when they cease,
    We are worse in peace:
What then remains, but that we still should cry
For being born, or, being born, to die ?

From this repellent piece of pessimism, with its precision of thought and polish of style, let us turn where we will to Shakespeare:

Let me not to the marriage of true minds
Admit impediments.   Love is not love
Which alters when it alteration finds,
Or bends with the remover to remove:
O, no! it is an ever-fixèd mark
That looks on tempests and is never shaken;
It is the star to every wandering bark,
Whose worth 's unknown, although his height be taken;
Love 's not Time's fool, though rosy lips and cheeks
Within his bending sickle's compass come;
Love alters not with his brief hours or weeks,
But bears it out even to the edge of doom:
If this be error and upon me proved,
I never writ nor no man ever loved.

Here is wisdom, the wisdom of the seer, not of the logician; here is beauty of thought and loveliness of poetic form; thought poetical, not epigrammatic; form in those free lines that mark the sure stroke of artistic mastery, as opposed to the thought of the admirably clear, cool, and subtle mind that is the antithesis of the poet. The epigram, quoted above, is certainly Bacon's, not only for the contemporary evidence but for its Baconian spirit of worldliness and its hard-eyed recognition of the vanity and futility of such a life as was his. But it is little to found the reputation of a poet on. Indeed, Bacon's touch with poetry is scarcely more serious than his momentary points of contact with the drama.

If we dare emulate for the moment the rhapsodical art of the late Mr. Swinburne, among the many vagaries and wanderings into darkness that egotistic singularity has begotten on crass ignorance none could be more unfortunate than any confusion of the lives, the characters, or the works of Francis Bacon with William Shakespeare. For, ransack Elizabethan England how we will, it would be impossible to find two minds of conspicuous prominence more radically different in their natures, their modes of thinking, and quality of achievement than were the minds of these two great men. The man, whatever his name, who wrote the plays which still issue under the name of Shakespeare in thousands of impressions yearly, was country born and acquainted with rural sports: moreover he possessed a knowledge of such things that came by nature. Again, he was a man absolutely free from the slightest suspicion of bookishness and pedantry, a man of "small Latin and less Greek." In the third place, the man that wrote the Shakespearean plays was one intimately conversant with the theater; not merely to the degree of assisting in the preparation of one or two masques for the entertainment of her majesty, but to the extent of many years of actual service, involving the ordeal of a rigid apprenticeship, the revision and refashioning of old work, the treading the boards as an actor, and that feeling of the pulse of the public which the clever manager learns to interpret with unfailing success. Lastly, the writer of these plays was a poet; a man

of lavish and exuberant imagination, pregnant with wisdom
and illumined with the purest vein of humor known to literature. To country breeding, the absence of all that makes
the bookish man, an intimate conversancy with the public
stage, and the qualities that combine to make the most consummate of poets and dramatists, might be added many other
characteristics which all would agree must have animated
the heart and brain of the author of these plays: his universal
sympathy and charity, his lofty ethics, his deep and noble
philosophy of life — but enough has been written.

Now, in view of all this, what sort of a man was Francis
Bacon? City born and courtly bred, with an ideal of a trim
clipped garden as "the greatest refreshment to the spirit of
man," with a knowledge of herbs and flowers, extensive (as
was all his knowledge) and pedantically scientific (as was
much of it). As to his acquaintance with contemporary
drama, Spedding declared that in all his study of Bacon he
had never seen any sign that the philosopher had ever read
a line of Shakespeare. A time-server and a trimmer, whom
the wise Queen Elizabeth mistrusted and the unwise King
James advanced; a scholar and an author distinguished for
his English prose, yet one, as we have seen, who feared lest
his mother-tongue might prove a bankrupt, as he put it, and
therefore entrusted the precious freight of his philosophy to
Latin; a philosopher who sought to revolutionize the processes
of human thought but rejected some of the most important
scientific discoveries of his own time; a jurist, the most
eminent of his day, self-convicted of corruption.

It is possible to treat with respect and accept so far as the
evidences appeal to reason, the scholars' proofs that parts
of Shakespeare as printed to-day are not his; that Fletcher's
hand is discernable in *Henry VIII*, and that other inferior
authors may have penned portions of other plays. The
influence of Lyly is patent in the earliest comedies, and Marlowe's is as unmistakeable in the earlier historical dramas.
Conceivable — although the present writer could not share
it — is a fancy that Ben Jonson transcended himself in the
writing of parts of *Julius Cæsar;* or that Spenser miraculously

wrote some passage or other of these plays, showing himself for the first and only time in his life a dramatist. But of all the men of Elizabeth's reign, great and little, gentle or common, poets or none, there is not one so infinitely removed, so absolutely alien, in character, spirit, and nature, in qualities of mind and of heart from the author of Shakespeare's plays as Francis Bacon. The man who wrote the Shakespearean dramas was one whose birth, and extraction, whose education, training, and experience in life were the precise counterpart of the little that we know and the more that we may with reason infer to have been Shakespeare's. These plays are Shakespeare's very own; and least of all things conceivable is the preposterous notion that they could in any part or parcel have been written by such a man as Bacon.

CHAPTER XIX

DONNE AND HIS PLACE AMONG LYRICAL POETS

WE know more of the outward events of the life of John Donne than of any poet or writer of his age, and yet he remains a personage strange and enigmatic, and a poet more often misjudged than appreciated. Donne's was a twofold greatness. A biographer, not long since, wrote a *Life of Donne* in which he confesses to little sympathy with his poetry.[1] He was writing of the famous Dean of St. Paul's, amongst the most learned of divines in an age of deep theological learning, the most brilliant and persuasive preacher of his day. Of Donne as a divine we have already heard in this book. But Donne would remain great in the history of literature with the Dean of St. Paul's neglected, in that he is the most original, the most independent, the most perverse, yet in some respects among the most illuminated of the poets of the latter days of Elizabeth. Nor is it possible to separate wholly these two aspects of Donne's career; for although there is little of the future divine in those strange and cynical erotic poems which formed so interesting a part of the exercises of his youth, still his poetry would be far from what it is to us were the spirituality of his later poems not to enter into account. On the other hand, it is the power of poetry in the divine as well as the beauty and sanctity of his life that endeared him to those whose privilege it was to know him, and made him a power for good in his day.

John Donne was born in London in 1573, the year of Jonson's birth. His father, also John Donne, was Master of the Ironmongers' Company and a man of wealth and prominence. His mother was Elizabeth Heywood, daughter of John Heywood, the famous epigrammatist and writer of interludes in the days of Henry VIII. Both families were

[1] *John Donne, Sometime Dean of St. Paul's*, by A. Jessopp, 1897.

stanch Roman Catholics; and they remained such, and suffered for their faith. Donne's education was superintended by his uncle, Jasper Heywood, a Jesuit of prominence and translator, with others, of Seneca's tragedies. In order to escape the difficulties of taking the oath of allegiance (which was made particularly offensive to them), it was the custom for Roman Catholic boys to go up to college very young; for the oath was not exacted of any under the age of sixteen. Donne and his brother, Henry, matriculated at Oxford when twelve and eleven years of age, John leaving when less than fourteen. There he formed a warm friendship with Sir Henry Wotton, which lasted through life. Both left Oxford, however, without a degree, and Donne probably traveled abroad, as we know that Wotton did, with the design (as we should put it) of entering the diplomatic service. In 1592 we find Donne again in England, a student at Lincoln's Inn and intimate with the young poet, Christopher Brooke, the friend of Browne and Wither. Donne certainly enjoyed extraordinary advantages in the study of science and language. His curiosity appears to have led him early to wide reading on a diversity of subjects, especially law and the dialectics of theology. But it does not appear that he became "a convinced opponent of Romanism" until the year 1603. Donne was attendant at the famous meetings at the Mermaid Tavern, where he met Shakespeare, Jonson, Drayton, Beaumont, and many lesser men. Reputation as a poet and a scholar came to Donne early. He was possessed of a competence; and his expectations were doubled on the untimely death of his only brother when but just of age. Donne spent his money, too, in the manner of a gentleman, frequenting the best literary and fashionable society. He seems to have been a man of handsome person and engaging manners; and he easily acquired a host of friends. But one thing stood against preferment. His uncle, Father Heywood — at one time "esteemed the Provincial of the English Jesuits" and lodged in the Tower for his activity in political intrigue — had long lived abroad, conspicuous among the proscribed recusants; and Donne was suspected of more than a sympathy with the old faith.

Donne began his literary career as a satirist, though he himself published nothing. To Donne's *Satires* we need not return. In 1596, when the expedition against the Spanish king was fitted out, Donne offered himself as a volunteer to the Earl of Essex and was accepted. He accompanied both expeditions against Spain; and in that against Cadiz formed an intimacy with Thomas Egerton, son of Lord Chancellor Ellesmere. The two descriptive poems, "The Storm" and "The Calm," belong to this period. Ben Jonson admired the latter and declared to Drummond that he had "by heart . . . that dust and feathers do not stir, all is so quiet." The passage to which Jonson alluded runs:

> The fighting place now seamen's rags supply;
> And all the tackling is a frippery.
> No use of lanthornes; and in one place lay
> Feathers and dust, today and yesterday.

There is no better illustration of Donne's uncompromising realism matched with his characteristic remoteness of thought than this which follows. He is speaking of the storm and its effects on his shipmates:

> Some coffined in their cabins lie, equally
> Grieved that they are not dead, and yet must die.
> And as sin-burdened souls from grave will creep
> At the last day, some forth their cabins peep
> And trembling ask what news and do hear so
> As jealous husbands what they would not know.
> Some sitting on the hatches, would seem there
> With hideous gazing to fear away fear.
> Then note they the ship's sicknesses, the mast
> Shaked with an ague and the hold and waste
> With a salt dropsy clogged, and all our tacklings
> Snapping, like too-too-high-stretched treble strings,
> And from our tattered sails rags drop down so
> As from one hanged in chains a year ago.

Indeed, nothing could be more discordant to the general acceptation of poetry than these harsh, vivid, and ingenuous lines. We are concerned neither with their place in literature nor

their qualities as poetry, but with their marked characteristics and divergences from the prevailing type of the moment.
And as to this, there can be no two opinions.

On his return from the Cadiz expedition the good offices
of his friend, young Egerton, procured Donne the post of
secretary to his exalted father the Lord Chancellor. This
post Donne held for four years, throwing himself heart and
soul into the amusements and the frivolities of the court, yet
reserving from every day some part to slake in study what he
calls "an hydroptic immoderate desire of human learning."
It was in these years that Donne acquired his great repute as
a wit and a poet, carelessly tossing off both verse and prose
(the latter in the form of "paradoxes" and problems), to be
read in clubs, discussed in ordinaries, and copied into manuscript commonplace books, the author taking not the least
heed as to the printing or preservation of either.

The lyrical poetry of a secular character which Donne has
left us lies in point of date of writing between 1592 and 1602.
It contains that fascinating, yet forbidding, group of poems
which add to all his other traits of idiosyncrasy the new note
of a frank and daring cynicism. The audacious outspokenness of several of these erotic poems has blinded readers to
their possible autobiographical significance. And yet these
poems give us really very little definite biographical information. They are often as cryptic as the *Sonnets* of Shakespeare themselves. Indeed, it is possible that we may make
too much of all these throes, and agonies, and intensities of
fleshly love. There is such a thing as the libertine in thought
as well as the roué in practice. Of the latter we hear very
little subjectively in literature. He wallows in his sty, and
even Circe takes little note of him save to feed him. It is
otherwise with the libertine in thought. It is the adventure,
the danger, the imaginativeness of the pursuit of unlawful
love — dare we call it the sporting instinct ?— which interests
him. The very cynicism of Donne's earlier erotic poetry
confirms this opinion. It was the same active insatiable
curiosity and interest in the fulness of life which caused Donne
on the one hand to dip into forbidden volumes of heresy,

alchemy, and pseudo-science, and on the other to court and
dally inaginatively with experiences which come not to those
that tread the beaten paths of virtue. Take, for example,
the famous song, "Go and catch a falling star," wherein one
who has journeyed far to see "strange sights" is compelled
to "swear"

> Nowhere
> Lives a woman true, and fair.

The concluding stanza of the lyric is even more outrageously
cynical:

> If thou find'st one, let me know,
>   Such a pilgrimage were sweet,
> Yet do not, I would not go,
>   Though at next door we might meet;
> Though she were true when you met her,
> And last till you write your letter,
>   Yet she
>   Will be
> False, ere I come, to two or three.

The poems of Donne came much into fashion from their
absolute originality, and it may be affirmed that he exerted
a powerful influence on the course of English poetry before
he was aware of it himself. Indeed, Donne's attitude towards his poetry throughout his life was that of the gentleman and courtier of his day, except that he was sincere in his
regard of poetry as a trifle: others often affected this attitude.
Donne was always an insatiable student. "His reading,"
says Jessopp, "embraced an extraordinary range of learning,
which his command of foreign languages and his great versatility tempted him to widen. He read with his pen in hand,
annotating, digesting, commenting. Nothing came amiss:
scholastic theology and casuistry, civil and common law,
history, poetry, philosophy, even medicine; and all these
subjects, not only in the language of the learned, but in the
vernacular of France, Italy and Spain."

In 1601 Donne crowned a romantic love story with an
imprudent marriage, clandestinely solemnized. There is

nothing to his discredit in the affair, although it was a serious matter in those days to marry a minor against her father's wishes. Anne More was a niece of Lord Ellesmere's second wife; and, as the daughter of Sir George More of Losely, was above the young secretary in wealth and station. Sir George was imprudent in leaving the young people together in his sister's household, and very insulting when Donne dared to ask for an alliance with his family. In short Sir George played the part of the irate father to perfection; had his new son-in-law, with his friend, Christopher Brooke, and his brother, who had participated in the marriage ceremony, committed to prison, and procured Donne's dismissal from the services of the Lord Chancellor, thus destroying once and for all his prospects in diplomacy. It mattered little that Sir George later repented, when he found that Donne was neither penniless nor without friends. Although he sought to undo the work of his passion and to reinstate his son-in-law with the chancellor, Lord Ellesmere replied that he had "parted with a friend and such a secretary as was fitter to serve a king than a subject; yet that, though he was unfeignedly sorry for what he had done, it was inconsistent with his place and credit to discharge and readmit servants at the request of passionate petitioners." The young people suffered from narrowness of means and worry for years. Children came to increase their needs; and sickness and death visited them. Donne's own health was always precarious and he dated many of his letters "from my hospital at Micham." Yet even in these times of depressed fortune, Donne was not without friends. Though young Sir Thomas Egerton had died in Ireland meanwhile, Sir Francis Wooley, whom Donne had also met as a shipmate on the Cadiz expedition, now befriended him. A tender friendship also subsisted between Donne and the Herberts, whom he had first met when their admirable mother was residing at Oxford for the education of Edward, afterwards Lord Herbert of Cherbury, and George, the devotional poet, then a little lad. To these years (as many letters which have been preserved attest) belong the foundations also of Donne's enduring friendships with Sir

Henry Goodere and with that engaging and munificent patron of poetry and learning, Lucy Countess of Bedford. Later Sir Robert Drury offered Donne and his family a home with him in his splendid mansion beyond Temple Bar. As to his marriage, it turned out ideal in its happiness and, when his beloved wife died, he cherished her memory.

It was during these years of waiting and intellectual depression that Donne wrote his strange prose treatise, *Biathanatos*, "a declaration of that paradox or thesis that self-homicide is not so naturally sin that it may never be otherwise." We can see in this subject what were some of the ponderings of this dialectic mind in a time of desperate fortune. This work, though known to his nearest friends, was not printed during Donne's life; and in a letter accompanying a manuscript of it sent to a friend much later, Donne describes it as "a misinterpretable subject . . . written by Jack Donne and not by Dr. Donne"; and adds: "Preserve it for me if I live; and if I die, I only forbid it the press and the fire." *Biathanatos* has been described as "a literary curiosity — a *tour de force*, unique in English literature, a survival of the old dialectic disputations, carried on strictly according to the rules of syllogistic reason, which the medieval schoolmen loved so well."

The steps by which Donne was drawn more and more into the religious controversies of his day we need not follow. *Ignatius his Conclave* is a fierce little satire in Latin and English and decidedly wanting in good taste. It was written about 1608 and is alone sufficient to attest the author's complete severance from the Jesuit influences of his youth. Donne was apparently well acquainted with Bacon and may have been one of "the good pens that forsake me not" that Bacon kept busy in the revision and Latinizing of his works. At some time prior to 1610, Donne became secretary to Lord Hay, afterwards Earl of Carlisle, who was at the moment high in the royal favor. This brought Donne into closer contact with the king, and a happy argument on the question of the oath of allegiance by Donne in the king's presence elicited the royal command that he put the case in writing. *The*

Pseudo Martyr, 1610, was the result, a work that gained an immediate popularity and confirmed King James in his determination that Donne should enter the church. This Donne was long reluctant to do from certain honest scruples and from a fear lest his motives might suffer misconstruction. There was perhaps another reason. With all his theological learning, Donne was a man of large and tolerant ideas. "You know," he writes to Sir Henry Goodere, "I never fettered or imprisoned the word religion; . . . immuring it in a Rome, or a Wittenberg, or a Geneva." The Christian sects, he continues, "are all virtually beams of one sun, and wheresoever they find clay hearts, they harden them and moulder them to dust. . . . They are not so contrary as the north and south poles; . . . they are connatural pieces of one circle." At last the king became importunate. Donne was ordained in 1615. No one knowing the man can hold his decision in anything but respect. A year later Donne became one of the royal chaplains; and in 1617, Dean of St. Paul's. He was a great and eloquent preacher, and a man of sweet and fervent piety. His ministrations, his sanctity, and his charity, all can be read in Walton's incomparable *Life*. Donne died in 1626.

There are more mistakes prevalent about Donne as a poet than about any one of even approximately equal rank. The first is the notion that Donne was a late Jacobean or Caroline writer, contemporary as a poet with Cowley. This error arises from the accident that the earliest extant edition of Donne's poetry is posthumous and dates 1633. Cowley's *Poetical Blossoms*, the appropriately named budding poetry of a precocious boy of thirteen, appeared in the same year. Donne would have been sixty, if alive. Without entering into the clear evidences which are at hand for all to use, Donne is an Elizabethan in his poetry in the strictest acceptation of that term, the forerunner of a remarkable movement, not soon assimilated or even imitated by his immediate contemporaries.

A more serious error is that which has arisen out of the term "metaphysical school of poetry." The word "metaphysics" was first associated with the poetry of Donne by Dryden in his *Discourse on Satire;* and Cowley is there charged with imitating Donne, which it is not to be questioned that he did. Although the mention of Donne is purely incidental, he is praised for "variety, multiplicity and choiceness of thought." Now this passage fell under the eye of the great Dr. Samuel Johnson when he was writing his "Life of Cowley" in *The Lives of the English Poets*. He expanded it into a sonorous critical dictum in which the word "metaphysical" was extended from an incidental trait of Donne and his late imitator, Cowley, to the distinguishing characteristic of a whole "school" of poetry; in which this "school" was thrown into violent contrast as "wits" with real poets, and in which only one thing was omitted concerning Donne, and that was the "variety, multiplicity and choiceness of thought" with which the judicious Dryden had credited him. This famous deliverance of Dr. Johnson's is a glaring example of the species of criticism which is worked up out of the critical dicta of others, a mystery unhappily not confined to the age of the Georges. We may give over expectation of a time when popular histories of literature will not discuss "the metaphysical poets" in eloquent passages expanded from Dr. Johnson's "Life of Cowley," as Dr. Johnson expanded the incidental words of Dryden. The instinct that bids each critic follow his predecessor has determined once and for all that the poetical indiscretions of the saintly Dean of St. Paul's, perpetrated thirty-five years before, shall be linked to all eternity to the clever imitations of a school-boy fifty years his junior. But let us turn from the discouraging negative function of criticism, the detection of error, to its positive mission, the affirmation — if we may be so fortunate as to find it — of truth.

The salient qualities of the poetry of Donne are, foremost, a contempt for mere form, shown in his disregard of the graces of diction as such, alliteration, choice of words for sound or smoothness, and other like tricks of the trade. Neither harshness of sound nor violence to meter deter him; and he repeats and uses the plain word where necessary to the force and rhetoric of the thought.

Some man unworthy to be possessor
Of old or new love, himself being false or weak
Thought his pain and shame would be the lesser,
If on womankind he might his anger wreak,
    And thence the law did grow,
    One might but one man know;
    But are other creatures so ?

It was with reference to such a line as the fourth that Jonson observed to Drummond that Donne "deserved hanging for not keeping accent." And yet there will be found a rhetorical value in even the roughness of Donne. His stanzas are often elaborate and always original, they are fitting to the subject in hand. Moreover, the roughness of Donne has been exaggerated. Secondly, Donne's contempt of form carried with it an absolute discarding of the poetical apparatus of the past. The gods of Greece and Rome dwell not with him, and though abundantly learned he scorns allusion or imitation, representing in this the very antithesis of Jonson. Donne's illustrations are powerful for their homeliness, vividness, and originality. He bids a lover ride "till age snow white hairs on thee." He craves "to talk with some old lover's ghost that died before the god of love was born"; Christ is addressed as the "strong ram that batterest heaven for me." Once more, Donne is not a nature poet, his work discloses no love of animals or of flowers. The forms of this world were nothing to him; he neither painted nature nor sought nature for his model. There is, for example, a strange absence of the sense of color in the poetry of Donne. When he uses color words at all, they are crude and perfunctory. On the other hand the abstractions of light and darkness are always before him. The relations of men to each other were likewise matters sealed. There is a completer absence of dramatic instinct in Donne than in any poet of his age. The concrete was nothing to him except as illustrative of the abstract. The reason for this, as for his want of an appreciation of nature, is to be found in the intense subjectivity of his poetry. It is related of him that he never saw, much less knew personally, the young maiden, Elizabeth Drury, whose untimely death he has immortalized in that strange and fascinating poem, "The Anatomy of the World." To him she is a beautiful abstraction, the symbol of all that is spiritual, divine, and permanent in this passing world. The symbol is not the real thing; the real is here the ideal. We must cross into the kindred sphere of speculative thought for the glow, the white passion, the power and subtlety of this remarkable work; and yet it remains poetry, for, however speculative its thought and eloquently rhetorical the expression, its real traffic is with the divine illusions and phantasmagoria of this world. The personality of Donne is ever present in his works; but it is not his bodily self but the spiritual part of him in these poems, sublimed, if it may be so put, into a universal meaning. Donne is himself the spiritual microcosm of the world. With him the one is all; and hence to such a man the body is but a veil for the soul. He speaks of the body of Elizabeth Drury as

> so pure and thin
> Because it need disguise no thought within,
> 'T was but a through-light scarf her mind to enrol
> Or exhalation breathed out of her soul.

So that

> We understand her sight; her pure and eloquent blood
> Spoke in her cheeks, and so distinctly wrought
> That one might almost say her body thought.

To Donne the soul alone is worthy of contemplation whose inner harmony is broken by too close a contact with the objective world. What seems a confusion of visual ideas really has this inner contemplative harmony to one to whom time and space are naught. By a natural step Donne "entertains a universal, almost Pantheistic faith in the unity and totality of his soul with all souls." In Donne will be found a romanticism of soul. His lyrics and satires are to be regarded as his struggle with sense. The sonnets, epistles, and "Anatomy of the World," these are the real Donne, though not alone the most poetical of his work.

Returning, Donne's originality shows itself in his themes which are of life, death, everything, and all; whatever he

touches he treats as an abstraction. Take for example such
lines as these, apostrophizing "Strong and long lived Death":

> The earth's face is but thy table; there are set
> Plants, cattle, men, dished for Death to eat.
> . . . .
> Nor will this earth serve him; he sinks the deep
> Where harmless fish monastic silence keep,
> Who (were Death dead) the roes of living sand
> Might sponge that element, and make it land.
> He rounds the air, and breaks the hymnic notes
> In birds', Heaven's choristers', organic throats,
> Which, if they did not die, might seem to be
> A tenth rank in the heavenly hierarchy.

His originality is likewise in his style, which in addition to the
negative qualities already noted displays a totally new range
of imagery derived from science, medicine, law, mathematics,
astronomy, alchemy, and the chemistry of the day. Not
"learned eccentric" as some one described the vocabulary
of Robert Browning at times, nor crammed for the nonce as
in Jonson's *Alchemist*, but the natural utterance of a mind
accustomed to think in technical terms.   In Donne's vocabulary there are many peculiar words, not technicalities, and
many words repeatedly used with a kind of fondness. His
must have been one of those minds that form strong associations about certain symbols, and use words with a deeper
significance than can ever reach him who runs as he reads.

When all has been said, there remains however that quality
by which Donne is chiefly known, namely, his use of conceit.
Of the conceit, its origin among the imitators of Petrarch, and
of Sidney's position as the popularizer of extravagant met-
aphors among the lyrists, we have already heard in this book.
That the conceit originated with Donne is no longer maintained by those who have knowledge on the subject; but it
is still held by some that Donne is responsible for its
prevalence in Jacobean poetry: a position equally untenable.
The mistake in this whole matter is the general confusion of
Donne with the "concettists" who preceded him, and who,
affected more or less by him, followed him. What may be

true of English concettists in general may not be true of Donne in particular and vice versa.   The confusion of Donne with Gongora is as bad as the confusion of Donne with Lyly.   That Donne is a concettist is unquestionable.   He often employs a thought which is far-fetched and ingenious rather than of natural and obvious meaning.   Moreover, it is true of the Donnian conceit (in contrast with the hyperbolical conceit of Sidney, the ingenuities of Cowley, and the antithetical wit of the next, the "classical", age), that the twist with Donne, if it may be so called, is in the thought rather than in the words.   Let us take a typical passage of Donne from a poem entitled "The Ecstasy."   The theme is of the spiritual nature of the ecstasy of love:

> When love with one another so
>   Interanimates two souls,
> That abler soul, which thence doth flow,
>   Defects of loneliness controls.
> We then, who are this new soul, know
>   Of what we are composed and made:
> For th' atomies, of which we grow,
>   Are souls, whom no change can invade.
> But O, alas! so long, so far
>   Our bodies why do we forbear?
> They are ours, though not we; we are
>   The intelligences, they the sphere;
> We owe them thanks, because they thus
>   Did us to us at first convey,
> Yielded their senses' force to us,
>   Nor are dross to us but allay.
> On man heaven's influence works not so,
>   But that it first imprints the air;
> For soul into the soul may flow
>   Though it to body first repair.

This passage is subtle, as is the whole poem, almost dialectic.   A keen, sinuous, reasoning mind is playing with its powers.   Except for the implied personification of the body regarded apart from the soul, the language is free from figure; there is no confusion of thought.   The new soul, the able soul, is that which, uniting the strength in the soul of each lover, "controls" loneliness in that union. This new soul is indestructible, because composed of the atomies (atoms we should say) which, being indivisible and the primal material of all things, are incapable of destruction. There is the distinctively Donnian employment of ideas derived from phys-ical and speculative science: the "atomies" with their indivisibility, a term of the physics of the day; the body is the "sphere" or superficies which includes within it the soul, a term of the old astro-philosophy; the body is not "dross" but an "allay," alchemical terms; the "influence" of heaven is the use of that word in an astrological sense, meaning "the radiation of power from the stars in certain positions or collocations affecting human actions and destinies;" and lastly, the phrase "imprints the air" involves an idea of the old philosophy, by which "sensuous perception is explained by effluxes of atoms from the things perceived whereby images are produced ('imprinted') which strike our senses." Donne subtly transfers this purely physical conception to the transference of divine influence. How different all this is to the earlier hyperboles of the Sidneian school, the rhapsodical extravagance of Crashaw, or the persistently clever ingenuity of Cowley, need be pointed out only to be understood. In Donne, even where the conceit in all its ingenuity does exist, it is again and again raised out of its class by a certain fervor, sincerity, and applicability that not only condones its extravagance but justifies it. Such is the famous image of the compass, best known of the Donnian conceits, yet none the less worthy of quotation once more. It occurs in a poem entitled "A Valediction Forbidding Mourning," written to his beloved wife, and runs thus:

> Our two souls therefore, which are one,
>   Though I must go, endure not yet
> A breach, but an expansion,
>   Like gold to airy thinness beat.
>
> If they be two, they are two so
>   As stiff twin compasses are two;
> Thy soul, the fix'd foot, makes no show
>   To move, but doth, if th' other do.

> And though it in the center sit,
>   Yet, when the other far doth roam,
> It leans, and hearkens after it,
>   And grows erect, as that comes home.
>
> Such wilt thou be to me, who must,
>   Like th' other foot, obliquely run;
> Thy firmness makes my circle just,
>   And makes me end where I begun.

A letter remains extant bearing date December, 1614, addressed by Donne to his friend Sir Henry Goodere in which he writes:

> One thing now I must tell you; but so softly that I am loth to hear myself, and so softly that if that good lady (Lady Bedford) were in the room with you and this letter, she might not hear. It is that I am brought to a necessity of printing my poems, and addressing them to my Lord Chamberlain. This I mean to do forthwith; not for much public view, but at mine own cost, a few copies. . . . I must do this as a valediction to the world before I take orders . . . and I would be just to my written words to Lord Harington to write nothing after that.

This edition, if ever actually printed, has perished; and, save for this mention, there is no word of it. We may believe that Donne bade a final farewell to his Muse two years before the death of Shakespeare. Even the divine poems, which include a few sonnets, hymns, transcriptions of the psalms, and the like, were doubtless all of them written before his ordination. Of the influence of Donne on what came after little need be said here. The poets that survived Shakespeare to write into the reign of King Charles — to name only the most important — were Jonson, Drayton, Chapman, Browne, and the Fletchers. Of these, the last three were wholly Spenserians, and Drayton remained to the end at least half such. Chapman went his ample, fantastic way and, so far as we can make out, wrote less and less after the completion of his translation of the *Odyssey*, published in the year of Shakespeare's death. But Jonson rated Donne at his due and a friendship honorable to both subsisted between them, Donne

penning more than one poetical epistle to Jonson. To Donne,
on the other hand, Jonson sent his *Epigrams* with verses
declaring,

> If I find but one
> Marked by thy hand, and with the better stone,
> My title's sealed.

In another epigram Jonson trumpeted his opinion of his
friend in lines beginning:

> Donne, the delight of Phoebus and each Muse,
> Who to thy one, all other brains refuse;
> Whose every work, of thy most early wit,
> Came forth example and remains so yet.

Jonson even paid the tribute of imitating what he conceived
to be the Donnian conceit in a little poem sent to Drummond
on "a Lover's Dust, Made Sand for an Hour-glass." But
the great dramatic satirist was much too self-centered and
independent to be affected by Donne or any one else, when
he had once laid his certain course, by theoretical compass
and classical chart, to the port of poetical celebrity. Among
the more important younger lyrists Drummond published the
first part of his *Poems* in 1616, having previously appeared
first in print three years earlier in *Tears on the Death of Mœl-
iades*, a pastoral name for Prince Henry. Thomas Carew
was but twenty in 1616; but Robert Herrick and George Herbert were both Carew's seniors, the one by five years, the
latter by three. Both must have begun to write poetry by
this time; but Herrick is the truest of the lyrical "sons of Ben"
and bettered his father's hard if noble favor with a beauty
all his own. Herbert remains the most certain of the successors of Donne to be affected immediately by his influences
in poetry; and Herbert, in his youth, as we have seen, was
personally intimate with Donne. A recent editor claims for
Herbert that "he devised the religious love-lyric and he introduced structure into the short poem."[1] With the long line
of lyrists before us and the wealth of their stanzaic variety
and invention, this last is obviously too large a claim, but in

[1] G. H. Palmer, *The Life and Works of George Herbert*, i, 57.

view of the inventiveness of Donne as to stanza and the intensity
of the passion of his secular love-songs, it may well be surmised that the poetry of Donne was George Herbert's immediate poetical inspiration and model. To Herbert, even more
certainly, Donne transmitted his own peculiar use of the
conceit, though Herbert is often quaintly ingenious where
Donne flashes unexpected illumination by the original bias
of his mind.

William Drummond, known as Drummond of Hawthornden from his estate near Edinburgh, was born in 1585, the
son of John Drummond, gentleman-usher to James before
he became King of England and knighted by that monarch
in 1603. The poet Drummond was educated at the University
of Edinburgh and in France, and joined his father at the
London court of the new Scottish king at the most impression-
able time of a young man's life. In several extant letters
which Drummond wrote home to friends in Scotland about this
time, he shows his interest and pleasure in the pageantry
and ceremonial of the court. But a list of his reading, also
extant, discloses him likewise busily engaged with poetry
and romance. His countryman Alexander's *Aurora, Euphues,*
the *Arcadia,* and the *Diana* of Montemayor; *Love's Labor's
Lost, A Midsummer-Night's Dream, Romeo and Juliet, Lucrece*
and *The Passionate Pilgrim* were among the books read by
this Scottish youth in 1606; and later we hear of many French
and Italian writers: of Daniel, and Davison's *Poetical Rhapsody* and (most significant) the *Arcadia,* read a second time.
In 1610, on the death of his father, Drummond gave up definitely his intent to follow the law and retired to his beautiful estate of Hawthornden to devote himself to poetry and
scholarly leisure. It was there that he planned to lead the
lady, who had inspired much of his sincere and beautiful
poetry and whose memory, on her untimely death in 1615,
before their marriage, he cherished for so many years. It
was at Hawthornden, four years later, that Drummond entertained Ben Jonson on that worthy's pilgrimage afoot to
Edinburgh; and doubtless Drummond's influence and appreciation of Jonson's poetry and reputation at the English court

procured for the English laureate the freedom of the city and other attentions which the citizens of Edinburgh accorded him.

The poetry of Drummond that made his repute is comprised in the little quarto of 1616. It consists of songs and sonnets, addressed for the most part to the lady to whom he was betrothed; of a collection of madrigals and epigrams, doubtless the earliest of his poetizing; and of a series of "spiritual poems," as the phrase went, entitled *Urania*, almost certainly the most recently written. Drummond's pattern and example is Sir Philip Sidney and his inspiration, Petrarch. To quote from a fragment printed with the *Poems* and called *A Character of Several Authors:* "Among our English poets Petrarch is imitated, nay surpassed in some things in matter and manner: in matter none approach him to Sidney." Later he continues: "Donne, among the Anacreontic lyrics, is second to none, and far from all second. . . . I think, if he would, he might easily be the best epigrammatist we have found in English." With the mention of Alexander, who is praised in this passage as only one Scotchman can praise another, we complete the list of the chief poetical influences on Drummond. But inspired by the work of other men though he was, this new poet of the last days of Shakespeare was far from devoid of a sweetness and gentle originality all his own. This sonnet, while perhaps not among the very best of Drummond, strikes the note of sincerity that marks all his threnodies for his lost Aurastella, as he somewhere calls her:

> As, in a dusky and tempestuous night,
> A star is wont to spread her locks of gold,
> And while her pleasant rays abroad are roll'd,
> Some spiteful cloud doth rob us of her sight;
> Fair soul in this black age so shin'd thou bright,
> And made all eyes with wonder thee behold,
> Till ugly Death, depriving us of light,
> In his grim misty arms thee did enfold.
> Who more shall vaunt true beauty here to see?
> What hope doth more in any heart remain,
> That such perfections shall his reason rein,

> If beauty, with thee born, too died with thee?
> World, plain no more of Love, nor count his harms;
> With his pale trophies Death hath hung his arms.

A greater originality characterizes this serious little poem, which the author denominates a madrigal:

> This life, which seems so fair,
> Is like a bubble blown up in the air
> By sporting children's breath,
> Who chase it everywhere,
> And strive who can most motion it bequeath:
> And though it sometime seem of its own might,
> Like to an eye of gold, to be fix'd there,
> And firm to hover in that empty height,
> That only is because it is so light.
> But in that pomp it doth not long appear;
> For even when most admir'd, it in a thought,
> As swell'd from nothing, doth dissolve in nought.

Drummond is not usually as free of conceit as these two quotations would seem to indicate; and his conceits, where he yields to hyperbole, are those of Petrarch, or rather Sidney, never those of Donne. Drummond loved the sonorous proper names of classical mythology as deeply as did Milton after him; and he delighted, like Milton again, in the recondite allusions involving them. Thus Pythagoras is the Samian; Boreas is Orithyia's lover; Venus, the Idalian star or the fair Erycine. Achelous' horn stands for a cornucopia; nightingales are "Pandionian birds," and birds in general, "Amphions of the trees." Equally dear to Drummond are unusual poetical words: brandon, cynoper, ramage, decore, panisks; and his originality is less in new figures than in a loving shaping of old material into a something different, yet reminiscent, like a faded fragrance, of some fair thing that we have known before. Drummond welcomed King James to Scotland, in 1617, in a panegyric of much poetic value called *The River Forth Feasting*. This act of the courtier he repeated with failing power, save for its adulation, in the *Entertainment of Charles* when that monarch, too, visited Scotland in 1633. In the year of the Shakespeare folio, 1623, Drummond published a book of devotional poetry of great beauty, entitled *Flowers of Sion*, in which he displays, as in his prose essay, *A Cypress Grove* (a treatise upon death, published in the same volume), a singularly Platonic type of Christian philosophy. Drummond's later life shows him interested in theoretical mechanics and seeking patents for the invention of various contrivances, chiefly warlike instruments. He was a giver of books to his university, Edinburgh, and was drawn into the vortex of the unhappy political controversies of the day towards the end of his life. He died in 1649.

To return in conclusion to Donne, it is somewhat disconcerting to find an author whom, not unlike to Walter Savage Landor in our own late century, the critics can not glibly classify as the founder of a school or the product of a perfectly obvious series of literary influences. Donne is a poet of this difficult type. For, just as Shakespeare touched life and mankind at all points, and, absorbing the light of his time, gave it forth a hundred-fold, so Donne, withdrawn almost entirely from the influences affecting his contemporaries, shone and glowed with a strange light all his own. Orthodoxy — or rather a restoration to orthodoxy — as to John Donne demands that we recognize him in his poetry as an Elizabethan, as strictly such as Shakespeare, far more so than Jonson; that while we grant Donne to be a concettist he was such from the originality and natural bias of his mind, not from affected singularity or a striving after effect; that his strange and fascinating poetry, so caviare to the general, yields a true and rich reward to him who will seek with labor and true faith; and, lastly, that Donne, next to Spenser and Jonson, exercised the most potent influence of his time on English poetry. Donne's highest contribution to literature, like Shakespeare's in a very different way, depends on that deeper element of modern poetry which we call poetic insight, a power in his case which, proceeding by means of the clash of ideas familiar with ideas remote, flashes light and meaning into what has hitherto appeared mere commonplace. No one, in short, excepting Shakespeare, with Sidney, Greville, and Jonson in lesser degree, has done so much to develop intellectualized emotion in the Elizabethan lyric as Donne. In comparison with all this the notions about a "metaphysical school," even a "rhetorical school of poetry" and the fiction of a fantastical prince of concettists, leading a generation of poetlings deliberately astray, become vagaries of criticism comparatively unimportant. Donne deserves the verdict of his friend, Ben Jonson, who called him "the first poet in the world in some things." But Donne is the last poet to demand a proselyting zeal of his devotees, and all those who have learned to love his witching personality will agree to the charming sentiment of his faithful adorer, Izaak Walton, when he says: "Though I must omit to mention divers persons, . . . friends of Sir Henry Wotton; yet I must not omit to mention of a love that was there begun betwixt him and Dr. Donne, sometime Dean of Saint Paul's; a man of whose abilities I shall forbear to say anything, because he who is of this nation, and pretends to learning or ingenuity, and is ignorant of Dr. Donne, deserves not to know him."

CHAPTER XX

DRAMA AT THE UNIVERSITIES, THE PASTORAL DRAMA AND THE MASQUE

F ROM Chaucer's time to Spenser's, English poetry owed most to the court. This we have seen in various lyrical forms, in fiction, and in the pastoral, to name no more. The old sacred drama had in it much of the folk; but when modern drama arose to succeed it, the first influences were those that belonged specifically to the society that surrounded the sovereign; and however soon these were rivaled and surpassed by the larger utterances of the popular drama they continued to develop in their own way, and what is more, to exert a decided influence on the popular drama besides. Thus Lyly was tutor to the young Shakespeare in comedy; Peele transferred his talents from the college and the court to the boards of the London playhouses; and Kyd, a satellite revolving in an outer orbit of the charmed Sidneian circle, furnished popularized Senecan tragedy to the same stage. It is the business of this chapter to trace the drama as it flourished at court after the time of Lyly, and to treat, in connection with this, the academic drama which in nature is of close kindred.

Scarcely anything secularly dramatic in England is as old as the practice of the performance of Latin plays at schools and colleges. It was out of this custom that such a play as *Ralph Roister Doister* came to be written and perhaps *Gammer Gurton* as well; for the substitution of an original play, Latin or English, was an obvious enough departure from the older acting of a comedy of Terence or Plautus. These performances were early used to celebrate important occasions and came to be a recognized feature of royal progresses and entertainments of other important personages. Thus in the year of Shakespeare's birth, when Elizabeth visited Cambridge, she was regaled not only with "scholastical exercises in phil-

osophy, physics, and divinity," but with comedies and tragedies at night "set forth partly by the whole university and
partly by the students of King's College." Similar festivities
attended the queen's visit to Oxford, two years later, and
many a forgotten name, such as Preston, Edwards, Gager,
and Legge, has been preserved in the complaisant accounts
of these old theatrical revels. Among men to become known
to the stage, Peele began his career, as we have seen, in college
plays at Oxford; and Nash narrowly escaped expulsion from
Cambridge for a libelous Latin comedy. A satirical quality
is almost invariably characteristic of the college play. The
satire is for the most part dependent on the close and intimate
relations of college life and it assumed familiarity, as it had
a right to do, with the classical education in vogue at the time
and smacks, at times to excess, of the school and the commons.
A famous play, *Pedantius*, of Cambridge in the early eighties,
obtrudes an absurd Ciceronian (by some believed a take-off
on Gabriel Harvey) into the midst of a comedy of Plautine
intrigue; and *Bellum Grammaticale*, a contemporary piece at
Oxford, elaborates after a medieval model an ingenious allegory of the parts of speech. At other times the immemorial
feud between town and gown becomes the subject of dramatic
treatment as in *Club Law*, acted 1599, at Cambridge, in which
certain townsmen were forcibly compelled to view themselves
outrageously lampooned in their own costumes, which had
been previously borrowed by the mischievous collegians with
that nefarious end in view.

Among strictly Elizabethan academic plays none are more
prominent or interesting than the trilogy known as "the
Parnassus plays," the work of an unknown author and acted
at St. John's College, Oxford, in the interval covered by the
years 1598 to 1602. The first of these is entitled *The Pilgrimage to Parnassus*. It details the career of a couple of
youths in their journey, by way of the well-known *trivium*,
through "the island of logique," "the pleasant groves of
rhetorique," and the harsher climate of philosophy, until
they reach "the laurel shady grove" upon Parnassus' top.
They are not without adventures by the way with the tavern-

er, the Puritan, and other typical personages of college life. This production is not much more than an interlude in length. But it was received so well that in a second part, *The Return from Parnassus*, the author undertook a far more elaborate presentation of "the progress of learning towards a settlement in life" in which he represents the same heroes, seeking preferment and rebuffed and abused on every hand. In a final play, the second part of *The Return from Parnassus*, the theme is still further amplified, and abuses of bribery and favoritism in the presentations of church livings are held up to the light. The disheartening moral is that there is no place for merit and learning in this world, unless both be supported by station, wealth, or at least by sycophancy. Incidentally these comedies exhibit several typical figures cleverly satirized, such as Gullio, the fool of fashion and patron of the poets, whose cheerful and impudent appropriation of the verses of other men's making, especially Shakespeare's, attests both the great poet's repute and the attitude of the superior young collegians towards his poetry. Gullio is exhibiting to Ingenioso his "vein in courting":

Gullio. Pardon, fair lady, though sick-thoughted Gullio makes amain unto thee, and like a bold-faced suitor 'gins to woo thee.

Ingenioso (aside). We shall have nothing but pure Shakespeare and shreds of poetry that he hath gathered at the theaters.

Gull. Pardon me, moi mittressa, ast am a gentleman, the moon in comparison with thy bright hue a mere slut, Antony's Cleopatra a black-browed milk-maid, Helen a dowdy.

Ingen. (aside), Mark, *Romeo and Juliet!* O monstrous theft! I think he will run through a whole book of Samuel Daniel's.

Gull. Thrice fairer than myself — thus I began —
The god's fair riches, sweet above compare,
Stain to all nymphs, more lovely than a man,
More white and red than doves and roses are!
Nature that made thee with herself had strife,
Saith that the world hath ending with they life.

Ingen. Sweet Master Shakespeare!

Gull. As I am a scholar.
These arms of mine are long and strong withal,
Thus elms by vines are compassed ere they fall.

Ingen. Faith, gentleman, your reading is wonderful in our English poets!

Gull. Sweet mistress, I vouchsafe to take some of their words and apply them to mine own matters by scholastical invention. Report then upon thy credit; is not my vein in courting gallant and honorable?

It may be surmised from the allusions of these plays that these "young sprouts of Apollo" regarded *Venus and Adonis* as the work on which chiefly rested the contemporary fame of Shakespeare. It was Ovidian in subject and manner, and it, like *Lucrece*, had been published by the regular channels and becomingly dedicated to lordship. Of the dramas, they were not quite so sure. The popular actors, Burbage and Kemp, are represented among the characters in the last of these plays, and doubtless their appearance and their manner-isms of speech and action were divertingly mimicked then as our popular actors are at times mimicked by the collegians of to-day. But though the world was ringing with the tri-umphs of Shakespeare and Jonson, the acknowledgment of their superiority is put into the ignorant mouth of Kemp, the morris-dancer, in the certainly satirical words: "Few of the university pen plays well; they smell too much of that writer Ovid, and that writer Metamorphosis, and talk too much of Proserpina and Jupiter. Why here's our Shakespeare puts them all down, aye, and Ben Jonson, too."

Few things are more persistent in the strictly academic plays than their employment of allegory. The minuteness of the parallels in the old *Bellum Grammaticale* would do credit to Priscian or William Lilly; and even more elaborate are the allegorical details of *Lingua*, a fluently written comedy by one Tomkins of Trinity College, Cambridge, often acted and in print by the year 1607. Therein the tongue is appro-priately conceived as a feminine personage possessed of the aggressiveness and activity of a modern "suffragette," who demands, for herself, full recognition as one of the senses. In an extraordinary number of scenes and with an aston-ishing number of characters, this struggle for recognition is detailed to the end which we regret to say was Lingua's discomfiture. The age of James was not the twentieth century. *Lingua* is an ably written drama and full of ingenious wit. It may be recommended to the reader who would learn how sumptuously and with what variety the personages of a private play were costumed in these old times. This drama of *Lingua* was acted at the house of an uncle of Oliver Cromwell, in 1603, to welcome King James on his progress up to London. And an absurd story, of later cavalier invention, makes Oliver himself the actor who impersonated the character, Tactus; and, learning in the play what it was to wear a crown, he bent all his energies thereafter to acquire one. Oliver was four years old in 1603.

But we may feel sure that, except on grand occasions when the colleges were visited by royalty, the academic play was a much simpler affair. A pleasing little burlesque, called *Narcissus*, served to enliven the Christmas festivities at St. John's College, Oxford, in 1602. In its persons, dialogue, and setting especially, we meet with as frank a satire on contemporary amateur theatricals as is Shakespeare's representation of Bottom and his "base mechanicals" of *The Midsummer-Night's Dream*. So, too, the several plays of 1607 at the same college, when Oxford seems for the nonce to have gone theatrically mad, were performed apparently on a stage erected in the refectory by pushing the tables together; and the properties were the fewest. An interesting contemporary account of these festivities informs us of the whole manner of their proceedings: how the collegians selected a Christmas prince who was installed with egregious solemnity and an appropriate Latin play; how tragedies in Latin and comedies for the younger sort in English were devised, rehearsed, and acted; and of their troubles in rehearsal, the accidents and triumphs of performances, and many like matters. Few of these lighter amateur productions are possessed of any literary, much less poetic, merit. The one dramatist whose work was strictly academic, to rise to literary distinction, was Thomas Randolph, and he belongs to the reign of King Charles. But these academic productions of the time of

Elizabeth and James are neither without their value nor without a deeper interest for their relations, though often remote, to their sister plays on the popular stage.

Concomitantly with satiric farce and allegory, Latin tragedy, with its imitation in English, continued to flourish at both the universities. In subject-matter these plays were preferably taken from classical history or myth. Two of the most famous Latin tragedies in their day were *Roxana*, 1592, the work of William Alabaster, praised for his poetry by Spenser, and *Nero* by Dr. Matthew Gwinne, printed in 1603. This latter tragedy, which is closely written and of great length, is rigorously grounded on the recognized classical authorities for the history of that degenerate Roman emperor, and owes its existence as completely as Jonson's *Sejanus* to Tacitus and Suetonius. Alabaster's *Roxana*, on the other hand, has recently been discovered to be little more than a translation of one of the dramas of the Italian, Luigi Groto. But Italian sources such as these were more frequently employed by the collegians for comedy and a long list of plays — few of them rising above mediocrity — can be made out for both colleges, levying on what may be called Plautus Italianized. Such a play, to name only one, is *Lælia*, 1590, a translation of *Gl'Ingannati* of Giovanni della Porta and a suggested source of Shakespeare's *Twelfth Night;* another translation from the same Italian dramatist is Tomkins' *Albumazor*, 1615, which Dryden mixed up for want of information as to its source with Jonson's *Alchemist;* a third is the celebrated *Ignoramus*, by far the most popular of all the academic comedies of its time. *Ignoramus* is the work of George Ruggle. The plot, which is far from wanting either in cleverness or wit, revolves about the character who supplies the title and whose coarse scheming, blundering, and jargon of dog Latin, bad English, and law French proclaim him the very embodiment of blatant, militant Philistinism. *Ignoramus* was acted for the first time at Cambridge before James in 1615 with a cast chosen, so Oxford hinted, with at least as much care to the social relations of the actors as to their histrionic abilities; and its success with King James (who journeyed up to Cambridge a second time to see the comedy repeated) was, we fear, as much due to its broad obscenities as to any designed encouragement of learning and the arts that governed the purposes of that learned monarch.

Further into the strictly academic drama our present design does not lead us. In Gwinne's *Nero*, English-Latin tragedy reached its height; *Ignoramus* was surpassed in wit and in decency by many following plays. The restrictive sphere of satire and allusion in such plays lent little to the popular comedy of manners which had long since outstripped it. The restrained and narrow rhetoric of Senecan tragedy was equally a thing of the past on the stage of London. On the other hand, plays at college were open from the first to outside influences, more especially those of the court than to those of the popular drama. Of the court influences on the academic drama the most important by far was pastoral; and we turn now to the consideration of pastoral drama during the period of this book.

It will be recalled that in a previous chapter a succession of literary fashions, so to speak, was noted as characteristic of the latter half of Elizabeth's reign. There was the time of the sonnet, for example, and that when lyrics were more specifically written to be set to music. Preceding both of these was the period of the pastoral, which tinged with its artificial ideals and its preciosity nearly every form of current literature. Thus the pastoral is rather a way of viewing nature and reproducing it in art than, in any strict sense, a variety of literature, much less a form of poetry. Quite enough has been said of the origin of the pastoral in the chapter which deals with its lyric form. In the pastoral, be it remembered (lest we become critical where criticism is unfair), we leave the actual world behind us to hark back to that golden age so besung by the poets, to dwell in the land where all swains are lovers and all nymphs are fair; where their work is the knotting of rushes or the piping of melodies, their play, the prettiest of innocent love-making — but who knows not Arcadia, though his life may no more have compassed it than his lips have tasted the springs of Helicon or his feet attempted the steeps of Parnassus ?

In Italy the step from pastoral romance to pastoral drama was soon taken by Tasso, whose *Aminta*, acted in 1573, was translated by Englishmen in the eighties; twenty years later came Guarini's *Il Pastor Fido*. But well before either of these famous regular pastoral dramas, English poets had employed the pastoral notion in masque-like devices and entertainments. Gascoigne used such figures among others in his speeches to Queen Elizabeth at Kenilworth in 1575, and Sidney in his *Lady of May*, three years later, gives us a lively little pastoral interlude. In Peele's court play, *The Arraignment of Paris*, and equally in several of the dramas of Lyly, we have a pastoral atmosphere breathed by the gods of Greece and Rome, incongruous to none but a classical purist who has forgotten intervening history. But in such a drama as Lyly's *Love's Metamorphosis*, the manners are pure Arcadia. The pastoral as an element entered into English comedies in other combinations. A "court element," as it has been called, combines with the pastoral in certain well-known plays; such, for example, as *Mucedorus*, an exceedingly popular little comedy, attributed to Lodge. In the inferior *Thracian Wonder*, much as in Sidney's *Arcadia*, the combination of the pastoral is with the heroic. More interesting is the contrast of ideas that arises from a combination of the conventions of the Italian pastoral with the English ideal of free rural life, embodied in the tales of the doings of Robin Hood. Such a drama as this Ben Jonson had in mind in the fragment of *The Sad Shepherd*, written we may feel certain, whatever the date, at least after the regular English pastoral plays, of which more shortly. Here a tale of Robin and his Maid Marian is interwoven with one of Æglamour, Mellifleur, and Amie, names redolent with the pastoral ideals; and huntsmen and shepherds rub against Puck-Hairy and the Witch of Paplewick. The robust English nature of Jonson could never have realized the rococo landscape of Arcadia or the tinted shepherdesses that dwell simperingly therein. In less striking contrast, these two elements appear once more in *As You Like It*. The ultimate source of Shakespeare's plot, as is well known, is the medieval *Tale of Gamelyn*, a plain English story of outlawry and vengeance. Into it there enters no woman's figure; and, in the end, the unjust eldest brother is slain and the two younger divide the estate. Lodge translated the story from England to the Arcadian forest of Ardenne, transformed "the maister outlawe" to the banished King of France, turned Gamelyn into the romantic lover, Rosader, and invented Rosalynd to match him, conveying a group of shepherds and shepherdesses into the forest for the human setting. Lodge's *Rosalynd* is more truly pastoral than any play of Lyly. Shakespeare in *As You Like It* restored the English setting and introduced his veritable English country, folk, Audrey and William, beside the pastoral figures of Silvius and Phœbe; using pastoral love-making in the delicious wooing of Orlando and Rosalind only for delightful burlesque. *As You Like It* is no true pastoral; and no more readily than Jonson, could the free romantic spirit of Shakespeare be bound within the conventions of a form of literature so exotic and conventional.

We reach now by process of elimination the slender products of the true pastoral drama in England. They consist of scarcely more than a half-dozen English plays within the lifetime of Shakespeare, only two of them, Daniel's *Queen's Arcadia* and John Fletcher's *Faithful Shepherdess*, ranking really high as poetry. Indeed, if we except *The Sad Shepherd* of Jonson, we must look forward to the *Amyntas* of Randolph, a product of the revival of pastoral drama in the reign of King Charles, for a play to match these two in its kind. Of Samuel Daniel and his work as one of the earliest of the sonneteers, pastoralists, and writers of narrative poetry, we have heard above. It was in 1605 that *The Queen's Arcadia* was acted at Christ Church College, Oxford before Anne, the queen of King James. Daniel, as we know, had visited Italy; and, while there, had met Guarini, author of *Il Pastor Fido*. This famous pastoral drama is Daniel's direct inspiration, and the English poet has preserved with a fidelity, complete but by no means slavish, the atmosphere and general *milieu* of the pastoral. The story, which involves no very original intrigue, sets forth the usual pastoral figures, illustrating love in its various phases and relations. But Daniel introduces, not without success, a corrupt returned traveler and "a subtle wench of Corinth" who complicate the plot and offer a happy foil, alike to the superlative virtue and the excessive gravity of the pastoral folk. A fair specimen of Daniel's Arcadian style may be caught from the following lament:

> O Silvia, if thou needs wouldst have been gone,
> Thou shouldst have taken all away of thee;
> And nothing left to have remain'd with me.
> Thou shouldst have carried hence the portraiture
> Which thou hast left behind within my heart,
> Set in the table-frame of memory,
> That puts me still in mind of what thou wert,
> Whilst thou wert honest, and thy thoughts were pure;
> So that I might not thus in every place,
> Where I shall set my careful foot, confer
> With it of thee, and evermore be told,
> That here she walked, and lean'd upon mine arm;
> There gathered flowers, and brought them unto me;
> Here by the murmurs of this rustling spring,
> She sweetly lay, and in my bosom slept;
> Here first she showed me comforts when I pined;
> As if in every place her foot had stept,
> It had left Silvia in a print behind.

As to the comedy of relief, it is in *The Queen's Arcadia* that the well-known descant upon tobacco occurs, a passage tuned to a nicety to the ear of the royal author of *A Counterblast to Tobacco*. After telling of the source of this "herb wrapped up in rolls from the island of Nicosia" and describing how

> This in powder made, and fired, he sucks
> Out of a little hollow instrument
> Of calcinated clay, the smoke thereof:
> Which either he conveys out of his nose,
> Or down into his stomach with a whiff;

he continues of the Arcadians, that in place of their former pleasant festivals and meetings:

> Now do they nothing else but sit and suck,
> And spit and slaver all the time they sit,
> That I go by and laugh unto myself,
>
> .   .   .   .
>
> That men of sense could ever be so mad
> To suck so gross a vapor that consumes
> Their spirits, spends nature, dries up memory,
> Corrupts the blood, and is a vanity.

As yet there had been no attempt to popularize the true pastoral drama, although several comedies since the time of Lyly had disclosed pastoral elements, in addition to those already mentioned, especially John Day's *Isle of Gulls* and *Humor out of Breath*. The first is a sprightly little piece, founded on an episode of Sidney's *Arcadia*, but converting the heroic tone of the original into satire and raillery. *Humor out of Breath*, while containing several charming scenes of a pastoral nature, is otherwise free from the conventions of the type. These comedies belong respectively to 1605 and a couple or more years after. It must have been about 1608 that Fletcher staged his poetic pastoral drama, *The Faithful Shepherdess*. According to the author's own account the play was a failure on the popular boards; and in a preface "To the Reader," when the drama came to print, Fletcher justifies his scheme and makes it plain that he accepted the pastoral conventions in their integrity. In the story the faithful shepherdess is Clorin who, her lover having died, has set up a bower near his grave wherein she lives the life of an anchoress and practises simple arts of healing. She is assisted in her work by a gentle satyr on whose original nature devotion to this pure mistress has wrought a miracle. . . . Clorin is sought in love by Thenot, whom she gently but firmly refuses, and at last repulses completely by a momentary pretense of yielding; for it was Clorin's constancy, not Clorin, that Thenot adored. Amoret, unkindly wounded by her lover, Perigot, who, practised on, has thought her false, is brought by the satyr to Clorin for cure; and so, too, is Alexis, justly wounded by a sullen shepherd on account of Cloe, a light-o'-love. All these and other shepherds and shepherdesses are cured or reclaimed in the end by the holy anchoress, who continues faithful to her dead love. Into the allegory alleged by some to underlie this story it is unnecessary to inquire. The lapses from decorum which stain this otherwise beautiful poem are doubtless best explained by the method of contrast which Fletcher invoked in his earlier plays with Beaumont and carried at times to excess. In execution and within the limits of its artificial kind, *The Faithful Shepherdess* leaves little to criticism. It became, despite its first failure, exceedingly popular on the stage and was admired by generations of poets. One need not turn far into its pages to find how much even Milton owed to it. The octosyllables given to the gentle-natured satyr are always particularly musical. Thus he offers his forest treasures to Clorin his benefactress:

> Here be grapes, whose lusty blood
> Is the learnèd poet's good,
> Sweeter yet did never crown
> The head of Bacchus; nuts more brown
> Than the squirrel's teeth that crack them;
> Deign, O fairest fair, to take them!
> For these black-eyèd Dryope
> Hath oftentimes commanded me
> With my claspèd knee to climb:
> See how well the lusty time
> Hath decked their rising cheeks in red,
> Such as on your lips is spread!
> Here be berries for a queen,
> Some be red, some be green;
> These are of that luscious meat,
> The great god Pan himself doth eat:
> All these, and what the woods can yield,
> The hanging mountain or the field,
> I freely offer, and ere long
> Will bring you more, more sweet and strong.

In *The Winter's Tale* will be found some of the most exquisite outdoor scenes in our drama. But they are pastoral only in the sense that they deal with shepherds and their life. Greene's prose tale of *Pandosto*, the source, is more pastoral than these scenes, and the atmosphere of the rest of the play is that of the court. The same thing is true of the rare comedy of Robert Daborne called *The Poor Man's Comfort*, 1613. This pretty romantic play, which has been almost completely forgotten, departs from one of the long accepted conventions of romance to leave the heroine a shepherdess, and no princess, even in the end. In 1614 Daniel returned to the pastoral drama with *Hymen's Triumph*, a shorter, maturer work though scarcely equaling the more elaborately planned *Queen's Arcadia*. *Hymen's Triumph* was acted before their majesties on the occasion of a noble wedding. The demands of such an event gave to Daniel's play much the sumptuousness in performance of the masque. It is written throughout in that admirable English diction that earned for the author in his own day the sobriquet "well-languaged Daniel." The continued touch of the pastoral with the universities is shown in a strange, but interesting and far from unpoetical, production called *Sicelides*, the work of Phineas Fletcher, author of *The Purple Island*, and intended for performance before the king at Cambridge in 1615. *Sicelides* is a piscatory comedy in which fisher-folk take the place of the shepherds of the pastoral. This was quite orthodox, at least on the example of the piscatory eclogue, a variety of the pastoral neither unknown to Sannazaro nor to Theocritus himself. The pastoral drama seems to have fallen into disfavor about this time. At least there are few, even inferior, specimens until the revival of the mode, some ten years later, in the reign of King Charles. Jonson's admirable fragment of a pastoral play has already been mentioned. *The Sad Shepherd* was never finished and never staged. In it, as in so many of his works, Jonson appears to have come into direct rivalry with Daniel, who was again and again the butt of Jonson's ridicule. It seems not unreasonable to believe *The Sad Shepherd* a production of about this period and that it was written to emulate the success of *Hymen's Triumph* rather than long before or (what is still more improbable) after all his immediate competitors for the favor of the court had ceased to write dramas of this kind.

Masking in the sense of revelry, taking more or less a dramatic form, is as old in England as the drama itself. The masque, as a specific variety of entertainment at court or among the nobility, was a development of the latest years of Elizabeth's reign and the time of James. Moreover, had it not been for the peculiar talents of Ben Jonson and the conjunction with him of Inigo Jones, the royal architect and ingenious designer of scenery and stage devices, the history of the English masque would have been far shorter and poorer. In the restrictive sense of the word with which we are alone concerned, a masque may be defined as a setting, lyric, scenic, and dramatic, for a court ball. It is an entertainment into which songs, dialogue, action, music, scenery, and costume all enter; but the nucleus is always a dance. The precise language of the day, for example, recognized in the "entertainment" a similar amplification of the speech of welcome, and in the word "barriers," a mock tournament, embellished with dialogue and action. Moreover, an examination of the works of the age will disclose an accurate use of these terms. In the masque, from the first, a distinction was drawn between "the masquers," as they were called, and the professional assistants in music, dancing, and acting. The masquers ranged from eight to sixteen, and were the titled people of the court. They were handsomely attired and grouped in positions heightened by scenic arrangement and mechanical contrivance; but little save the creation of an imposing show was expected of them. As the masque developed, it was soon found necessary to enlist the services of professional actors and singers for the presentation of the more premeditated parts. But care was taken not to bring these people into touch with the masquers. As to the parts of the masque, there was first the appearance of the masquers, with their march or descent from their "sieges" or seats of state in the scene, and their first dance: all this was called the "entry"; then there was the "main" or principal dance. All up to this was planned and premeditated. Then followed two extemporal parts,"the dance with the ladies" and the "revels," the latter made up of galliards, lavoltas, and corantos. Lastly, there was the closing march or "going out." That the masque is a purely exotic by-form of the drama, derived mainly either from Italy or from France, can hardly be held in view of the long preparation for it in the annals of the festivities at the English court; but that foreign influences affected its nature and the course of its development in England is not to be denied.

The earliest examples of a masque fulfilling the technical conditions, mentioned above, are to be found in the account of the festivities known as the *Gesta Grayorum*, "betwixt All-Hollantide and Christmas," 1594. This is the most elaborate "Christmassing" recorded, and its solemnities included a complete royal mock court with all the ceremonials thereof: feastings, dancing, dramas, masques, and what not. Of the three masques of the *Gesta Grayorum*, the *Masque of Proteus* presages nearly all the elements subsequently to be so highly developed in the next reign. This production was the work of two well-known young men, Francis Davison, editor a few years later of the last of the lyrical anthologies, *The Poetical Rhapsody*, and Thomas Campion, the musician and lyrist. This masque is important only for its historical position. It involved an obvious enough compliment to the queen, who is likened to "the adamantine rock" that draws all hearts.

With the accession of Elizabeth's successor, a new impetus was given to masquing and entertainments of every kind. The king's progress up to London and through the metropolis to his court was one continued scene of welcome in which the "entertainment" in its technical sense was resorted to again and again. The chief rival poets, on the way, were Jonson and Daniel; and the latter in his *Vision of the Twelve Goddesses*, acted in January, 1604, presented the first of the noble series of court masques which grace the annals of King James. Daniel's masque is everything that a masque should be except dramatic. That want Jonson supplied in his *Masque of Blackness* a year later, adding a wealth and richness of poetic imagination and ingenuity of detail that placed him, at once

without a rival, the accepted entertainer of the court.   This
is not the place in which to list Ben Jonson's masques.   His
activity in this respect continued for thirty years during which
he put forth nine entertainments, three barriers, two anti-
masques and no less than two-and-twenty masques proper,
some of them of extraordinary completeness.   Jonson wrote
more than three times as many masques as all his competitors
— Campion, Daniel, Beaumont, Chapman, Marston, and
Browne — together; and their quality in general may compare to advantage with the best.   In *Hymenæi*, wherein Jonson used his notion of the humors and affections issuing from
the microcosm or globe figuring a man, in the admirably
startling contrasts of the fine *Masque of Queens*, in *The
Golden Age* in which Pallas turns the Iron Age and all his
attendant evils into statues, and in *Pleasure Reconciled to
Virtue* (wherein the character Comus may have been suggested to Milton), we have examples of the poetic beauty,
dramatic aptitude, inventive ingenuity, and resourcefulness
that make Jonson the great master of the masque.

All of these masques were sumptuously "furnished" and
ingeniously staged by the skill of Inigo Jones.   In *Hymenæi*
gigantic golden figures of Atlas and Hercules were the support-
ers of the scene; in the *Viscount Haddington's Masque*, 1608,
golden pilasters, "charged with spoils and trophies, . . . all
wrought round and bold" supported "overhead two personages,
Triumph and Victory, in flying postures and twice as large as
the life, in place of the arch, and holding a garland of myrtle
for a key."   This framing of the scene, utterly in contrast with
the practice of the popular stage, was frequent thereafter.
In *The Masque of Queens*, "an ugly hell   .   .   .   flaming
beneath, smoked unto the top of the roof," and afforded the
setting for the antimasque of witches.   Novelty and surprise
was carefully preconcerted for the moment of the appearance
of the masquers, who were attired with a variety and splendor
of costume that readily explains the extravagant cost of these
spectacles.   At times the masquers were "discovered" sitting
in a glittering temple, or seated in "a great concave shell";
at others they descended from the clouds, or emerged from

"a microcosm or globe." This last is described as "filled with countries and those gilded; where the sea was expressed, heightened with silver waves. This stood, or rather hung (for no axle was seen to support it), and turning softly discovered the first masque." Landscapes and especially the sea were again and again represented, the waves in motion, with Tritons and sea-horses "bigger than life" among them, and even ships, sailing to and fro. Careful effects were those of light and clouds "made artificially to swell and ride like the rack," and the moon in a "heaven, vaulted with blue silk and set with stars of silver which had in them several lights." Even the modern Wagnerian device of the rise of steam to obscure a part of the scene was not unknown to these ingenious performances; and there it was further refined, after a classical precedent, into "a mist of delicate perfumes."

Not the least service that Jonson rendered to the masque was the development of its dramatic capabilities in the element of relief. This was called the antimasque and was always entrusted to professional hands. Thus, in *The Masque of Queens*, the antimasque is a bevy of witches grotesquely contrasted with the beautiful queens that follow. *Mercury Vindicated from the Alchemists* opens with a vivacious scene in which that volatile deity escapes from the furnace of Vulcan and "imperfect creatures with helms and limbecks on their heads" figure in the dances; and in *Love Restored* the scene opens with a satiric little sketch of the difficulties that a plain man experiences in gaining access to these spectacles. In two of Jonson's works of this kind the antimasque has usurped the whole scene and the masque proper fallen out of existence For example, *The [Anti]masque of Christmas* introduces that personage of good cheer with his sons and daughters, Carol, Wassel, and Minced-pie; and the later *Gipsies Metamorphosed* is a humorous if vulgar rendering of a bit of actual low life, appreciated by the king to Jonson's enrichment for the same reason that his majesty so hugely enjoyed *Ignoramus*.

Jonson's activity in the masque carries us well over into the time of Charles. But there were other notable masques of the days of King James as well as Jonson's. In 1610

Daniel furnished *Tethys' Festival* for which Inigo Jones devised no less than three changes of scenery. Novel features of this masque were Daniel's attempt to restrict the performers in it to "great personages," and its extraordinary cost, reckoned at £1600, more than double Jonson's previous masque of that year, *Love Free'd from Ignorance*. In 1613 three masques of unprecedented grandeur were furnished by nobles and by gentlemen of the Inns of Court to grace the marriage of the Princess Elizabeth to the Palsgrave. The first of these was *The Lords' Masque* by Campion. The scene changed four times and the masquers were stars and golden statues called to life. Chapman's masque, which followed the next day, was presented by the gentlemen of the Middle Temple and Lincoln's Inn and exhibited the novel departure of a sumptuous procession to the masquing place by land, in which appeared cars triumphal and a cavalcade attended by two hundred halberdiers, all gorgeously attired. Chapman's work is over-elaborate and its effect could not have been otherwise than tedious. The third grand masque for this wedding was that of Beaumont, presented by the gentlemen of the Inner Temple and Gray's Inn. This was to have been preceded by a water pageant, planned to move up the Thames from Winchester House in a gallant flotilla with music, torches, and the booming of ordnance. But this plan was only partially carried out, as even the Jacobean powers of endurance in pleasure gave out on this third consecutive day of masquing and feasting. Beaumont's masque was performed, however, a few days later, and with the success which its poetic merit deserved. It is of interest to recall that Beaumont offered this masque in his capacity of a member of the Inner Temple, not as a notable writer for the popular stage (a thing that he was content to conceal); and secondly that Sir Francis Bacon, then solicitor-general, was chiefly responsible for the expenses of its furnishing. Another masque on which, as we have seen, Bacon is said to have expended £2000 was the *Masque of Flowers*, 1614, the work of three gentlemen of Gray's Inn. Among Jacobean masques, those of Campion are conspicuous for the care which the author bestowed on the music both vocal and instrumental. A masque of poetical quality and — for the masque — of singular coherency of plot is that of William Browne, entitled *Ulysses and the Sirens,* 1615. The masque continued to rise in expense and sumptuousness until it became in the next reign an impoverishment to the royal purse and a scandal to the serious minded.

As to the nature of the Jacobean masque, its oldest inheritance was allegory, which it derived directly from the morality and the allegorical devices, long in vogue in previous courts. But the allegory of the morality was ingenious and didactic; that of the masque was artistic and eulogistic, and by the necessities of the case modeled on simpler lines. To the cultivated people of the court, suggestion was commonly sufficient, and as Jonson well put it, "a writer should trust somewhat to the capacity of the spectators, especially in these spectacles; where men, besides inquiring eyes, are understood to bring quick ears, and not those sluggish ones of porters and mechanics, that must be bored through with narratives." The Jacobean masque abounds, as might be expected, in classical and mythological personages, imagery, and allusion. This was no affectation in an age in which education came to men, and women too, chiefly by means of the classics. Jonson's ancient lore stood him in good stead in his masques; but he by no means escaped the pedantry of classical reference and learned quotation, a weakness which Daniel and others were quick to see and caustically report. Neither coherency nor anything like unity of design can be said ever to have distinguished the masque, and even satire — except for certain personal lampoons in the antimasquing parts of Jonson's work — was kept decorously in leash in the royal presence. In a consideration of the masque it must be remembered that this was only the most highly elaborated of a large variety of like entertainments that signalized almost every important social function of the day. Speeches of welcome and farewell; pageants, interludes, and processions; Maying, Christmassing, and wassailing; sham tournaments, mock courts with all their ceremonials — such were the incessant pleasures of the day. For example, the lord mayor was installed with elaborate pageantry year after year. More than thirty of these productions between the years 1580 and 1629 remain extant to disclose the character of this civic pageantry, and some of the "shows" are by the hands of the best poets of their time, Peele, Munday, Dekker, Middleton, Marston, and Shirley. Even Jonson's activity was not wholly absorbed by the court.

That the popular stage should reflect this fashion of the day was in the very nature of things. Nearly all the dramatists who wrote in the reign of James employ the elements of the masque more or less organically in plays. To mention only Shakespeare, there is an antic-dance of satyrs in *The Winter's Tale* and a betrothal masque in *The Tempest*, as likewise an antimasque of "strange shapes"; while into *Cymbeline* has been thrust a "dream" with Jupiter descending "on an eagle," a paltry stage device which only a contemporary demand for such stuff could justify or excuse. A more important matter is the more general effect which the extravagant and ingenious settings of masques at court must have had on the plays of the London theaters. It seems impossible to believe, as some have believed, that the popular stage was little affected by the devices of Inigo Jones. That an alert and captious audience such as that of Shakespeare, in his later days, should have remained content with bare boards, when the court plays were set handsomely in perspective and with change of scene, is altogether defiant of the probabilities. There must certainly have been under the influences of such examples a gradual improvement alike in the staging and the costuming of popular dramas, although the precise degree of this change must remain a matter indeterminable. And yet the college plays, the pastoral drama, and the masque remain exotic and, at least during the lifetime of Shakespeare, without the direct current of drama that flowed from Marlowe to Shirley; the first because of the collegian's uninformed and conscious attitude of superiority towards the popular drama, together with the tradition that perpetuated the following of ancient models or their Italian imitations, the pastoral, because its conventional ideals mark the antithesis of the English conception of free country life; and lastly the masque, for its restriction to the entertainment of royalty and because, in its thoughtless pursuit after novelty and its wanton expense and display, the drama evaporated out of it.

CHAPTER XXI

SHAKESPEARE AND THE NEW DRAMA OF FLETCHER

IN any history of the literature or poetry of the times of Elizabeth and James, the drama must bulk large, not only because of Shakespeare, Jonson, and the rest, but because in no other literary form of that age was expression so untrammeled and life capable of representation, both so faithfully and so ideally. In the previous pages we have endeavored to represent this drama in its sudden rise from the immaturities of the first plays in regular dramatic form to the height of comedy in Dekker, Shakespeare, and Jonson, and the summation of tragedy in Marlowe, Shakespeare, and Webster. We have been more concerned with the variety of Elizabethan drama in its range — from the dainty cleverness of Lyly or the poetic fancy of Dekker to the imaginative fulness of Shakespearean comedy, from the actualism of *Arden* or the melodrama of Kyd to the passionate idealism of Juliet or the mastery of terror which *Lear* or *The Duchess of Malfi* depict — than we have been concerned with individual authors in the integrity of their careers. The group of dramatists popularly known as Shakespeare's predecessors fell early out of the race. Dekker, Chapman, Jonson and Middleton, who began writing in the middle nineties, all continued to write after Shakespeare's death, although the distinctive work of every one of them falls strictly within his lifetime. Marston, Webster, and Tourneur condensed their shorter dramatic careers into a period almost coincident with the last ten years of Shakespeare's life. So that of the great Elizabethans in the drama that remain — Beaumont and Fletcher, Massinger, Ford, and Shirley — only the last three are strictly post-Shakespearean. Beaumont was always an amateur, and he gave up writing for the stage early. The triumphs that gave to Fletcher the succession to Shakespeare's primacy were made before the latter's death. In the present chapter our concern is with the relations and characteristics of Beaumont and Fletcher as dramatists, with the Fletcherian dramatic departure called tragicomedy and its bearings on the group of Shakespeare's plays known as "dramatic romances." It was tragicomedy, in the hands of Fletcher, that developed a new variety of the romantic drama which was potently to affect what came after; for it is in his plays that we meet, almost for the first time, the exaggerated romanticism that led through successive steps in the next reign to the heroic play of Davenant and Dryden.

While it is obvious that no actual combination of tragic and comic elements could justify so contradictory a term as tragicomedy, the word was employed by writers of the time of James to denote a romantic drama involving serious passion, yet ending happily: and such plays speedily acquired an extraordinary popularity. Tragicomedy is not necessarily melodrama, but it easily degenerates into such. Its dangers are false sentiment and perverted ethics; and it is liable to sacrifice the logic of events to dramatic surprise. The truest tragicomedy is that in which the circumstances of the drama and its clash of personalities are such that the outcome is naturally uncertain. *The Merchant of Venice* trembles in the balance between tragedy and comedy in the supreme scene of the trial, and only Shylock's final hesitancy to accept, with his own destruction, a full and final revenge preserves the drama within the latter category.

Of John Fletcher we have already heard in this book as a writer of comedies in the manner of Middleton and as the author of a poetical pastoral drama, *The Faithful Shepherdess.* Fletcher was born in 1579, the son of Richard Fletcher, Dean of Peterborough and later Bishop of London. The bishop's brother was Giles Fletcher, author of the sonnet-sequence, *Licia*, and both his sons, Giles the Younger and Phineas Fletcher have found their place in the pages above as followers of the Spenserian allegorized pastoral. John Fletcher, the dramatist, thus came of a notable and literary family. He attended Bene't College, Cambridge, as a pensioner in 1591;

and, as a younger son, received no patrimony except a part of his father's library. Much praised and esteemed by his contemporaries and frequently mentioned for his poetry, we know surprisingly little what manner of man Fletcher was, and his relations to his fellows, Shakespeare, Beaumont, Massinger, and the rest, are vague and derivable for the most part by inference. The custom of Fletcher's age habitually associated his name with that of Francis Beaumont, a man five years his junior, of much the same station in life, but of whom we know rather more. Beaumont was likewise a younger brother. His father was Sir Francis Beaumont of Grace Dieu in Leicestershire, a justice of the Common Pleas. Young Beaumont received his education at Broadgate's Hall, Oxford, where he was admitted a gentleman commoner in 1597, and at the Inner Temple, for which society we have already found him writing a masque under the patronage of Sir Francis Bacon. We do not know when Beaumont and Fletcher became intimate; not unlikely it was through the acquaintance of each with Ben Jonson, who drew to himself alike from his convivial habits, his geniality, and his learning and poetry, the Bohemian spirits of his day, and held them in allegiance at the Mermaid and later in the famous Apollo room of the Devil Tavern. We are certain that there was personal friendship and collaboration between Fletcher and Beaumont; and we are equally sure that the publication, in the folio of 1647, of the collected plays of the former with those in which the latter had shared, has had the effect of giving greater weight to this association than is at all warranted by the facts. In this very volume we may feel sure that there are more than twice as many plays in which Fletcher's collaborator or reviser was Philip Massinger. And when it is recalled that Beaumont died a young man in 1616, just a month before Shakespeare, while Fletcher continued an active dramatist up to his death by the plague nearly ten years later, enough has been said to make patent that the expression, "the plays of Beaumont and Fletcher," applied to any large body of dramas in which the latter had a hand, is a pure misnomer.

The most conspicuous difference between these two authors consists in the fact that Fletcher was a professional dramatist; Beaumont was not. Beaumont does not appear to have sanctioned the publication of any of his works, his name appearing during his lifetime only on the title of his *Masque of the Inner Temple and Gray's Inn*. It seems not improbable that the two young men began authorship independently, Fletcher in that direct picturing of London life that we associate with the name of Middleton; Beaumont in a closer following of Jonson's comedy of humors to which he added a quality of burlesque all his own. Beaumont, it has been surmised, first wrote for the Children of Paul's from about 1604 to 1606 or 1607, Fletcher's earliest unaided work being for the Children of his Majesty's Revels. In 1610 both authors were writing for the King's company, having brought with them work previously written together. Tradition relates that Beaumont's part in this collaboration was advisory and critical; and even Ben Jonson, his senior by ten years, addressed him enthusiastically in an epigram beginning: "How I do love thee, Beaumont, and thy Muse," and elsewhere with a deference surprising in a man of Jonson's temper. However, it is not to be questioned that Beaumont did more than advise and criticize in some of the dramas attributed to him and Fletcher in their immortal partnership. Indeed, without the charmed Shakespearean circle, there is no question of criticism relating to Elizabethan drama that has been so much argued and exploited. Into its niceties the purposes of this book can not demand that we enter. But this much must be said, for Beaumont falls entirely within our period, however the Fletcherian plays at large may extend beyond it. A consideration of work which we have reason to believe only Beaumont's discloses — according to the critics — that he was the truer Elizabethan, that is, his was the higher artistic earnestness. A genius for tragedy, a deeper insight into character, especially in the realization of the nature of his women, a power of pathos, a breadth of humor and good-natured satire — all these things are posited of the younger dramatist. While in contrast, Fletcher is accused of a want of artistic seriousness, allowed to possess "a pretty, playful fancy," abundant wit but a lighter quality of humor, and a more superficial insight into human nature and conduct. Fletcher's genius is clever, ready, and off-hand, but often careless and morally irresponsible: and the styles of the two men bear out this contrast. Beaumont, after the custom of the older dramatists, employs prose and rime at times to vary his blank-verse, the phrasing of which exhibits a moderate freedom not unlike the self-contained and more carefully wrought verse of Jonson. Beaumont is, moreover, as careful as Jonson himself as to the numbering of his syllables, seldom admitting a redundancy to alter the strict decasyllabic character of his lines.

> Presumptuous Iris, I could make thee dance,
> Till thou forgott'st thy lady's messages,
> And ran'st back crying to her. Thou shalt know
> My power is more; only my breath and this
> Shall move fix'd stars, and force the firmament
> To yield the Hyades, who govern showers
> And dewy clouds, in whose dispersèd drops
> Thou form'st the shape of thy deceitful bow.

In contrast with these lines from Beaumont's *Masque*, we may take these opening words of *Bonduca*, as unquestionably Fletcher's in his confirmed later manner:

> The hardy Romans! oh, ye gods of Britain!
> The rust of arms, the blushing shame of soldiers!
> Are these the men that conquer by inheritance?
> The fortune-makers? these the Julians,
> That with the sun measure the end of nature,
> Making the world but one Rome and one Cæsar?
> Shame, how they flee! Cæsar's soft soul dwell's in 'em,
> Their mothers got 'em sleeping, Pleasure nursed 'em;
> Their bodies sweat with sweet oils, love's allurements,
> Not lusty arms.

Here all is in contrast. The style is easy and rapid; the construction loose, cumulative, and at times rambling; the verse distinguished by an incessant use of redundant syllables, commonly at the end of each line, transmuting the usual measure of ten syllables to one habitually of eleven with a pause at the end of each line. To speak technically, the hendecasyllabic verse end-stopped is characteristic of Fletcher as it is characteristic of no other poet within the range of English letters; and out of this departure in dramatic verse, Fletcher made not only a novel, but a remarkably successful and adaptable medium for the conveyance of dramatic dialogue.

With these criteria of contrast, scholars have portioned out the parts of those plays which, from their dates or for other reasons, may be supposed to be the work of both Beaumont and Fletcher, with a further corrective, referable to a later revision in some cases by Massinger. The last-named dramatist does not concern us, as his work falls beyond our period. In general it may be said that these tests of authorship are satisfactory; but it is easy to exaggerate their importance and to forget that after all joint authorship, in a product like a play, means the presence of both authors throughout, or we can expect no such unity as even these Elizabethan productions often present. The present writer professes a profound distrust of the glib assignments of scenes, passages, and lines to given authors and given periods of their activity; and he believes that, in the Beaumont-Fletcher-Massinger group of plays, Beaumont has been assigned, in general, rather too large a part, and Massinger much too subtly traced.

With King James a few years on his throne, the taste of the time had undergone certain changes and modifications. While we can hardly say that men had surfeited of tragedy, at least they had become less fond of that strong wine, or rather, of the wholesome drug in shape of a moral application which it frequently involved; and they preferred to go home pleased rather than thoughtful. Again, the new performances at court, called masques, suddenly developed, as we have seen, into extraordinary cost and splendor, and the popular stage was immediately affected. The craving, too, and demand for novelty strained the drama in every direction to make the realistic more actual and coarse, the romantic more extravagant and unnatural; to deepen the motives of passion and crime, if such were possible, and lighten comedy into greater

frivolity, farce, and fantasticality. At this juncture came
Fletcher, one of the cleverest playwrights in the range of
letters, to combine the courage of the innovator with a ready
aptitude for seizing the occasion. The result was the invention
of a new kind of romantic drama, founded on contrast and
heightened situation, which proceeded with great rapidity of
action and was carried on, to a certain degree, by means of
personages more or less presented in types. This novel
drama he served in the new, lithe, and supple variety of blank-
verse described above, so colloquial that it did away with the
necessity of interlarded prose and yet retained the power to
become eminently poetical at need.

The typical play of this new class is *Philaster*, referred to
in an epigram of Davies of Hereford in 1610, and the work
of both Beaumont and Fletcher. *Philaster* abounds in contrasts. There is first the usurping king and the true prince
Philaster, in his rôle as the true lover and as a noble gentleman,
also set off against the ignoble voluptuary, Prince Pharamond.
Both are suitors to the peerless princess, Arethusa, whose
steadfastness and pure love is thrown into relief as compared
with the wanton conduct of her waiting-woman, Megra; and
whose love, requited by Philaster, is once more contrasted
with the pathetic, unrequited devotion of the page, Bellario,
who serves Philaster and aids him in his courtship of Arethusa,
though actually a maiden devotedly in love with him. We
have here a drama of sentimental interest thrust into the
midst of elements heroically tragic. The action is swift,
full of event and of varied emotion; and the personages are
governed by prearranged ruling qualities from first to last.
Types are the result. *Philaster* gave to the drama the heroic
but unreasoning hero; the blunt, out-spoken soldier; the disconsolate and love-lorn maiden; and the semi-comic poltroon.
None the less *Philaster* is in many respects an admirable
drama and deserving of the popularity that it long enjoyed.
Its novelty must have been startling in its time; and while the
heroic conception of some of its characters, especially the
prince, has given him an irrational inconsistency and sapped
somewhat the moral basis of his conduct, the poetry of the

play, its sentiment and pathos, are worthy of all the praise that they customarily receive. The source of *Philaster* has not been discovered by the indefatigable seekers in the quarries of literature, and although a more or less direct influence of the Spanish *comedias de capa y espada* has been surmised, the ingenious plotting of *Philaster* is doubtless the invention of the authors.

The likelihood of this origin is strengthened when we find almost the same range of material employed again and again with ingenious variety to repeat the same effective result. *The Maid's Tragedy, Cupid's Revenge*, and *A King and No King*, all first staged between 1609 and 1611, are plays closely resembling *Philaster* in plot, construction, style and characterization; and further examples of this likeness are not far to seek within the range of the Beaumont-Fletcher-Massinger plays. On the other hand these general likenesses are readily exaggerated. *The Maid's Tragedy* is a powerful drama in which the heroic but unreasoning hero becomes the bewildered and unstable Amintor; and the evil and spiteful trull, Megra (in *Philaster*), is replaced by the tragic figure of Evadne, wrought to evil by ambition atoned in death. In *A King and No King*, correspondingly, the heroic Philaster is replaced by the pseudo-king, Arbaces, intentionally represented as a boaster and ignoble, while Spaconia, who corresponds to the love-lorn maidens, Euphrasia and Aspasia of the other two plays, is a young woman of resources and contrives in the end to keep her prince for herself.

An ingenious theory, which has somehow obtained much currency through the sanction of recognized authority,[1] extends the criteria of this group of Beaumont and Fletcher to the later work of Shakespeare. This theory holds, in a word, that Shakespeare was seriously affected, in these latest romances, by the new Fletcherian tragicomedy, and that this influence worked to the detriment of Shakespeare's art, destroying especially the strong lines of his characterization and

[1] See especially A. H. Thorndike, *The Influence of Beaumont and Fletcher on Shakespeare*, 1901, and his excellent edition of *The Maid's Tragedy* and *Philaster*, 1906.

reducing his art to the measure of the man he imitated.   This theory would make Imogen, Hermione, Perdita, and Miranda women less vital than their elder sisters of tragedy or comedy, and regard them as the kindred of the heroines of Fletcher. Now if the list of Shakespeare's plays be examined, we shall find besides the clearly defined group of comedies, histories, and tragedies, several about which there may well arise a doubt as to whether they belong to any of these accepted categories. *Troilus and Cressida*, which we have already considered, is a problematic drama, too serious and bitter for comedy yet rising neither to the height of tragic passion nor disposing of its dramatis personæ in death to expiate crime.   So, too, *Timon of Athens*, though it concludes with the death of the hero, is rather a biographical narrative dramatized than a tragedy as that term is ordinarily employed. *Timon* is a story of the ancient world; and perhaps as classically set forth as we could expect of the master of romantic art, with Painter's *Palace of Pleasure* as an immediate model. But *Troilus* is redolent of medieval romance; and so too is *Pericles*, doubtless on the stage by 1608.   In short, to the three dramas, *Cymbeline*, *The Winter's Tale*, and *The Tempest*, usually included in this group called "dramatic romances," we may add *Troilus*, *Timon*, and *Pericles* before, and perhaps *The Two Noble Kinsmen*, if Shakespeare had a hand in it, after.   Common characteristics of these plays are considerable looseness in construction, recalling the epic qualities of the old chronicle plays; far less strenuous passion than that of the tragedies; and though there is comedy in them all, merriment is far from their dominant tone.   Once more, these dramas delight in strange lands or wanderings over unknown seas, in shipwreck and other adventure, in children and kindred lost or estranged, found and reconciled.   Moreover, these dramas at times trespass imaginatively, as in *The Tempest*, on the supernatural.   It may be noted in passing that these are elements altogether distinguishable from the courtly atmosphere of intrigue and the incessant dramatic contrast of the *Philaster* group.

Pericles, Prince of Tyre, was first published in 1609 and

went through five quartos before it was collected into the third folio of Shakespeare's works in 1664. The story of *Apollonius of Tyre*, of which *Pericles* is a dramatized version, is one of the most generally diffused in fiction; and the immediate sources of the drama appear to have been the tale as told by Gower in his *Confessio Amantis*, and the prose version of Lawrence Twine in his *Pattern of Painful Adventures*, 1576. The circumstance that *Pericles* was not included in the first folio, that the workmanship is exceedingly unequal, and the text corrupt has caused doubt to be cast on Shakespeare's sharing in it; and William Rowley and George Wilkins, a minor dramatist who published a novel on the subject about the date of the play, have been named as Shakespeare's possible collaborators. There are scenes unmistakably Shakespeare's, however, in *Pericles*, no matter what inferior hand may have supplied the wooden choruses spoken by Gower, and several unworthy scenes. As to Shakespearean quality, few scenes are lovelier than that in which the distracted Pericles, sunk in melancholy, is restored to his faculties by the sweet singing of his own lost daughter.

> *Pericles.* I am great with woe, and shall deliver weeping.
> My dearest wife was like this maid, and such a one
> My daughter might have been. My queen's square brows;
> Her stature to an inch; as wand-like straight;
> As silver-voic'd; her eyes as jewel-like
> And cas'd as richly; in pace another Juno;
> Who starves the ears she feeds, and makes them hungry,
> The more she gives them speech. Where do you live?
> *Marina.* Where I am but a stranger. From the deck
> You may discern the place.
> *Per.* Where were you bred?
> And how achiev'd you these endowments, which
> You make more rich to owe?
> *Mar.* If I should tell my history, it would seem
> Like lies disdain'd in the reporting.
> *Per.* Prithee, speak.
> Falseness cannot come from thee; for thou look'st
> Modest as Justice, and thou seem'st a palace
> For the crown'd Truth to dwell in. I will believe thee,

> And make my senses credit thy relation
> To points that seem impossible; for thou look'st
> Like one I lov'd indeed. What were thy friends?
> Didst thou not say, when I did push thee back —
> Which was when I perceiv'd thee — that thou cam'st
> From good descending?
>   *Mar.* So indeed I did.

And so the beautiful lines run on to the joy of certainty:

>   *Per.* O Helicanus, strike me, honored sir;
> Give me a gash, put me to present pain;
> Lest this great sea of joys rushing upon me
> O'erbear the shores of my mortality,
> And drown me with their sweetness. O, come hither,
> Thou that beget'st him that did thee beget;
> Thou that wast born at sea, buried at Tarsus,
> And found at sea again! O Helicanus,
> Down on thy knees, thank the holy gods as loud
> As thunder threatens us. This is Marina.
> .   .   .   .
> Now, blessing on thee! Rise, thou art my child.
> Give me fresh garments. Mine own, Helicanus;
> She is not dead at Tarsus, as she should have been,
> By savage Cleon. She shall tell thee all;
> When thou shalt kneel, and justify in knowledge
> She is thy very princess.

All this and much more of Pericles we may feel assured is the very Shakespeare.

Pericles may be said to unite the "romance" with the tale of adventure as *Timon* touches classical story. So *Cymbeline* combines the apparently discordant elements of legendary chronicle history with the "romance." *Cymbeline* was first printed in the folio and may be dated about 1609. The legendary history of King Cymbeline, Shakespeare derived from his habitual source, Holinshed's *Chronicles*, the romantic story from some version (French, Italian, or English) of a tale of the *Decameron* of Boccaccio. In fact, all the features of the wager of Posthumous, the repulse of Iachimo, the false tokens, the attempted punishment and wandering of Imogen are to be found in a tale of exceedingly wide diffusion, a point to be remembered when "the indefensible conduct of Post-humous" is dilated on by the psychologic critic.   To the present author *Cymbeline* is one of the most beautiful of the Shakespearean plays.   He does not look for a closely-knit and intricately-woven plot in a drama of this kind, and can enjoy, without strictures, a story that straggles from Britain to Rome and back again and unites a romantic tale of the Renaissance with a hotchpotch of legendary battles.   Tragic as is the theme of a pair of married lovers parted for the nonce by villainous practices, he does not look for the storm of passionate agony that destroyed Othello in every story involving jealousy; and he registers no complaints that King Cymbeline is not King Lear.   Moreover, he feels that he can appreciate the wholly adequate portraiture of the Iachimo without discant on the stronger acid with which the picture of Iago is bitten in, and delight in the sweet wifely devotion of Imogen without remembering that Cleopatra, on the stage in the previous year, is a more astonishing personage.   Wisdom, poetry, happiness of phrase, and sufficiency in dramatic portraiture, so far as dramatic portraiture comports with the quality of the play, all are as characteristic of *Cymbeline* as of other and earlier plays of Shakespeare.   It is time to protest against the "discovery" that Shakespeare was prematurely old and decaying in his genius at forty-five, careless in his art, and content to leave his throne to sit on the footstools of his younger contemporaries.

The *Winter's Tale*, on the stage by 1610 or 1611, is a dramatized version of *Pandosto*, one of the most pleasing pastoral stories of Shakespeare's old competitor, Robert Greene.   But when we say of any play of Shakespeare's that it is "a dramatized version," we are really noting one of its most trivial similarities to something that has gone before, a thing perhaps little more important than a mention of the material out of which the David of Michael Angelo had been chiseled or the Perseus of Cellini cast.   Shakespeare, in *The Winter's Tale*, preserves the life of Hermione instead of permitting her, after her original, Bellaria in Greene's story, to die of grief.   Shakespeare's King Leontes, when his un-

reasonable jealousy and his wicked defiance of the oracle have
lost him his wife and children, spends years, we are led to
infer, in repentance and remains true to the memory of his
unparalleled queen. This makes possible the reconciliation
in the end and the joy and hope that springs from the restoration of the lost ones and Perdita's marriage to her Prince
Florizel. But it is not only in these and in several minor
changes that Shakespeare betters Greene's plot for dramatic
use, but in the invention and introduction of new characters.
Antigonus, incomparable Paulina, Mopsa, Dorcas, the clown,
and above all Autolycus — all these are Shakespeare's invention. Where in all Vagabondia shall we find so fascinating,
so disreputable a rogue as Autolycus?

> When daffodils begin to peer,
>   With heigh! the doxy over the dale,
> Why, then comes in the sweet o' the year;
>   For the red blood reigns in the winter's pale.
>
> The white sheet bleaching on the hedge
>   With heigh! the sweet birds, O, how they sing!
> Doth set my pugging tooth on edge;
>   For a quart of ale is a dish for a king.
>
> .   .   .   .

My traffic is sheets; when the kite builds, look to lesser linen.
My father nam'd me Autolycus, who being, as I am, litter'd under
Mercury, was likewise a snapper-up of unconsidered trifles. With
die and drab I purchas'd this caparison, and my revenue is the silly
cheat. Gallows and knock are too powerful on the highway; beating
and hanging are terrors to me; for the life to come, I sleep out the
thought of it.

Last of the plays of Shakespeare comes *The Tempest*,
acted, we know, during the festivities attending the marriage
of the Princess Elizabeth to the Palsgrave in 1613, along with
many other plays and the grand masques of Campion, Chapman, and Beaumont, though certainly not written (as some
have over-ingeniously surmised) for the occasion. In the
autumn of 1610, news of the shipwreck of an English vessel,
the Sea Venture, on the island of Bermuda, reached London.
To the strangeness of the tropical landscape and the fact that

the island was overrun by wild hogs, the superstition of the
sailors had added that it was visited by strange sounds and
haunted by the devil. Several pamphlets appeared on the
topic. On this hint of the moment, Shakespeare seems to
have constructed the plot of *The Tempest*, adding to the conception of a sea-isle haunted by unclean beasts (embodied in
Caliban), the enchantment of Ariel, breathing in musical
zephyrs and doing the will of a beneficent magician. The
story of *The Tempest* is slight enough. It has recently been
referred with confidence to "a collection of mediocre stories"
entitled *Noches de Invierno* by an obscure Spanish author,
Antonio de Eslava, published at Pamplona in the year
1609. But, once more, do we read *The Tempest* any more
than we read *A Midsummer-Night's Dream* only for the story?
And are we to expect any more of these lovely citizens of an
enchanted island — with their ministering spirits and demons,
even of their foils of the world without, on whom enchantments
work miracles — those strong lines of personality that belong
to the personages of Shakespeare whose struggle is with the
primary passions of human nature? Delicacy and elevation,
as terms applied to the imagination, are not synonymous with
weakness and attenuation. It is not "the big pow-pow manner," as Sir Walter Scott somewhere calls it, that alone in-
dicates genius and the maintenance of poetic power. There
are defects in *The Tempest*, exquisite production of a controlled
imagination that it is; but these are less, if at all, the defects
of failing powers, or due to the imitation of lesser men, than
of that carelessness as to things in which he is not immediately
interested which Shakespeare shows everywhere, but in smaller
degree than almost any of his contemporaries among the
dramatists. *The Tempest* was an immediate success and with
The Winter's Tale continued popular long after the author's
death, to be revived after the Restoration. There are those
whose imaginations can not reach to the dramatist's art, and
who therefore disbelieve in that high impersonality in which
the author loses himself in his creations. To such *The Tempest* is only a last leaf in what they call Shakespeare's autobiography, and explainable as an elaborated allegory in which

Shakespeare took leave of the stage in the person of the magician Prospero, abjuring his art in the well-known passage,
concluding:

> I 'll break my staff,
> Bury it certain fathoms in the earth,
> And deeper than did ever plummet sound
> I 'll drown my book.

To those who recognize the larger nature of drama, who can
grasp the idea of an art higher than that of the egotist, in the
power of the true dramatic poet to thrill with a responsive
sympathy for the emotion of any one of his personages, however differently situated in life and feeling from himself, there
is no need to interpret Prospero (nor any other of the characters
that crowd his pages) as a projection of Shakespeare himself
into his creative work.

On the external side there is not much to chronicle as to
the last years of the great poet's life. There seems reason to
believe, from lately discovered material, that Shakespeare
was later in London than 1611, the usual date set by the
biographers for his retirement to Stratford. It may be doubted
if he gave up the stage altogether; though he must have parted
with his shares in the Blackfriars and the Globe at some time
between 1613, when he is recited in a legal document as a
sharer, and the date of his death, when he was no longer such.
Whatever the date of Shakespeare's retirement, he must have
left in the hands of his company some plays incomplete and
unfinished. We know that his position as chief dramatist
to the King's company was immediately filled by Fletcher,
and abundant evidence exists to show the association of the
two men for a time in their craft. For example, in 1653 a
bookseller named Moseley licensed for publication a play
described as "*The History of Cardenio* by Fletcher and Shakespeare." This was doubtless the play described as *Cardenno*
or *Cardenna*, twice acted by the company of Shakespeare in
1613. No trace of it exists, and it is doubtful if Moseley obtained the right to publish it. *The Double Falsehood*, a
drama on what was doubtless the original in the Spanish of

Cervantes of *Cardenio*, was published as Shakespeare's by Theobald in 1727; but there are no traces of the master's hand in it.

Two plays, the work of Shakespeare and Fletcher, survive. These are *The Two Noble Kinsmen* and *Henry VIII*. The former was first printed in 1634, with this statement on the title: "by the memorable worthies of their time, Mr. John Fletcher and Mr. William Shakespeare." Many critics have agreed to accept this ascription of authorship, though differences of opinion have arisen as to how much is Shakespeare's and whether parts, at one time attributed to him, may not be revisions by the hand of Massinger. If Shakespeare is in *The Two Noble Kinsmen*, his part is confined to the main plot, Chaucer's *Knight's Tale of Palamon and Arcite*, already twice dramatized on the English stage. As for the rest of *The Two Noble Kinsmen*, it is not notable among the dramas of Beaumont and Fletcher, in the second folio of whose works, that of 1679, it was included. The question of authorship in *Henry VIII* is not dissimilar. It was during a performance of this play in June, 1613, that a blazing wadding from a cannon on the stage of the Globe Theater ignited the thatch on the roof and burned the edifice to the ground. There is no proof that this was a first preformance, and it seems reasonable to believe (on the basis of allusions in the prologue of *Henry VIII* to a play of Samuel Rowley, entitled *When You See Me You Know Me*, 1604), that an earlier form of the Shakespearean play at some time existed. It is much more likely that Shakespeare should first have used such a subject when the recent death of Queen Elizabeth caused a momentary revival of interest in her history and in that of her parents, than it is to think that Shakespeare revived, without assignable reason, a kind of drama, out of fashion in 1613 for nearly ten years. None the less we may feel sure that the play of *Henry VIII* as we have it is of approximately the latter period, and the hand of Fletcher seems unmistakable in it. The parts of King Henry, Katherine of Aragon, and Cardinal Wolsey for the most part, are written in the best manner of Shakespeare. Those who hold the alternative view, which assumes that

Shakespeare, in the parts that resemble Fletcher, deliberately imitated the latter, must explain why the mimicry was confined only to certain scenes and followed only the minor personages.

Let us return to the dramatic career of Beaumont and Fletcher within the period of Shakespeare's life. Aside from Beaumont's *Masque* and his *Woman Hater*, 1606, a frank following of the Jonsonian comedy of humors, to Beaumont's single authorship is now usually assigned the diverting burlesque of the old heroical drama, *The Knight of the Burning Pestle*, 1607, a satire which the influence of Jonson, once more, may have suggested, and one by no means appreciated by the bourgeois auditors of the old plays therein ridiculed. On the other hand, Fletcher, too, indulged in experiment; and his attempt to popularize the exotic pastoral drama in *The Faithful Shepherdess* was, as we have seen, not more successful. There seems reason to believe that another early effort of Fletcher was the comedy entitled *The Woman's Prize or the Tamer Tamed*, an entertaining sequel to Shakespeare's *Taming of the Shrew*, described above as the play in which Katherina, having died early, is succeeded by a second wife, Maria, who proceeds to tame the valiant Petruchio in a manner as vigorous as it is resourceful and complete. It was by way of such experiments that these clever young dramatists made their way to the inventive comedy of manners that Fletcher especially later practised and to the new drama of Philaster-type already described.

Fletcherian comedy includes an interesting group of dramas of London life in which Middleton's art is at times bettered. Such plays are *The Scornful Lady* and *Wit at Several Weapons*, repeating several familiar comedy figures; *Monsieur Thomas*, in which a diverting variety of scapegrace who gives his name to the play is treated in foil with another of Fletcher's witty and capable women. Even better is *Wit Without Money*, in which the right of a free spirit to scorn what all men love is upheld with results which, thanks to another clever and understanding woman, the world does not always mete out to such unthrifts. *The Night Walker or the Little Thief* is intricate and well plotted; but it descends in its representation of the lower haunts of the London of its day to a realism that outdoes Middleton at his lowest and suggests the degenerate comedies of Restoration times. All these plays fall between 1607 and 1615 and the dates of their writing, as well as the relations of the authorship of most of them, remain in dispute among the critics. In several plays Fletcher carried the comedy of contemporary manners over into foreign countries, sketching, none the less, from his countrymen about him. *The Coxcomb*, of indeterminate scene, mingles characters with Italian and English names, and combines a plot containing romantic elements with comedy of manners. Ricardo, the hero, seems in his weakness for the wine-cup and his remorse for the consequences of that weakness, a reminiscence of Cassio. Other examples of such plays within our period are *The Captain*, an unpleasing story, the scene Venice; and *The Honest Man's Fortune*, laid in Paris. In this last excellent comedy is set forth the effects, on true friends and false, of a loss of fortune in the case of a gentleman, Montaigne, of admirable character and fortitude. Both these plays have been dated near to 1613. In the latter, Fletcher was only the ruling spirit of four collaborators.

More akin to the tragicomedies of Philaster-type for the romantic element in them are such comedies as *The Beggars' Bush*, which has been thought to have been originally the work of Beaumont, and the several beautiful tragicomedies in which Fletcher laid under contribution the wealth of story which the literature of Spain, then in the height of its bloom, was spreading over Europe. Although *The Knight of the Burning Pestle* is directly referable to *Don Quixote*, it was not until a year or two before Shakespeare's death that Fletcher, apparently, showed English dramatists the way to the treasures of Spanish literature. Strange as it may seem, there is no reason to believe that Fletcher was acquainted with the Spanish language, for all his sources of this kind are traceable in translations, principally French. Even more strange is it that no one of the contemporaries of Shakespeare has as yet been proved to have borrowed unmistakably from the contemporary Spanish drama. Cervantes and several of his countrymen furnished material to the playwrights of the later time of James and of Charles, but all these sources are in fiction. The drama of Lope de Vega and Cervantes had practically no touch with that of Shakespeare and Fletcher. In *The Chances*, 1615, perhaps Fletcher's earliest play on a Spanish original, levy is made on the famous *Novelas Exemplares* of Cervantes with the result of a very charming comedy, somewhat hardened in line and broadened in humor as compared with its admirable original. *The Chances* continued long a popular play. Of none of the other Spanish plays in which Fletcher had a hand can we be sure that they were written within the period before us.

With respect to Fletcherian tragedy, there can be little question of the excellence of *The Maid's Tragedy* however its "Philaster-types," if critics will so have it, were staled on the later stage by incessant repetition. There is a quality so truly heroic in worldly and wicked Evadne, suddenly awakened from the security of her sin to the enormity of it, there is something, too, so pitiful in the faltering Amintor, whose spaniel-like fidelity to the king who has wronged and outraged him almost as man was never wronged and outraged before, that we are carried away by the originality of their story as well as by the pathos of the unhappy page-maiden Aspasia and the pervading poetic spirit of the whole drama. Fletcher never bettered *The Maid's Tragedy*. Perhaps he never again in tragedy worked in such perfect adjustment with his friend Beaumont. But several other Fletcherian tragedies are memorable. Passing *Cupid's Revenge*, a lesser play of the Philaster-group, we find the next tragedy, now to be placed before 1614, in *Bonduca* which from its subject, the clash of ancient Britain with Rome, suggests the background of *Cymbeline*. *Bonduca* is a signal example of Fletcher's happy art in construction. The story of Boadicea and that of Caractacus, in defiance of history, are happily combined in one plot; and the touch of a genuine pathos infused in the invented story of the little Prince Hengo. Fletcher's Caratach is a fine heroic character, sure to be effective in the hands of a robust and declamatory actor; and the difficult war scenes

are handled with a restraint and ability to suggest where
portrayal is impossible, that causes us to realize how far we
have traveled from the crude realism of the old chronicle
plays. In the following passage we can feel Fletcher's power
of pathos. Caratach is in flight with the little Prince Hengo
whom he has preserved among many perils, and the Roman
soldiers are close upon their tracks:

> *Caratach.* How does my boy?
> *Hengo.* I would do well; my heart's well;
> I do not fear.
> *Car.* My good boy!
> *Hengo.* I know, uncle,
> We must all die; my little brother died,
> I saw him die, and he died smiling; sure,
> There's no great pain in 't, uncle. But, pray, tell me,
> Whither must we go when we are dead?
> *Car.* Strange questions! —   [*Aside.*
> Why, the blessed'st place, boy! ever sweetness
> And happiness dwells there.
> *Hengo.* Will you come to me?
> *Car.* Yes, my sweet boy.
> *Hengo.* Mine aunt too, and my cousins?
> *Car.* All, my good child.
> *Hengo.* No Romans, uncle?
> *Car.* No, boy.
> *Hengo.* I should be loth to meet them there.
> *Car.* No ill men,
> That live by violence and strong oppression,
> Come hither; 't is for those the gods love, good men.
> *Hengo.* Why, then, I care not when I go, for surely
> I am persuaded they love me: I never
> Blasphemed 'em, uncle, nor transgressed my parents;
> I always said my prayers.
> *Car.* Thou shalt go, then,
> Indeed thou shalt.
> *Hengo.* When they please.
> *Car.* That's my good boy!
> Art thou not weary, Hengo?
> *Hengo.* Weary, uncle!
> I have heard you say you have marched all day in armor.

Car. I have, boy.

Hengo. Am not I your kinsman?

Car. Yes.

Hengo. And am not I as fully allied unto you
In those brave things as blood?

Car. Thou art too tender —

Hengo. To go upon my legs? they were made to bear me.
I can play twenty mile a-day; I see no reason,
But, to preserve my country and myself,
I should march forty.

Car. What wouldst thou be, living
To wear a man's strength!

Hengo. Why, a Caratach,
A Roman-hater, a scourge sent from Heaven
To whip these proud thieves from our kingdom. Hark!
                                        [*Drum within.*

Scarcely less interesting is the only other tragedy of Fletcher
that falls within our scope, *Valentinian*, also now to be placed
before 1614. This contribution of Fletcher to tragedy on
classic story is almost as pervasively romantic in tone as that
which touches the field of chronicle history. Here, out of an
obscure anecdote of Procopius, the dramatist has constructed
a tragedy in which, although his favorite types — the lustful
tyrant, the steadfast wife, the bluff heroic soldier — recur, all
is so adequately and so admirably expressed and handled with
so sure a hand that we wonder why the Fletcherian art, notwithstanding, does not fully satisfy.[1]

Fletcher, when all has been said, is the completest of English dramatists, and this was alike his distinction and his serious limitation. The poetry of Marlowe, more commonly his
passion, bore forward his drama, until he attained the control
of *Edward II*, and even then the art of tragedy was as yet form-
ative. Jonson was the playwright of theory, though often of

[1] The only two other plays of Fletcher, usually dated prior to
1616, are *Thierry and Theodoret* which, however, based on an earlier
play, is, as we have it and for its political allusions, properly placed
after 1617. *Love's Cure*, sometimes placed at 1606, is founded on a
play of De Castro, printed in Spain for the first time about a month
before Fletcher's death. It is probably not his.

most triumphant practice. But he went ever his own way,
gratified and complaisant if the public went with him, stubborn
and intractable when the tide was against him. Shakespeare
had the finer gift, to seem to follow where he really led, to guide
his public and raise it to an appreciation of his own artistic
standards. This he did less by the persistent presentation of
ideals, impossible of attainment, than by that human element in
his art that offers to each man some one intimate point of
contact thus to touch life at innumerable points. Fletcher
was above all an adaptable genius. There was a great dramatic literature behind him to warn him and to guide There
were the great men, his fellow dramatists, practising their art
around him. And there was the stage itself, with its traditions
and its practical lessons, and that difficult, exacting, and untam-
able Jacobean audience. To all these things Fletcher readily adjusted himself and determined from the first that his auditors should have what they craved. To this end he toned
up his plays, heightening every contrast, hastening the rapidity
of the action, sharpening the surprise of climax and the unex-
pectedness of the outcome. And in this process he unknit the
sequence of cause and effect. The plays of Fletcher and his
group are less true to the ethics of life and of art than the
greater drama that preceded them. Dryden thought that
Fletcher could draw a better gentleman for the stage than could
Shakespeare; and, as to the conventions, doubtless, of social
life and intercourse, the gentlemen of Fletcher's drawing were
nearer in their conduct and conversation to the gentlemen
of Dryden's time than were the latter to the larger and more
universally veritable figures of Shakespeare. Elizabethan
drama rose rapidly from the flats of *Gorboduc* and *Gammer Gurton*, reaching beetling cliffs in Marlowe, and heights that pierced
the sky, with much that was more pleasant and habitable at
lower levels in the royal domain of Shakespeare and his immediate fellows. Fletcher leads us downward in a long, but not too
precipitous decline, diversified from time to time with highland
kindred to the mountainous region that we have left behind us;
reproducing much of its fauna and, in particular, its lovely poetical flora. There are other highlands on the broad map of Eng-

lish drama; but they concern us not. The range of Elizabethan
drama, too, is to be measured by its depths as well as by its
heights, by its deserts as well as by its cultivatable lands.
To vary the figure, there has been no drama of such an ampli-
tude of vibration, so tuned to respond, a universal resonator,
to the infinite varieties and degrees of the emotions and pas-
ions of men.

When Shakespeare died, in April, 1616, King James was at
the height of his reign; and the Stuart tenets of absolute king-
ship in church and state had already hardened the Puritan temper and provoked the parliamentary struggle that, leading
inevitably to rebellion, was to cost his son and successor his
throne and his life. These things concerned the future, and
as yet little affected English daily life. The king's weak and
disgraceful rule, on the other hand, was more patent to the
world; his infatuation for his favorites, his condoning of folly
and worse, the extravagance that prompted extortion and ille-
gal taxation, the corruption of the courts, and the suppression
of Parliament: these were some of the portents of the day.
And yet to the superficial observer, the times were prosperous and the arts were as flourishing as in the days of Elizabeth.
Richard Hakluyt died in the same year with Shakespeare;
with him closed the long and interesting chapter of England's
early maritime adventure. An occasional pamphlet or drama
of old fashion, or a belated adventurer, like Captain John
Smith, might respond to the memory of the perils and escapes,
the bravery and heroic daring that made the old sea-dogs
the terror of the Spanish ocean. But with the execution of
Raleigh, two years later, the last of the old Devonian heroes
was gone, and the sons of the men who had hunted the Armada
to the Hebrides and back into the Irish sea, now contemplated
with indifference the alliance of an English prince with an In-
fanta of Spain. But if one form of English prose had lost its
old insular national spirit, English style in general continued to
develop into a simpler and less labored instrument for the expression of the complexities of modern thought, leaving Euphuism and Arcadianism behind it, and much of its Latinism as

well, though still destined to undergo a relapse into the florid,
the cumbrous and involved, before it reached the reasonable
directness of Dryden.   As to the varieties of prose, none followed in the reign of the second Stuart which had not been
abundantly presaged before King James had been long on his
throne.   The pamphlet and occasional broadside continued,
assuming more and more the character of the newspaper that
was yet to be, and taking on with the trend of the time an in-
creasingly bitter political and satirical nature.   Wither is an
example of a sweet poet and amiable man turned to the
austerity of Puritanism and the rancor of the libeler by
this spirit of his day.   The essay, for the same reason, was
succeeded in popular esteem by the "character," wherein
much was sacrificed to the"palpable hit"; and even history,
as later with Clarendon, was conceived as meriting praise
when it sparkled with the wit of satirical portraiture cleverly
essayed.

Among new books in prose, in the closing years of Shakespeare's life, were Daniel's *History of England* and Hall's *Contemplations*, Alexander's completion of the *Arcadia*, Raleigh's
History of the World, Selden's *Titles of Honor*, and his *History
of Tithes*.   Camden's *Annals of Queen Elizabeth* appeared in
1615.   In this same year Breton's *Characters* showed the
immediate influence of the second edition of Bacon's *Essays*,
published three years earlier.   As to Breton's pamphlets at
large, of the thirty or more titles attributed to him, at least
twenty had appeared by 1616.   Dekker, too, to mention only
one other pampheteer, had put out some thirteen booklets of
this class — few of them reprinted — up to this date.   But
later editions of old books, better than new, disclose contemporary taste.   In 1610, Foxe's *Book of Martyrs* reached a sixth
edition, not to be reprinted until 1632.   The year 1612 saw the
fourth edition of North's *Plutarch;* the following year the
Arcadia in a sixth, and *Euphues* in a ninth issue.   Lower down
in the scale of fiction, Munday's *Palmerin of England* attained
a third edition in 1616, his *Amadis de Gaule*, a second three
years later.

As to non-dramatic poetry, Spenser, Sidney, Drayton, and

Daniel were the four most popular Elizabethan poets.   The first collected edition of Spenser appeared in 1611, following thirteen issues of separate poems or partial collections, within the poet's life. *Astrophel and Stella*, after three editions in the single year 1591, was always reprinted with the *Arcadia*, thus issuing for the seventh time in 1613. Daniel edited his non-dramatic poetry four times in his lifetime (he died in 1619) and there were fifteen separate editions of his poems, and dramas besides; while Drayton edited the third and best edition of his works in 1619, three more appearing later, and issued, besides, seventeen separate editions of individual works. One of the most popular poems of the time was Warner's *Albion's England*, which reached an eighth edition by 1612; a fourth edition of Sir John Davies' *Nosce Teipsum* appeared in 1618, a fifth before the date of the Shakespeare folio. Fletcher's *Christ's Victory and Triumph*, Browne's *Britannia's Pastorals*, and Wither's *The Shepherd's Pipe* disclose the continued popularity of the Spenserian mode between 1610 and 1616.   Lower in the scale of literature, Davies of Hereford had issued a dozen pamphlets in verse, Breton more than a score up to the same date; whilst in translation the year 1616 was signalized by the final collection of *The Whole Works of Homer* by Chapman, a sixth edition of the earliest parts, and this, besides the laborious poet's other activities in the drama and in nearly a dozen other volumes of original verse.   Well may we pause to consider such an activity (only partially indicated here) in a metropolitan community that had not yet reached two hundred thousand souls, the center of a nation scarcely numbering three millions; a community, moreover, in which the proportion of readers by reason of illiteracy must have been perhaps three in ten, and one in which the high proportionate cost of books must still further have limited the possible number of purchasers.

But the most important single volume, published in the year of Shakespeare's death, was the first folio of the collected works of Ben Jonson.   Jonson is the earliest English dramatic poet so to appear, and the only one to superintend such an edition of his works himself.   His popularity demanded a second edition in 1632, which was completed in 1641, some four years after the poet's death. Jonson is also the only Elizabethan dramatist who saw a collected edition of his own works in print; for although a larger number of Shakespeare's plays, singly and in quarto, "escaped into print" during his lifetime than of any other playwright, the great dramatist had been dead seven years before the famous first folio of 1623 was printed. Jonson's works were published, for a third time, in 1692; the two folio editions of the plays of Beaumont and Fletcher date 1647 and 1679. But Shakespeare demanded publication four times — in 1623, 1632, 1663–1664, and 1685 — within the period up to 1700. Only two other of Shakespeare's actual dramatic contemporaries were collected even imperfectly before the time of the Restoration: these were Lyly, whose *Six Court Comedies* dates 1632, and Marston, whose *Works*, containing an equal number of his plays, appeared in the next year.

In the drama, the exit of Shakespeare and the next few years marked a momentous change. Henslowe died in the same year with Shakespeare and with him passed away the old methods of theatrical management; for his son-in-law, Alleyn the actor, now long since retired and married to his second wife, a daughter of Dr. Donne, the poet and Dean of St. Paul's, had put away his humble and sordid past, and had founded Dulwich College to preserve therein *Henslowe's Diary* and other treasures for the antiquarian of our Elizabethan drama. In 1619 Richard Burbage died. Burbage had made the title rôles of Shakespeare as Alleyn had made those of Marlowe. With these two gone, and some of the elder comedians as well, the older ways of acting, too, must have suffered a change which, in view of the greater prevalence of melodrama, senti mentality, masquing, and scenic display, could scarcely have been altogether a change for the better. But although the drama, strictly Elizabethan, was now succeeded in the popular esteem by tragicomedies and comedies of contemporary life, and its range and artistic appeal was becoming more and more restricted, with Puritanism withdrawn from the theaters and the more serious-minded intent on the political struggle impending, we must remember that Shakespeare's plays and the earlier successes of Marlowe, Jonson, and others still held the stage with Fletcher and Shirley and what came after.

The age of Shakespeare knew, as every age in English-speaking lands since has known, that in Shakespeare the world has alike its truest dramatist and its greatest poet. To escape his rule and sway it is not in the nature of ignorance nor criticism to effect, however the alien moralist may display the limitations of his own comprehension or native Philistinism may deliver its diatribes against Shakespeare's poetry, his ethics, or his art. It is not in the nature of things human to withstand forever the inroads of time. The beautiful imagery of the poets that tells of gold-laden galleons, lying in the depths of the ocean, their treasures jeweling the floor of the sea, is denied by the stubborn facts of science. Sea-water is the universal solvent wherein even gold is tarnished and all at last reduced to the universal slime. So, too, the wealth of this great literature of Shakespeare and his fellows must yield perceptibly to the universal solvent, time; what was bright becomes tarnished, what was vitally significant, recoverable by the plodding student alone, to him an object of curious lore far more than the inevitable reality or the adored ideal that it was to the man of Elizabeth's day. Yet who will say that this is all? Homer still lives, and he is bold who will set limits to his immortality. And there remains, too, in this incomparable literature of the greatest age of modern times, more than enough that will continue sound, significant, and potent for generations and generations to come, long after our petty triumphs of to-day shall have perished irrevocably from the memories of men.

BIBLIOGRAPHY

This bibliography makes no pretensions to completeness. Its chief concern is the representation, in a condensed form, of the literary activity of the writers discussed in this book; its second, an indication as to where these authors may be read in modern available editions. Works of critical comment have been to a large degree ignored, not from a want of appreciation of the admirable results of modern scholarship, but from a conviction that, in the study of literature, a knowledge at first hand of what the author has written is the one supreme and important thing.

The following items are arranged first by the name of the author; secondly by title, where the book is anonymous or the work of several authors. A few subject-titles are added where the matter is not otherwise covered. A few abbreviations, mostly obvious, are employed. An exponent (thus 1632^2) means that more than one edition was issued in the same year. Well known collections, such as *Dodsley's Old English Plays*, and *Chalmers' English Poets* are alluded to by the author's name only. *Garner* signifies *Arber's English Garner*, new edition by Sidney Lee; *D. N. B.*, the *Dictionary of National Biography*.

ADDLINGTON, WILLIAM, fl. 1565. *The Golden Ass of Apuleius.* 1566, four edd. to 1596. *Tudor Translations*, ed. C. Whibley, 1892.

ALABASTER, WILLIAM, 1567–1640. *Roxana Tragedia*, 1632, Controversial works and a few scattered poems.

ALEXANDER, SIR WILLIAM (Earl of Stirling), 1567–1640. *Aurora*, 1604; *Monarchic Tragedies*, 1603–1607. See *Seneca.*

ALLOTT, ROBERT, fl. 1600. Editor of *Wit's Theater;* extracts from ancient authors, 1599; *England's Parnassus*, 1600, repr. Park, *Heliconia*, 1815, and C. Crawford, 1912.

ANDREWS, Lancelot (Bishop of Winchester), 1555–1626. Russel, *Life and Works*, 1863; Church, in *Masters of English Theology*, 1877.

ANTON, ROBERT, fl. 1616. *Moriomachia*, 1613; *Philosophers'*
Satires, 1616; *Vice's Anatomy*, 1617.

Arden of Feversham, 1592, 1599, 1633. Ed. Bullen, 1887; ed.
Bayne, *Temple Dramatists*, 1897.

ARMIN, ROBERT, fl. 1610. *Fool upon Fool*, 1605, repr. as *A Nest*
of Ninnies, 1608, in *Sh. Soc. Publ.*, 1842. *The Two Maids of*
Moreclacke, 1609. Reprint, J. S. Farmer, 1913.

AWDELEY, John, fl. 1559–1577. *Fraternity of Vagabonds*, 1565,
three edd. Repr. *The Shakespeare Library*, 1907.

BACON, FRANCIS, 1561–1626. *Controversies in the Church*, 1587;
Essays, 1597, 1612, 1625; *The Advancement of Learning*, 1605, ed.
Chase, 1906; *De Sapientia Veterum*, 1609; *Certain Considerations*
touching the Plantation in Ireland, 1609; *Novum Organum*, 1620–
1658 in various separate publications, ed. Fowler, 1878; *History of*
Henry VII, 1622; *De Dignitate et Augmentis Scientiarum*, 1623;
Apophthegms, 1624; *Psalms*, 1625; *Sylva Sylvarum*, 1627; *The New*
Atlantis, 1629; *Maxims of the Law*, 1630; and various other post-
humous publications, 1638–1671. Collected ed. Spedding, Ellis and
Heath, 1889–93, 10 vols. See also Spedding, *Life and Times of*
Bacon, 1878, 2 vols.; and Church, in *Men of Letters Series*, 1889;
Essays often reprinted. Poems, ed. Grosart, *Fuller Worthies' Mis-*
cellanies, i, 1870. See Bibliography, *Cambridge History of Litera-*
ture, 1910, vol. iv. J. E. G. de Montmorency, *Great Jurists*, 1914.

BALDWIN, WILLIAM, fl. 1559. See *Mirror for Magistrates*.

BARNES, BARNABE, 1569?–1609. *Parthenophil and Parthenope*,
1593; repr. *Garner, Sonnets*, i; *A Divine Century of Spiritual Sonnets*,
1595, repr. Park, *Heliconia*, ii. 1815. *The Devil's Charter*, 1607, ed.
McKerrow, *Materialien zur Kunde*, vi, 1904.

BARNFIELD, RICHARD, 1574–1627. *The Affectionate Shepherd*,
1594; *Cynthia*, 1595; *Lady Pecunia*, 1598, 1605; the last two reprinted
by Collier, *Reprints*, 1866, i. Poems, ed. Arber, *English Scholar's*
Library, 1882, and Garner, *Longer Elizabethan Poems*, 1903.

BARRY, DAVID LORD, *Ram Alley*, 1611, 1636, 1639, Dodsley x.

BASSE, WILLIAM, 1583–1653. *Sword and Buckler*, 1602; various
elegies and commendatory poems, between 1602 and 1653; *Pastorals*,
first printed by Collier, *Miscellaneous Tracts*, 1870; *Polyhymnia*, first
printed in *Poetical Works of W. B.*, ed. Bond, 1893.

BASTARD, THOMAS, 1566–1618. *Chrestoleros*, 1598. Poems, ed.
Grosart, *Occasional Issues*, 1880.

BEAUMONT, FRANCIS, 1584–1616. *Salmacis and Hermaphroditus*,
1602; *Poems*, 1640, enlarged 1653, and reprinted as *The Golden*

Remains of Beaumont and Fletcher, 1660. All these are doubtfully Beaumont's. *Masque of the Inner Temple and Gray's Inn*, 1613. Plays with Fletcher, ed. A. Glover and A. R. Waller, 10 vols. 1905–12; C. M. Gayley, *Beaumont as Dramatist*, 1914.

BEDINGFIELD, THOMAS, d. 1613. *Cardanus' Comfort*, 1573; *The Florentine History of Macchiavelli*, 1595; repr. *Tudor Translations*, 1905; and other works.

Bellum Grammaticale, 1635. Not reprinted. See *Sh. Jahrbuch*, xxxiv; and Chambers, iv. 374.

Bible, Erasmus, New Testament, Lat. (with Gk. text), 1516, various edd. and Latin paraphrases, to 1524. Tyndale, *New Testament* in English, 1525[2], facsimile repr. Fry, 1862, ed. Arber, 1871; *Pentateuch*, 1530, some forty edd. of these two (usually together) to 1553. Coverdale *Bible* (complete), 1535[2] (one of these, the first *Bible* printed in England); 1537, *New Testament*, 1538, revised; whole *Bible*, 1539; Matthews, 1537, 1539; Taverner, 1539; *Great Bible*, 1539, 1540[3], 1541[3]. Whittingham, 1557 (part), *Geneva Bible*, 1560, eighty-six edd. to 1611; *Bishops' Bible* (Parker), 1568, revised 1572, twenty edd. to 1606; *Rheims New Testament*, 1582, *Douay Old Testament*, 1609, few edd.; *Authorized Version* or *King James' Bible*, 1611. Upwards of a score of edd. to 1616.

F. H. A. Scrivener, *The Authorized Edition of the Bible*, 1884; A. S. Cook, *The Bible and English Prose Style*, 1892; F. A. Gasquet, *The Old English Bible*, 1897; R. G. Moulton, *The Literary Study of the Bible*, 1899; A. Wright, *A General History of the Bible*, 1905; J. H. Penniman, *A Book About the English Bible*, 1918, containing a valuable bibliography.

BLENERHASSET, THOMAS, 1550?–1625?. *The Second Part of the Mirror for Magistrates*, 1578. See *Mirror for Magistrates*.

BODENHAM, JOHN, fl. 1597. Reputed editor of *Wit's Commonwealth*, 1597; *Belvedere or the Garden of the Muses*, 1600, repr. *Spenser Society*, 1875; *England's Helicon*, 1600, ed. Bullen, 1887.

?BOWER, RICHARD. *Appius and Virginia*, 1575, repr. *Dodsley*, iv.

BRAITHWAITE, RICHARD, 1588?–1673. *The Golden Fleece*, 1611; *The Poet's Willow*, *The Prodigal's Tears*, and *The Scholar's Medley*, all in 1614; *A Strappado for the Devil*, 1615; and many more later tracts in verse or prose.

BRETON, NICHOLAS, 1545?–1626?. *The Works of a Young Wit*, *A Flourish upon Fancy*, both 1577, the latter in part reprinted in Park, *Heliconia*, 1815; *Pasquil's Madcap*, *Fool's Cap*, *Pasquil's Pass*, all 1600, the first also 1605; *The Soul's Harmony*, 1602; *The Passionate*

Shepherd, 1604, and fifteen other volumes of verse to *An Invective Against Treason*, 1616. *Wit's Trenchamour*, 1597; *A Packet of Madcap Letters*, 1603, many edd. to 1685; *An Old Man's Lesson*, 1605; *Characters upon Essays*, 1615; *The Good and the Bad*, 1616, 1648 and seventeen other prose pamphlets to *Fantastics*, 1626.

Some seventeen other works have been attributed to Breton; see bibliography in Morley, *English Writers*, xi. Collected ed. Grosart, 1879 (not quite complete), 2 vols. See Tappan, *The Poetry of B. Publ. Mod. Lang. Asso.*, 1898; Kuskop, *B. und seine Prosaschriften*, 1902.

BRIGHT, TIMOTHY, 1551 ?–1615. *Abridgement of Foxe's Book of Martyrs*, 1581, 1589; various medical pamphlets; *Characterie*, "an art of short, swift and secret writing," 1588; repr. J. H. Ford, 1888.

BRINSLEY, JOHN, fl. 1612. *Ludus Literarius, or the Grammar School*, 1612, 1627. G. W. McClelland, *Brinsley and the Grammar School Education of His Day*, 1916.

BROOKE, ARTHUR, d. 1563. *Romeus and Juliet*, 1562. Ed. Munro, *The Shakespeare Library*, 1908.

BROOKE, CHRISTOPHER, d. 1628. *The Ghost of Richard III*, 1614; contributor to *Britannia's Pastorals*, 1613, and *The Shepherd's Pipe*, 1614. See Browne, William, and Wither. Ed. Grosart, *Fuller Worthies' Miscellanies*, 1872, iii.

BROOKE, LORD, see Greville, Fulke.

BROWNE, WILLIAM (of Tavistock), 1591–1643 ?. *Britannia's Pastorals*, 1613–16, 1625; *The Shepherd's Pipe*, 1614; *Masque of the Inner Temple* (*Ulysses and Circe*), in *Works*, ed. Davies, 1772, 3 vols.; *Poems*, ed. G. Goodwin, *The Muses' Library*, 1894. See also F. W. Moorman, *William Browne*, 1897.

BRYDGES, JOHN (Dean of Salisbury). Alleged author of *Gammer Gurton*. See Ross, in *Anglia*, xix; but see Stevenson, William.

BRYSKETT, LODOWICK, fl. 1571–1611. *Discourse of Civil Life*, 1606[2].

BUC, SIR GEORGE, d. 1623. *Daphnis Polystephanos*, 1605, 2nd ed. (under title *The Great Plantagenet*), 1635; *The Third University of England*, 1615; *History of Richard III*, 1646.

BYRD, WILLIAM, 1538 ?–1623. Musician and publisher of music; probably not a poet. *Psalms, Sonnets*, 1588; *Songs of Sundry Natures*, 1589, 1610; *Second Book of Songs*, 1611. All in *Garner, Shorter Poems*, 1903.

CAMDEN, WILLIAM, 1551–1623. *Britannia*, 1586, six edd. to 1607, transl. 1610, 1637; repr. R. Gough, 1806, 4 vols.; *Remains Concerning*

Britain, 1605, seven edd. to 1674; *Annals*, 1615 and nine edd. to 1688, repr. ed. Hearne, 1717, 3 vols. Other minor works.

CAMPION, EDMUND, 1540–1581. See Simpson, *Edmund Campion*, a *Biography*, 1867.

CAMPION, THOMAS, d. 1619. *Poemata*, 1595, 1619; *A Book of Airs*, 1601; *Observations in the Art of Poesy*, 1602; *The Lord's Masque*, pr. Nichols, *Progresses of King James*, 1828, ii; *Two Books of Airs*, 1613; *Songs of Mourning*, 1613; *Counterpoint*, 1613; *Third and Fourth Book of Airs*, 1617; *Works* (complete), ed. Bullen, 1889. Selections, E. Rhys, *The Lyric Poets*, 1895. The Song Books also in *Garner, Shorter Poems*, 1903. Ed. S. P. Vivian, *English Poems*, 1910. *Observations, Elizabethan Critical Essays*, 1904.

CAREW, RICHARD, 1555–1620. *Godfrey of Bulloigne*, transl. 1594. Repr. Grosart, *Occasional Issues*, 1881. See *Retrospective Review*, 1821, and Koeppel in *Anglia*, xi.

CAREY, ROBERT (Earl of Monmouth), 1560–1639. *Memoirs*, first printed by Walpole, 1759. "Account of the death of Elizabeth," *Garner, Stuart Tracts*, 1903.

CECIL, WILLIAM (Lord Burleigh), 1520–1598. *Certain Precepts for the Well-ordering of a Man's Life*, 1617, six edd. to 1783. In later ones called *Lord Burleigh's Advice to his Son*.

CHAPMAN, GEORGE, 1559 ?–1634. *The Shadows of Night*, 1594. *The Tears of Peace*, 1609; *Andromeda Liberata*, 1614; and seven other publications of original verse to *A Justification of Nero*, 1629.

Ovid's Banquet of Sense, 1595; *Hero and Leander*, completed, 1598; Homer, *Iliad*, 1598–1611; *Odyssey*, 1614; *Whole Works of Homer*, 1616; *Hymns*, etc., 1624; *Hesiod*, 1618; Juvenal, *Satire V*, 1629.

The Blind Beggar of Alexandria, 1598; *A Humorous Day's Mirth*, 1599; *All Fools*, 1605; *Eastward Hoe* (with Jonson and Marston), 1605[3]; *Monsieur D'Olive*, 1606; *The Gentleman Usher*, 1606; *Bussy D'Ambois*, 1607, five edd. to 1657; *The Conspiracy of Byron*, 1608, 1625; *May Day*, 1611; *The Widow's Tears*, 1612; *The Revenge of Bussy D'Ambois*, 1613; *Pompey and Caesar*, 1631[2], 1653; *The Ball*, 1639; *Chabot*, 1639 (these two with Shirley); *Alphonsus of Germany*, and *Revenge for Honor*, both 1654, are not by Chapman. Dramatic Works, ed. Pearson, 1873, 3 vols.; Complete Works, ed. Shepherd (inferior), 1874–75, 3 vols. Selected dramas, ed. *Mermaid* (Phelps), 1895; *Belles Lettres Series* (Boas, 1905, Parrott, 1907), four plays, 2 vols. Homer, ed. Hooper, 1857, 5 vols. Plays, ed. T. M. Parrot, *Tragedies*, 1910, *Comedies*, 1914.

Characters. See Hall, Joseph; Overbury; Breton. H. Morley, *Character Writing of the Seventeenth Century*, 1891; Greenough, *Studies in the Development of Character Writing*, 1898; Whibley, in *Blackwood's*, 1909; R. Adlington, *A Book of " Characters,"* 1924.

CHESTER, ROBERT, 1566 ?–1640 ?. *Love's Martyr*, 1601; repr. *New Sh. Soc.*, 1878; *Poems* with Salusbury, ed. C. Brown, 1914.

CHETTLE, HENRY, 1564–5 ?–1607 ?. *Kind-Heart's Dream*, 1593, repr. *Sh.Allusion Books,New Sh. Soc.*,1874; *Pierce Plain's Apprenticeship*, 1593; *Downfall and Death of Robert, Earl of Huntington* (2 parts with Munday), 1601, repr. Hazlitt's *Dodsley*, viii, 1874; *Patient Grissil* (with Dekker and Haughton), 1603, repr. *Sh. Soc.*, 1841; *Hoffman*, 1631, repr. Ackermann, 1894, with bibliography. *England's Mourning Garment*, 1604, also in *Sh. Allusion Books*, as above.

Chronicle Plays. See Schelling, *The English Chronicle Play*, 1902; and Bibliographical Essay, *Elizabethan Drama*, 1908, by the same.

CHURCHYARD, THOMAS, 1520 ?–1604. Between *Shore's Wife* contributed to *The Mirror for Magistrates*, ed. 1563, and *Churchyard's Good Will*, 1603, some forty tracts in verse mostly, moral, devotional, historical, personal, elegiac, etc. The best is *The Worthies of Wales*, 1587, ed. *Spenser Soc.* 1871. Select works are reprinted in Nichol's *Progresses of Queen Elizabeth*, *The Harleian Miscellany*, and Collier's *English Poetical Miscellanies*.

College Drama. F. S. Boas, *University Drama*, 1914; G. C. Moore Smith, *College Plays*, 1923.

CONSTABLE, HENRY, 1562–1613. *Diana*, 1592, 1594, *Garner*, Sonnets, ii; *Spiritual Sonnets*, first pr. Park, *Heliconia*, ii. Ed. Hazlitt, complete, 1859.

Contention between the Houses of York and Lancaster, 1 and 2, see Pseudo-Shakespeare.

COOKE, JOSHUA, fl. 1602. *How a Man may Choose a Good Wife*, 1602, repr. *Dodsley*, ix.

COOPER, THOMAS (Bishop of Winchester), 1517 ?–1594. See *Marprelate Controversy*.

CORYATE, THOMAS, 1577–1617. *Crudities*, 1611; repr. Glasgow, 1905, 2 vols; *Coryate's Crambe*, 1611; *The Oldcombian Banquet*, 1611; *Traveller of the English Wits*, 1616; *Letter from Agra*, 1616.

COVERDALE, MILES, 1488–1568. See *Bible*.

CRANMER, THOMAS (Archbishop of Canterbury), 1489–1556. *Remains, Parker Soc.*, 1844–6, 2 vols.; and see *Bible*.

Criticism, Elizabethan Poetic, and Verse. See Haslewood, *Ancient*

Critical Essays, 1811, 2 vols.; Schelling, *Elizabethan Verse Criticism*, 1893; Saintsbury, *History of English Criticism*, 1900–1904, 3 vols. G. G. Smith, *Elizabethan Critical Essays*, 1904.

Cromwell, Chronicle History of Thomas Lord, 1602, 1613, Hazlitt, *Doubtful Plays of Shakespeare*, 1887. See Pseudo-Shakespeare.

DABORNE, ROBERT, fl. 1613. *The Christian Turned Turk*, 1612; *The Poor Man's Comfort*, 1655, both reprinted in Anglia, xx, xxi, 1897–98.

DANETT, THOMAS, fl. 1600. *Description of the Low Countries*, 1593; *History of Comines*, 1596.

DANIEL, SAMUEL, 1562–1619. *Delia*, 1591; *Delia* with *The Complaint of Rosamund*, 1592², 1594; *Cleopatra*, 1594; *Civil Wars*, 1595–1609; *Musophilus*, 1599; *Defense of Rime*, 1602; *Vision of the Twelve Goddesses*, 1604; *Philotas*, 1605; *The Queen's Arcadia*, 1606; *Tethys' Festival*, 1610; *History of England*, 1612–1617; *Hymen's Triumph*, 1615. Five collective edd. of varying contents, 1599 to 1623. Ed. Grosart, *Huth Library*, 1885, 5 vols.; *Selections* with Drayton, H. C. Beaching, 1899. *Inedited Poems*, Philobiblon Soc., 1854.

DAVIES, JOHN (of Hereford), 1565?–1618. *Microcosmus*, 1603; *Wit's Pilgrimage*, 1610–11; *The Scourge of Folly*, 1611; and nine other poetical booklets between 1602 and 1617. *The Writing Schoolmaster*, first known ed., 1633. Collected ed. Grosart, *Chertsey Worthies' Library*, 1878, 2 vols.

DAVIES, SIR JOHN, 1569–1626. *Orchestra*, 1596, 1622; *Nosce Teipsum*, 1599, and six other edd. to 1697; *Epigrams*, n. d.; *Hymns to Astraea*, 1618. Irish tracts and legal papers, 1612 to 1656. Coll. ed. Grosart, *Fuller Worthies' Library*, 1869–76, 3 vols.; ed. Morley, 1889.

DAVISON, FRANCIS, 1575?–1619. *Poetical Rhapsody*, 1602, 1611, 1621, repr. Bullen, 1890, 2 vols.

DAY, JOHN, 1574–1640. *The Isle of Gulls*, 1606², 1633; *The Travails of Three English Brothers*, 1607; *Humor out of Breath*, 1608; *Law Tricks*, 1608; *The Parliament of Bees*, 1641; *The Blind Beggar of Bethnal Green*, 1659. Collected ed. Bullen, 1881, 2 vols. See also *Nero and other Plays, Mermaid Series*, 1888.

DEE, DR. JOHN, 1527–1608. The author of seventy-nine works in Latin and English from *A Supplication for the Preservation of Ancient Writers and Monuments*, 1556, to *The Private Diary of Dr. Dee*, first printed by Halliwell-Phillipps, Camden Society, 1842, and later in part by J. E. Bailey, 1880.

DEKKER, THOMAS, 1570?–1641?. Twenty pamphlets from

Canaan's Calamity, 1598, 1618, to *Wars, Wars, Wars*, 1628; chief among them *The Wonderful Year, The Bachelor's Banquet*, both 1603; *The Dead Term, The Bellman of London*, both 1608; *Lanthorn and Candlelight*, 1608, 1609; *Four Birds of Noah's Ark*, 1609, *The Gulls' Hornbook*, 1609, repr. the King's Classics, 1895. *Old Fortunatus, Comedy of*, 1600; *The Shoemakers' Holiday*, 1600, six edd. to 1657; *Satiromastix*, 1602; *Patient Grissel*, 1603; *The Honest Whore*, 1604, six edd. to 1635; *Northward Hoe*, 1607; *Westward Hoe*, 1607; *The Whore of Babylon*, 1607; *Sir Thomas Wyatt*, 1607, 1612; *If It be Not Good the Devil is in It*, 1612; 2nd part of *The Honest Whore*, 1630; *Match Me in London*, 1631; *The Wonder of a Kingdom*, 1636. Four pageants, one for King James, the rest for the Lord Mayors, between 1604 and 1629. See Percy Soc., x. Collective edd: Dramas, ed. Shepherd, 1873, 4 vols.; Mermaid ed. five plays, 1887. Non-dramatic Works, ed. Grosart, 1884, 5 vols. M. T. Hunt, *Dekker*, 1911.

DELONEY, THOMAS, 1543–1600. *The Gentle Craft*, 1598, many edd. to 1696, repr. Lange, *Palæstra*, xviii, 1903; *Thomas of Reading*, [1599 lost], six edd. to 1636, repr. Thoms, *Early English Prose Romances*, 1858. *The Garland of Good Will*, 1604, eight edd. to 1664, repr. Percy Soc., xxx, 1853; *Strange Histories*, 1607, four edd. to 1681; *John of Newberry*, eighth ed. 1619, ten others to 1672, repr. R. Sievers, *Palæstra*, xxxvi, 1904. Broadside ballads, between 1583 and 1591. *Complete Works*, ed. F. O. Mann, 1912.

DICKENSON, JOHN, fl. 1594. *The Shepherd's Complaint* (in hexameters), n. d.; *Arisbas, Euphues amidst his Slumbers*, both 1594; *Greene in Conceipt*, 1598. Repr. Grosart, *Occasional Issues*, vi., 1878.

DONNE, JOHN, 1573–1631. *Ignatius his Conclave, Biathanatos*, 1608; *Pseudo Martyr*, 1610; *An Anatomy of the World*, 1611, 1612, 1621, 1625; *Elegy on Prince Henry*, 1613; Various *Sermons* singly issued, 1623–33; *Moral Sentences*, 1631; *His Funeral Sermon*, 1632 and other edd.; *Poems*, 1633, six edd. to 1669; *Eighty Sermons*, 1640; *Fifty Sermons*, 1649; *Essays in Divinity*, 1651; *Letters to Several Persons*, 1651, 1654; *Twenty-six Sermons*, 1669. Collected edd. Grosart, 1872, 2 vols.; ed. E. K. Chambers, *The Muses' Library*, 1896, 2 vols.; *Poems*, ed. H. J. C. Grierson, 1912.

DOWLAND, JOHN, 1563?–1626?. *The First Book of Songs*, 1597, five edd. to 1613; *The Second Book of Songs*, 1600; *The Third and Last Book of Songs*, 1603; *A Pilgrim's Solace*, 1612, all in Garner, *Shorter Poems*, 1903. See E. H. Fellowes, *English Madrigal Verse*, 1920.

Drama. See F. E. Schelling, *Elizabethan Drama*, 1908, 2 vols., T. Brooke, *Tudor Drama*, 1912; Schelling, *Elizabethan Playwrights*,

1925. See also W. W. Greg, *A List of English Plays, Bibliographical Society*, 1900; E. K. Chambers, *The Elizabethan Stage*, 4 vols., 1923.

DRANT, THOMAS, d. 1580. Latin verses and English sermons, 1564 to 1574. *Horace, his Art of Poetry, Epistles and Satires Englished*, 1567; parts of the *Iliad* unpublished.

DRAYTON, MICHAEL, 1563–1631. *The Harmony of the Church*, 1591, Percy Soc., 1843, vol. vii.; *Idea the Spheherd's Garland*, 1593, 1606, repr. *Spenser Soc.*, 1891, 3rd ed. 1619, repr. *Garner, Sonnets*, ii, 1904, 4th ed. 1620; *Legends of Gaveston, Matilda, Robert of Normandy, Cromwell*, each separate, 1594–1607 in several edd.; *Idea's Mirror*, 1594, seven edd. to 1620, repr. *Garner, Sonnets*, ii, 1904, and often elsewhere, ed. Esdaile, with Daniel's *Delia*, 1908; *Mortimeriados*, 1596 (repr. Collier, Roxburghe Club, 1856), altered into *The Barons' Wars*, 1603, 1605 (repr. *Spenser Soc., Poems*, 1888); *England's Heroical Epistles*, 1598, five other edd. variously combined to 1603; *The Owl*, 1604; *Polyolbion*, 1613, repr. Hooper, 1876; Spenser Society, 1890; *The Battle of Agincourt*, 1627 (repr. Garnett, 1893); *The Muses' Elizium*, 1630 (repr. with *Nymphidia*, 1896); and nine other separate publications in verse. Ten collective edd. of varying contents between 1605 and 1637.

The dramas of Drayton are lost, except possibly for his share in *The Merry Devil of Edmonton*, 1608, Dodsley, x: and *Sir John Oldcastle*, 1600. A complete ed. of Drayton, projected by Hooper, gave out on the completion of *Polyolbion and Hymns of the Church*, 1876, 3 vols.; Selections: by Bullen, 1883; by Garnett, *The Battle of Agincourt*, 1893; *Nymphidia and The Muses' Elizium*, 1896. Selections, with Daniel, ed. Beaching, 1899. See also Elton, *Introduction to Drayton*, 1895, and Whitaker, *Drayton as a Dramatist*, Publ. Mod. Lang. Asso., 1903.

DRUMMOND, WILLIAM (of Hawthornden), 1585–1649. *Tears on the Death of Meliades*, 1613, 1614; Poems, 1616², 1656, 1659; *Forth Feasting*, 1617; *Flowers of Sion*, 1623, 1630²; *The Cypress Grove*, 1623, 1655; *Entertainment of King Charles*, 1633; *History of Scotland*, 1655; *Works* collected by Ruddiman, 1711; *Conversations with Ben Jonson*, Sh. Soc., 1842. Modern ed. Turnbull, 1890; ed. W. C. Ward, *Muses' Library*, 1894, 2 vols.; see also Masson, *Drummond of Hawthornden*, 1873. Ed. L. E. Kastner, 1913.

DYER, SIR EDWARD, 1540–1607. See Hannah, *Raleigh and Other Courtly Poets*, 1875, and ed. Grosart, *Fuller Worthies' Library*, iv, 1872.

EDEN, RICHARD, 1521 ?–1576. *The Decades of the New World*,

1555; *The History of Travel*, 1577; and other translations of voyages and science. See Arber, *The First Three English Books on America*, 1885.

EDWARDS, RICHARD, 1523?–1566. *Damon and Pithias*, 1571, Dodsley, i; and see *Miscellanies*.

ELIZABETH, QUEEN, 1533–1603. Various translations, ed. C. Pemberton, *Early English Text Soc.*, 1899; see Flügel in *Anglia*, xiv, 1891. For specimens of the queen's letters, Camden Soc., 1849. *England's Parnassus*, see Allott, Robert.

Essay, The. See Bibliography, *Cambridge History*, 1910, vol. iv; also Littleboy, *Relations between French and English Literature*, 1895; and Upham, *French Influence in English Literature*, 1908.

Euphuism, see C. G. Child, *John Lyly and Euphuism, Münchener Beiträge*, vii, 1894; Bond, *Works of Lyly*, 1902, 3 vols.; Fuillerat, *John Lyly*, 1910.

Every Woman in her Humor, 1609, Bullen's *Old Plays*, iv.

Fair Em [n. d.], 1631; Simpson, *School of Shakspere*, 1878, vol. ii.

FAIRFAX, EDWARD, d. 1635. *Godfrey of Bulloigne*, 1600, 1624, repr. Routledge, *British Poets*, 1868; *Twelve Eclogues*, in part first printed in Cooper's *Muses' Library*, 1737. See *Anglia*, xii.

FENTON, SIR GEOFFREY, 1539?–1608. *Certain Tragical Discourses*, 1567, repr. *Tudor Translations*, 2 vols., 1898; *Guevara's Golden Epistles*, 1575, 1577, 1582; *The History of Guicciardini*, 1579, and other translations.

Fiction, Elizabethan, see Jusserand, *The English Novel in the Reign of Elizabeth*, 1895; and Bibliography in *Cambridge History of Literature*, vol. iii.

FIELD, NATHANIEL, 1587–1633. *A Woman is a Weathercock*, 1612; *Amends for Ladies*, 1618, 1639; ed. Mermaid, *Nero and Other Plays*, [n. d.].

FITZGEOFFREY, CHARLES, fl. 1601. *Affaniae* (Latin epigrams), 1601. Ed. Grosart, *Occasional Issues*, xvi, 1881. Also *Sir Francis Drake*, 1596.

FLETCHER, GILES (the elder), 1549?–1611. *Of the Russe Commonwealth*, 1591, Hakluyt Soc., ed. E. A. Bond, 1856; *Licia* and *The Rising to the Crown of Richard III*, 1593, repr. Grosart, *Fuller Worthies' Miscellanies*, iii, 1872; *Licia* also in *Garner, Sonnets*, ii.

FLETCHER, GILES (the younger), 1588–1623. *Christ's Victory and Triumph*, 1610, 1632, 1640. Ed. Grosart, *Early English Poets*, 1876; ed. W. T. Brooke, n. d.

FLETCHER, JOHN, 1579–1625 (including plays with Beaumont). *The Woman Hater*, 1607[2], 1648, 1649; *The Faithful Shepherdess*, n. d., five edd. to 1665; *The Knight of the Burning Pestle*, 1613, 1635[2]; *Cupid's Revenge*, 1615, 1630, 1635; *The Scornful Lady*, 1616, seven edd. to 1651; *The Maid's Tragedy*, 1619, seven edd. to 1661; *King and No King*, 1619, seven edd. to 1661; *Philaster*, 1620, seven edd. to 1652; *Thierry and Theodoret*, 1621, 1648, 1649; *The Two Noble Kinsmen* (with Shakespeare?) 1634; *The Elder Brother*, 1637[2], five edd. to 1661; *The Bloody Brother*, 1639, 1640; *Monsieur Thomas*, 1639; *Wit Without Money*, 1639, 1661; *The Night Walker*, 1640, 1661; *Rule a Wife and Have a Wife*, 1640; *Beggars' Bush*, 1641[2]; *The Wildgoose Chase*, 1652 (folio form). Collected edd. First folio, 1647, contains thirty-four other plays; the following are mentioned in the text: *The Woman's Prize*, *The Coxcomb*, *The Captain*, *Love's Cure*, *Wit at Several Weapons*, *The Chances*, *Bonduca*, *Valentinian*. Second folio, 1679, reprints all the plays of the first folio and all of the quartos just enumerated except *Beggar's Bush;* it adds *The Coronation* from the quarto of 1640, a play later claimed by Shirley. Third folio (repr. of the second), 1711. Critical edd. begin with Theobald and others, 1750, 10 vols.; and continue to Weber, 1812, 14 vols.; and Dyce, 1843–46, 11 vols. Recent edd. are that of A. Glover, *Cambridge English Classics*, 1905, 10 vols. to 1912; and the *Variorum Ed.* by various scholars (Bullen), also 1905, 4 vols. discontinued. *Barnavelt* was first printed by Bullen, *Old English Plays*, ii, 1883.

FLETCHER, PHINEAS, 1582–1650. *Locustae*, 1627; *Britain's Ida*, 1628; *Sicelides*, 1631; *The Purple Island, Piscatory Eclogues, Miscellanies*, etc., 1633; other lesser books. *Poems*, ed. Grosart, *Fuller Worthies' Miscellanies*, 1869, 4 vols.

FLORIO, JOHN, 1553–1625. *Italian and English Dictionary*, 1598; *Montaigne's Essays Englished*, 1603, 1613, repr. J. H. McCarthy, 1889. Ed. Saintsbury, *Tudor Translations*, 1892–93. Other works between 1578 and 1603.

FORD, EMANUEL, fl. 1607. *Parismus*, 1598, 2nd part, 1599, many subsequent edd.; *Ornatus and Artesia*, 1607 and other edd.; *Montelion*, earlier edd. lost, 1633, and later edd. See Dunlop, *History of Fiction*, 1814.

FORMAN, DR. SIMON, 1552–1611. *Diary, Camden Society*, 1843. The parts relating to Shakespeare were first reprinted by Collier, *New Particulars, etc.*, 1836.

FORTESCUE, THOMAS, fl. 1570. *The Forest or Collection of Histories*, 1571. Not reprinted.

FOXE, JOHN, 1516–1587. *Acts and Monuments* (*Book of Martyrs*), 1562, and eight other edd. to 1684. Earlier Latin edd. Strassburg, 1554; Basel, 1559–1562. Ed. Stoughton, 1877, 8 vols. *Christus Triumphans*, 1556, five later edd. to 1677.

FRAUNCE, ABRAHAM, fl. 1587–1633. Tasso-Watson, *Aminta*, transl. 1587; *The Arcadian Rhetoric*, 1588; *The Lawyer's Logic*, 1588; *The Countess of Pembroke's Emanuel*, 1591; repr. Grosart, *Fuller Worthies' Miscellanies*, iii. 1871; *The Countess of Pembroke's Ivychurch*, 1591–92; and other works.

GAGER, WILLIAM, fl. 1580–1619. *Ulysses Redux, Meleager*, both 1592. Other works not printed.

GASCOIGNE, GEORGE, 1525?–1577. *A Hundreth Sundry Flowers*, 1572; *The Posies of G.*, 1575; *The Whole Works*, 1587. These contain *The Steel Glass*, separately published, 1576, repr. Arber, *English Reprints*, 1868; the plays, *Supposes, Jocasta, The Glass of Government*, 1575; *The Adventures of Master F. I.* 1572; and *Certain Notes of Instruction;* besides other tracts. Ed. Cunliffe, *Cambridge English Classics*, 1907–9, 2 vols. See also Schelling, *Life and Writings of G.*, 1893; *A Hundreth Sundry Flowers*, Haslewood Books, 1926.

GIFFORD, HUMPHREY, fl. 1580. *A Posie of Gilliflowers*, 1580; ed. Grosart, *Occasional Issues*, 1875.

GILBERT, SIR HUMPHREY, 1539?–1583. *Discourse of a New Passage to Cataia*, edited by Gascoigne, 1576; *Queen Elizabeth's Academy*, pr. E. E. Text Soc., 1869.

GOLDING, ARTHUR, 1536?–1605?. *Seneca de Beneficiis*, 1558; Aretino's *History of the Goths in Italy*, 1563; *Caesar*, transl. 1565; *Ovid's Metamorphosis*, 1565, 1567, repr. *The King's Library*, ed. Rouse, 1904.

GOOGE, BARNABE, 1540–1594. *Eclogues, Epitaphs and Sonnets*, 1563; ed. Arber, *Reprints*, 1871. Various translations, 1560 to 1579.

GOSSON, STEPHEN, 1555–1624. *The School of Abuse*, 1579, 1587, repr. Arber, *Reprints*, 1868; *Ephimerides of Phialo*, 1579, 1586; *Plays Confuted*, 1582; *Pleasant Quips for Upstart New-Fangled Gentlewomen*, 1595.

GOUGH, HENRY, fl. 1570. *Offspring of the House of the Ottomans*, 1570.

GRAFTON, RICHARD, fl. 1543–1595. Besides edd. of Harding's and of Hall's Chronicles, 1543 and 1548, in which Grafton was printer and reviser; *Abridgment of Chronicles*, 1562, five edd. to 1572; *Chronicle at Large of England*, 1586–69, 2 vols., two edd. *Manual of English History*, 1595.

GREENE, ROBERT, 1560?–1592. Thirty pamphlets between
Mamillia, [1580], 1583; and *Greene's Vision*, 1592, chief among them
Planetomachia, 1585; *Euphues his Censure to Philautus*, 1587;
Penelope's Web, 1587; *Perimedes*, 1588; *Pandosto*, 1588, ed. P. G.
Thomas, *Shakespeare Classics*, 1907; *Menaphon*, 1589; *The Spanish
Masquerado*, 1589; *The Mourning Garment*, 1590, 1616; *Farewell to
Folly*, 1591, 1617; *Philomela*, 1592, 1631; *A Quip for an Upstart
Courtier*, 1592³, 1606, 1620, 1635; the Conycatching tracts, 1592.
The Black Book's Messenger, 1592, *A Groatsworth of Wit*, 1592,
eight edd. to 1637, repr. Saintsbury, *Elizabethan and Jacobean
Pamphlets*, 1902; *Greene's Repentance*, 1592.

    Friar Bacon and Friar Bungay, 1594, four edd. to 1655; ed. A. W.
Ward, with *Faustus*, 1892; *Orlando Furioso*, 1594, 1599; *Selimus*,
1594, 1638, both in Malone Soc., 1907, 1908; *James IV*, 1598; *Alphonsus of Aragon*, 1599; *George a Greene*, 1599, doubtfully accepted
as by G. *Life and Complete Works*, ed. Grosart, *Huth Library*, 1881–
86, 15 vols.; *Plays and Poems*, ed. J. C. Collins, 1905, 2 vols.;
Dramas, ed. Dickinson, *Mermaid Series*, 1909.

    GREVILLE, SIR FULKE (Lord Brooke), 1554–1628. *Mustapha*,
1609, *Certain Learned and Elegant Works*, 1633; *Life of Sidney*,
1652; repr. ed. Brydges, 1816, 2 vols.; also by N. Smith, 1907. *Remains*, 1670. Collective ed. Grosart, 1870, 4 vols.

    GRIFFIN, BARTHOLOMEW, d. 1602. *Fidessa*, 1596, *Garner,
Sonnets*, ii.

    Grim the Collier of Croydon, Gratiae Theatrales, 1662, Dodsley, viii.

    GRIMALD, NICHOLAS, 1519–1562. See *Yale Studies*, 1925.

    GRIMESTONE, EDWARD, fl. 1610. *General Inventory of the His-
tory of France*, 1607; *History of the Netherlands*, 1608; *History of
Spain*, 1612; and other like works, none reprinted. See Boas in
Modern Philology, iii, 1905.

    GROVE, MATTHEW, fl. 1587. *Pelops and Hippodamia, Epigrams,
Songs and Sonnets*, 1587. Repr. Grosart, *Occasional Issues*, 1878.

    GUILPIN, EDWARD, fl. 1598. *Skialetheia*, 1598, repr. Collier
Miscellaneous Tracts, 1868; and Grosart, *Occasional Issues*, 1878.

    GWINNE, MATTHEW, 1558?–1627. *Nero*, 1603, 1639; *Vertumnus*,
1607; other works, J. Ward, *Lives of Gresham Professors*, 1740.

    HAKE, EDWARD, fl. 1579. *News Out of Paul's Churchyard*,
1568, 1579, *Isham Reprints*, 1872; many devotional and commendatory works.

    HAKLUYT, RICHARD, 1552?–1616. *Divers Voyages Touching
America*, 1582, ed. J. W. Jones, *Hakluyt Soc.*, 1850; *Four Voyages*

into Florida, 1587; *The Principal Navigations*, 1589, enlarged 1598–
1600, 3 vols. repr. ed. Goldsmid, 1884; new ed. Glasgow, 1903–05,
12 vols.; *Galvano's Discovery of the World*, 1601; repr. Bethune, 1862;
Virginia Richly Valued, 1609, ed. Rye, W. B., 1851; *Discourse concerning Western Discoveries* (wr. 1584), first printed by *Maine
Historical Society*, ed. Woods, 1831, ed. Deane, *Hakluyt Soc.*, 1877.

HALL, ARTHUR, 1540 ?–1604. *Ten Books of Homer's Iliad*, 1581.

HALL, JOSEPH, 1574–1656. *Virgidemiarum Six Books*, 1597–
98, 1599, 1602; *Mundus Alter et Idem*, 1605, 1607, transl. by Healey
as *The Discovery of a New World*, 1608, repr. Morley, *Universal
Library*, 1885; *Characters of Virtues and Vices*, 1608; *Epistles*, 1608,
2 vols.; *Contemplations on Scriptures*, 1612–1626, 6 vols. *Works*, ed.
Wynter, 1863, 10 vols.; *Poems*, ed. Grosart, 1879; *Satires*, ed. S. W.
Singer, *The Muses' Library*, 1907.

HANNAY, PATRICK, d. 1629. *Epigrammaton Centuriae Sex*,
1616; other later verses. Collective ed., 1622, repr. *Hunterian Club*,
1875.

HARBERT, WILLIAM, fl. 1604. *A Prophecy of Cadwallader*, 1604.
Ed. Grosart, *Fuller Worthies' Library*, 1870.

HARINGTON, SIR JOHN, 1561–1612. *Orlando Furioso*, transl.
1591, 1607, 1634. (*Apology of Poetry* prefixed, repr. Haslewood.
Ancient Critical Essays, ii, 1811–15); *Epigrams*, 1613, five edd. to
1634. Various political and other tracts, most important a *View of
Ireland in* 1605, ed. Macray, 1879; *Nugae Antiquae*, 1769–75, ed.
Park, 1804; *Epigrams*, ed. N. E. McClure, 1926.

HARMAN, THOMAS, fl. 1567. *A Caveat for Common Cursetors*,
1566 (lost), 1567. Repr. *New Sh. Soc.*, 1880, and *The Shakespeare
Library*, 1907; F. Aydelotte, *Elizabethan Rogues*, 1913.

HARRISON, WILLIAM, 1534–1593. *Description of England*, prefixed to Holinshed's *Chronicles*, 1577, 1587; ed. Furnivall, *New Sh.
Soc.*, 1877–1881. Abridgement, *Camelot Series*, n. d.

HARVEY, GABRIEL, 1545 ?–1630. Various *Letters*, 1580, 1592,
1593; Pierce's *Supererogation*, 1593; *The Trimming of Thomas
Nash*, 1597. Latin works, 1577–78. Collected ed. Grosart, *Huth
Library*, 1884–85, 3 vols.

HAUGHTON, WILLIAM, fl. 1598. *A Woman will Have her Will*,
1616, 1626, 1631, otherwise called *Englishmen for my Money*, Dodsley,
x. Ed. A. C. Baugh, University of Pennsylvania, 1917.

HAYWARD, SIR JOHN, 1564–1627. *History of Henry IV*, 1599;
Union of England and Scotland, 1604; *Lives of Three Norman Kings*,
1613; *Sanctuary of a Troubled Soul*, 1616, many edd.; other devotional

pamphlets; *Edward VI*, 1630, 1636; *Beginning of the Reign of Elizabeth*, 1636 (*Camden Society*, repr. 1840); *History of Henry III and IV*, with Cotton, 1642.

HENSLOWE, PHILIP, d. 1616. *Henslowe's Diary*, ed. Collier, *Sh. Soc.*, 1845 (unsafe); ed. Greg, 1904–1908, 2 vols. (authoritative).

HEYWOOD, JASPER, 1535–1598. See Seneca Translated.

HEYWOOD, THOMAS, 1575?–1650. *Edward IV*, 1600, five edd. to 1626; *If You Know Not Me*, 1605, eight edd. to 1623; *A Woman Killed with Kindness*, 1607, 1617; *The Fair Maid of the Exchange*, 1607, three edd. to 1637; *The Rape of Lucrece*, 1608, four edd. to 1638; *The Golden Age*, 1611; *The Silver Age*, 1613; *The Brazen Age*, 1613; *The Four Prentices of London*, 1615, 1632; *The Fair Maid of the West*, 1631; *The Iron Age*, 1632; *The English Traveller*, 1633; *The Lancashire Witches*, 1634; *A Maidenhead Well Lost*, 1634; *Love's Mistress*, 1636, 1640; *A Challenge for Beauty*, 1636; *Royal King and Loyal Subject*, 1637; *The Wise Woman of Hogsdon*, 1638; *Fortune by Land and Sea*, 1655; *The Captives*, Bullen, *Old Plays*, iv, 1883.

Troia Britannica, 1609; *An Apology for Actors*, 1612, repr. Sh. Soc., 1841; *Gunaikaion*, 1624; *England's Elizabeth*, 1632; *The Hierarchy of Blessed Angels*, 1635; *Pleasant Dialogues and Dramas*, 1637; *The General History of Women*, 1657. Elegies, Epithalamia, six city Pageants (for which see *Percy Society*, x, 1843), additional translations and pamphlets. *Dramatic Works*, ed. Pearson, 1874, 6 vols. See K. L. Bates, ed. *Heywood*, *Belles Lettres*, 1919.

HIGGINS, JOHN, 1545–1602. See *Mirror for Magistrates*.

Histriomastix, 1610, probably by Marston, *School of Shakspere*, 1878.

HOBY, SIR THOMAS, 1530–1566. *The Courtier of Count Baldessar Castilio*, 1561, five edd. to 1603. Repr. *Tudor Translations*, 1900.

HOLINSHED, RALPH, d. 1580?. *Chronicles of England, Scotland, and Ireland*, 1577, 1586–87. Repr. 1807–08, 6 vols. See also Boswell-Stone, *Shakespeare's Holinshed*, 1896.

HOLLAND, PHILEMON, 1552–1637. Livy's *Roman History*, 1600; Pliny's *History of the World*, 1601; Plutarch's *Morals*, 1603; Suetonius, *Twelve Caesars*, 1606, repr. *Tudor Translations*, ed. Whibley, 1899; Marcellinus, *Roman History*, 1609; Camden's *Britannia*, Englished, 1610; Xenophon's *Cyropaedia*, 1632.

HOLYDAY, BARTEN, 1593–1661. *Persius' Satires*, translated, 1616, 1617, 1635, 1673; *Technogamia*, a comedy, 1618, 1630; and other later works.

HOOKER, RICHARD, 1554–1600. *Ecclesiastical Polity,* four books, 1594. 1604; *Book V,* 1611, 1617; *Books VI, VIII,* 1648, 1651; *Book VII,* 1862. *Sermons* and *Tracts,* ed. Church and Paget, 1888, 3 vols. See L. S. Thornton, *Hooker's Theology,* 1923.

HOPKINS, RICHARD, d. 1594 ?. Granada's *Prayer and Meditation,* 1582, 1592, 1612; Granada's *Memorial of a Christian Life,* 1586, 1599, 1612, 1625.

HOWELL, THOMAS, fl. 1568. *New Sonnets and Pretty Pamphlets,* 1567–68; *The Arbor of Amity,* 1568; *Howell his Devise,* 1581. Ed. Grosart, *Occasional Issues,* viii.

HUGHES, THOMAS, fl. 1587. *The Misfortunes of Arthur,* 1587, ed. Grumbine, 1900.

HUME, TOBIAS, d. 1645. *First Part of Airs,* 1605; *Captain Hume's Musical Humors,* 1607. See Rimbault, *Bibliotheca Madrigaliana,* 1847.

HUNNIS, WILLIAM, fl. 1530–1597. *A Hive full of Hunney,* 1578; *Seven Sobs,* 1583; *Hunnis' Recreations,* 1588. See Stopes, in *Sh. Jahrbuch,* xxvii, and repr. 1892 for an account of Hunnis.

Jack Drum's Entertainment, 1601, *School of Shakspere,* 1878.

JAMES I, KING, 1566–1625. *Essays of a Prentice,* 1584, repr. Arber, *Reprints,* 1869; *Demonology,* 1597; *Basilikon Doron,* 1599; *True Law of free Monarchies,* 1603; *A Counterblast to Tobacco,* 1604; religious meditations and political tracts. Collected ed. 1616, 1619, 1689; a convenient ed. of extracts by Rait, *A Royal Rhetorician,* 1900.

J. C., *Alcilia, Parthenophen's Loving Folly,* 1595. Repr. W. Wagner, *Sh. Jahrbuch,* x, 1875. *Garner, Longer Poems,* 1903.

JEWELL, JOHN (Bishop of Salisbury) 1522–1571. *Works,* 1609. Ed. Ayre, 1845–50, 4 vols.

John, The Troublesome Reign of King, 1591. Ed. Furnival, facsimile repr. 1888.

JOHNSON, RICHARD, 1573–1659 ?. *The Nine Worthies of London,* 1592; *The Seven Champions of Christendom,* 1596–97, fourteen edd. to 1690; *A Crown Garland of Golden Roses,* 1612, seven edd. to 1685, repr. Percy Soc., vi, 1842; *Walks in Moorfields,* 1607; *Look on Me, London,* 1613; both repr. in Collier, *Early English Popular Poetry,* vol. ii, 1864; *Tom Thumb,* 1621; *Tom a Lincoln,* 1631, twelve edd. to 1682. Several other like pamphlets.

JONES, ROBERT, d. 1616. *Book of Songs,* 1601; *First Set of Madrigals,* 1607; *Ultimum Vale,* 1608; *A Musical Dream,* 1609; *The Muses' Garden of Delights,* 1610, ed. W. B. Squire, 1901.

JONSON, BEN, 1573–1635. *Every Man Out of his Humor,* 1600[2];

Cynthia's Revels, 1601; *Every Man in his Humor*, 1601; *Poetaster*, 1602; *Sejanus*, 1605; *Eastward Hoe* (with Chapman and Marston), 1605[3]; *Volpone*, 1607; *The Case is Altered*, 1609[2]; *Catiline*, 1611, 1635; *The Alchemist*, 1612; *The Silent Woman*, 1612?, 1620. (All in folio 1616 except *The Case is Altered*.)

King James' Entertainment, 1604; *Hymenæi*, 1606; *The Viscount Haddington's Masque*, 1608; *The Queen's Masques* [*of Blackness* and *of Beauty*], 1609, *The Masque of Queens*, 1609; *Love Freed from Ignorance*, 1612?; *Oberon, Love Restored, Mercury Vindicated, The Golden Age*, and three other pieces, folio 1616. *Epigrams, The Forest*, both folio 1616.

The New Inn, 1629, 1631; *Bartholomew Fair*, four other comedies, *The Sad Shepherd*, folio 1640; *The Masque of Lethe*, 1617; *Neptune's Triumph*, 1623; *The Fortunate Isles*, [n. d.]; *Chloridia*, 1630?; *Love's Triumph*, 1630; these and twelve other masques and entertainments, folio 1640; *Execration upon Vulcan and Divers Epigrams*, quarto, 1640; *Horace Art of Poetry, The Masque of Gipsies*, and *Epigrams*, octavo, 1640; *Discoveries, English Grammar*, folio 1640 with contents of folio 1616. *Leges Convivales*, in third folio, 1692, with all the foregoing. Modern collective edd., Gifford, 1816, 9 vols.; Cunningham-Gifford, 1875, 9 vols; Mermaid, ed., n. d. 3 vols. *Complete Works*, ed. Simpson and Herford, 1925, 3 vols. in progress. M. Castelain, *Ben Jonson*, 1909.

KNOLLES, RICHARD, 1550–1610. *General History of the Ottoman Turks*, 1603.

KYD, THOMAS, 1557?–1595. *Soliman and Perseda* [1593?], 1599[3]; *Spanish Tragedy*, 1592? twelve quartos to 1633, repr. ed. Schick, *Archive*, xc, and *Temple Dramatists*, 1898; *Cornelia*, 1594, 1595; *The First Part of Jeronimo*, 1605, is not by Kyd. Three pamphlets between 1588 and 1592. Collective ed. Boas, 1901.

Larum for London, A, 1612, Simpson. *School of Shakspere*, 1872.

LEGGE, THOMAS, 1595–1607. *Richardus Tertius, Sh. Soc.*, 1844.

Leir, The History of King, 1605, repr. Malone Society, 1907; also *Shakespeare Classics*, ed. S. Lee, 1907.

LITHGOW, WILLIAM, 1582–1645. *A Total Discourse of the Rare Adventures and Painful Perigrinations*, 1614, complete in 1632.

Locrine, The Tragedy of, 1595, repr. Malone Society, 1908. See Pseudo-Shakespeare.

LODGE, THOMAS, 1558–1625. *Defense of Poetry and Stage Plays*, 1579, repr. *Sh. Soc.*, 1853; *An Alarum for Usurers*, 1584, repr. in the same; *Rosalynd*, 1590 and eight other edd. to 1642, often repr'd., ed.

Greg, *Shakespeare Classics*, 1907, and sixteen other romances, translations, and moral tracts including *A Margaret of America*, and *Wit's Misery*, both 1596; *A Treatise on the Plague*, 1603; *The Works of Seneca*, 1614; and *A Summary upon Du Bartas*, 1621. *Scillæ's Metamorphosis*, 1589, 1610; repr. Chiswick Press, 1819; *Phillis*, 1593, *Garner Sonnets*, ii; *A Fig for Momus*, 1595. Repr. Auchinleck Press, 1817. *The Wounds of Civil War*, 1594, Dodsley, vii; *A Looking-glass for London*, 1594, 1598, 1602, 1617. *Works*, ed. Gosse (exclusive of the plays), *Hunterian Club*, 1872–82.

LOK, HENRY, fl. 1593–1597. *Ecclesiastes, whereunto are annexed sundry Sonnets of Christian Passions*, ed. Grosart, *Fuller Worthies' Library*, 1871.

London Prodigal, 1605, Tyrrel, *Doubtful Plays of Shakespeare*. See Pseudo-Shakespeare.

Lust's Dominion, "by Marlowe," 1657. Ed. Pickering, *Marlowe*, 1826, iii.

LYLY, JOHN, 1553-4—1606. *Euphues*, 1579[2] and twelve other edd. to 1636; *Euphues and his England*, 1580[2], and eleven edd. to 1636. Repr. Arber, 1868. *Campaspe*, 1584[2], 1591; *Sapho and Phao*, 1584, 1591; *Endimion*, 1591; *Gallathea*, 1592; *Midas*, 1592; *Mother Bombie*, 1594, 1598; *The Woman in the Moon*, 1597; *The Maid's Metamorphosis*, 1600; *Love's Metamorphosis*, 1601. *Pap with a Hatchet*, 1598, has been attributed to L. Collective edd.: *Six Court Comedies*, 1632; ed. Fairholt, 1858, 2 vols.; complete *Works*, ed. Bond, 1902, 3 vols. See also A. Feuillerat, *John Lyly*, Rennes, 1910.

LYNCHE, RICHARD, fl. 1596–1601. *Diella, Certain Sonnets*, 1596, repr. *Garner, Sonnets*, 1904; *The Fountain of Ancient Fiction*, 1599.

Lyrics, Elizabethan. *Lyrical Poems*, Percy Society, xiii, 1844; Arber, *English Garner*, 1879–83, 8 vols.; Bullen, *Lyrics from Song Books*, 1887, *More Lyrics from Song Books*, 1888, *Lyrics from the Dramatists*, 1889–90, *Lyrics from Romances*, 1890, Garner, *Shorter Elizabethan Poems*, 1903; Schelling, *Book of Elizabethan Lyrics*, 1895; F. I. Carpenter, *English Lyrical Poetry*, 1906.

MACHIN, LEWIS, fl. 1607. *Eclogues* with Barkstead's *Mirrha*, 1607; *The Dumb Knight*, with Markham, 1608, 1633. Repr. Dodsley x.

Madrigal. See F. A. Cox, *English Madrigals in the Time of Shakespeare*, 1899. Also T. Oliphant, *Musa Madrigalesca*, 1837, and E. H. Fellowes, *English Madrigal Verse*, 1920.

MANNINGHAM, JOHN, d. 1622. *Diary*, ed. Bruce, *Camden Society's Publ.*, 1868.

MARKHAM, GERVAIS, 1568–1637. *Ariosto's Satires*, 1608, 1611; thirty or more pamphlets on horsemanship, husbandry, angling, archery, the art of letter-writing, and other subjects between 1593 and 1654. Repr. *Tears of the Beloved*, 1600; *Marie Magdalene's Tears*, 1601, ed. Grosart, *Fuller Worthies' Library*, 1871.

MARLOWE, CHRISTOPHER, 1564–1593. *Tamburlaine*, 1590, 1592, 1605, 1606; *Edward II*, 1594, four quartos to 1622; *Dido* (with Nash) 1594; *Hero and Leander*, 1598², seven edd. to 1637; *Lucan's Pharsalia* (Book I), 1600; *Ovid's Amores*, 3 edd. n. d. ; *Massacre at Paris*, 1600 ?; *Faustus*, 1604 (first extant quarto) and seven other edd. to 1631; *The Jew of Malta*, 1633 (first extant quarto). *Lust's Dominion*, 1657, is not Marlowe's. Collective edd. Bullen, 1885, 3 vols.; Mermaid ed. 1887; ed. Tucker Brooke, 1910. And see J. L. Hotson, *The Death of Marlowe*, Harvard Press, 1925.

MARSTON, JOHN, 1576–1634. *Pigmalion's Image*, 1598, 1613, 1638; *The Scourge of Villainy*, 1598, 1599². *Antonio and Mellida*, 1602; *The Malcontent*, 1604³; *The Dutch Courtezan*, 1605; *The Fawn*, 1606²; *Sophonisba*, 1606; *What You Will*, 1607; *The Insatiate Countess*, 1613, 1616, 1631; one or two other plays doubtfully his, and two masques. *Tragedies and Comedies*, 1633. *Works*, ed. Bullen, 1887, 3 vols.

Martin Marprelate Controversy, 1587–1590. Preliminary works: *A Defence of the Government*, by Bridges, 1587; *Diotrephes*, by J. Udall; *The Demonstration of Discipline*, anon. (both Puritan replies), 1588. Puritan tracts: *The Epistle; The Epitome; A Supplication to Parliament*, by Penry; *Hay any Work for Cooper; The Protestation;* with others, in all nine tracts, all 1589. Church pamphlets: *An Admonition*, etc., by T. Cooper; *Mar-Martin; Anti-Martinus; Pasquil of England; Martin's Month's Mind; Pap with a Hatchet; An Almond for a Parrot;* with other tracts, in all some eighteen, all 1589 or early in 1590. Bacon, *Controversies of the Church*, 1587. On the topic see Arber, "Introductory Sketch to the M. M. Controversy," *English Scholars' Library*, viii, ix, xi, xv, wherein several of the tracts are reprinted. See also W. Pierce, *An Historical Introduction to the Marprelate Tracts*, 1908; and Bibliography in *Cambridge History of Literature*, 1909, vol. iii.

Masque, H. A. Evans, *English Masques*, 1897; R. Brotanek, *Die englischen Maskenspiele, Wiener Beiträge*, 1902; P. Reyher, *Le Masque Anglais*, 1909; see also W. W. Greg, *A List of Masques*, etc., 1902. Simpson and Bell, *Designs by Inigo Jones*, 1924. [Important.]

MELBANCKE, BRIAN, fl. 1583. *Philotimus, the War betwixt Nature and Fortune*, 1583. See Brydges, *British Bibliographer*, ii.

MELVILLE, JAMES, 1556–1614. *Diary*, pr. for the Bannatyne Club, 1829.

MELVILLE, SIR JAMES, 1535–1617. *Memoirs of his own Life*, 1683; repr. for the Bannatyne Club, 1827.

MERES, FRANCIS, 1565–1647. *Palladis Tamia, Wit's Treasury*, 1598, 1634. Repr. in part, *New Sh. Soc.*, 1874. Also certain religious works.

Merry Devil of Edmonton, 1608, five edd. to 1655. See Drayton.

Microcynicon, Six Snarling Satyres, by T. M. Gent, 1599. (Not by Middleton.)

MIDDLETON, THOMAS, 1570–1627. *The Wisdom of Solomon Paraphrased*, 1597; *Blurt, Master Constable*, 1602; *Michaelmas Term*, 1607, 1630; *Your Five Gallants*, 1607 ?; *The Phoenix*, 1607, 1630; *The Family of Love*, 1608; *A Trick to Catch the Old One*, 1608², 1616; *A Mad World my Masters*, 1608, 1640; *The Roaring Girl*, 1611; *A Fair Quarrel*, 1617², 1622; *The Inner Temple Masque*, 1619; *The World Well Tossed at Tennis*, 1620; *A Game at Chess*, 1625⁴; *A Chaste Maid in Cheapside*, 1630; *The Changeling*, 1653, 1668; *The Spanish Gipsy*, 1653; *Two New Plays: More Dissemblers Besides Women, Women Beware Women*, 1657; *No Wit, No Help like a Woman's*, 1657; *The Mayor of Queenborough*, 1661; *Anything for a Quiet Life*, 1662; *The Witch*, first pr. 1778 by Reed; eight pageants between 1613 and 1626. See *Percy Society*, x; and several pamphlets. Works, ed. Dyce, 1840, 5 vols.; Bullen, 1885, 8 vols.

Mirror for Magistrates, ed. Baldwin, 1559, 1563 (Sackville's work first included), 1571, 1574, 1575, 1578; *The First Part of the M. for M.*, ed. Higgins, 1574, 1575; *The Second Part of the M. for M.*, ed. Blennerhasset, 1578; *The M. for M.* "with the addition of divers tragedies," ed. Newton, 1587; *M. for M.* "newly enlarged," ed. Niccols, 1610. Repr. Haslewood, 1815, 3 vols.

Miscellanies (Lyrical). *Tottel's Miscellany* (Songs and Sonnets by Wyatt, Surrey, and others, ed. Grimald), 1557, seven edd. to 1587, repr. Arber, 1870; *The Paradise of Dainty Devices*, ed. Edwards, 1576, eight edd. to 1600, repr. Brydges, *British Bibliographer*, iii, 1810; *A Gorgious Gallery of Gallant Inventions*, ed. Proctor, 1578, repr. Park, *Heliconia*, i, 1815; *A Handful of Pleasant Delights*, ed. Arber, 1878; also reprinted by H. E. Rollins, Harvard, 1925; *The Phoenix Nest*, editor R. S. (unknown) 1593, repr. *Heliconia*, ii; *England's Helicon*, ed. Bodenham, 1600, 1614, repr. Bullen, 1887; *A Poetical Rhapsody*, ed. Davison, 1602, 1611, 1621, repr. Bullen,

1890, 2 vols. Collective ed. Collier, *Seven English Miscellanies*, 1867, includes all of these but *A Handful of Pleasant Delights*.

More, Sir Thomas, The Play of, Malone Reprints, 1911; A. W. Pollard and others. *Shakespeare's Hand* in this play, 1923.

MORLEY, THOMAS, fl. 1594. *Canzonets*, 1593; *Madrigals*, 1594, 1600, 1601; *The First Book of Ballets*, 1595, and ten other like works to *The Triumphs of Oriana*, 1601, repr. *Garner, Shorter Poems*, 1903.

MORYSON, FYNES, 1566–1616. *An Itinerary Containing Ten Years' Travel*, 1617. Ed. Hughes, as *Shakespeare's Europe*, 1903; also in part (as to Ireland) in 1735 and by Morley, *Carisbrook Library*, 1890.

Mucedorus, A Most Pleasant Comedy of, 1598, sixteen edd. to 1668. Dodsley, vii.

MULCASTER, RICHARD, 1530 ?–1611. *Positions for the Training up of Children*, 1581; *Elementary of the Right Writing of the English Tongue*, 1582; *Catechismus Paulinus*, 1599. See Quick, *R. M. and his Elementary*, 1893; Klackr, *Leben und Werke R. M.'s*, 1893.

MUNDAY, ANTHONY, 1553–1633. A score of pamphlets, tracts, and broadsides verse and prose from 1577 to 1611, chief among them *The Mirror of Mutability*, 1579; *Sundry Examples*, 1580; *The Taking of Campion*, 1581, etc. M.'s principle stories and romances translated are, *Zelauto*, 1580; *Paladino of England*, 1588; *Palmarin d'Oliva*, 1588–1597; *Palmendos*, 1589, 1653; *Amadis de Gaule*, 1589–1619; *Gerileon of England*, 1592; *Sir John Oldcastle*, 1600 (with others); *The Downfall* and *The Death of Robert Earl of Huntingdon*, 1601, repr. *Dodsley*, viii; *Palmerin of England*, 1602, five edd. to 1664; *Primaleon of Greece*, 1619, (lost ed. 1595); *John a Kent*, a play, pr. *Sh. Soc.*, 1851. Civic pageants, eight between 1605 and 1623, see *Percy Soc. Publ.*, x. Also M. St. C. Byrne, *Library*, 1923.

Narcissus, a Twelfth Night Merriment, ed. M. L. Lee, 1893.

NASH, THOMAS, 1567–1601. *The Anatomy of Absurdity*, 1589, 1590; *A Countercuff to Martin Junior, Martin's Month's Mind, The Return of Pasquil of England*, 1589; *Pasquil's Apology*, 1590, these four Marprelate Tracts; *Astrological Prognostications*, 1591; *Pierce Penniless, Four Letters Confuted*, both 1592, the last repr. 1593; *Christ's Tears over Jerusalem*, 1593, 1594, 1613; *The Terrors of the Night*, 1594; *The Unfortunate Traveler or Jack Wilton*, 1594, repr. ed. Gosse, 1892; *The Tragedy of Dido*, 1594 (pr. in edd. of Marlowe); *Have With You to Saffron-Walden*, 1596; *Lenten Stuff*, 1600; *Summer's Last Will*, 1600, *Dodsley*, viii. Collective ed. Grosart, *Huth Library*, 1883–85, 6 vols.; McKerrow, 1904–10, 5 vols. Several of Nash's tracts were reprinted by Collier in his *Reprints, Temp. Eliz. and Jac. I;* see also *Selections from Elizabethan Critical Essays,* ed. G. G. Smith, 1904.

NAUNTON, SIR ROBERT, 1563–1635. *Fragmenta Regalia,* 1641, ed. Arber, *Reprints,* 1870.

NEVILE, ALEXANDER, 1544–1614. See Seneca Translated.

NICCOLS, RICHARD, fl. 1610. See *Mirror for Magistrates.*

NORTH, SIR THOMAS, 1535?–1600?. *The Dial of Princes,* 1557; *Philosophy of Doni,* 1570, 1601, ed. Jacobs, *Earliest English Version of the Fables of Bidpai,* 1888; *The Lives of the Noble Grecians and Romans,* by Plutarch, 1597, eight edd. to 1676. Modern ed., *Tudor Translations,* 1895; also *Shakespeare's Plutarch,* ed. Skeat, 1875.

NORTHBROOKE, JOHN, fl. 1570. *A Treatise wherein Dicing, Dancing and Vain Plays are Reproved,* 1577, 1579. *Sh. Soc.,* 1843.

NORTON, THOMAS, 1532–1584. See Sackville.

NUCE, THOMAS, d. 1617. See Seneca Translated.

Oldcastle, Sir John, The first part of, see Pseudo-Shakespeare.

OVERBURY, SIR THOMAS, 1581–1613. *The Character of a Wife,* 1614; *Characters with a Wife "now a Widow,"* 1614, 1615[4] 1616[3], sixteen edd. to 1638, repr. *Carisbrook Library,* 1891; *Works,* ed. Rimbault, 1856. E. A. Parry, *The Overbury Mystery,* 1925.

OWEN, JOHN, d. 1622. Epigrams in Latin, four edd., each adding to the last between 1606 and 1613. Collected 1624 and often after; Englished, 1619, and six edd. to 1678 by various hands; transl. French, German, and Spanish.

OXFORD, EARL OF, EDWARD DE VERE, 1550–1604. Verse contributed mostly to contemporary anthologies. Collected by Grosart, *Fuller Worthies' Library,* 1872.

PAINTER, WILLIAM, fl. 1557. *The Palace of Pleasure,* 1566, 1569, 1575; "the second time," 1567, 1575. Ed. Jacobs, 1890, 3 vols.

PARKER, MATTHEW (Archbishop of Canterbury), 1504–1575. For Bibliography see *D. N. B.,* xliii.

Parnassus Plays, The. *The Pilgrimage to Parnassus;* 1, *Return Return from Parnassus;* 2, *Return from Parnassus,* 1606. All in ed. W. D. Macray, 1886; the last also ed. O. Smeaton, 1905. printed.

PARSONS, ROBERT, 1546–1610. For the thirty-two items of his controversial writings between 1580 and 1612 see *D. N. B.,* xliii. P.'s most popular work was *A Christian Directory,* 1582, 1585, and other edd. *Leicester's Commonwealth,* 1584, 1641[2], 1661, was repudiated by him as not his.

Pastor Fido, Il, of Guarini, translated, "by a kinsman of Sir

Edward Dymocke," 1602. See W. W. Greg, *Pastoral Poetry and Pastoral Drama*, 1906, p. 242.

Pastoral, The. See especially W. W. Greg, *Pastoral Poetry and Pastoral Drama*, 1906; and the collection of *English Pastorals*, by E. K. Chambers, 1895. Also V. M. Jeffery, in *Mod. Lang. Rev.*, 1924.

Pedantius, see Wingfield.

PEELE, GEORGE, 1552 ?–1598 ?. *The Arraignment of Paris*, 1584; *Edward I*, 1593, 1599; *Battle of Alcazar*, 1594, repr. Malone Soc., 1906; *The Old Wives Tale*, 1595, repr. by the same 1908, *David and Bethsabe*, 1599. Eight or more pageants and pieces of occasional verse between 1585 and 1592. *Merry Conceited Jests*, 1607, six edd. to 1671. Collective ed. Bullen, 1888, 2 vols.

PEMBROKE, MARY, COUNTESS OF, 1555 ?–1621. *A Discourse of Life and Death*, 1592, 1600; Garnier's *Antonie*, 1592, ed. Luce, *Litterar-historische Forschungen*, iii, 1897.

PENRY, JOHN, fl. 1587. See Marprelate Controversy.

PERCY, WILLIAM, d. 1648. *Coelia*, 1594; repr. Garner, *Sonnets*, 1904, ii; Four plays, ed. Lloyd, for Roxburghe Club, 1824, 2 vols.

PETTIE, GEORGE, 1548–1589. *Palace of Pettie his Pleasure*, 1576, five edd. to 1613. Ed. Gollancz, 1908.

PHAER, THOMAS, d. 1560. *Seven Books of the Æneid*, 1558; *Nine Books*, 1562; 1573 (completed by Twyne to twelve books); 1583; six further edd. to 1620.

Playhouse, see Stage.

PORTER, HENRY, fl. 1600. *The Two Angry Women of Abington*, 1599[2], Dodsley, vii. And see Gayley, *Representative Comedies*, 1903.

PRESTON, THOMAS, fl. 1560. *Cambises*, 1570?, 1585? Repr. Manly, *Specimens*, ii, 1897.

PROCTOR, THOMAS. See Miscellanies.

Proteus and the Rock Adamantine, Masque of, Gesta Grayorum, 1688, repr. Nichols' *Progresses of Elizabeth*, ii.

PSEUDO-SHAKESPEARE. *Locrine, The Lamentable Tragedy of*, 1595; *Sir John Oldcastle*, 1600[2]; *Cromwell, The Chronicle History of Thomas Lord*, 1602, 1613; *The London Prodigal*, 1605; *The Puritan or the Widow of Watling Street*, 1607; *A Yorkshire Tragedy*, 1608, 1619; *Pericles, Prince of Tyre*, 1609[2], eight edd. to 1635; all of these plays were added to Shakespeare's in the third folio 1664, and reprinted in the fourth, 1685. See R. Sachs, in *Sh. Jahrbuch*, xxvii, 1892; and A. F. Hopkinson, *Shakespeare's Doubtful Plays*, 1890–95; also *Shakespeare Apocrypha*, ed. C. F. Tucker Brooke, 1908, who reprints them.

Pulpit, The English. See Bibliography *Cambridge History of Literature*, 1910, vol. iv.

PURCHASE, SAMUEL, 1575?–1626. *Purchase his Pilgrimage*, 1613, 1614, 1617, 1626. *Purchase his Pilgrim*, 1619; *Hakluytus Posthumus* or *Purchase his Pilgrims*, 1625, repr. Glasgow, 1905, 20 vols.

Puritan, The, 1607. See Pseudo-Shakespeare.

Puritan Attack on the Stage. Northbrooke, *A Treatise wherein Dancing and Vain Plays are Reproved*, 1577; Gosson, *The School of Abuse*, 1579; Munday?, *A Second and Third Blast of Retreat from Plays*, 1580; Lodge, *A Defence of Poetry, Music and Stage Plays*, 1580?; Gosson, *Apology of the School of Abuse*, 1581; Gosson, *Plays Confuted in five Actions*, 1582; Field, J., *A Godly Exhortation*, 1583; Stubbes, *Anatomy of Abuse*, 1583, five edd. to 1593; Whetstone, *A Touchstone for the Time*, 1584; Rankins, *A Mirror of Monsters*, 1587; Rainolds, *The Overthrow of Stage-plays*, 1599; Heywood, *Apology for Actors*, 1612; Greene, J., *A Refutation of the Apology*, 1615; Field, N., *Remonstrance*, 1616; Anon., *A Short Treatise Against Stage Plays*, 1625. On the general subject see E. N. S. Thompson, *The Controversy between the Puritans and the Stage, Yale Studies*, 1903.

PUTTENHAM, GEORGE, 1532–1590?. *The Art of English Poesy*, 1589, repr. Arber, 1869; *Partheniades*, first pr. ed. Haslewood, *Art of English Poesy*, 1811. See *Rev. of Engl. Studies*, 1925.

RAINOLDS, DR. JOHN, 1549–1607. *De Romanae Ecclesiae Idolatria*, 1596; *Overthrow of Stage-Plays*, 1599.

RALEIGH, SIR WALTER, 1552–1618. *A Report of the Fight about the Isles of Azores*, 1591, repr. by Hakluyt, 1595, and Arber, 1871; *Discovery of the Empire of Guiana*, 1596², repr. by Hakluyt, 1598, ed. Schomburgk, Hakluyt Society, 1848. The *History of the World*, 1614, fourteen edd. to 1687, repr. Edinburgh, 1820, 6 vols. *Prerogatives of Parliament*, ed. by Milton, 1658. *Poems now first Collected*, 1813. Contained in Hannah, *Raleigh and other Courtly Poets*, 1870. Bibliography by Brushfield, 1908.

RANKINS, WILLIAM, fl. 1587, d. 1601. *A Mirror for Monsters*, 1587; *The English Ape*, 1588; *Seven Satyres*, 1598. No play of R. is extant.

REYNOLDS, JOHN, fl. 1606. *Dolarny's Primrose*, 1606; *Epigrammata*, 1611; *The Triumphs of God's Revenge Against Mudrer*, 1622–24; and other pamphlets.

Richard II, A Tragedy of, first printed by Halliwell-Phillipps, 1870. See *Sh. Jahrbuch*, xxxv.

Richard III, The True Tragedy of, 1595, repr. *Sh. Soc.*, 1844.

RICHE, BARNABE, fl. 1574–1624. *Don Simonides*, 1581, 1584; *Riche his Farewell to the Military Profession*, 1581, 1606, repr. *Sh. Soc.*, 1846; *Brusanus, Prince of Hungaria*, 1592. Other pamphlets see Haslitt, *Handbook*, 503-506.

ROBINSON, CLEMENT, see *Miscellanies*.

ROGERS, THOMAS, d. 1616. *Celestial Elegies*, 1598, repr. Roxburghe Club, *Lamport Garland*, 1887. Also the author of many religious tracts between 1576 and 1608.

ROWLANDS, SAMUEL, 1573?–1628?. *The Letting of Humor's Blood in the Head-Vein*, 1600, seven edd. to 1613; *'T is Merry When Gossips Meet*, 1602, seven edd. to 1675; *Greene's Ghost*, 1604, 1626; *Diogenes Lanthorne*, 1607, eight edd. to 1659; *Doctor Merry-man*, 1607, thirteen other edd. *Guy of Warwick*, 1607, twelve other edd.; and twenty other like pamphlets of similar vogue. Collected ed. Gosse, *Hunterian Club*, 1880, 3 vols.

ROWLEY, SAMUEL, d. 1633?. *When You See Me You Know Me*, 1605, four edd. to 1632; *The Noble Soldier*, 1634.

ROWLEY, WILLIAM, 1585–1642. *A Search for Money*, 1609; repr. *Percy Society*, x, 1840; *A New Wonder*, 1632, Dodsley, xii; *A Match at Midnight*, 1633; Dodsley, vii; *All's Lost by Lust*, 1633; *A Shoemaker a Gentleman*, 1638, both repr. by Stork, *Publ. University of Pennsylvania*, 1910; *The Witch of Edmonton*, 1658; Mermaid ed. Dekker, 1887; *The Birth of Merlin*, 1662, ed. Warnke and Proescholdt, 1887.

RUGGLE, GEORGE, 1575–1622. *Ignoramus*, 1630^2, 1658, 1659, 1668 and four later. Transl. by Codrington, 1662; by Ravenscroft, 1678. See Dissertation by J. L. Van Gundy, Jena, 1905.

SABBIE, FRANCIS, fl. 1595. *The Fisherman's Tale*, 1595, repr. Halliwell-Phillipps, 1867; *Pan's Pipe*, 1595; repr. by Bright and Mustard in *Modern Philology*, vii, 1910. *Adam's Complaint*, 1596.

SACKVILLE, THOMAS (Earl Buckhurst), 1530–1608. *The Complaint of the Duke of Buckingham*, in *The Mirror for Magistrates* ed. 1563, and subsequent edd.; *Gorboduc* (with Norton), 1565, 1570, 1590, repr. Manly, *Specimens*, ii, 1897. For other works see *Athenae Cantabrigienses*, ii.

SANDYS, GEORGE, 1578–1644. *The Relation of a Journey*, 1615, six edd. to 1673; *Ovid's Metamorphosis*, transl. 1621–1626, 1628, 1632, 1640, 1656; *Paraphrase of the Psalms*, 1636; *A Paraphrase upon the Divine Poems*, 1638; *Solomon*, 1641^2, 1642.

Satire, Elizabethan, see R. M. Alden, *The Rise of Formal Satire in England, Publications of the University of Pennsylvania*, vii, 1899.

SCOLOKER, ANTONY, fl. 1604. *Daiphantus*, 1604. *Garner, Longer Elizabethan Poems*, 1903.

SCOTT, REGINALD, 1538–1599. *The Hop Garden*, 1574; *The Discovery of Witchcraft*, 1584, repr. ed. Nicholson, 1886.

SELDEN, JOHN, 1584–1654. *Latin and English Writings*, 1610; *Notes on Polyolbion*, 1612, 1613; *Titles of Honor*, 1614; *History of Tithes*, 1618; *Table Talk*, 1689 and many edd. *Works*, ed. Wilkins, 1726, 3 vols.

Seneca, translated. *Troas*, 1559, *Thyestes*, 1560, *Hercules Furens*, 1561, these three by Jasper Heywood; *Œdipus*, 1563, by Alexander Nevile; *Medea, Agamemnon*, both 1566, *Hippolytus*, and *Hercules Œtaeus*, 1581, these four by John Studley; *Octavia*, [n.d.], and *Thebais*, by Thomas Nuce, who collected the work as *Seneca his Ten Tragedies Translated*, 1581. Repr. Spenser Society, 1887. 2 vols. See J. W. Cunliffe, *The Influence of Seneca*, 1893; Kastner and Charlton, Introduction, *Works of Sir William Alexander*, 1921.

SHAKESPEARE, WILLIAM, 1564–1616. Quartos: *Venus and Adonis*, 1593, eleven edd. to 1675; *Lucrece*, 1594, eight edd. to 1611; *Titus Andronicus*, 1594, 1600, 1611; *Richard II*, 1597, five edd. to 1634; *Richard III*, 1597, eight edd. to 1629; *Romeo and Juliet*, 1597, four edd. to 1637; 1 *Henry IV*, 1598, eight edd. to 1639; *Love's Labor's Lost*, 1598, 1631; *The Passionate Pilgrim*, 1599, (2nd ed. lost), 1612; *The Merchant of Venice*, 1600, four edd. to 1652; *Henry V*, 1600, 1602, (1619); *Much Ado About Nothing*, 1600; 2 *Henry IV*, 1600; *A Midsummer-Night's Dream*, 1600, (1619); *The Merry Wives of Windsor*, 1602, 1619, 1630; *Hamlet*, 1603, 1604–05, 1611, 1637; *King Lear*, 1608, (1619), 1655; *Troilus and Cressida*, 1609[2]; *Pericles*, 1609, four issues to 1619; *Sonnets*, 1609, 1640; *Othello*, 1622, 1630, 1655. Folios: First folio (contains these and the rest of the plays except *Pericles*), 1623; Second folio, repr. of the first, 1632; Third folio (contains all of the foregoing, *Pericles*, and six plays not Shakespeare's), 1664; Fourth folio, a reprint of the third, 1685. The fifteen additional quartos of single plays issued after the first folio, all of them, except *The Taming of the Shrew*, 1631, are reprints of former quartos. R. M. Alden, Variorum ed. of the *Sonnets*, 1916.

The best of many reproductions of the Sh. folios is that of the first by Lee, 1902; and all four by Methuen & Co., 1903–06. The quartos were reproduced under the superintendence of Furnivall, 1880–89, also by photography. Important works on the Bibliography

BIBLIOGRAPHY

of the early edd. of Sh. are Lee, *Bibliographical History of the First Folio*, 1905, and Pollard, *Shakespeare Folios and Quartos*, 1909, and his *Shakespeare's Fight with the Pirates*, 1920. Critical edd. of Sh. began with Rowe, 1709; and through the edd. of Pope, 1723–25; Theobald, 1733; Johnson, 1765; Capell, 1767; Malone, "the first Variorum," 1790 and many more to Dyce, 1857; Halliwell, 1853–65; the Cambridge ed., 1863–66. A new Variorum ed. was begun by H. H. Furness in 1873, still in progress; a new Cambridge ed. by Quiller-Couch and Wilson, 1921–27, 10 vols.

In addition to the *Life of Sh.* by Halliwell-Phillipps, 1881, most important of a score of recent biographies are those of Fleay, 1886, Dowden, 1893, Brandl, 1894, Brandes, 1896, Lee, 1898, Rolfe, 1904; Raleigh, 1907; Alden, 1922; Adams, 1925. See also the bibliographies of *The Cambridge History* and the present writer's, *Elizabethan Drama*, 1908, and *Elizabethan Playwrights*, 1925.

SHELTON, THOMAS, 1531–1620. *The Delightful History of the Witty Knight, Don Quixote*, 1612, 2nd part, 1620, 1652, 1675; ed. Kelly, *Tudor Translations*, 1896, 3 vols.

SIDNEY, SIR PHILIP, 1554–1586. *Arcadia*, 1590, reproduced ed. Sommer, 1891; sixteen edd. to 1674; *Astrophel and Stella*, 1591³, repr. *An English Garner*, 1904; *Defense of Poesie* (*An Apology for Poetry*), 1595, 1598 with *Arcadia* and thereafter so printed, ed. Cook, 1890; *Certain Sonnets*, 1598, ed. of *Arcadia; The Lady of May*, 1613 ed. of the same; *Psalms*, first printed 1823. *Poems*, ed. Grosart, 1873, 3 vols.; *Miscellaneous Works*, ed. Gray, 1829; ed. Flügel, *Astrophel and Stella*, 1889. Life by Greville, 1652; Symonds, *Men of Letters*, 1886; *Complete Works*, ed. A. Feuillerat, 4 vols., 1922–26.

SMITH, WILLIAM, fl. 1596. See Sonnet Sequences.

Sonnet Sequences and like Lyrical Collections. Puttenham, *Partheniads*, 1579. Gifford, *Posie of Gilliflowers*, 1580. Watson, *Passionate Century of Love*, 1582. Soothern, *Pandora*, 1584, Munday, *Banquet of Dainty Conceits*, 1588. Sidney, *Astrophel and Stella*, 1591. Constable, *Diana;* Daniel, *Delia*, 1592. Barnes, *Parthenophil;* G. Fletcher, *Licia;* Lodge, *Phillis;* Watson, *Tears of Fancy*, 1593. Barnfield, *Affectionate Shepherd;* Drayton, *Idea's Mirror;* Percy, *Coelia; Willobie his Avisa; Zepheria*, 1594. Barnes, *Century of Spiritual Sonnets;* Chapman, *A Coronet for his Mistress Philosophy;* E. C., *Emaricdulph;* J. C., *Alcilia*, 4 edd., Davies, *Gulling Sonnets;* Spenser, *Amoretti*, 1595. Griffin, *Fidessa*, Lynche, *Diella;* Smith, *Chloris*, 1596. Breton, *Arbor of Amorous Devices;* Lok, *Sundry Sonnets;* Tofte, *Laura*, 1597. Tofte, *Alba, the Month's Mind*, 1598;

The Passionate Pilgrim (Shakespeare), 1599. Chester, *Love's Martyr*, 1601. Alexander, *Aurora;* Breton, *The Passionate Shepherd;* Scoloker, *Daiphantus*, 1604. *Dolarny's Primrose*, 1506. Drummond, *Poems*, 1607. Shakespeare, *Sonnets*, 1609. Davies, *Wit's Pilgrimage*, 1610. Browne, *Caelia*, [1616]. Wither, *Fidelia*, 1617. Davies, *Hymns to Astræa*, 1618. Wither, *Fair Virtue*, 1622. Greville, *Cælica*, 1633. Constable, *Spiritual Sonnets* 1815. See Schelling, *Elizabethan Lyrics*, 1895; S. Lee, Introduction to *English Garner, Elizabethan Sonnets*, 1904; Crow, *Elizabethan Sonnet-Cycles*, 1896–98.

SOUTHWELL, ROBERT, 1562–1595. *Saint Peter's Complaint*, 1595[3]; eight edd. to 1615; *Mæoniæ*, 1595, 1596, 1597; some half-dozen prose tracts between 1593 and 1595, chief among them, *Mary Magdalen's Tears*, 1594 and three other edd.; and *The Triumphs over Death*, 1595, 1596. Collected works, ed. Grosart, *Fuller Worthies' Library*, 1872.

SPEED, JOHN, 1552 ?–1629. *History of Great Britain*, 1611, 1623, 1632, 1650; *Genealogies in Scripture*, 1611, 33 edd. to 1640.

SPENSER, EDMUND, 1552–1599. *Epigrams* and *Sonnets* in *The Theater for Worldlings*, 1569; *The Shepherds' Calendar*, 1579, six edd. to 1611; *The Faery Queen*, 1590–96, 1609, ed. Warren, 1896–1900; *Complaints*, 1591; *Daphnaïda*, 1591, 1596; *Colin Clout's Come Home Again, Amoretti, Epithalamium*, 1595; *Four Hymns, Prothalamium*, 1596, ed. Winstanley, 1907; *A View of the Present State of Ireland*, 1633. Collected Works, first folio 1611 (second folio only of *The Faery Queen*), ed. Child, 1855, 5 vols.; *Globe* ed., by Hales and Morris, 1869; Grosart, 1882–84, 10 vols; J. C. Smith, 1910, 3 vols., in progress. Lives: Church, Men of Letters, 1879; Dowden, 1888; and see Bibliography in *Cambridge History of Literature*.

Stage, Elizabethan. See bibliography in Schelling, *Elizabethan Drama;* also G. T. Reynolds, *Mod. Philol.* 1911; A. H. Thorndike, *Shakespeare's Theater*, 1916; J. Q. Adams, *Shakespearean Playhouses*, 1917; and Chambers, *Elizabethan Stage*, 1923, vol. iii.

STANIHURST, RICHARD, 1547–1618. *Four Books of Vergil*, 1582, 1583, repr. Arber, *English Scholar's Library*, 1880; *Description* and *History of Ireland* contributed to Holinshed, ed. 1577; several Latin religious tracts.

STAPLETON, THOMAS, 1535–1598. *History of the Church of England*, 1565; many controversial writings. *Opera Omnia*, 1620, includes the *Apology for Philip II*.

STEVENSON, WILLIAM, fl. 1550. *Gammer Gurton's Needle*, 1562–3 (*Diccon of Bedlam*, Stationers' Register, this ed. lost); 1575. In Gayley, *English Comedies*, 1903. As to authorship, see Bradley in *Athenæum*, Aug. 6, 1898, and Chambers, *Mediæval Drama*, ii, 457.

STILL, JOHN, 1543–1608. Sometime reputed author of *Gammer Gurton's Needle*. See Stevenson, William.

STOW, JOHN, 1525–1605. Editor of Chaucer, 1561, assisting in Speight's ed. of the same, 1598; *Summary of English Chronicles*, 1565, ten edd. to 1604; editor, Matthew of Westminster, 1567, of Matthew of Paris, 1571, of Thomas of Walsingham, 1574; *Annals of England*, 1573, five edd. to 1631; *Survey of London*, 1598, four edd. to 1633.

STUBBS, Philip, fl. 1580–1593. *The Anatomy of Abuse*, two parts, 1583, four edd. to 1595. Repr. *New Sh. Soc.*, 1877 and 1882. Several religious tracts between 1581 and 1593, for which see *Sh. Soc. Papers*, iii and iv, and Collier, *Broadside Black Letter Ballads*, 1868.

STUDLEY, JOHN, fl. 1566–81. See Seneca Translated.

Stukeley, The Famous (Chronicle) History of Captain Thomas, 1605, Simpson, *School of Shakspere*, 1878.

SURREY, EARL OF (Henry Howard), 1517 ?–1547. See Miscellanies; ed. F. M. Padelford, 1920.

SWETNAM, JOSEPH, fl. 1615. *The Arraignment of Women*, 1615, five edd. to 1690; and other satirical pamphlets. See Grosart, repr. *Swetnam the Woman Hater*, 1620, *Occasional Issues*, 1880.

SYLVESTER, JOSHUA, 1563–1618. *A Canticle of the Victory at Ivry*, 1590; fragments of transl. of *La Semaine*, 1592–1605; *Du Bartas, his Divine Weeks and Works*, 1606, six edd. to 1641. Also several minor works, mostly translations. Collective ed. Grosart, *Chertsey Worthies' Library*, 1880, 2 vols.

Taming of a Shrew, The, 1594. Repr. *Sh. Quartos*, 1886; *Shakespeare Classics*, ed. Boas, 1908.

TARLTON, RICHARD, d. 1588. See Halliwell-Phillipps, ed. *Tarlton's Jests*, *Sh. Soc.*, *Publ.* 1844. *Famous History of Henry V*, 1598, facsimile ed. Furnivall, 1887.

Thracian Wonder, The, "Webster and Rowley," *Two New Plays*, 1661. Dyce's *Webster*.

TOFTE, ROBERT, d. 1619 ?. *Two Tales of Ariosto*, 1597; *Laura*, 1597, *Garner, Sonnets*, ii; *Alba the Month s Mind*, 1598, Grosart, *Occasional Issues*, 1880; Boiardo, *Orlando Innamorato*, 1598.

TOMKINS, THOMAS, 1614. *Albumazar*, 1615, 1634, 1668; *Lingua*, 1617, five edd. to 1657 doubtfully by Tomkins. Dodsley, ix and xi.

Tom Tyler and his Wife, 1661, ed. Schelling, *Mod. Lang. Publ.*, xv, 1900.

Tottel's Miscellany, 1557. See Miscellanies.

TOURNEUR, CYRIL, 1575–1626. *The Transformed Metamorphosis*, 1600; two or three panegyrics, between 1609 and 1613; *The Revenger's Tragedy*, 1607; *The Atheist's Tragedy*, 1611. *Plays and Poems*, ed. Collins, 1878, 2 vols. Ed. A. H. Thorndike with Webster, 1912.

Tragedy, for the Bibliography of, see Bibliographical Essay, Schelling, *Elizabethan Drama;* and A. H. Thorndike, *Tragedy, Types of English Literature*, 1909.

Tragicomedy. See A. H. Thorndike, *The Influence of Beaumont and Fletcher on Shakespeare*, 1901; and Schelling, *Elizabethan Drama*, chapter xvii; F. H. Ristine, *Tragicomedy*, 1910.

Translators. For an excellent bibliography of English translation during this period see *The Cambridge History of English Literature*, vol. iv, 1910. Also, W. J. Harris, *The First Printed Translations of Great Foreign Classics*, 1909; T. G. Tucker, *The Foreign Debt of English Literature*, 1907.

Trial of Chivalry, The, 1605. Bullen, *Old Plays*, vol. iii.

TURBERVILLE, GEORGE, 1530–1594?. *Epitaphs, Epigrams, etc.*, 1567[2], 1570, 1597, Collier *Reprints*, vol. ii; *Eclogues of Mantuan*, 1567, 1572, 1594, 1597; *Heroical Epistles of Ovid*, 1567, five edd. to 1605; *A Plain Path to Virtue*, 1568; *The Book of Falconry*, 1575; *The Noble Book of Venery*, 1575; repr. together, 1611; *Tragical Tales* (chiefly from Boccaccio), 1576, 1587, repr. Edinburgh, 1837.

TUSSER, THOMAS, fl. 1525–1580. *A Hundredth Good Points of Husbandry*, 1557; *Five Hundreth Points of Good Husbandry*, 1573, fifteen edd. to 1672; repr. *English Dialect Society*, 1878; *The Book of Huswifery*, 1562, appended to edd. of the last.

Two Tragedies in One (Yarington, R.), 1601. Repr. Bullen, *Old Plays*, iv.

TWINE, LAWRENCE, fl. 1576. *The Pattern of Painful Adventures*, [1576?], 1595, 1607. Repr. *Shakespeare's Library*, 1843.

UDALL, JOHN, 1560?–1592. See Martin Marprelate Controversy.

UDALL, NICHOLAS, 1505?–1556. *Flowers of Latin Speaking out of Terence*, 1533, several later edd.; *Apophthegms of Erasmus*, 1542; *Ralph Roister Doister*, 1566, repr. Arber, 1869, in Gayley, *Representative Comedies*, 1903, and Adams, *Pre-Shakespearean Drama*, 1924.

Valiant Welshman, The, 1615, 1663; repr. by Kreb, *Münchener Beiträge*, 1902.

Voyages. See *Garner, Travelers' Tales*, 1903, 2 vols. E.

J. Payne, *Voyages of Elizabethan Seamen*, 1893–1900, 4 vols.;
J. A. Froude, *English Seamen in the Sixteenth Century*, 1901. Bibliography, *Cambridge History of English Literature*, vol. iv, 1910 and
see Hakluyt.

WADESON, ANTHONY, fl. 1600. *Look About You*, 1600. Dodsley,
vii.

WARNER, WILLIAM, 1558–1609. *Pan his Syrinx*, 1584, 1597;
Albion's England, completed by accretions in nine edd., 1586 to 1612;
repr. *Chalmers' English Poets*, 1810, vol. iv. *Menaechmi of Plautus*,
transl., 1595.

Warning for Fair Women, A, 1599, Simpson, *School of Shakspere*,
1878.

War of the Theaters, see J. H. Penniman, monograph of that
title, *Publications of the University of Pennsylvania*, 1897; R. A. Small,
in *Forschungen zur englischen Sprache*, i, 1899; H. C. Hart, in *Notes
and Queries*, series ix, 1903; and the Introduction ed. by Penniman
of *Poetaster* and *Satiromastix, Belles Lettres Series*, 1913.

Wars of Cyrus, The, 1594, repr. *Sh. Jahrbuch*, xxxvii, 1901.

WATSON, THOMAS, 1557–1592. *Hecatompathia or the Century
of Love*, 1582, repr. Arber, 1869; *Italian Madrigals Englished*, 1590;
The Tears of Fancy, 1593, Garner, *Sonnets*, i, 1904. Latin verses
in transl. of Greek and Italian authors between 1581 and 1592.

Weakest Goeth to the Wall, The, by "Webster and Dekker," 1600.

WEBBE, WILLIAM, fl. 1568–1586. *A Discourse of English Poetry*,
1586, repr. Arber, 1870.

WEBSTER, JOHN, 1580 ?–1625. *Sir Thomas Wyatt, Westward Hoe,
Northward Hoe* (all with Dekker) and each in 1607; *The White
Devil*, 1612, 1631, 1665, 1672; *The Duchess of Malfi*, 1623, 1640,
1678, 1708; *The Devil's Law Case*, 1623; *Appius and Virginia*, 1654;
two new plays: *A Cure for a Cuckold, The Thracian Wonder*, "by
Webster and William Rowley," 1661, neither of them Webster's.
Works ed. Dyce, 1830, 4 vols.; Mermaid Series, *Webster and Tourneur*,
contains the two great tragedies as does *Webster* ed. Sampson, *Belles
Letters*, 1904; R. Brooke, *Webster and Elizabethan Drama*, 1616.

WEELKES, THOMAS, fl. 1597. *Madrigals*, 1597, repr. Musical
Antiquarian Society, 1845; *Ballets and Madrigals*, 1598, 1608;
Madrigals for Viols and Voices, 1600; *Madrigals*, 1600; *Airs or
Fantastic Sprites*, 1608. Also contributions to other musical collections.

WEEVER, JOHN, 1576–1632. *Epigrams*, 1599; *The Mirror of
Martyrs*, 1601, repr. *Roxburghe Club*, 1873; *Agnus Dei*, "a thumb
book," 1606; *Ancient Funeral Monuments*, 1631.

WHETSTONE, GEORGE, fl. 1576–1587. *The Rock of Regard*, 1576; repr. *Collier Reprints; Remembrances* (metrical lives), 1577–85; *Promos and Cassandra*, 1578, repr. *Shakespeare's Library*, ed. Collier-Hazlitt, 1875; *An Heptameron of Civil Discourses*, 1582, 1593 (under title *Aurelia*); and other prose tracts.

WHITEHORNE, PETER, fl. 1560. *The Art of War* of Macchiavelli, 1560, 1573. *Tudor Translations*, 1905.

WHITGIFT, JOHN (Archbishop of Canterbury), 1530 ?–1604. For Bibliography see *D. N. B.*, lxi.

WILBYE, JOHN, fl. 1598–1614. Two sets of *Madrigals* in 1598 and 1608. Also contributor to other musical collections. Ed. J. Turle, 1840–41, and ed. Budd, 1846.

WILKINS, GEORGE, fl. 1608. *The Miseries of Enforced Marriage*, 1607; repr. Dodsley, x; *The Travails of Three English Brothers*, 1607, Bullen, ed. Day. *The Painful Adventures of Pericles, Prince of Tyre*, 1608.

WILLES, RICHARD, fl. 1558–1573. Latin poems, 1573; editor with Richard Eden of *The History of Travel*, 1577; and of articles in Hakluyt's *Voyages*.

Willobie his Avisa, 1594, five edd. to 1635. Ed. Grosart, *Occasional Issues*, 1880.

WILMOT, ROBERT, fl. 1568–1619. *Tancred and Gismund*, 1591, Dodsley, vii.

WILSON, ROBERT (the elder) fl. 1584–1600. *The Three Ladies of London*, 1584; *The Three Lords and Three Ladies of London*, 1590, both in *Dodsley*, vi; *The Cobbler's Prophecy*, 1594, repr. *Sh. Jahrbuch*, 1897; *The Pedlar's Prophecy*, 1595.

WILSON, SIR THOMAS, fl. 1550. *The Rule of Reason, Containing the Art of Logic*, 1551, seven edd. to 1580; *The Art of Rhetoric*, 1553, five edd. to 1585.

WINGFIELD, ANTHONY, or FORSETT, EDWARD. *Pedantius*, 1631. Ed. J. C. M. Smith, *Materialien zur Kunde*, 1905.

WITHER, GEORGE, 1588–1667. *Prince Henry's Obsequies*, 1612, 1617; *Epithalamia*, 1613, 1620; *Abuses Stript and Whipt*, 1613, 1614, 1615, 1617; *A Satyre*, 1615; *The Shepherd's Hunting*, 1615, 1620; *Fidelia*, 1617², 1619, 1620; *Wither's Motto*, 1621²; *Fair Virtue*, 1622. *Works*, 1620 (a surreptitious volume), *Juvenilia*, 1622, 1626, 1633. The rest of Wither's copious bibliography belongs to controversy and uninspired religious edification. Mod. edd. *Spenser Soc.*, 1870–83, in 20 parts. Selections ed. Morley, *Companion Poets*, 1891.

Woodstock, The Tragedy of Thomas of, see *Richard II*.

WOTTON, HENRY, fl. 1580. *A Courtly Controversy of Cupid's Cautels*, 1581.

WOTTON, SIR HENRY, 1568–1639. *Elements of Architecture*, 1624; *Ad Regem*, 1633; *The State of Christendom*, 1637; *Reliquiæ Wotton-ianae*, 1651, four edd. to 1685. Poems, ed. Dyce, 1842; with Raleigh, ed. Hannah, 1870.

YARINGTON, ROBERT, fl. 1600. *Two Lamentable Tragedies*, 1601, Bullen, *Old Plays*, iv.

Yorkshire, Tragedy, The, 1608, 1619. See Pseudo-Shakespeare.

YOUNG, BARTHOLOMEW, d. 1621. Guazzo's *Civil Conversation*, 1586; *Amorous Fiametta*, 1587; Montemayor's *Diana*, 1598, in part repr'd. Collier, *Sh. Library*, ii, 1843.

YONGE, NICHOLAS, d. 1619. *Musica Transalpina*, 1588, words reprinted in *Garner, Shorter Poems*, 1903.

Zepheria, see Sonnet Sequences.

A SUPPLEMENTARY LIST,

adding to the items already noted a few important collections, some recent editions of authors not already included in the foregoing Bibliography, and a selection of works of commentary.

ADAMS, J. Q. *The Dramatic Records of Sir Henry Herbert,* 1917.

ALBRIGHT, E. M. *Dramatic Publications in England, 1580–1640,* 1927.

ARONSTEIN, P. *Thomas Heywood,* Anglia, 1913.

AULT, N. *Elizabethan Lyrics,* 1925.

BIBLIOGRAPHY. *The Year's Work in English Studies,* 1919–1924, 5 vols.; *Bibliography of English Language and Literature,* Modern Humanities Research Association, 1925–1926; *American Bibliography,* Publ., Modern Language Asso., 1921 to date; and *The American Year Book,* 1915–1919.

BOAS, T. S. *Shakespeare and the Universities,* 1923.

Bodley Head Quartos, ed. G. B. Harrison, 1923–1925, 12 vols., in progress. [Elizabethan Prose Tracts.]

BOND, R. W. *Early Plays from the Italian,* 1911.

BRADLEY, A. C. *Shakespearean Tragedy,* 1904.

BRADY, G. K. *Samuel Daniel, a Critical Study,* Abstract of Thesis, Illinois University, 1923.

BRETT, C. *The Minor Poems of Michael Drayton,* 1907.

BRIDGE, F. *O Mistress Mine, Shakespeare's Music,* 1923.

BRIE, T. *Lyly und Greene,* Englische Studien, 1910.

BRIGGS, W. D. *Studies in Ben Jonson,* Anglia, 1913–14.

BROOKE, C. F. T. *Shakespeare's Plutarch,* 1909.

BRUSHFIELD, T. N. *Bibliography of Raleigh,* 1908, 2nd ed.

BULLEN, A. H. *A Collection of Old English Plays,* 4 vols., 1882–1885.

Elizabethans, 1924. (Contains essays on Breton, Campion, Daniel and others.)

BYRNE, M. ST. C. *The Elizabethan Home* Discovered in Two Dialogues by Claudius Hollyband and Peter Erondell, 1925.

Anthony Munday and His Books. Bibliographical Society Trans. n. s., i, 4, 1921, and The Library, 1923.

Cambridge History of English Literature, The. Edited by A. W. Ward and A. R. Waller, 14 vols., 1907–1916. (Vols. iii to vi include the period of this volume.)

CAMPBELL, L. B. *Scenes and Machines on the English Stage,* 1923.

CARPENTER, F. I. *A Reference Guide to Edmund Spenser,* 1923.

CHAMBRUN, L. *Giovanni Florio, un apôtre de la Renaissance en Angleterre,* 1921.

CHEFFAND, P. H. *George Peele,* 1913.

CHEVELLEY, A. *Thomas Deloney, le roman des métier au temps de Shakespeare,* Paris, 1926.

COURTHOPE, W. J. *A History of English Poetry,* 1893–1910. (Vols. ii and iii concern the period of this volume.)

COWLING, G. H. *Music on the Shakespearian Stage,* 1913.

CRAWFORD, C. *Collectanea,* 2 vols., 1906.

Ed. *England's Parnassus,* 1913.

CREIZENACH, W. *The English Drama in the Age of Shakespeare,* 1916. [A translation of Band iv of the *Geschichte.*]

CROLL, M. W., and CLEMONS, H. *Euphues: the Anatomy of Wit Euphues and His England* by John Lyly, 1916.

CROLL, M. W. *The Works of Sir Foulke Greville,* Diss., 1903.

CUNLIFFE, J. W. *Early English Classical Tragedies,* 1912.

DE SELINCOURT, E. *Spenser's Minor Poems,* 1910.

ELLIS-FERMOR, U. M. *Christopher Marlowe,* 1927.

ELLISON, L. M. *The Early Romantic Drama at the English Court,* 1917.

England's Helicon. New Reprint, 1925, *Haslewood Books.*

FAIRHOLT, F. W. *Lord Mayors' Pageants,* 2 vols., 1843–1844. [*Percy Society,* xxxviii, xliii.]

FARMER, J. S. *The Tudor Facsimile Texts,* 184 vols., 1907–1914; Early English Drama Society, 1906; Recently Lost Tudor Plays, 1907. (Texts of old plays.)

FAUSET, H. I. *John Donne, a Study in Discord,* n. d. [1923].

FEUILLERAT, A. *Documents relating to the Office of the Revels in the time of Queen Elizabeth,* 1908. (Materialien, xxi.)

GAYLEY, C. M. *Representative English Comedies,* 3 vols., 1903–1914.

Gesta Grayorum, Francis Davison?, Malone Society, 1914.

GILDERSLEEVE, V. C. *Government Regulations of Elizabethan Drama,* 1908.

GRAVES, T. S. *The Court and the London Theaters During the Reign of Elizabeth,* 1913.

GREG, W. W. *A List of English plays* written before 1643 and printed before 1700, 1900.

A List of Masques, Pageants, etc., 1902.

GRIERSON, H. J. C. *Metaphysical Poems of the Seventeenth Century,* 1921.

Haslewood Books, 1924–1926. (Reprints of Elizabethan Verse and Prose.) 14 vols. in progress.

HATCHER, O. L. *John Fletcher, a Study in Dramatic Method,* 1905.

HERFORD, C. H. *A Sketch of Recent Shakespeare Investigation,* 1923.

HOOD, C. M. *The Book of Robert Southwell,* 1926.

HUBBARD, G. *On the Site of the Globe Playhouse,* 1923.

HUGHES, C. *The Itinerary of Fynes Moryson,* 1907–1908.

JORDAN, J. C. *Robert Greene,* 1915.

KASTNER, L. E. *Thomas Lodge as an Imitator of Italian Poets,* Mod. Lang. Rev., 1907.

KELLNER, L. E. *Restoring Shakespeare,* a Critical Analysis of Misreadings, 1925.

KEYNES, G. *Bibliography of the Works of Dr. John Donne, Dean of St. Paul's,* 1914.

LAWRENCE, J. W. *The Elizabethan Playhouse,* 2 vols., 1912, 1913.

LEE, SIR S. *The French Renaissance in England,* 1910.

LUCAS, F. L. *Shakespeare and Elizabethan Tragedy,* 1922.

MACDONAGH, T. *Thomas Campion and the Art of English Poetry,* 1913.

MCKERROW, R. B., ed. *The Gulls' Handbook,* King's Library, 1904.

Malone Society, Collections, vol. i, 1907–1911; vol. ii, pt. i, 1913; and *Reprints,* 1907–1927, in progress. (Texts, Documents and Commentary on Elizabethan Drama.)

Materialien zur Kunde des älteren englischen Dramas, edited by W. Bang, Louvain, 43 vols., 1902–1914.

Mermaid Series, The Best Plays of the Old Dramatists, 22 vols., 1887–1895.

MERRILL, L. R. The Life and Poems of Nicholas Grimald, *Yale Studies*, 1925.

MURRAY, J. T. *English Dramatic Companies*, 2 vols., 1910.

NEILSON, W. A. *The Chief Elizabethan Dramatists Excluding Shakespeare*, 1911.

NICHOLS, J. *The Progresses and Public Processions of Queen Elizabeth*, 3 vols., 2nd ed., 1823.

The Progresses, Processions and Magnificent Entertainments of King James the First, 4 vols., 1828.

NIEDIG, W. J. *The Shakespeare Quartos of 1619*, Mod. Philol., 1911.

NOBLE, R. *Shakespeare's Use of Song*, 1923.

ONIONS, C. T. *Shakespeare's England*, 2 vols., 1916. (An important coöperative work.)

PATTERSON, R. F. *Conversations of Ben Jonson with Drummond of Hawthornden*, 1922.

Pedantins. See ed. Moore Smith, G. C., Materialien, 1905.

The Phœnix Nest, new ed., *Haslewood Books*, 1926.

POLLARD, A. W., *The Foundations of Shakespeare's Texts*, 1923.

The Holy Bible. Reprint of the Authorized Version, of 1611, with an Introduction, 1911.

REYHER, P. *Les Masques anglais*, 1909.

REYNOLDS, G. F. *What We Know of the Elizabethan Stage*, Mod. Philol., 1911.

Some Principles of Elizabethan Staging, Mod. Philol., 1905.

William Percy and His Plays, Mod. Philol., 1914.

ROBERTSON, J. M. *Shakespeare and Chapman*, 1917.

SCHELLING, F. E. *Foreign Influences in Elizabethan Drama*, 1923.

Typical Elizabethan Plays, 1926 (exclusive of Shakespeare.)

SCOTT, M. A. *Elizabethan Translations from the Italian*, 1916.

SEEMANN, M. *Sir John Davies, sein Leben und seine Werke*, Wien, 1913.

SHEAVYN, P. *The Literary Profession in the Elizabethan Age*, 1909.

SIMPSON, E. M. *A Study of the Prose Works of John Donne*, 1924.

SIMPSON, P. *The Portraiture of Humors*, his ed. of *Every Man in His Humor*, 1919.

SMITH, C. G. MOORE. *Harvey's Marginalia*, 1917.

MERRILL, L. R.   The Life and Poems of Nicholas Grimald, *Yale Studies*, 1925.

MURRAY, J. T.   *English Dramatic Companies*, 2 vols., 1910.

NEILSON, W. A.   *The Chief Elizabethan Dramatists Excluding Shakespeare*, 1911.

NICHOLS, J.   *The Progresses and Public Processions of Queen Elizabeth*, 3 vols., 2nd ed., 1823.

The Progresses, Processions and Magnificent Entertainments of King James the First, 4 vols., 1828.

NIEDIG, W. J.   *The Shakespeare Quartos of 1619*, Mod. Philol., 1911.

NOBLE, R.   *Shakespeare's Use of Song*, 1923.

ONIONS, C. T.   *Shakespeare's England*, 2 vols., 1916.   (An important coöperative work.)

PATTERSON, R. F.   *Conversations of Ben Jonson with Drummond of Hawthornden*, 1922.

Pedantins.   See ed. Moore Smith, G. C., Materialien, 1905.

The Phœnix Nest, new ed., *Haslewood Books*, 1926.

POLLARD, A. W.,   *The Foundations of Shakespeare's Texts*, 1923.

The Holy Bible.   Reprint of the Authorized Version, of 1611, with an Introduction, 1911.

REYHER, P.   *Les Masques anglais*, 1909.

REYNOLDS, G. F.   *What We Know of the Elizabethan Stage*, Mod. Philol., 1911.

Some Principles of Elizabethan Staging, Mod. Philol., 1905.

William Percy and His Plays, Mod. Philol., 1914.

ROBERTSON, J. M.   *Shakespeare and Chapman*, 1917.

SCHELLING, F. E.   *Foreign Influences in Elizabethan Drama*, 1923.

Typical Elizabethan Plays, 1926 (exclusive of Shakespeare.)

SCOTT, M. A.   *Elizabethan Translations from the Italian*, 1916.

SEEMANN, M.   *Sir John Davies, sein Leben und seine Werke*, [W]ien, 1913.

SHEAVYN, P.   *The Literary Profession in the Elizabethan Age*, [190]9.

SIMPSON, E. M.   *A Study of the Prose Works of John Donne*,

[SI]MPSON, P.   *The Portraiture of Humors*, his ed. of *Every [Man] in His Humor*, 1919.

[SM]ITH, C. G. MOORE.   *Harvey's Marginalia*, 1917.

A SUPPLEMENTARY LIST,

adding to the items already noted a few important collections, some recent editions of authors not already included in the foregoing Bibliography, and a selection of works of commentary.

ADAMS, J. Q.   *The Dramatic Records of Sir Henry Herbert*, 1917.

ALBRIGHT, E. M.   *Dramatic Publications in England, 1580–1640*, 1927.

ARONSTEIN, P.   *Thomas Heywood*, Anglia, 1913.

AULT, N.   *Elizabethan Lyrics*, 1925.

BIBLIOGRAPHY.   *The Year's Work in English Studies*, 1919–1924, 5 vols.; *Bibliography of English Language and Literature*, Modern Humanities Research Association, 1925–1926; *American Bibliography*, Publ., Modern Language Asso., 1921 to date; and *The American Year Book*, 1915–1919.

BOAS, T. S.   *Shakespeare and the Universities*, 1923.

Bodley Head Quartos, ed. G. B. Harrison, 1923–1925, 12 vols., in progress.   [Elizabethan Prose Tracts.]

BOND, R. W.   *Early Plays from the Italian*, 1911.

BRADLEY, A. C.   *Shakespearean Tragedy*, 1904.

BRADY, G. K.   *Samuel Daniel, a Critical Study*, Abstract of Thesis, Illinois University, 1923.

BRETT, C.   *The Minor Poems of Michael Drayton*, 1907.

BRIDGE, F.   *O Mistress Mine, Shakespeare's Music*, 1923.

BRIE, T.   *Lyly und Greene*, Englische Studien, 1910.

BRIGGS, W. D.   *Studies in Ben Jonson*, Anglia, 1913–14.

BROOKE, C. F. T.   *Shakespeare's Plutarch*, 1909.

BRUSHFIELD, T. N.   *Bibliography of Raleigh*, 1908, 2nd ed.

BULLEN, A. H.   *A Collection of Old English Plays*, 4 vols., 1882–1885.

Elizabethans, 1924.   (Contains essays on Breton, Campion, Daniel and others.)

BYRNE, M. ST. C.   *The Elizabethan Home* Discovered in Two Dialogues by Claudius Hollyband and Peter Erondell, 1925.

Anthony Munday and His Books.   Bibliographical Society Trans. n. s., i, 4, 1921, and The Library, 1923.

Cambridge History of English Literature, The. Edited by A. W. Ward and A. R. Waller, 14 vols., 1907–1916. (Vols. iii to vi include the period of this volume.)

CAMPBELL, L. B. *Scenes and Machines on the English Stage,* 1923.

CARPENTER, F. I. *A Reference Guide to Edmund Spenser,* 1923.

CHAMBRUN, L. *Giovanni Florio, un apôtre de la Renaissance en Angleterre,* 1921.

CHEFFAND, P. H. *George Peele,* 1913.

CHEVELLEY, A. *Thomas Deloney, le roman des métier au temps de Shakespeare,* Paris, 1926.

COURTHOPE, W. J. *A History of English Poetry,* 1893–1910. (Vols. ii and iii concern the period of this volume.)

COWLING, G. H. *Music on the Shakespearian Stage,* 1913.

CRAWFORD, C. *Collectanea,* 2 vols., 1906.

Ed. *England's Parnassus,* 1913.

CREIZENACH, W. *The English Drama in the Age of Shakespeare,* 1916. [A translation of Band iv of the *Geschichte.*]

CROLL, M. W., and CLEMONS, H. *Euphues: the Anatomy of Wit Euphues and His England* by John Lyly, 1916.

CROLL, M. W. *The Works of Sir Foulke Greville,* Diss., 1903.

CUNLIFFE, J. W. *Early English Classical Tragedies,* 1912.

DE SELINCOURT, E. *Spenser's Minor Poems,* 1910.

ELLIS-FERMOR, U. M. *Christopher Marlowe,* 1927.

ELLISON, L. M. *The Early Romantic Drama at the English Court,* 1917.

England's Helicon. New Reprint, 1925, *Haslewood Books.*

FAIRHOLT, F. W. *Lord Mayors' Pageants,* 2 vols., 1843–1844. [*Percy Society,* xxxviii, xliii.]

FARMER, J. S. *The Tudor Facsimile Texts,* 184 vols., 1907–1914; Early English Drama Society, 1906; Recently Lost Tudor Plays, 1907. (Texts of old plays.)

FAUSET, H. I. *John Donne, a Study in Discord,* n. d. [1923].

FEUILLERAT, A. *Documents relating to the Office of the Revels in the time of Queen Elizabeth,* 1908. (Materialien, xxi.)

GAYLEY, C. M. *Representative English Comedies,* 3 vols., 1903–1914.

Gesta Grayorum, Francis Davison?, Malone Society, 1914.

GILDERSLEEVE, V. C. *Government Regulations of Elizabethan Drama,* 1908.

GRAVES, T. S. *The Court and the London Theaters During the Reign of Elizabeth,* 1913.

GREG, W. W. *A List of English plays* written before 1643 and printed before 1700, 1900.

A List of Masques, Pageants, etc., 1902.

GRIERSON, H. J. C. *Metaphysical Poems of the Seventeenth Century,* 1921.

Haslewood Books, 1924–1926. (Reprints of Elizabethan Vers and Prose.) 14 vols. in progress.

HATCHER, O. L. *John Fletcher, a Study in Dramatic Meth* 1905.

HERFORD, C. H. *A Sketch of Recent Shakespeare Inv* tion, 1923.

HOOD, C. M. *The Book of Robert Southwell,* 1926.

HUBBARD, G. *On the Site of the Globe Playhouse,*

HUGHES, C. *The Itinerary of Fynes Moryson,* 1907

JORDAN, J. C. *Robert Greene,* 1915.

KASTNER, L. E. *Thomas Lodge as an Imitator* Poets, Mod. Lang. Rev., 1907.

KELLNER, L. E. *Restoring Shakespeare,* a Critic Misreadings, 1925.

KEYNES, G. *Bibliography of the Works of L* Dean of St. Paul's, 1914.

LAWRENCE, J. W. *The Elizabethan Playho* 1913.

LEE, SIR S. *The French Renaissance in I*

LUCAS, F. L. *Shakespeare and Elizabeth*

MACDONAGH, T. *Thomas Campion a* Poetry, 1913.

McKERROW, R. B., ed. *The Gulls' F* 1904.

Malone Society, Collections, vol. i, 1913; and *Reprints,* 1907–1927, in ᵖ and Commentary on Elizabethan Dr

Materialien zur Kunde des älte by W. Bang, Louvain, 43 vols., 19

Mermaid Series, The Best Play 1887–1895.

Ed. *Victoria* by A. Fraunce, Materialien, 1906.

SPINGARN, J. E. *Literary Criticism in the Renaissance*, 1908.

SWINBURNE. *The Age of Shakespeare*, 1908.

SYKES, H. D. *Sidelights on Shakespeare*, 1919.

SYMONDS, A. *Studies in Elizabethan Drama*, 1920.

THOMPSON, SIR E. M. *Shakespeare's Handwriting*, 1916.

The Autograph MS. of A. Munday. Bibliographical Society, 1916.

THOMPSON, E. N. S. *The Controversy Between the Puritans and the Stage*, 1903.

Elizabethan Dramatic Collaboration, Engl. Stud., 1909.

Literary Bypaths, 1922.

THOMPSON, G. A. *Elizabethan Criticism of Poetry*, Chicago Diss., 1914.

THORNDIKE, A. H. *The Influence of Beaumont and Fletcher on Shakespeare*, 1901.

The Relations of Hamlet to Contemporary Revenge Plays, 1902.

WALLACE, C. W. *Shakespeare, the Globe and Blackfriars* (privately printed, 1909.)

The Children of the Chapel at Blackfriars, 1908.

WATT, H. A. *Gorboduc and Ferrex and Porrex*, Wisconsin, 1910.

WARD, A. W. *History of English Dramatic Literature to the Death of Queen Anne.* 2nd ed., 3 vols., 1899.

WILSON, F. P. *The Plague Pamphlets of Dekker*, 1925.

WILD, L. H. *A Literary Study of the Bible*, 1922.

WITHERSPOON, A. M. *The Influence of Robert Garnier on Elizabethan Drama*, 1924.

YOUNG, F. B. *Mary Sidney, Countess of Pembroke*, 1912.

INDEX

Actors, see players
Adams, Thomas, 315
Admiral's players, the, 81, 96, 183, 229, 232
Æschylus, 250, 271
Alabaster, William, alluded to by Spenser, 52; his *Roxana*, 383
Alamanni, 318
Albright, V. E., 87
Alençon, Duc d', 70
Alençon, Marguerite d', 49
Alexander, Sir William, his *Aurora*, 135; 373; the *Monarchic Tragedies* of, 240; praised by Drummond, 374; his completion of Sidney's *Arcadia*, 422
Allen, Cardinal, 298, 302
Alleyn, Edward, 67, builds the Fortune theater, 84; creation of the title rôles of Marlowe, 87; Hieronimo in *The Spanish Tragedy*, a favorite rôle of, 94; 96; his association with Henslowe and success as an actor, 100, 101; befriends Dekker, 173; founds Dulwich College, 182; 183, 232, 424
Amyot, Jaques, Bishop of Auxerre, translator of Plutarch, 273; Sir Thomas North meets, 278
Anacreon, imitated by Sidney, 27; 246
Andrews, Launcelot, notable in theological controversy, 307; his eloquence, 315
Angelo, Michael, 410
Anne, Queen, of James I, 386, her Children of the Revels, 82, 402
Anthologies of lyrics, 22, 191, 192
Antiquarian studies, books of, Camden's, 292, 293; Selden, Speed and Cotton, their interest in, 297; Stow and his, of London, 297, 298; Wotton and, 298

Anton, Robert, his *Vice's Anatomy*, 327
Apuleius, translated, 273
Aquinas, Thomas, 312
Arcadianism, 43, 44
Archer, W., 85 note
Arden of Feversham, 89, 90; most notable of the murder plays, 184, 185; why not by Shakespeare, 184, 185; 250
Areopagus, the, 25, 26; Spenser and the, 46
Argyle, Countess of, 135
Ariosto, Spenser and, 47, 48, 56; 112; translated, 280, 281; 318
Aristophanes, 235
Aristotle, 268
Armin, Robert, his jests, 104; his satirical tracts, 329
Arnold, Matthew, 44, 277
Arundel, Earl of, interested in madrigals, 195
Ascham, Roger, 4; on English prose, 8, 9; on classical versification in English, 26; 39, 54, 299
Aubrey, John, 47, his opinion of the Latin of Shakespeare, 151; on Jonson's Carlo Buffone, 234
Audeley, John, his *Fraternity of Vagabonds*, 328
Augustine, St., 290
Babington conspiracy, the, 106
Bacon, Anthony, 347
Bacon, Francis, 4, 9, 13, 34, Breton dedicates his *Essays* to, 107; protests against religious controversy, 115, 338; 151, 169, 219, 249, 272, 291, 293, on the plagiarism of Hayward, 294; 298, 299; on the administration of Ireland, 300; Jonson's opinion of, 306; 313; influence of the *Essays* of, 335; reasons for the prominence of, 337; his life, 337-342; his friendship with Essex, 338-340; rivalry with

his age, 29; his criticism of
contemporary drama, 29; of
alliteration, 29; his lofty ideals,
29; the poetry of, 29-33;
Astrophel and Stella, 29-32;
biographical import of, 30, 31;
Petrarchan inspiration in, 30;
French influences on, 31; poetry of the *Arcadia*, 32; popularization of the conceit by, 32,
33; services of, to literature,
33; the *Arcadia* of, 42-44;
prose style of, 43, 44; *The
Shepherds' Calendar* dedicated
to, 45; and Spenser, 47-49; 51;
alluded to in *Colin Clout*, 52,
53; 62, 76, 101, 121, 123, 125,
126, 127, his use of conceit, 128,
129, 131, 134, 137; genuine nature of, 141, 149, 155, 169, 191,
194, 219; empirical classicism
of, 246; source of the underplot
of *King Lear* in the *Arcadia*,
265; 281; his interest in Spanish, 284; 299, 301; Greville's
Life of, 304; 349, 351, 368, 369;
an example to Drummond, 374,
375; 376; his *Lady of May*,
385; 388, 422
Simier, M. de, 71
Skelton, John, 46, 104, 317
Smith, Captain John, 421
Smith, Henry, "pulpiter," 315
Smith, William, sonneteer, 131
Socrates, 37
Somerset, Earl of, see Carr, Sir
Robert
Song-books, Elizabethan, 194-201;
popularity of, 196, writers of,
196-200; relation of words to
music in the, 197
Songs of the drama, early, 201;
of the predecessors of Shakespeare, 201; of Dekker, 202,
203; of Shakespeare, 203-206; of
Fletcher, Jonson and other playwrights, 206-208
Sonnet, introduced by Wyatt, 21;
decade of the, 128; equally
indebted to France and Italy,
129; *Astrophel and Stella*, 129;
other earlier sequences, 129;
French influence on the, 129,
130; borrowing not plagiarism,
130; height of the fashion of
the, 130, 131; form of the, 131;

varieties of the, 131, 132; the
devotional, 132, 133; as an occasional poem, 133, 134; conceit in the, 134; after-history of the, 135; the five great
sequences of the, 137; *Idea*, 137,
138; *Amoretti*, 139-141; the
Sonnets of Shakespeare, 141-
146, their imitative nature, 142;
difficulties about, 142; publication and dedication of, 142, 143;
story of, 144; the "other poet,"
144; Southampton and, 144,
145; autobiographical interpretation of, 145; poetic quality
of, 145, 146
Sophocles, 29, 250, 267, 271
Southampton, Henry Wriothesley,
third Earl of, a patron of
Shakespeare, 141; and Shakespeare's sonnets, 143, 144; *Venus
and Adonis* and *Lucrece* dedicated to the, 149; an adherent
of Essex, 192; 216; an enemy of
Bacon, 341
Southey, Robert, 315
Southwell, Robert, 125; his devotional poetry, 125, 126; a concettist, 128; 193, 213, 249
Spagnuoli, Battista, see Mantuan
Spanish influence, supposed in
Philaster, 406; on English
drama, 416, 417
Spanish Moor's Tragedy, The,
100
Spedding, J., 294, 343, 346, 352,
355
Speed, John, continuator of Stow,
294; his *History of England*,
294, 297
Spencer, Gabriel, actor, killed in
duel by Jonson, 229
Spenser, Edmund, 19, 23; his poetry that of the coterie, 24; and
the Areopagus, 25, 26, 28; life
of, 45-48; 50, 51, 53, 55, 56;
early translations, 46; and the
Areopagus, 46; lost works of,
47; *The Shepherds' Calendar*,
48-50; in Ireland, 50-52, 54, 55;
not poet laureate, 52; and
Shakespeare, 52, 53; *Colin
Clout*, 52, 53; *The Faery
Queen*, 56-62; nature of the
genuis of, 61, 62; 69, 80, 95; 104,
111; Nash on 112; 121; songs of